More praise for *Tragic Muse:*

~

"Brownstein cannot conceal the fervent affection that she feels for the skinny, vulgar, libidinous, ultra-French, immutably Jewish, epoch-making genius who is her subject. Happily for us. Her strong feeling for Rachel touches every page of this attractively written, finely intelligent book."—Stanley Kaufmann, *Salmagundi*

"After reading this book, one gets the impression that the celebrity stage and screen leading ladies who follc —Calev Ben-David, *The Jerusalem Report*

D0731292

"A fascinating take on the reigning tragedienne of mid-nineteenth-century Europe, Rachel Brownstein's book mixes ideas about gender, ethnicity, and theatricality with panache."—Susan Gubar

"An epic meditation, rich with detail on the history of the stage, of Jews in France, of journalism and its role in creating a Rachel."—*Kirkus Reviews*

"In mid-19th-century France, when large, languorous, pastel looks were all the rage for women, Rachel Félix, a wiry, fiery, working-class Jew, revitalized French classical theater and invented the profession of superstar. She was an actress whose life and death became spectacles for her insatiable audiences. Rachel Brownstein examines her own identification with her namesake, deepening a lively, probing biography into an investigation of selfhood and Jewishness."—*Voice Literary Supplement*

"Rachel Brownstein's boldly imagined and historically fascinating tale captures all the odd and remarkable features of this particular woman, as well as the eternally teasing paradoxes of female stardom. The rapport between subject and biographer extends beyond their shared names in this stunning and eminently enjoyable act of literary empathy."—Molly Haskell

"More than just a life, *Tragic Muse* is an analysis of what is meant to be a woman, an actress and a Jew from a wretchedly poor family in mid-19th-century France." —Oliver Bernier, *The Wall Street Journal*

"Analyzing art, literature, and the artifacts of popular culture, Brownstein raises interesting questions about the impulse to elevate—or reduce—famous people to the level of abstraction. *Tragic Muse* celebrates the vitality of a woman who, while doomed by her own success, remained true to the selves she invented." —Bill Jones, *Arkansas Democrat-Gazette*

~

Tragic Muse

Rachel thumbing her nose, photograph by Dragon

Tragic Muse

Rachel of the Comédie-Française

~

Rachel M. Brownstein

Duke University Press   Durham and London   1995

© 1993 Rachel M. Brownstein
First paperback printing by Duke University Press, 1995
Originally published by Alfred A. Knopf, Inc., 1993

*Grateful acknowledgment is made to the following for permission to reprint
previously published material:*
Columbia University: Excerpt from "A Company of Actors (The Comédie-Française)" from
Papers on Acting IV by Françisque Sarcey (Columbia, 1926). Reprinted by permission from
the Brander Matthews Dramatic Museum Collection, Rare Book and Manuscript Library,
Columbia University. Doubleday: Excerpt from *George Sand in Her Own Words*, edited by
Joseph Barry (Doubleday, 1979); excerpt from *The Goncourt Journals, 1851-1870*, translated
from the journal of Edmond and Jules de Goncourt, edited by Louis Galantière (Doubleday
Doran, 1937). Reprinted by permission of Doubleday, a division of Bantam, Doubleday,
Dell Publishing Group, Inc. Oxford University Press: Excerpt from *Heine's Jewish Comedy*
by S. S. Prawer (Oxford University Press, 1983); excerpt from"Rachel in Russia," Annenkov
quoted in Senelick (Theatre Research Press Int'l III, February, 1978). Reprinted by permission of Oxford University Press, Oxford, England.

Library of Congress Cataloging-in-Publication Data
Brownstein, Rachel M.
Tragic muse: Rachel of the Comédie Française / Rachel M. Brownstein.
p.   cm.   Originally published: New York: Knopf: distributed by Random House, 1993.
Includes bibliographical references and index.   ISBN 0-8223-1571-8
1.Rachel, 1821?–1858. 2.Comédie-Française. 3.Theater—France—History—19th century.
4.Theater and society—France. 5.Actors—France—Biography. I.Title.
PN2638.R3B7   1995   792'.028'092—dc20   [B]   94-30101   CIP

~

Contents

~

Acknowledgments

I AM GRATEFUL to the National Endowment for the Humanities and the CUNY Research Foundation for financial support and encouragement, and to the archivists and helpful staffs of libraries here and abroad, especially the Bibliothèque de la Comédie-Française, the Bibliothèque de l'Arsénal, and the Cabinet des Estampes of the Bibliothèque Nationale in Paris; The Theatre Museum, London; The Hebrew University of Jerusalem; the Harvard Theatre Collection, Harvard College Library; and the Performing Arts Library at Lincoln Center of the New York Public Library. And I thank Mme Sylvie Chevalley for advice and materials, as well as tea.

This book could not have been written without the sustaining encouragement of Nancy Miller and Alice Kaplan—my friends, colleagues, and insightful readers and advisers. Also invaluable has been the help of Shale Brownstein, Gabriel Brownstein, Carolyn Heilbrun, Elizabeth Houlding, Geoffrey Nunberg, Sandy Petrey, my knowledgeable agent Georges Borchardt, and my editors Elisabeth Sifton and Susan Ralston. I thank Adrienne Munich and Robert Viscusi, editors of the volume of *Browning Institute Studies* (vol. 13, 1985) in which an early version of my discussion of Arnold and Brontë first appeared; J. D. McClatchy of *The Yale Review;* and the members of the responsive audiences who listened to me talk about Rachel at the City University and elsewhere. For assistance, insights, inspiration, and input of various kinds, I am grateful to Bonnie Anderson, Louis Asekoff, Christina Boufis, Richard Brickner, Daniel Brownstein, Ezra Brownstein, Mary Ann Caws, Myriam Chapman, Lore and Morris Dickstein, Susannah Driver, Linda Dunne, Diana Fane, Gina Fisch-Freedman, Helene P. Foley,

Anne Humpherys, Deborah Interdonato, Gerhard Joseph, Juliet Koss, Barbara Newman, Marie-France Racine, Laura Slatkin, Claire Sprague, Jane P. Tompkins, Count Charles-André Walewski and Countess Walewski, Wendy Wipprecht, Joseph Wittreich, and especially Jane Richmond, who read the final manuscript and made last-minute improvements. She shares with Henry James the credit for suggesting my title.

~

Introduction

STARS ARE MADE UP of fictions; we acknowledge this when we call them fabulous, legendary. Images as well as actual persons, they seem more and less real than the rest of us, and therefore suggest that personal identity is bound up in illusions, stereotypes, social and literary conventions. Fortunes were made in Hollywood by exploring the phenomenon: the dead or distant actress is and is not a person apart from the face that fills the screen, the unique and familiar image—larger than life—that we call by her name.

Stars are remarkable for doubleness above all; perhaps they represent doubleness. They seem to be both singular and reminiscent, simultaneously false and true. As such they reflect, reveal, and focus a problem that has preoccupied Western culture for at least two hundred years: the shape and depth of individual character, the outlines of the integral, coherent self, the relation between the substance of a self—sometimes called character—and appearances, self-presentations, temporary social roles.

A star is someone whose roles shape her character and get conflated with it, whose personal life appears to be spectacular as we watch it get theatrically played out. The process is peculiarly charged when she is a woman, and representative, in this culture, of the private or inner life. A problematically public woman, the star is accessible to all, but also entirely self-possessed. We don't know quite what to make of her; we wonder about what she makes, has made, of herself; credulous and cynical by turns, we applaud and enviously debunk her. The contradictions and connections between selves and others are palpably part of a star's identity—if she may be said to have one.

Stars are signs of anxiety about identity. The glamour that distinguishes them from everything bourgeois belies their origins: they are products of bourgeois individualism, emblems of it. The word "star" was first used in English, of actors, in the 1820s. The earliest stage stars were David Garrick and Mrs. Siddons in England, and Talma and Rachel in France: before them, people came to the theater for the play. A star's fans (from "fanatics") come rather to see a person, or perhaps the very idea of one: when *la grande Rachel* visited her in prison, the condemned murderess Marie Lafarge told her she regretted having missed her in some of her roles, having not seen her "toute entière." Simply by being herself, a star poses the question of whether and how coherent, integral identity hangs on performances and fictions.

This study of the nineteenth-century tragic actress Rachel is about the paradoxes she presented, the way her image worked as a thrilling, telling oxymoron. In the traces of her that remain, I look for the conditions and contradictions that generate stars, and the specific ones that made this one. My approach has resulted in what might be called a postmodern biography. That is, it is not a sequential narrative of the story of a life; it does not seek to isolate and define some inner essence of Rachel; and it is self-conscious about the position from which I am writing. Locating my subject amid the clashing cultural currents of her time, I see her now as mere spume on the waves and then as riding them, sometimes brilliantly navigating for her own ends. I pay more attention to how she was seen than I do to her own subjectivity: my interest is the person in performance, the star. But although I call Rachel a cultural construct and read her as if she were a text or a collation of texts, I do not mean to present her as only a shimmer of language. Rachel actually lived and made money and loved and fell ill and died in history, and she was exceptionally faithful to her own past—to her family and to her repertoire. But for reasons that I hope will become clear, I think the best way to know what she was and what she meant is to look at her through other people's eyes. It is also the only way we have now. Influenced by what I have read and lived through, then, I read her not as the unique and integral self she seemed to be, but as a function of her personal effects.

RACHEL WAS the reigning tragedienne in Europe from the late 1830s to the mid-1850s—mock queen of a culture that had mixed, vexed feelings about royalty. In the France of her time—post-Napoleonic and post-Restoration, post- and pre-revolutionary, and then imperial once more—concern with both personal and national distinctiveness was intense. The nation's identity was being debated and defined, from the 1830s, as its history was rewritten in numerous volumes by men with different political agendas for its future. The very flood of words suggested that a people could be what it said it was: France, after all, had become a republic, an empire, and so on through a succession of utterances. As Balzac showed in a series of novels he called *La Comédie humaine*, this was a society in which the most interesting and enterprising individuals might decide to change their names, assume new characters, improvise selves and lives. Napoleon's example and his idea of the career open to talent inspired the ambitious; Guizot's exhortation, "Enrichissez-vous!," directed their energies; and as writers like Stendhal and Balzac considered and reflected on their countrymen's strivings, they encouraged people to reimagine themselves.

Sometimes called one of the four muses of the romantic stage, Rachel, they say, stood for Tragedy as Marie Taglioni stood for Dance, Maria Malibran for Opera, and Marie Dorval for Drama. But she is not quite assimilable into the company of stage Marys: she had a different relation to her different art. While dance, opera, and drama flourished as if naturally in a society enamored of spectacle, poetic High Tragedy was popular only through the agency of Rachel—only because she had revived it, and only when she performed it. Theater historians remember her for single-handedly bringing back to life an old-fashioned genre soon after her contemporaries had pointedly rejected it. In the first decade of the Bourgeois Monarchy, she stirred memories of past glory—of the ancien régime and the Napoleonic empire, of ancient Greece and Rome, of some ideal literary time beyond time. She moved audiences to reflect on how France had survived, and how it had changed. Astonishingly and ironically, by performing courtly dramas that had been dismissed as elitist, artificial, and irrelevant to modern life, she became a popular star. She made an enormous amount of money: as Mae West would save Paramount, as Deanna Durbin would save Universal, as Marilyn Monroe would save Hollywood, Rachel saved the Comédie-Française.

Contradictoriness was her strength. While connoisseurs commended her art as perfectly traditional, she was also romantically original. Therefore advocates of both classicism and romanticism loved and hated her: and response to her was nearly always intense.

She became famous before sound and moving images could be recorded, and her ephemeral art is gone. From what people wrote, we can guess she was one of those unexpectedly breathtaking performers who, like the unlikely-looking actor in Isaac Babel's story "DiGrasso," convinces audiences that "there is more justice in outbursts of noble passion than in all the joyless rules that run the world." But at the same time she seemed to stand for the rules of art. By making heterogeneous crowds thrill to Racine's high-minded, formally exigent lines of verse, she helped call into question the line between control and passion, elite and popular culture, and art and nature, high and low, in general.

Like the other women performers of her time—the opera divas and ballet dancers and romantic actresses—Rachel was understood to stand for Nature and Instinct and Passion and Beauty. But she also represented their opposites, standing also for the lapidary word. Her face and her skinny body were unprepossessing. Her voice was rough and deep—it had bronze tones, they said later, comparing it to Sarah Bernhardt's golden ones. Critics spoke with respect of her "male talent." But the image of the priestess of high grim art hardly accorded with the sensational rumors about her private life. This Tragic Muse was no dignified, married, English Mrs. Siddons, but a woman who lived like a Parisian courtesan, a pleasure-loving, jewel-collecting demimondaine. And her parents were Jewish peddlers from Alsace; people said they barely spoke French. The darling of queens and statesmen had risen from nowhere, as legend requires, to become a star. And by keeping her family close to her, she seemed perversely and arrogantly to insist on the fact that she had come to center stage from the nation's murkiest margins. You could see her as a heroine of the new age of opportunity for all, or argue from a distance, as Matthew Arnold did, that the contradictory forces of modern life were gloriously resolved in her image. Or you could say, more accurately, I think, that she challengingly embodied opposites, made the force of social, psychological, and aesthetic conflicts felt—and therefore became a star.

RACHEL ELUDED stereotypes and evoked them. She inflected and combined images that were already compelling to the popular mind: the priestess of art, the stage queen risen from the gutter, the virgin and the virago. As a woman, an actress, and a Jew, who commanded respect and made large sums of money, she focused and braided together a set of anxieties about sex and power, about national and sexual as well as personal identity. Questions of who she really was, and who or what she stood for, were central to her figure's fascination. She stood for passion and restraint, therefore for romanticism and classicism; for foreignness and also for France, the monarchy, republic, and empire; for Woman's duplicity and the greed peculiar to Jews. The clash of symbolic meanings was noisy and resonant, the echoes warning against easy interpretation. From the beginning people were saying she was not really sincere, inspired or gifted—not, as we say now, for real. Hostile critics condemned her as a puppet of her father or the Comédie-Française, or ascribed her success to claques and powerful journalists. Meanwhile she herself flamboyantly mocked the roles of Actress and Tragedy Queen, seemed to flaunt the fact that she was a fiction and a fabrication, someone making herself up.

~

Tragic Muse

CHAPTER ONE

~

Tragedy

Tragedy is an imitation of an action.

ARISTOTLE, *Poetics*

The arts differ according to the nature of their medium; well, the actor's medium is—himself.
His own face, his body, his life is the material of his art; the thing he works and moulds to draw out from it his creation.

COQUELIN, *The Art of the Actor*

I (to bored man at cocktail party, who has asked me what I'm working on): A book about an actress. Her name is Rachel. Like mine, only French. She was a nineteenth-century actress—a *tragédienne*.

He (with sudden interest): Oh, really? What did she die of?

IN SPITE OF a cold wet fog like a pall over Paris, crowds began to gather in the Place Royale as early as eight in the morning. Henri IV, building up his monarchy around 1600, had designed the square as the elegant center of a new *quartier* in the marshy area known as the Marais; by the middle of the nineteenth century, in an enlarged city, it was tucked away behind busy avenues, an island in a poor and populous Jewish section. The matching rose-brick Renaissance buildings with their graceful arcades enclosed a quiet orderly space that was reminiscent of the ancien régime, and as separate from the modern world as a stage set. Renamed Place de l'Indivisibilité during the Revolution, and again later, more euphoniously, after the distant mountainous *département* of the Vosges, the square remained the Place Royale for most Parisians. The old regal name seemed most appropriate to the occasion on Monday, 11 January 1858, as people gathered to mourn the early death of the woman who for most of her brief life had been France's *reine de théâtre*, Rachel of the Comédie-Française. A grand state funeral would be the elaborate last act of her reign and her tragedy, the ultimate appropriation of the woman by the nation.

She had made her debut at the state theater almost twenty years earlier, at the age of only seventeen. So thorough was her youthful triumph that soon she was assured a coveted place as a *sociétaire*, or full member, of the elite company. (She became a *sociétaire* at twenty-one.) Through three different regimes—from the last decade of the July Monarchy, through the Second Republic, and into the early years of the Second Empire—she dominated the stage on the rue de Richelieu, recognized as a queen there even by republicans. The tragic royal roles she played adhered to her, informed the way she held her head and bore her body, the way other people regarded her. Dignity like hers, vested in the body, seems to be innate: Rachel exuded that rare utter confidence in her own choices and instincts, her own intrinsic worth, which commands admiration and respect. "You have that in your countenance which I would fain call master," says Kent, disguised, to the humbled, still regal King Lear; pressed to define it, he says, "Authority." Rachel's contemporary Théophile Gautier, a poet and critic who disliked French high tragedy, wrote of her that she had "that supreme gift which makes great tragediennes, authority." To the Victorian novelist Charlotte Brontë she seemed a "stage empress." In the history of the European theater, Rachel is remembered as the first international dramatic star.

Her great success was an extraordinary personal achievement, as well as a sign of what was on her audience's mind. While on the one hand it was astonishing that an obscure young actress should be hailed as the queen of tragedy in Paris in the mid-nineteenth century, the phenomenon expressed the preoccupations of that time and place: the cult of heroic personality, the concern with national identity, the value placed on performance and self-creation, the grandiosity and theatricality of the world that Balzac's novels describe. Born in 1821, the year Napoleon died, Rachel was the product of an age that was nostalgic for heroes and suspicious of them. These mixed feelings surely helped to produce its glut of performing heroes and heroines, or stars: the divas Pasta and Malibran, the dancers Taglioni and Elssler, the romantic actors Frédérick Lemaître and Marie Dorval, Jenny Lind the Swedish Nightingale, Pauline Viardot, the mime Deburau. Mocking power in the extra-theatrical world as they dominated their audiences, these accomplished people captured the popular imagination by illustrating a pervasive idea, that one could make oneself up into something significant, that the self could take on a meaning beyond itself.

What is an actress, asks Balzac, but the stir she makes in the world? Controversy and disputes increase her fame. It was Balzac who called his era an age of paper, and the papers helped Rachel to make her name. The busy *feuilletonistes*—daily reviewers, literary essayists, gossipy columnists— vigorously praised and damned her various performances, and argued about the sources and the soundness of her gifts. Representing and misrepresenting her was one way of engaging in larger controversies, and those, in turn, aggrandized her.

In Rachel's day as in ours the force of theatrical entertainments was generated between pairs of poles: elite and popular, traditional and original, literary and spectacular, mainstream and fringe, legitimate and subversive. History and politics, as always, informed the categories. France's primary theatrical company, the Comédie-Française, was the heir to the nation's most exalted sense of itself. It had been created in 1680 by an edict of King Louis XIV, which combined two existing repertory companies. The king charged the new national company with the duty of preserving the great dramatic works written during his reign: the comedies of Molière and the tragedies of Corneille and Racine. These tragedies, written in rhyming alexandrines— verses of twelve syllables—faithfully followed the rules of art according to Aristotle and the Roman poet Horace, which had been rephrased and reissued by the seventeenth-century French poet and critic Boileau. Usually based on ancient plays or stories, classical French tragedies were constrained by rigid rules as to time, place, and action. The so-called unities required the plot to take place within twenty-four hours, in a single place, unimpeded by subplots. Courtly *bienséances,* or rules of seemliness, imposed further constraints, relegating bloody action to the wings and insisting on a limited, periphrastic vocabulary, in which love, for instance, was always a flame and often a fetter. The dramatic force of dilemmas was intensified (or eviscerated, depending on your taste) by the insistent balance and antithesis: as every line had its rhyming mate, and each heroine or hero had a confidant, every

personal struggle was waged between opposed abstractions. Torn by conflict-
ing allegiances, arguing like brilliant lawyers, the characters lived intensely in
a world of polarizing moral issues.

The members of the company of actors that enjoyed unique rights to
those plays tended to be adepts at one or another of the kinds of roles that
recurred in the repertoire: brave heroes or heavy fathers, young princesses or
scornful queens. Over the years, they developed and codified a set of gestures
and inflections based on the early recommendations of the poet-playwrights,
which were painstakingly passed on through generations of actors proud to
be in the state company's employ. The Revolution caused the tragic repertoire
to pass out of its sole possession, and other theaters to rival its power, but
the *sociétaires* of the Théâtre-Français remained the acknowledged aristocrats
of players. Elsewhere, actors were treated like servants by their managers,
who could throw them in jail for disobedience; here, they had a share in the
decisions and the profits of the company. Their statuesque bearing and incan-
tatory, often bombastic delivery marked their commitment to a high aesthetic
ideal and strict rules that were suggestive of, and derivative from, other
legitimacies. Playing ancient Greeks and Romans in the cast-off silks of courtiers, they reflected and affirmed the values of the court of the Sun King.
While in fact they were at least close cousins of raffish wandering players—
the acrobats, ballad-singers, and mimes of the fairgrounds—they seemed to
be members of a different, higher class.

Court theater, like street theater, cannot but reflect power politics and
engage with them. The radical social and political changes that came at the
end of the eighteenth century were signaled and reflected at the theater that
had been designed as a showcase for absolutism. The aristocrats who saw
Beaumarchais's *Le Mariage de Figaro* in 1784 were clearly given to understand
that their privileged situation was threatened; in the years after 1789, the
Comédie-Française was rent by schism, as the country was. Renamed the
Théâtre de la Nation, it declined as new rival theaters were licensed, and
prolific writers of melodrama—Pixérécourt and his followers—satisfied the
taste for thrills that had been whetted by tragedy on a national scale, complete with lurid spectacles in the streets. The blurring of genres under the
influence of German and English romanticism, the popularity of opera, the
development of theatrical machinery for spectacular visual effects, all helped
to lessen the appeal of the old plays in the new century. Though Napoleon's
taste for tragedy reaffirmed its stature, the state theater's hold on the popular
imagination became ever weaker after his fall. In 1826, the death of the

emperor's favorite actor, the tragedian François-Joseph Talma, was mourned as the death of tragedy.

In February 1830, the Théâtre-Français was the scene of a historic fight as followers of Victor Hugo, the leading enemy of old-fashioned tragedy, cheered his drama, *Hernani*, loudly enough to drown the jeers of traditionalists. The "Battle of *Hernani*" was viewed at the time as a sign of the triumph of the new romantic drama; in fact the vogue would last only a few years, until the failure of Hugo's *Les Burgraves* in 1843. But the rejection of neoclassical tragedy and traditional declamatory acting was emphatic and decisive. In the late 1830s, as melodramas drew crowds to the so-called boulevard theaters and the increasingly lavish productions at the Paris Opéra, the best actors of the state company were aging; the theater on the rue de Richelieu, which was partly subvened by the state, was losing money.

It was saved, to everyone's astonishment, in the fall of 1838, by a new young actress's electrifying renditions of familiar roles—Corneille's Camille and Emilie, Racine's Hermione and Roxane. Die-hard conservatives hailed Rachel for bringing the dead back to life—not only Racine and Corneille, but Aeschylus, Sophocles, and Euripides right behind them. (Although in fact she never played and probably never read the ancient Greeks, some of her fans saw in her a pure classical ideal that had eluded even Racine.) Some writers called her a daughter of the dead to deprecate her, but others used the same phrase with the opposite intention: one of the plays written (but never produced) for her, years later, was entitled *La Fille d'Eschyle*. She was criticized as a mere banner for the political right to band behind: "Mademoiselle Rachel est un principe!" one critic wrote, attacking Rachel's fans. More loudly, she was praised as an uplifting avatar of the *patrimoine*, or cultural legacy of the nation, as a priestess of Art, as the precious embodiment of a lost ideal. Alfred de Musset described her as the crucible in which Racinian gold was purified. Rachel seemed persuasively to embody both the glory of France and eternal beauty—and to make them newly thrilling.

But the symbol of classical standards came quickly into vogue for very romantic reasons: Rachel was a striking anomaly, an original, a phenomenon. Novelty and genius were the reigning modern values: though her diction and bearing were awesomely perfect and traditional, Rachel seemed inspired. She was visibly wracked by her great roles; she seemed to embody the fever of the mind in creation, to suffer the burden of Racine's genius and her own, to be—though only an actress—the very image of an *artiste maudite*, an outcast from ordinary society who is maddened by a vision of truth and tormented by the need to speak it. Among the strongest singers of her praises, from the first, had been Musset, who called on his fellow poets to write new modern tragedies for Rachel, and Théophile Gautier, the poet and critic who, in long hair and a red plush waistcoat, had led the forces of romantic rebellion who packed the house for the Battle of *Hernani*, coming to the theater hours before performance time, eating garlicky supper sausages in the dark stalls, and crowding out, then drowning out, the conservative opposition. Gautier disputed the view of Rachel as classical: for her most acute critic, her glittering nervous brilliance was quintessentially modern. He reflected that

> Rachel, who triumphed so magnificently in the old tragedies, was marked by distinctively modern qualities, in talent as in beauty.— This slender young girl, so thin she could make a belt of her diadem, this supple-bodied child, with her thin and delicate hands, tiny feet, prominent brow, dark-flashing eyes, lip arched in a scornful sneer, in no way resembles those women of ancient times, with narrow hips and thick waists, broad shoulders and low foreheads, which we find in Greek and Roman statues; all of the unhealthy passion of our own time agitates her fragile, anxious limbs, which draw their strength from nervous energy, as the ancients drew theirs from a physical source.—This modern fever of hers which always perceptibly boils beneath the cold surface of old tragedy is one of the unrecognized and unacknowledged reasons for the young tragedienne's success.

Stendhal, who had argued in a celebrated essay that Shakespeare was better than the colder, more formal Racine, found Rachel's Racinian heroines marvellous: there had been nothing like it in France for two hundred years, he wrote of the actress. She put Shakespeare in Racine, people said.

Quickly embraced as the darling of reactionary Catholics and aristocrats and the carefully cultured bourgeoisie of the Faubourg Saint-Germain, Rachel also appealed to ordinary people in Paris and the provinces and eventually abroad, in spite of her old-fashioned repertoire and her want of conventional healthy female good looks—or perhaps, as Gautier implies, because of that. She was a waif with burning eyes, not sexually appetizing as an actress is supposed to be. She lacked the stature expected of a tragedienne: her waist, Musset wrote ungallantly, was the size of an arm of Mlle George, the (still living) *grande tragédienne* of Napoleon's day. On the other hand, she seemed made for tragedy—and by it. She had been born in poverty, and on her face and body the marks of deprivation were legible; as she threw herself into her roles she seemed to consume herself in performance, to act out her own doom. The spectacle of her suffering thrilled sensation-seekers. Tuberculosis haunted her for years, and toward the end newspapers across the world were publishing bulletins about the progress of her mortal illness. Biographies were ready for the press when the news of her death came: readers were avid for the least details of the tragedienne *in extremis,* especially the most morbid ones. Her dying was lamented and also celebrated—by moralists as her just deserts, by aesthetes as her appropriate end, by the muddled legions of her fans as the ultimate accolade and a perverse vindication, proof that she was tragic, was Tragedy.

The mourners who drifted into the Place Royale early that January morning in 1858 were not, on the whole, the ones who had rejoiced at the rebirth of mandarin art. This was the popular audience that the guardians of taste deplored—the people who, they said, had coarsened Rachel's play as she worked for their applause, the poor Jews who proudly packed the galleries to support her, and other elements of the new masses of an increasingly crime-ridden city, who were aroused by her violent stage passions as they also were by vulgar melodrama. The impudent poor girl clever enough to pass in high society appealed to the popular imagination. Her frank acknowledgment of her lowly origin was attractive. She relished her enormous successes, and the idea that she was worthy of them. Enjoying the royal "we," she wrote merrily home from one tour abroad, "What can I tell you about our triumphs? They continue to be as great as our gifts are." Her arrogance was fabulous, and her vulgarity. People loved the story that, after dining in London with the flower of the English aristocracy, she declared she longed to "disenduke" herself; they laughed about the battered guitar she passed off as the one she had strummed as a child street performer, which she hung on the wall of her luxurious salon, then sold at an exorbitant price to a besotted admirer. Having thrilled audiences as Racine's murderous Roxane, and inspired a contemporary playwright to write her the role of Judith, the biblical heroine who kills Holofernes, she burnished her criminal image by laying out a display of ornamental daggers on a table in her home. And everyone knew these details of her furnishings: *le tout Paris* flocked to the salon she ran on Thursdays, and gossiped about the outrageous lavishness of her house. Rachel was a creature of publicity, a star more than half-created by strategically deployed rumors and the new machinery of the penny press, by columnists and caricaturists.

Later, some would claim that the grand state funeral was a flop. They pointed out that Rachel had been in retirement, dying, for two and one-half years and that her star had been in decline for some time earlier. "They wanted to orchestrate a final triumph for the great tragedienne," Michaud's 1880 *Biographie universelle* declared, "but only a crowd of curiosity-seekers came." But who can characterize such a crowd? People came to the funeral as they had come to the theater to see her, to put their own persons close to a celebrity's; to mourn and savor the death of a glamorous, still-young woman; to invite the mixed pleasures of pity and terror; to relish the fact that they themselves were still alive; to enjoy the evidence that the high and mighty also fall. Above all they came to bear witness to—to be reassured of—the idea that reason and order, the massed forces of civilization, can make something intelligible of death.

WHEN SHE FIRST MOVED into the apartment at 9 Place Royale, already mortally ill, Rachel had remarked with bitter irony that the rooms would just do to accommodate her mourners. In another mood, she might have observed that the large square could serve as a lobby and anteroom, a liminal space where people could come together as they do in Racinian tragedy. But the former street performer would have been amused by the sight of so many chilled spectators content to stay outdoors on her account on a wintry day when long stretches of the Seine were icebound. (Some six years before, on a very hot evening, she had had to be cajoled into acting *en plein air* before the Czar of Russia and the King of Prussia, on the beautiful Island of Peacocks in the great lake of the park in Potsdam.) By noon on the day of the funeral people were jostling for good vantage points on the wet gravel; a few men and boys climbed into the leafless trees. This was not the first time Rachel had kept them waiting, some joked, alluding to performances canceled without explanation, also to the fact that announcements that the funeral would be on Friday had been posted on the walls of the Théâtre-Français before the train from the south had arrived, late, with the body. (A rumor circulated that, in a characteristic effort to avoid expense, her family had had the corpse put into a common deal packing case, sent to the railway to be forwarded to Paris as merchandise, and stowed in the luggage van, whereupon it had been stolen by a lover, who sought, as one early biographer wrote, "to inter the precious remains in his own grounds, and erect there a monument over which he might mourn unseen by profane eyes.") Rachel had often been criticized for womanly caprice—in other words, for withholding herself. The sense that she was ungenerous was perhaps retaliatory, a response to her coercive power onstage. In 1847, the Russian writer Alexander Herzen had described the complex knot of pleasure and pain and compulsion that bound together the audience, the role, and Rachel:

> Her acting is fascinating; while she is onstage, no matter what happens, you cannot take your eyes off her; this weak and fragile being dominates you; I cannot imagine that anyone would not abandon himself to her power during the performance. I imagine I can still see that proud pout, that sharp, whip-like glance.

Her body seemed an image of her self-disciplining will, the pleasurable pain she inflicted on audiences. Herzen read in "those finely chiseled, expressive features, molded by the passions" evidence that suffering had empowered her to inflict suffering; her extreme thinness was seen as a sign of her wasting away, burning up. Ambivalence was the common response to her. In *Villette*, Charlotte Brontë's narrator-heroine, overwhelmed by the intensity of the actress she calls Vashti, describes the conflict she imagines to be going on within the other woman, and feels within herself, as she watches her. Her prose imitates the structure of her experience, strophe contradicting antistrophe:

> It was a marvellous sight: a mighty revelation.
> It was a spectacle low, horrible, immoral.

For Brontë, Rachel's power was wrenchingly ambiguous: was she wonderful or terrible, a victim of hell or its tyrant queen? Countess Marie d'Agoult (who wrote fiction as Daniel Stern) heard with disdain the accents of a much-reviled race in the tragedienne's harsh, scornful tones. Perceived with mixed feelings—not to say mutually contradictory ones—Rachel was imagined as a person divided against herself. But on the day she was buried the more hostile responses were muted: the crowd was oppressed by the chilly, wet weather and the nearness of the dead body, the solemn sense of doom satisfactorily fulfilled.

Straining to identify the black-hatted, bearded men passing in and out of Number 9, onlookers gaped as well at another house on the square: Number 6, the home of Victor Hugo, the poet, playwright, novelist, statesman, and popular hero. Hugo was now in exile from the country he had served and stood for, stranded like Prometheus, like Napoleon, living on the isolated rocky island of Guernsey, victim of an emperor he had derided as *Napoléon le petit*. In their time the dead actress and the banished writer had been associated, first as antagonists, then briefly as collaborators. Hugolians were conspicuous among the early critics who dared Rachel to venture outside the classic repertoire. When after much taunting and urging she finally agreed to play Tisbe in Hugo's *Angelo*, she not only managed the feat of memorizing her unrhymed lines, but thoroughly and brilliantly identified herself with the self-immolating romantic heroine. Gautier, who always saw Rachel as some stirring variant on a marble statue, praised her perfect delivery of "those lines in which ideas resound like bronze armor on a warrior's shoulders . . . that style so firm, so precise, so masterful, in which meaning emerges as in a bas-relief, from under a chisel." With her characteristic wry emphasis on money and class and her own legend, Rachel herself wrote that the role of the Venetian courtesan could be played only by a woman who, like Tisbe, had risen from miserable poverty to sleep on satin sheets. Hugo dressed her for the part (also undressed her, the gossips tattled); the tangle of prejudices—misogynist, antitheatrical, anti-Semitic—tightened as it always did around Rachel, as scandalmongers repeated the angry imprecations that the playwright's jealous mistress, Juliette Drouet, had scribbled against the Jewess.

Now that both playwright and actress were respectively exiled and dead, it seemed appropriate to mourn them together, as if the man-god of romanticism and the most exalted of the era's stage goddesses had been a matched pair, types of genius and glory, giants of a great past. Better, almost, than they themselves had done, their twinned ghosts adumbrated what each one had quite differently represented: the grandeur of romantic heroic individualism and the sense that it was gone for good, that it perhaps had never been, or had been only an illusion. At noon the atmosphere, in the gray dampness, was of a twilight of the gods.

FUNERALS WERE FAVORITE SPECTACLES in nineteenth-century Paris. They functioned sometimes to make public amends for private indignities, always to identify and honor the nation's heroes and thus, in effect, the nation itself. At the end of the eighteenth century in Paris, a king had been beheaded with a conspicuous lack of ceremony; three regimes later, the bodies of the martyrs of the divisive June Days of 1848, surrounded by a uniformed guard, were solemnly paraded through the streets by a government eager to keep the peace and assert its own permanence. Like a biography, a funeral appropriates a life and celebrates death as an agent of closure; the private is given public expression for public—which is to say political—reasons. The burial of a person identified with the nation provides an occasion to express the continuing vitality, to define and clarify the identity, of the body politic.

The event that best epitomizes the genre was the so-called Second Funeral of Napoleon, which had made a theater of all Paris in the winter of 1840, early in Rachel's tenure as *reine de théâtre* and midway through the reign of Louis-Philippe. The idea for the show came from the minister Adolphe Thiers; that he had been turned out of power by the time the ceremony was held, and that therefore it was underfinanced, augmented its already considerable comic dimension.

Not only nostalgic about Napoleon's lost glory but covetous of it, the politicians of the July Monarchy aimed to bring him theatrically back by staging a belated funeral for the ashes that were still stowed on St. Helena. A party of sailors was sent to the island in the spring, in a frigate ridiculously named the *Belle-Poule* and correctively festooned with imperial eagles. It was commanded by the Citizen King's third son, the twenty-two-year-old Prince de Joinville, who flaunted princely or youthful disdain for navy regulations in the form of a blond beard. The expedition took six months. During the seafaring stages, at least, it continued to seem adventurous: heady with his mission of stealing the glory of the past, Joinville imagined he sighted pirates on the way home with his precious cargo, and commanded that all movables be scuttled, which only increased discomfort on board. Difficulties multiplied after the ship docked in France, as the men proceeded very slowly by riverboat from Le Havre to Paris: cheering crowds lined the banks to honor the dead emperor, but Joinville had to sleep in a room with twenty others, on top of a table with a common sailor stretched out beneath him on the floor.

The day on which Napoleon's ashes were finally to reach the Invalides, 15 November, was wintry, with a few gusts of snow. The young actor Edmond Got, who—probably after the fact—chose to begin his journal with an account of that day, recalled snow six inches deep; Mary Shelley, visiting Paris, had to give up her chance to watch "the immense assemblage of people and military" because of "the intense cold," although she regretted missing a "sight exceedingly worth witnessing." Wind whipped the flags that lined the Champs-Elysées, where huge plaster statues of heroes, painted to look like bronze or marble, had been erected. There was a painted Arc de Triomphe over the door of the Hôtel des Invalides, and on top of the real Arc was a huge portrait of the emperor standing in a chariot, surrounded by allegorical statues of Fame, Glory, and Grandeur. From the Neuilly side, Victor Hugo noted, one saw only the struts supporting the canvas. A hundred thousand spectators watched the long cortège: the gendarmerie and

The Entry of Napoleon's Ashes into Paris,
from a contemporary lithograph

grenadiers, with generals and marshals among them; the national guard on horseback in interminable legions, rifles reversed; the crew of the *Belle-Poule*; finally the emperor's chariot itself, with eighty-six legionnaires carrying the flags of the eighty-six *départements*, a forest of flags that looked to Hugo like a marching field of gigantic dahlias. An animal said to be the emperor's own horse—it would have had to be more than twenty years old—marched with them. Temporary scaffolding erected for the event transformed the Place des Invalides into an amphitheater. Hugo paid for a seat in the stands, and, with the others who could afford such a luxury, stamped his feet on the planking for warmth. Poorer spectators stood along the streets, where one man was crushed beneath a wheel and another was wounded when a celebratory cannon went off. Hugo measured the warmth of Napoleon's reception as the cortège proceeded: the emperor, he wrote, was received piously by the people in the streets, more coldly by the bourgeoisie on the seats of the esplanade, and insolently by the deputies under the dome of the Invalides.

The playwright mocked the cheap pomp of plaster and decorative *tissu-de-verre*, swatches of which were sold as souvenirs the next day. But even he felt a solemn thrill as Joinville intoned, "Sire, je vous présente le corps de l'empéreur Napoléon." The handsome young man had high style (preserved in his likeness on one of the bas-reliefs around Napoleon's tomb). In an account of the spectacle written for the English public, William Makepeace Thackeray described Joinville: "a tall, broad-chested, dark-eyed young prince, with a great beard (and other martial qualities no doubt) beyond his years. As he strode into the Chapel of the Invalides on Tuesday at the head of his men, he made no small impression, I can tell you, upon the ladies assembled to witness the ceremony." Hugo noted that the mother of the matinee idol also behaved well, receiving her son for the first time in six months in public, without gushing, in the manner of a queen rather than a mother. To his theater-man's eye it seemed that the royal family, though inadequately backed by the government, performed quite creditably.

Only a few months after his great performance the dashing young prince de Joinville became the lover of Rachel, the first in a series of Napoleonic amorous connections. A second was Napoleon's own illegitimate son by the Polish countess Walewska; another, Arthur Bertrand, marched behind Joinville at the Second Funeral, alongside his father, General Bertrand, who had been Napoleon's steward at St. Helena. (Arthur had been born on the island, and was presented to the emperor by his mother as the first Frenchman to arrive there without British permission.) Yet another of Rachel's Napoleonic conquests was the republican Prince Napoleon-Joseph-Charles-Paul Bonaparte, nicknamed Plon-Plon and Nap, the son of the emperor's brother Jérôme Bonaparte, once King of Westphalia; and hardly the least of the lot was Charles-Louis-Napoleon Bonaparte, who became Napoleon III. Imperial splendor accrued to her through her lovers—obliquely, ironically. Stories were told about her imperiousness and exigence as a mistress, and the power plays she enjoyed. It was said that the Jewess was a "mad Messalina" who required her lovers to cry out blasphemies at the crucial moment. Rachel's reputation for taking and dismissing men at her pleasure made her a formidable image of sexual voracity: people said the carriage in which she toured the provinces was fitted out with a bed where she entertained a new man each night. She was notorious for demanding—and giving away—valuable gifts from her admirers. But it was also clear that she made her real money on her feet, not her back, by her own awesome gifts as an actress of high tragedy. Rachel was a vivid variation on the theme of the courtesan; she revised and corrected the sentimental stereotype, of which one example is Balzac's slavish little (Jewish) actress Coralie, who assures Lucien de Rubempré that her body will be a stepping-stone to his success. In Rachel's case, *her* success was the point. "Chère grande," her friends sometimes began their letters. ("Rachon," she liked to sign herself, or "Votre tragédienne ordinaire.")

TUBERCULOSIS CONSUMES SLOWLY and painfully. Rachel first coughed blood as early as 1841, when she was only twenty, but for years she hotly denied that she had the fearful disease. In 1848, after a visit to a victim of tuberculosis, she wrote that any other death was preferable. Her favorite younger sister died of it in 1854. Pallor and feverish intensity like hers were conventionally read in her time as signs of the malady; long before she fell ill in earnest, she embodied its metaphorical dimensions. Tuberculosis in the nineteenth century was elaborately overread. "Like all really successful metaphors," Susan Sontag observes, "the metaphor of TB was rich enough to provide for two contradictory applications." It was imagined as a "disease of the will," also interpreted as a sign of "a failure of will or an overintensity." As cancer does today, tuberculosis then seemed to pose the mind-body question in its most painful form, and with it questions about design and accident, personal integrity and control, guilt and punishment. For that reason tuberculosis was moralized and gendered: in a man (like Keats) it was read as a sign of genius, while in a woman (like Violetta in *La Traviata)* it seemed to signify both "consumption" by sexual desire, and punishment for desiring. In either case it nightmarishly literalized metaphor. As Rachel sickened and suffered and died, tuberculosis seemed to attest to her noble consuming spirit and "male talent," and also her corrupt female body; to signify both her unwomanly ambition and willfulness and her having gracefully given up; to mime and therefore simultaneously validate and undo the actress, whose art was to misrepresent her real self, to make the feverish and fearful real.

Death sanctioned Rachel as its own image, and also enrolled her in the glamorous, amorous company of tubercular romantic women: fictional heroines like Violetta and Marguérite Gautier, and their sisters from real life whose stories a Dr. Cabanès authoritatively retold in a 1925 book he shamelessly entitled *Poitrinaires et grandes amoureuses.* (Citing the physician who attended Rachel in her last illness, he asserted that she had caused lesions to develop in her lungs by stopping her breath and heartbeats to play death scenes.) Her final decline was slow but steady after 1855, when she caught cold on an unheated train between Boston and New York. On the advice of doctors, she exhausted herself in pursuit of promised health, going to Cuba to seek the sun, returning across the Atlantic to France, visiting a spa at Ems, then sailing to Egypt for a milder climate, and coming home again. During hot days and nights on a barge on the Nile, she coughed constantly and, with the nineteenth-century industriousness that seems so implausible now, she—largely unschooled and notoriously ungrammatical—kept up her extensive, lively correspondence, doing business, reporting on the sights and the people she met, and tirelessly dramatizing herself. To her young son in France, the pretty mother playfully describes the airy light clothes she wears all day in the heat, sketching an engaging self-portrait; signing off to a theatrical colleague, she who had played Cleopatra notes bitterly that she blots her letter with the dust of queens. In the end, in a villa in Le Cannet, in the south of France, where she finally waited to die, she took time to write a will circumventing French law by leaving more money to her children than she was allowed to do, through her sister Sarah (who failed, however, to follow through); she had time to go through her old love letters, which she tied together with ribbons in packets, tucked into baskets of fruit, and sent back to the writers, with greetings for the new year she did not expect to see. Toward the very end she sent her parents away so as not to suffer the pain of seeing their pain: she was always exquisitely aware of her audiences' responses. Only her longtime servant Rose Halff, and Sarah Félix, the sister, older by two years, who had embarrassed and annoyed her and had been her closest friend since childhood, were with her at the very end.

SARAH SUPERVISED the funeral arrangements; presumably she was responsible for assembling the minyan of local Jews who had chanted Hebrew prayers beside the deathbed. (The neighbors said they saw sudden gusts of wind whip flames above the building at the very moment Rachel died.) From Le Cannet, the body was taken to Nice, where it was embalmed and placed in a double coffin, a lead box inside a walnut one, before being shipped by train, in a special car, to Paris. The stations along the way became makeshift theaters or temples: in Marseilles the grand rabbi presided over a funeral service in the station; the actors of the Grand Theater of Lyons came to the station there to render homage. At 6 o'clock on Saturday morning, the remains arrived in Paris and were taken to the apartment on the Place Roy-

Comité
DE L'ASSOCIATION
de Secours Mutuels
DES
ARTISTES DRAMATIQUES
Rue de Bondy, 68.

Les Obsèques de **MLLE RACHEL** auront lieu demain Vendredi 8 Janvier, à onze heures du matin; on se réunira à son domicile, PLACE ROYALE, 9, *au Marais*.

Le Comité de l'Association des Artistes Dramatiques prie les Membres de la Société de considérer le présent avis comme Billet de faire part.

Pour le Comité,

LE PRÉSIDENT-FONDATEUR,

Bon TAYLOR.

Typ. JULES-JUTEAU, r. St-Denis, 341.

ale. Delayed at first by the Jewish sabbath, the funeral was again put off till Monday, when groups began to gather in the morning, at first huddling against the weather under the arcades, then growing, spreading, and filling the square.

The invitation specified that the funeral would begin at eleven in the morning. At 1 o'clock the coffin, draped in a white cloth embroidered with silver stars, was finally carried outside and laid on the hearse. Three crowns— of laurel, cypress, and gold—were placed on it; by some accounts, there was also another made up of the flowers called immortelles. Drawn by six horses caparisoned in black, the hearse began its slow progress through the narrow streets toward the Place de la Bastille, then on across the avenues to the cemetery at Père Lachaise, where Balzac's Père Goriot had been buried and Eugène Rastignac, another *arriviste,* had looked down and vowed to revenge himself on Paris by conquering it. At the head of the procession rode eleven municipal guardsmen on horseback, followed by thirty on foot, brass-helmeted and splendid in close-fitting blue uniforms trimmed with red, white, and gold. Behind the hearse walked Grand Rabbi Isidore of Paris, followed by Jacques and Raphaël Félix, the dead woman's father and brother, and after them her younger son, ten-year-old Gabriel Félix, holding the hand of Michel Lévy, the founder of the publishing house of Calmann-Lévy, a family friend, a relative of the rabbi, and one of Rachel's most faithfully devoted lovers. (Six months later, he would marry a twenty-year-old named Amélie Rachel Raba.) The dead woman's older son, the grandson of Napoleon I, had remained at his school in Switzerland. Other family members and friends followed, and then the actors of the Comédie-Française and the personnel of the theater, and representatives of the government, of the Académie Française, of the Association of Dramatic Artists. Some of the notables' names still mean something to us: Théophile Gautier and Paul de Saint-Victor, both of whom wrote memorably about Rachel; the acerb Prosper Mérimée, who had thought her vulgar; Henry Murger, who immortalized the Parisian *vie de bohème;* the pioneer journalist Emile de Girardin, another sometime lover and longtime friend; the waspish critic Sainte-Beuve; Augier, Ponsard, Legouvé, and Scribe, who had written plays for her; her rivals Mlles Judith and Plessy of the Comédie-Française; Mlle George, who had spitefully but wrongly predicted that someday Rachel would end up old and fat and poor like her. The actress Virginie Déjazet, who had also sadly outlived her glamour, was there as well; she wept while throwing violets into the grave, mingling her lamentations for poor Rachel and for herself, enviously and, as it turned out, wrongly prophesying that at her own death there would not be so fine a turnout.

Some six hundred carriages and thirty to forty thousand people on foot followed the hearse. According to one newspaper account, several detachments of cavalry were on hand to keep order. By the time the procession reached the cemetery, over one hundred thousand mourners surged forward dangerously toward the open grave, and the wrought-iron gates had to be closed to control the crowd.

Nearly twenty years later, in his "Letter from Paris" to the *New York Tribune*, Henry James reported the death of Mlle Déjazet. "She has had the funeral of a crowned head," he observed, noting that one hundred fifty thousand people followed her to the grave. With a typical Anglo-Saxon mix of envy and disdain he reflected that "there could not be a better example of the ingrained Parisian passion for all things theatrical than this enormous manifestation of homage to the memory of a little old lady who was solely remarkable for the assurance with which she wore trousers and sang free and easy songs." Edith Piaf's death would bring Parisians out to mourn in the streets; so would Yves Montand's. But actors had not always been rendered such homage in Paris. The great actress Adrienne Lecouvreur, who died in mysterious circumstances in the middle of the eighteenth century, had had no funeral at all: her body was dissolved on a bed of lime beside the river at night. Voltaire, in a poem eulogizing her, had deplored the way France treated actors, and pointed out that England, in contrast, honored them. On a January day some forty years before Rachel's funeral, indignant crowds of enthusiastic mourners had burst open church doors to accommodate the coffin of Mlle Raucourt, late of the Comédie-Française, protesting the Church's refusal to grant her Christian burial. For until the hard Catholic line against the theater was softened in 1849 by the Council of Soissons, actors were urged to repudiate the stage before dying (or marrying, or having their children baptized). As late as the funeral of Mlle Mars, in 1847, the priests had taken refuge in their carriages so as to avoid having to hear a eulogy for an actress. But by 1858 burying an actor respectably in state presented less of a problem—especially when she happened to be a Jew.

RACHEL'S FOUR PALLBEARERS had been chosen carefully: representing the theatrical world were Baron Taylor, president of the Association of Dramatic Artists, who as royal commissioner had led the funeral of the great Talma; and Geffroy, a *sociétaire* of the Comédie-Française and also a painter, whose 1840 group portrait of the company set a fashion for distinguishing Rachel from other actors by portraying her costumed as an immortal, or an abstraction, in toga and laurel wreath. Literature was represented by Auguste Maquet, president of the Commission of Dramatic Authors, and the imposing portly figure of Alexandre Dumas *père*. Maquet had extended and elaborated not only the legend of sexy, imperious Rachel but the idea of her doubleness and duplicity, by writing *Valéria et Lycisca* (1851) with Jules Lacroix, a play in which she created the double role of a Roman empress like Messalina—here exonerated—and her criminal doppelgänger, a prostitute. The connection between Rachel and Dumas was more problematic. Once, when she was living in faithful domesticity with Walewski, Dumas had written to propose becoming her lover—if not then, later on; when she rejected him on the same sheet of paper, disdainfully returning the offending lines which, she wrote, had doubtless flowed accidentally from his prolific pen, he became her enemy. He was only temporarily and mildly mollified by her choice of his *Mlle de Belle-Isle* for her first foray into romantic drama, in 1850. Dumas had led the chorus of Paris journalists who attacked Rachel as greedy and vulgar and virtually treasonous for going on tour to America— Hermione deserting Orestes to follow Barnum, as one caricaturist styled her, a woman contemptibly willing, for love of the dollar, to betray the dignity of France and render Racine's immortal lines in Iroquois! Under the circumstances, the choice of Dumas as pallbearer was so odd that even he was moved to comment on it. "Why was I chosen?" he asked rhetorically, after the funeral, in his paper *Le Monte-Cristo*, and answered himself smugly, "Because I'm me!" He meant he stood for France: proudly, he described how workers in blue blouses had pushed through the crowd to shake his hand. (Rachel's good friend and former lover, the playwright François Ponsard, once described Dumas in a letter to her as "a tedious charlatan.")

WHILE THEY PROBABLY did choose Dumas as a sign that the nation had forgiven its errant queen, the Félix family itself was not in a forgiving mood. Rachel had died unreconciled with her teacher, Samson of the Comédie-Française. He was understood to be the benefactor of her youth, the actor who had urged the national company to accept her. He had handed down to her the legacy of Talma and of Mlle Clairon; he had painstakingly rehearsed and advised her; he was popularly understood to be a vital part of her life. His absence was noted, and he was missed. Everyone knew the story of the furious encounter between Samson and Jacques Félix early in Rachel's career, when the actor had thrown the peddler down a flight of stairs after smashing a plaster statuette of his daughter that stood on his desk and threatening to break her just as he had made her. Félix had been demanding more money for Rachel (that is, for himself) on the ground that she had made an astounding two hundred thousand francs in six months for the Théâtre-Français; Samson, representing the company, had insisted on keeping to the terms of the contract she and her father had signed. The less dramatic but more decisive second round of the battle had been won in court by Félix and his lawyer Adolphe Crémieux, who had argued successfully that because Rachel had signed as a minor the contract was invalid. (It was this debate that eventually provoked the Comédie-Française to fix the uncertain date of Rachel's birth with a legal certificate.)

This was the first of a long series of arguments about Rachel's artistic and financial independence—the extent to which she was a free agent. The Comédie-Française—constituted by Louis XIV, subvened by the state, recognized as the epitome of dramatic art—was the source of her repertoire, her style, and her authority: only its traditions and its status and its style of tragedy could have made her *la grande Rachel*. On the other hand, having restored its fortunes, was she not entitled to go on and make a fortune for herself beyond its walls? To what extent was she bound to be a company woman? Maneuvering to put in power men who would comply with her demands, insisting on long vacations in which she could tour the provinces and abroad, bargaining by threatening to resign or retire, Rachel wrangled with the Théâtre-Français for years, largely without her father's help. But biographers have preferred to focus on the early part of her history, the story of a passive, dependent girl torn by divided loyalties to her biological father and to Samson, her father in art, both of whom believed they legitimately owned her. The drama of fathers and daughters is every bit as compelling as that of fathers and sons; and Rachel had unforgettably acted a daughter's role, as Camille in Corneille's *Horace* and also—before she ever appeared at the Théâtre-Français—in *La Vendéenne*, the melodrama written for her, in which she had made her Paris debut. The daughter role stuck, and offstage her father stuck to her, haunting the wings. "She's my daughter; it's only right that she make money for me," Félix supposedly insisted, with the logic of the poor. Samson rejoined—and many agreed with him—that the high art of the Comédie-Française, which he had taught her to embody, was vulgarized and ruined when she sought to supplement her income by performing outside Paris with incompetent actors, before ignorant audiences.

Legend casts Rachel's "father in art"—more respectable and dignified, more bourgeois and French—as a more plausible author of her being than the vulgar peddler. More and less explicitly, more and less anti-Semitically, Rachel's admirers resisted the inexplicable fact that the compelling exponent of the most refined and most French of poets had no education and, as one historian put it, "not a drop of French blood." The figures of Samson and Félix lend themselves to allegory: Samson the representative of nurture and art versus Félix the brute, whose claim to Rachel was merely natural. The conflict is between the state and the tribe, civilized Frenchman and Wandering Jew—with the actress of course cast as the passive product of one or another. Samson disputed the romantic pictures of Rachel as a magically inspired genius, insisting it was her hardworking teacher who effectively made her an actress and also civilized her into social life. It was said that Samson preferred Rachel to his own daughters; the actress and her teacher quarreled with a violence they did not impose on their biological families. The personal struggle was between generations and sexes; between a lesser artist and a greater one; between a functionary of an institution and a creative, independent egotist; between the advocate of a cultural establishment and all that such an establishment must define as wild and alien in order to assert its own authority. It was a clash of personalities, writes one biographer, explaining that Samson had "the temperament of a bureaucrat . . . respectful of authority," while Rachel "belonged to a race without roots [racines]." But on another level, the issue was precisely roots—and what was in question was whether Rachel's were legitimate. Loyalty to Samson was in effect allegiance to a distinctive art, institution, culture, and nation—all of which depended on assuming that the Félixes were different, other and inferior. By refusing to relinquish her loyalty to her family, Rachel challenged and undermined the French national ideal which she had come, with Samson's connivance and help, to represent.

At her death, she had not healed a breach made in 1853 and confirmed in 1854, when Samson had refused Michel Lévy's request that he speak at the funeral of her best-loved sister, the gifted twenty-five-year-old actress Rébecca Félix, "ma gentille et parfaite petite Rébec," as she called her. Although Samson, overcome by emotion, had broken down and praised the young actress at the graveside, and her brother Raphaël Félix had thanked him for his words, Rachel herself did not forgive him for his initial refusal. Directly after the ceremony, the mourning star fled with Lévy to the country; she never saw Samson again. But when he heard the news of Rachel's death, her teacher—who had published verses praising and also admonishing her from the start of her career—went so far as to prepare a eulogy of his greatest student, which he planned to deliver in spite of a bad cold (his wife recorded pettishly) and the weather. A clear note from Jacques Félix kept him at his fireside. It was inappropriate, Rachel's father wrote, that Samson should appear on this occasion.

. . .

THERE WAS, therefore, no official speech in the cemetery on behalf of the Comédie-Française, whose glory Rachel had restored and made her own. All accounts of the funeral stress the lack of such a eulogy, the absence of Samson, the "triumph" of the former peddler with the funny foreign accent over the man who had been a colleague of Talma. Had nature, in the form of the paternal Jew, vengefully come in the end to claim its own and challenge the pretensions of high art? Félix had written severely to the administrator of the Comédie-Française in the letter warning Samson away: "You may take me at my word, sir, since I have found the strength and courage to write to you at this moment." Rachel's biographers have mocked the possibility that he had grammar enough to phrase the letter himself, and the absurdity of a man of his class and kind professing "a pained sense of what is absolutely proper." It is entirely possible that Félix did have editorial help, as his daughter sometimes seems to have had with her official correspondence; but those who refuse to grant him a sense of what was appropriate seem to me to show their culturally determined hand.

"And so the history of Rachel begins and ends with Papa Félix": James Agate concluded his 1928 biography with this little flourish of contemptuous irony. In the biographical act of foregrounding the struggle between Samson and Félix for center stage at the graveside, we accept the conventional terms that deny Rachel agency and define her as a man-made thing. Rejecting it, or critically examining it, we cannot help seeing how misogyny is linked with other prejudices. The story of the conflict between the gross Jew and the gentleman-actor is hardly on the same level of anti-Semitism as the anecdote about the grand rabbi's turning to the Rothschild standing beside him at Rachel's funeral to get information about the stock market between two psalms (a story, by the way, that only got "recalled" at the time of the Dreyfus affair). Félix and Samson did in fact figure in Rachel's life as opponents and probably, in one another's minds, as opposites. But to polarize them—peddler and representative of the state theater, outsider and insider, (low) blood and (high) culture—is to enter a minefield of binary oppositions, where Rachel is blown out of the picture. It is better to focus directly on her figure, which provocatively invites such thinking while it also challenges and ultimately upsets it.

THE FUNERAL WAS a forum for interpretations. There were three eulogies, all political, two with the contentious flavor and form of arguments in a debate. First, Grand Rabbi Isidore, having pronounced the Hebrew prayers over the dead, contradicted, in French, the talk that Rachel had converted or ever planned to convert. Rumors that she was about to do so had circulated for years, since she had first been taken up by Mme Récamier's Catholic circle. She herself had denied them, at one point, in a letter to a newspaper ("I had always believed that an artist's private life was not in the domain of publicity, which evidently is not your view. . . . But nothing can authorize crossing certain boundaries—of the truth. Please inform your readers that the piquant story of my conversion is altogether without foundation"). But she had also, more privately, encouraged hopes of converting her. There was, for example, the bishop she had met on the ship back to France from Egypt, who had had a Mass for her recovery said at Malta. She thanked him, she reported, but made it clear he should abstain thereafter from talking to her of religion. ("We talked food all the way to Marseilles: he was an eating prelate," she reported.) More seriously, she flirted with the pious, star-struck young Gabriel Aubaret, whom she met in Egypt, and with his hopes of her conversion. After her return to France, she became quite close with his Catholic family, and he believed he was on the verge of bringing her into the church when, weak though she was, she suddenly fled to Paris, fabricating a story that one of her children was seriously ill.

The plain fact was that she had never repudiated her Jewishness. The rabbi at the funeral declared she had found ample satisfaction for the needs of her heart, and the demands of her beautiful intellect, in the old and good faith of her fathers. ("All that we can say of Mlle Rachel is, that to her other immoralities she has not added that of apostasy," was one Jewish newspaper's different, bitter comment.) Then Bataille, vice-president of the Society of Dramatic Artists, kept up the argument against the enemies of Judaism. At some length, he said that in spite of what people said Rachel had been very generous.

The final denial was the most ambitious—of death itself, by Jules Janin. The powerful critic of the *Journal des débats* had made Rachel a star with his reviews, which effectively defined the terms through which she would be seen evermore. He would continue to further her fame, and feed on it, by refashioning those reviews into a book. Janin was a man full of words and of himself, always ready to seize the day: once, in a week when there were no new plays, he had devoted a column to "Le Mariage du critique," a review of his own (second) wedding. The funeral of the greatest star he had ever discovered, whom he had so influentially described, moved the man of a thousand pens (as he styled himself) to an orgy of self-reflexiveness. At Rachel's graveside, he praised the silenced actress's audience, now his, and the death that had brought the assembly before him. He mourned the loss of all the brilliant artists of the generation of 1830, in whose number he implausibly included not only Rachel but her sister Rébecca Félix, who had been a small child in those great days. His periods swelled. He lamented the absence of the only man capable of mourning all the immense griefs and losses, without naming Hugo, the modern Prometheus who had been banished to a rock in the ocean. Praising glory in spite of the pains it entailed, he ended by applauding the people present, as lovers of beautiful things, faithful to the good, hopeful of immortality in this world and the next. For all his auditors, he wished the sole and supreme recompense, to be followed to the grave by pity, and sympathy, and respect, and—returning the focus, predictably, to himself—such a funeral as this one. Rachel was effectively reduced to an occasion for rhetoric.

SHE HAD REHEARSED her end throughout her public life as if attempting to anticipate, mock, or master it: she expired on stage memorably as Phèdre and also as Adrienne Lecouvreur, the great eighteenth-century actress, who, like Phèdre, was a victim of her own ill-judging love. When Rachel actually did die on 3 January 1858, she could not but do so theatrically. The setting was a villa in the south of France borrowed for the event from the uncle of the playwright Victorien Sardou. He was a man of bizarre tastes who had decorated the house in a fantastic medley of styles—Moorish, neo-classical, Renaissance—as a sort of museum or monument to the sciences and the arts. In one room, there was an immense leafless stucco tree, representing the tree of knowledge, whereon the names of celebrated scientists were engraved. The bedroom was lugubriously decked out as if for a dying trage-dienne. One visitor described its salient features:

> In the half-light of an alcove resembling a chapel is a strangely con-structed alabaster bed, designed to resemble an organ, with its pipes topped by ancient masks. At the foot, facing the head, is a statue of Polymnia, which evokes the memory of classical beauty by the folds of her tunic—a kind of beauty misplaced here in this masterpiece of bad taste. It is in this bed, which forewarns of the coldness of the tomb, that Phèdre went to sleep, never again to awaken.

One shudders to think what she must have made of the masks and the statue in her final fevers. Stories circulated about how she bore her dying: with a fine romantic defiance of the effects of high fever on the extremities, it was said that she begged her father to bring her the coffers of jewels she had collected from lovers and potentates, so that she could cool her fingers in them. After she died, her body was draped in white and crowned with laurel, and sketched by Mme Frédérique O'Connell; one version of the portrait later became the treasured property of Sarah Bernhardt. Ernest Legouvé, one of the authors of *Adrienne Lecouvreur,* had gone to Le Cannet to see her on her deathbed, and although he was turned away from the door he elaborately described her dying, still unregenerately the actress, self-consciously assuming statuesque postures even at the very end, mimicking the marble muse at the foot of her bed. As late as 1908 the *maison mortuaire de Rachel* was an obligatory stop for tourists in Le Cannet, who—the English especially, it was said—continued to pillage what detachable souvenirs remained.

IS IT POSSIBLE to locate Rachel's specificity, individuality, uniqueness— the person herself rather than what she represented or seemed to stand for— beneath or beyond the layers of spectacle and symbol and stereotype? Alfred de Musset, who addressed the actress as "chère muse" in at least one letter, defined her image by enthusiastically declaring, in 1838, that Rachel *was* Tragedy; soon after she died, the painter Jean-Léon Gérôme would spell this out in an idealizing memorial portrait of her entitled *La Tragédie* that was exhibited at the Salon of 1861. Against its own best interests, this repellent but unforgettable work demands contrast with Sir Joshua Reynolds's much more famous portrait, *Mrs. Siddons as the Tragic Muse* (1784), which portrays the distinguished English tragic actress undergoing apotheosis with roseate aplomb. In Gérôme's painting, a highly finished academic work, a boneless figure is slouched against a stagy background architectural. The tremulous face of stricken Phèdre, which Gérôme copied from a photograph by Nadar, is too small and stylized here to have much force. Swathed in a scarlet tragedy toga, wreathed with glaucous laurel, Tragedy is surrounded by a suffocating clutter of symbolic artifacts: a Grecian pillar hung with a plaque inscribed with names of tragic heroines; a sort of group tombstone that bears the names in Greek letters of Aeschylus, Sophocles, and Euripides, and beneath them Corneille's and Racine's names; a grimacing greenish tragedy mask. On top of the Ionic column at her side stands a fierce little statue, seemingly of an archaic priest or priestess, mouth open as if in a howl. Its extended hands hold out what appear to be snakes. The many names in the picture are painted to look chiseled into the various stone surfaces; the stone on which the figure stands, the plinth at the painting's base, bears the name, in large letters, "J.-L. Gérôme." Reynolds gracefully said, apropos of his own scrawled

Rachel as Phèdre, photograph by Nadar

signature, that he hoped to go to eternity on the hem of Mrs. Siddons's garment; Gérôme's makes us notice that Rachel's name is absent. The label fixed to the frame reads *La Tragédie*. The female figure dwarfed by Tragedy's regalia seems to be its sick, apprehensive victim, a woman who dreads becoming her own monument. This sad, frail creature's burden is the dead weight of allegory; she cowers at the approach of an unseen power that can only be limned by symbols—like herself. Is she a sign among other signs, or a woman destroyed by representation—by being taken, by taking herself, for a sign? Where Reynolds depicted the living Mrs. Siddons in the conventional but splendid role of Muse, Gérôme seems to brood uneasily, about the problems of separating Rachel from what she stood for. Rather than Tragedy embodied, the figure in his painting seems to be a trapped creature struggling against dissolution.

"It is the fate of actors to leave only picture postcards behind them," Virginia Woolf once wrote. The postcard shop at the Théâtre-Français invites us to consider the mailable colored reproduction of Gérôme's Rachel alongside what is sold as its complement, a picture of Delacroix's 1853 painting of the tragic actor François-Joseph Talma, who had died in 1826. The circumstances in which these two paintings of dead actors were produced were very different: Gérôme's commission came from Rachel's sister, who would sell the portrait to the Théâtre-Français, while Delacroix's was from the state. Talma is portrayed in the role of the tyrant Néron in Racine's *Britannicus*. He is seated on a golden throne to which the viewer must look up; lions' heads adorn its arms. His feet—shod in light golden Grecian sandals, not encumbered, as Rachel's are, by the heavy-soled archaic cothurni—are ready to lift him; his nervy left hand clenches the armrest, pressing fingers into the lion's open eye. The actor crowned with laurel is identified with an emperor: not only with the bloodthirsty Roman Nero, who loved to playact and paid people to applaud him, but also with that other tyrant and devotee of the theater, Napoleon I, who had preferred Talma above all actors—and perhaps, most ambiguously, with the man who had just made himself the second emperor, Louis-Napoleon, whose minister commissioned the portrait of Talma (and portraits of other heroes) in the course of making the political point that the new regime was continuous with legitimate governments of the past.

THE CONTRAST WITH the Rachel portrait is dramatic. To begin with, Talma's figure takes up the whole canvas, while Rachel's is diminished by its architectural context. The man's high-colored, open, mobile face, the flash of his large eyes, the strong grip of hand and poise of foot, are theatrical and vital; scarlet drapery swags and swirls to suggest movement; though his subject is a man long dead, Delacroix's theme is action and acting, life not death, the present not the lost past. A feminist reading of the difference is tempting: the man is portrayed as powerful agent, the woman as victim and vessel; the man's portrait is full of verve and light and movement, the woman's overemphatically enclosed. On the Rachel postcard, the gold frame of the Gérôme portrait, regularly buttoned with rosettes, serves as a border; the Talma runs to the edges. Gérôme's scarlet tragedy toga encases the female figure,

Mrs. Siddons as the Tragic Muse, after the
painting by Sir Joshua Reynolds, 1784

Delacroix's emphasizes the free mobility of the strong man. Talma is a man in action, Rachel an icon of a woman personifying an abstraction. But it would be wrong to read the portraits as simple opposites. It was common-place to compare Rachel to Talma; Gérôme knew the Delacroix portrait; and Delacroix painted Talma after having seen (and also dined with) Rachel. Recalling the tragedian in 1853, Delacroix had to be paying oblique homage to the tragedienne who had revived, with Corneille and Racine, the memory not only of Aeschylus but of Talma as well.

Painting Talma as Néron, in the age of Louis-Napoleon, Delacroix raised subtle questions about the reigning tyrant. Perhaps one ought not to make too much of the casual cruelty with which Talma-Néron sticks his finger in the eye of the lion carved on his throne; but the choice to depict the actor in that role rather than another, and in the act of rising, has clear reference to the concerns of the painter's moment. By the early 1850s, Rachel had altered people's view of classical tragedy. She had revised Talma's repertoire by emphasizing the importance of women's roles; she had made the old plays immediate and modern; and by feminizing the genre of tragedy, she had intensified its ironic dimension. When *Britannicus* was produced at the Théâtre-Français in 1848, for example, it was no longer Néron's play: all eyes were on the actress who dared, at the age of only twenty-seven, to play the role of Agrippine, the emperor's mother. The vivid portrait of Talma as Néron conveys the power in the world of an actor's art—Talma's, and also Rachel's—and wryly comments on the theatricality and the limits of power, in Rachel's manner.

Delacroix never did a full-scale portrait of her; neither did his rival Ingres, although Rachel at one point negotiated with him (she bowed out when he demanded too many sittings). In the works of the painters of her time, her influence can be traced and has been: she is said to have been the model for the dark-haired, pale, and muscular Semitic beauty in Delacroix's painting *La Sibylle au Rameau d'Or (The Cumaean Sibyl)*. But it is hard to sort out the features of this particular actress from the general vogue for dark-eyed exotics documented by both academic and romantic painters, including Chas-sériau, Delacroix, and the young Courbet. Rachel's popularity coincided with an aesthetic-erotic vogue for exotic women. Travel to the East, after Napo-leon, had helped to create a taste for Semitic feminine beauty; ringing changes on the type, artists sought models whose appeal ranged from the languidly sensual to the decadent. This orientalist enthusiasm was criticized: one of the patriotic young men of 1848 in Flaubert's *L'Education sentimentale* (1869) laments the taste for dark, thin women—and, at the same time, for "the women of antiquity"—declaring, "when all's said and done, a tart is a lot more fun than the Venus of Milo. Let's be Frenchmen, for God's sake. . . . We must go from brunettes to blondes." Later, the Goncourts deplored as anti-erotic the vogue for "thin, gaunt, flat, bony women, slight to hold in your hands, with . . . infinitely little place on them for amorous exercises: chlorotic women looking spectral and unhealthy—on their faces nothing but their minds." Rachel, wanting in flesh and beauty, was widely regarded, especially after her death, as the original for this Goncourtian paradigm.

Like all actors, she was to some extent typecast by her body; what they called her homeliness may have made it easier for men to take her seriously as an artist. A charcoal sketch of Rachel by Delacroix, very different from his statuesque sibyl, suggests as much: it portrays the actress in performance, a plain woman throwing her whole soul into the imaginative work of acting. Was she in fact ugly? What are we to make of the delicate little miniature that depicts an adorably fine-featured Rachel as the heroine, crowned with flowers, of *Le Moineau de Lesbie,* a slight pseudoclassical play written to exploit her charm and seductiveness?

In a celebrated early statue by Auguste Barre, Rachel is the pure Roman virgin Camille of Corneille's *Horace.* She is dewy and distraught and vivid in the English painter William Etty's appealing portrait, which (oddly, in spite of Henry James's clear allusion to Gérôme's, in the novel) decorates the cover of one paperback edition of *The Tragic Muse.* Rachel is prim and tight, even gnomish, in pictures by other artists. The glossy oils of the star by Amaury-Duval and Dubufe insist on her severe elegance and glamour; in Lehmann's 1851 painting she looks benign and graceful but unbeautiful; and in the portrait by Müller which she is supposed to have preferred she could pass for Charlotte Brontë, dowdy and domestic. Hostile caricatures depict her as a sullen, negroid Jewess or a hideous skeleton. On sheet music of *La Marseillaise* printed in 1848, line drawings show her as a version of the central figure in Delacroix's 1830 painting *Liberty Leading the People,* simplified and commercialized to suit the bourgeois revolution.

The few photographs we have of Rachel are as mutually contradictory as the other visual images, and, in their different ways, as disappointing. In private life, she huddles up and stares at the camera, blurry-faced, intense only around the unreadable eyes; or she poses, worn and faded, three months before her death, in front of a crudely painted scenic backdrop. In another photo, she is elegant but ugly; then again, clear-faced and pensively pretty, much more than the *jolie laide* men conceded she was when they acknowl-

Photograph said to be of Rachel, photographer and date unknown

edged that she wore clothes well. Time, moods, and illnesses changed her looks. The staged shots of Rachel in action show her frozen for muscle-aching minutes so the camera can catch Hermione's mouth twisted in scorn, Camille's operatic despair, the slant-mouthed sneer of Athalie asquat.

She is elusive: her voice, not her body, was the source of her power in the theater. She was very young when she first became famous, and she actually grew during the early years of her celebrity; costumes, roles, camera angles dramatically altered her. The sole constant in portraits of Rachel is that she is always dark, not fair, and always inaccessible, either "on" for the camera or guarded-looking, with something in her eyes (a slight cast?) that suggests she is away. Though nothing about her is coy, she will not meet the interlocutory gaze.

Language seems preferable to this embarrassment of contradictory visual riches—even the bland, flat description on her 1856 passport, comforting in its plainness: "Age, 35 years; Height, 1.6 meters; Hair, brown; Forehead, high; Eyebrows, brown; Eyes, brown; Nose, aquiline; Mouth, average; Chin, round; Face, oval; Complexion, pale." And still savory is the lovingly, long-ingly detailed description Samson set down years after her death, taking obvious pains to account for (and correct) the flaws that others had ascribed to her:

> Rachel was below average in height; she had a rounded forehead; deep-set eyes that, without being large, were very expressive; a straight nose, with a slight curve. Her mouth, studded with small, well-placed white teeth, was at once mocking and proud. Her neck was perfectly attached to her shoulders; her small head, with its low forehead, sat graciously upon it. She was terribly thin, but dressed so artfully that her thinness almost became a kind of beauty. Her gait and her gestures were easy, all her movements supple, her entire person filled with distinction. She had, to use a current expres-sion, the hands and feet of a duchess. Her contralto voice had little range, but having a most acute ear she used it with the utmost skill, managing the finest and most delicate inflections. When she first began to speak, there was a slight huskiness to her voice that soon disappeared.

He attributed the differences in descriptions of her to both real and imaginary changes wrought by time and subtler agents:

When she first appeared on the French stage she had not yet attained her full height; there was a sort of confusion, if I may be permitted to put it thus, in her small features and closely set eyes, and she was declared to be ugly. Later, she was said to be beautiful. She was in fact neither, not entirely one or the other, but both, depending on the time, the day, the expression on her face.

THE PLAYERS of Greek tragedy wore masks. Roland Barthes remarks that, historically, "the first actors separated themselves from the community by playing the role of the Dead: to make oneself up was to designate oneself as a body simultaneously living and dead: the whitened bust of the totemic theater, the man with the painted face in the Chinese theater, the rice-paste makeup of the Indian Katha-Kali, the Japanese No mask." For Barthes, a photograph is a death's head, "a kind of primitive theater, a kind of *Tableau Vivant*, a figuration of the motionless and made-up face beneath which we see the dead." To find the life in it, he continues, one connects with a *punctum*, responds to a particular detail; in the idiosyncratic response one locates the otherwise stilled life, the vital moment the photographer caught, stopped, and preserved. Though most photographs of Rachel defy such engagement (the exception, perhaps, is my frontispiece), Barthes's interactive model—which echoes the relation of the spectator and the actor in the theater—strikes me as the best available for the biographer. Any other approach, I think, involves as much self-projection.

We can only hope to fan a flicker of life from a photograph, however. The vital presence of singers and actors inheres in what Barthes called the "grain" of the voice. One cannot hope to find the "real" Rachel any more than one can revive and reevaluate her art. The weird, authoritative tones that compelled her audiences are lost for good; when one of her admirers attempted to set down her cadences by musical notation, he could mark the rises and falls, but not the timbre, which permanently eludes us. This warns against trying to locate and represent some essence of Rachel, and encourages the different project of reconstructing her by *bricolage*, out of the words and images that record other people's perceptions of her.

CHAPTER TWO

~

Stars

Don't think it's so easy to bury people of my race and merit.
Letter from RACHEL to her mother

I would not advise an author to take as subject of a tragedy an action
as modern as this. . . . Tragic characters must be viewed with a different eye from the one with which we commonly look upon characters whom we have seen so closely.
JEAN RACINE, Second Preface to *Bajazet*

She is unique; she is Elizabeth; there's only one. Perhaps with the
exception of Her Majesty the Queen.
Director RICHARD BROOKS of Elizabeth Taylor,
in a television interview

RACHEL IS STILL REMEMBERED in France. There is an Avenue Rachel at Père Lachaise cemetery, where the name on the pediment of her
tomb, a miniature Grecian temple, reads, *tout court*, Rachel. Her portrait
hangs in a conspicuous place in the Théâtre-Français, and sitting on a red
plush seat in the audience there one can breathe an air that is still, as Henry
James found it, "thick with associations." In 1876, when the distinctive
horseshoe-shaped house was even less changed than now, James reflected,
"Even if I had never seen Rachel, it was something of a consolation to think
that those very footlights had illumined her finest moments and that the

The tomb of Rachel at
Père Lachaise Cemetery, Paris

echoes of her mighty voice were sleeping in that dingy dome." (Criticizing
a similar phrase of Jules Janin's, Samson scornfully observed that an echoing
theater wouldn't be much good.) Modern Paris is the home of Rachel's—and
Napoleon's—descendants. And in one winter week there today you might be
able to see four or five of the plays Rachel performed in. Every schoolchild
in France still memorizes the great harangues, confessions, arguments—the
monologues called *tirades*—from the tragedies by Corneille and Racine; a
little more than a decade before Rachel's debut, Stendhal had protested that
Shakespeare was the greater poet, but Racine continues to be honored and
performed in France, where his works are considered the finest essence of a
patrimoine uniquely bound up in language. Although the favorite spectacle
of French people today may well be Baudrillard's America, the name of
Rachel still rings a bell in Paris, evoking a past when theatricality was naive
and high culture glamorous.

Cultivated European Jews may also recall that Rachel was a very great

actress, and the subject of many biographies. But most people I know who
know her name at all came to it, as I did, through Charlotte Brontë, whose
last novel, *Villette*, describes an actress who cannot but be Rachel. The language insists on the phenomenon of the star: "She rose at nine that December
night: above the horizon I saw her come. She could shine yet with pale
grandeur and steady might; but that star verged already on its judgment-day.
Seen near, it was a chaos—hollow, half-consumed: an orb perished or perishing—half lava, half glow. . . . What I saw was the shadow of a royal Vashti:
a queen, fair as the day once, turned pale now like twilight, and wasted like
wax in flame." We are invited to identify this "shadow of a royal Vashti" as
Rachel partly because the only proper name she has is but loosely attached
to her: the indefinite article even suggests that the odd name Vashti is generic.
And Lucy Snowe, the heroine of *Villette*, is not a reliable narrator; the actress,
we think, may be a Vashti only in her mind. Single, Semitic, and biblical,
the name resembles Rachel's. It is also suggestive on its own, especially in a
text that makes much of names: we know from Charlotte Brontë's letters
that Lucy Snowe's name was meant to suggest her coolness (Brontë had
considered "Frost"). Vashti is the name of the queen who gets cast off by
her husband, in the Book of Esther, because she rebelliously refuses to display
her beauty, at his behest, before a group of partying men. The actress in
Villette is another kind of rebel, a woman who defies men's rules and requests
by boldly putting herself on display.

From Lucy's point of view this Vashti is immodestly famous. But the
Englishwoman is drawn, paradoxically, by her reputation—as she puts it, "a
name that thrilled me—a name that, in those days, could thrill Europe"
(Lucy also happens to have been invited to the theater to see Vashti by a
man she is in love with). She is even more thrilled when she sees the actress
performing, and she conveys her excitement and awe so vividly—if turgidly—
that almost all biographies of Rachel in English have gratefully borrowed
from Lucy's description in the "Vashti" chapter of *Villette* to suggest what
the actress was like on the stage: "Scarcely a substance herself, she grapples
to conflict with abstractions. Before calamity she is a tigress; she rends her
woes, shivers them in convulsed abhorrence. Pain, for her, has no result in
good; tears water no harvest of wisdom: on sickness, on death itself, she
looks with the eye of a rebel. Wicked, perhaps, she is, but also she is strong;
and her strength has conquered Beauty, has overcome Grace, and bound
both at her side, captives peerlessly fair, and docile as fair."

If Brontë's contemporaries would have had no trouble identifying the
original of the performer whose very name thrilled Europe, they might have

been a little disturbed by Lucy Snowe's assertion that, at the time of writing, the actress's great name's "once restless echoes are all still; she who bore it went years ago to her rest: night and oblivion long since closed above her." For although Rachel had been reported to be ill, pale, and suffering for years, she was not in fact dead at the time Brontë was writing, and did not die until five years after *Villette* was published, two years after Charlotte Brontë herself died. When Brontë saw her in London in the summer of 1851, she did seem to be fading; but the text inclines one to suspect that there were also other reasons why the novelist who admired her enough to immortalize her in the very same move killed her off.

The English writer and the French actress were almost exact contemporaries; both of them were small, not beautiful women, and passionately ambitious artists; both survived beloved younger sisters who died of tuberculosis (Rachel visibly promised to die of it herself the summer that Brontë saw her); and there the resemblance ends. But as Chapter 22 of *Villette* and Brontë's letters suggest, the withdrawn writer from Yorkshire felt intensely and disturbingly connected to the flamboyant foreign actress who seemed to be her opposite and complement. Shocked by Rachel's fierceness and self-assertiveness, Charlotte Brontë was also moved to compassion for the frail woman, very nearly her own age, who seemed possessed by terrible passions, "devils which cried sore and rent the tenement they haunted, but still refused to be exorcized." Watching Rachel, she felt the other woman's emotions, felt herself possessed by an ungodly force she dared not name. "I shall never forget it," she reported in one of several letters she wrote about Rachel; "she made me shudder to the marrow of my bones: in her some fiend has certainly taken up an incarnate home. She is not a woman—she is a snake—she is the ———." The chapter called "Vashti" in *Villette*'s hot center seems to stop the narrative as dead as that sentence stops, bringing Lucy-Brontë to a pitch of eloquence, an ecstatic empyrean, where her own story is forgotten. So narrow is the focus on the actress that Lucy's more ordinary life fades away; the set piece threatens to dissolve the novel. But ironically, the theatrical episode proves crucial to the plot: Lucy's companion's response to Vashti reveals him to be callous and conventional and unworthy of Lucy's love, and at the theater he meets the woman he will marry. Turning away from stolid English John Graham Bretton, Lucy will begin to admit she loves someone more like Vashti, the violently emotional French teacher, Paul Emanuel. In effect, seeing Vashti changes her life.

Villette tells us nothing about the play or the details of Vashti's performance, focusing as it does on Lucy's response to the actress; only by recalling

Rachel (and extrapolating from Lucy's love story) can we guess (as we must) that the play she sees must be *Phèdre*, the tragedy of a woman's uncontrollable, unrequited love. Both the performance and the chapter end abruptly, when the actress's stage agon is interrupted by a cry of "Fire!" but the only real danger proves to be the panic of the crowd. The anticlimactic end raises the question of whether this woman who seemed to set the whole theater aflame with emotion was anything but a figment of the overheated imagination, the enthusiasm of deluded playgoers and the dangerous emotions that Lucy Snowe, striving to live up to her own cool name and exterior, seeks to banish. *Villette* asks scornfully whether the star who thrilled Europe in the 1840s and 1850s was nothing but a big name, a being of illusory genius and substance.

Many of Brontë's critics, reading her letters and reading her in Lucy, have raised the related question of whether the violent Vashti's power was all in the novelist's head, born of a repressed English spinster's problematic identification with a sexy French actress. "I neither love, esteem, nor admire this strange being, but (if I could bear the high mental stimulus so long), I would go every night for three months to watch and study its manifestations," Brontë wrote in her own person, of Rachel. Her pronouns pointedly avoid gender, too prudishly, almost as if she were daring psychoanalytic interpretation. Brontë's intense ambivalence suggests that Rachel stirred the self that she denied, reflected her secret desires for not only passionate action but public acknowledgment and applause. The French actress seemed shockingly and temptingly and threateningly like her hidden self—a self she half-hoped she might have hallucinated. In *Villette*, Lucy Snowe gives the reader grounds for dismissing the power of the actress as an illusion, which only seems to start a fire in the theater. But *Villette* also insists on "Vashti's" historicity—her having "a name that, in those days, could thrill Europe." Doing so, it invites us to shift the focus from the mind of Charlotte Brontë to Rachel.

I STARTED OUT reading about Rachel from what I took to be Brontë's question of how real she was, how distinct from the emotions of those who applauded and talked about her, how knowable. After years of sifting through the verbal and visual traces of her, I am unable and unwilling to answer it. The only conclusion I have come to is that this is the big question that faces all biographers, only more boldly and dramatically when the subject is an actress and a star.

For in the actor's case the question is complicated by another question:

would people other than her contemporaries have thought Rachel was wonderful? As Delacroix reflected in his journal, performers are the only artists whose contemporaries judge them once for all; unlike painters, he wrote, they have no recourse to posterity's reevaluation. (Films and tapes have changed this, to some degree.) *Villette* shows that Lucy Snowe's character and circumstances determine her peculiar perfervid view of Vashti; other people (like her companion, John Graham Bretton) see actors similarly, through the scrims, and within the limits, of their own emotional lives. Like Lucy, who takes seriously "a name that thrilled Europe," they are influenced for good and ill by other people's opinions; as Lucy's are, their perceptions are affected by the dominant assumptions of their culture, even when they reject them. For like Lucy they cannot but hear, and grapple with, received ideas—pervasive feelings about feeling, ideas about the nature of men, women, art, and the self.

According to one encyclopedia, Rachel was "the greatest actress France, or perhaps the world, has ever known." With her the reign of the actress began, write theater historians, pointing to her successful struggles for control of her time and money. She was personally of unprecedented interest to her fans. "Rachel," writes Jean Duvignaud, "was probably the first actor to go beyond the frame of mere notoriety and actually put her life onstage, where each of its events was transformed into an image of destiny—an abstraction of destiny made by transposing the memory of adventures played out in theaters." Not only the heroines she played and the structure of the plays she starred in shaped her self and her life story; the lives and legends of dead performers did, too. In a play written for her, she created the role of the eighteenth-century tragedienne Adrienne Lecouvreur; Alfred de Musset praised her as a second Malibran, after the diva who had died in 1836 and inspired him to write an elegy. Stars are translations, re-presentations, of other stars. Richard Avedon photographed Marilyn Monroe as Jean Harlow; the headline of one French newspaper's review of a recent biography of Rachel stressed the ragged street singer she had been, dubbing her the "môme Piaf" of tragedy. Marilyn Monroe probably didn't know how close she came to imitating a nineteenth-century tragic actress when, in her heyday, she placed the humble musical instrument she claimed to have played as a child—an old white piano, not a guitar—in her luxurious living room.

Images of other celebrated women impose themselves on a star, blurring and also aggrandizing her. The individual becomes generic; history melts into metaphor; fictions and their creators become one. The artistic and literary women of her era informed Rachel's image. For example, George Sand's

Consuelo (1842), a novel about a singer, was dedicated to Pauline Viardot, the novelist's great friend and the diva Malibran's sister; obliquely, it also invited readers to recall Rachel, who like Sand's heroine had been an impoverished child singer rescued by a kindly chorus-master, and had risen from destitution to become famous. (The web of associations was strengthened by gossip connecting Rachel and Musset, who had also been Sand's lover.) Sand's novel invoked romantic fiction as well as theatrical history—specifically, the eponymous heroine of Germaine de Staël's novel *Corinne, or Italy* (1807), who writes poetry and recites it to great applause. Like *Corinne*, *Consuelo* is the story of a brilliant woman performer; and just as *Corinne* did, it allows its readers to confuse its fictional performing heroine—I owe the phrase and the insight to Ellen Moers—with the famous woman author behind her, whose performance is the novel. Germaine de Staël, the author who irritated Napoleon, came to be called "Corinne" after the heroine she named for the Roman poet Corinna; scandalous Aurore Dudevant boldly named herself George Sand: both writers were kinds of stars, admired by the reading public as fashioners of their own unique and reminiscent images, as types and antitypes of Woman.

Stars like Rachel, whom other women see as their reflections and their opposites, seem to act out the struggle between individual and stereotype. Comparing her own different gifts of variety and mobility to a tragedienne's stark severity, Ellen Terry wrote of Sarah Bernhardt, "on the stage she has always seemed to me more a symbol, an ideal, an epitome, than a *woman.*" She added, "It is this quality which makes her so easy in such lofty parts as Phèdre." In her biography of Ellen Terry, Nina Auerbach describes the ways the English actress's career was constrained and informed by Victorian images of pure and loving womanliness, some of which she embodied while she rebelled against others. Rachel shocked and stirred Charlotte Brontë because she daringly transcended conventional womanliness, being foreign and bold as well as brilliant, and emphatically not bourgeois—and representing Tragedy.

But other people, Brontë knew, saw her differently. "He judged her as a woman, not an artist: it was a branding judgment," Lucy Snowe writes of her companion, John Graham Bretton. He dislikes Vashti, and metaphorically he brands her as a criminal or an animal might be branded. Unmoved by her appeal to the spirit, as Lucy is, he insists on her (female) body: he is disturbed—just as Lucy is exhilarated—by suspicions of sexual sources or analogues of her stage passions. He insists that *woman* and *artist* are opposites, that women cannot be artists, that actresses like Vashti cannot be women.

The slide is easy, the position commonplace: misogyny casually exacerbates what Jonas Barish has called "antitheatrical prejudice." Where actors are considered less than artists, because what they show and sell is their bodies and selves, actresses are seen as lesser yet. Critics have argued persuasively that sexist connotations are implicit in the feminine suffix.

While the attitudes toward actresses in nineteenth-century England differed in important ways from attitudes in France, in both countries they were deeply and fundamentally contradictory. On the one hand actresses were condemned for pretending to be who they weren't—and weakening what characters they had by pretense. They were also rated for merely playing themselves. In the misogynist imagination, actresses are false—artful, artificial, duplicitous, like women in general—and on the other hand excitingly, transgressively true to the passions and the imagination. In a culture that confusedly conceived of female sexuality as an excess of either nature or artifice, they were taken to stand for Woman. In a world where ladies did not work for money, they were taken to be like prostitutes. Dignified by tragedy, Mrs. Siddons and Rachel were exceptions that proved the rule that sex is at the heart of the questions an actress raises about morality, aesthetics, character, and truth. Proved, but did not break it. An actress, however lofty, is a public woman (in France a *femme publique* is a prostitute) who provokes in those who admire her more or less prurient curiosity about the parts she keeps hidden, which are easily imagined to be deeper and more interesting than what she shows (hence the interest in her offstage life). In a review of a biography of Rachel subtitled *Her Stage Life and Her Real Life*, Virginia Woolf insisted—in defense of art more than privacy—that the titular distinction was false: "It is when we feel most that we live most," she wrote; "and we cannot believe that Rachel, married to a real man, having real children, and adding up real butcher's bills, would have lived more truly than Rachel imagining the passions of women who never existed." Does an actor live most fully while pretending to be someone else, on the stage? How important, then, or real, is the offstage life? An actress may be a dramatic test case of human knowableness, the biographical subject par excellence.

SHAKESPEARE HAS IT that the actor holds, as 'twere, the mirror up to nature; players are "the abstract and brief chronicles of the time," Hamlet tells Polonius. The modern star reflects the society that constructs her. In the mid-nineteenth century, as the age of mechanical reproduction began and technology made possible the dissemination of cheap newspapers, engravings of portraits, plaster casts of statues, caricatures, and photographs, stars were born of collaborative efforts. As the media burgeoned, images begot fresh images. "Players and painted stage took all my love,/And not those things that they were emblems of," Yeats wrote in "The Circus Animals' Desertion." The more present they were, actors seemed the less real—nothing more than emblems.

On the other hand, lovers of the theater continued to feel, as we still do, that the actors with whom they shared moments of strong emotion were their fellows and intimates. Men lament the loss of their own youth, mourning dead actresses, Jules Janin wrote self-pityingly. When Marie Dorval died, Gautier wrote that "it seemed to us we had lost an intimate friend; a part of our soul and our youth goes to the grave with her; when one has long followed the transformations of an actress's life in the theater, when one has wept, loved, and suffered along with the woman impersonating the fantasies of poets, it is hard not to believe that the magnetic connection created between her luminous figure on the stage, and you in the gloom of the audience, is not reciprocally felt." The mechanism that psychologists call projection-identification falls short of describing the connection between men and women in the audience and those different others who are bright with meanings.

On the day Rachel died in Le Cannet, Delacroix, in the journal largely devoted to his own artistic development, copied out Gautier's review of her Phèdre: "Like all true artists, Rachel grows greater in spirit, ardor, and violence as her career continues. Instead of cooling off, she burns more brightly: experience serves to make her freer, more expansive, more impetuous. What she used to do with nuances, she now conveys by a masterful and dazzling tone." The painter, clearly, was seeing Rachel in his own image, as Charlotte Brontë had done.

It is appropriate that people's reflections of and on Rachel should be all we have of her. Submitting to her audience's gaze while her voice took their minds over, she destabilized the opposition of self and other—and male and female, subject and object, creator and creation, High and Low. ("La Jeune Rachel et la vieille Comédie-Française" is the title of an early pamphlet about her.) A star is rather like Stendhal's image of the beloved, an ordinary branch transformed by the adhering crystals generated by the lover's imagination. Rachel, who reflects and exemplifies the crosscurrents and contradictions of her culture, was their epiphenomenon and product: she would not have been without them. The star appropriated myths her moment provided—of the actress, of the artist; the men and women who painted and wrote about her helped Rachel to make herself up—as the biographer must, pretending perforce that she was and still is to some extent an integral individual, knowable and real.

BIOGRAPHY, advocacy at the very least, turns easily into role-playing; the biographer who comes to resemble her subject is as familiar as the walker who looks like her dog. For much of the time I worked on this book, I insisted to anyone who raised the inevitable eyebrow that I myself was *not* playing Rachel—was not pretending to be French or an actress, glamorous or tragic. When I first began to think and talk about "my" actress—to appropriate her?—no one would let me get over my nominal likeness to her. Just naming my subject hung the question in the air: was I meaning coyly to draw attention to myself? The matter of our name straightaway and economically raised that very good question attendant on any biographical project: Who does she think she is? (An actress raises that question all by herself.) I have driven my friends to invent elaborate periphrases so as to avoid saying the name, or to say it with exaggerated archness; others have felt compelled to let me know that they all too clearly recognize the dark forces that brought a middle-aged, middle-class American professor to "identify" with a glamorous French actress. And then there is G., my earnest and complicated colleague, who carefully pronounces Rachel's name (not mine) as if it were Hebrew—*à la juive*, as it were—his gutturals giving me to understand that he understands the important thing about her, perceives the unspoken, tragic, soul-to-soul connection between myself and my subject.

About whether people with the same name identify with one another—whatever that means—knowledgeable persons seem to be divided. At the first annual picnic of Bob Josephs in Prospect Park in Brooklyn, on 9 June 1985, two couples grappled with the issue. Martha Joseph, the wife of a Bob from Flint, Michigan, tried to explain how she felt about being in a group of people who were related in name only. "There's a kinship, you know what I mean? There's a feeling like automatically you're O.K.," she said. Her husband added, "It's an ego trip to see other little parts of yourself walking around." But another Mrs. Joseph said that for her part, "Well, it's different." And, "Darn sure different," added her Bob.

"AND YOUR NAME AGAIN IS . . . ," the brisk British telephone voice says impatiently. The librarian has reluctantly agreed to let me go through the archives for materials relating to the great French tragedienne who performed to worshipful crowds in London nearly every summer in the

1840s; she wants me to hear that she's made a great exception for an American researcher who neglected to write ahead for an appointment. I repeat my surname; to underscore my gratitude, I spell it out, and add my first name. "Oh, how appropriate," she takes the time to perkily rejoin.

What's odd, of course, is that I should be taken aback. But the sense of its being, precisely, *in*appropriate that my subject has my name on it has nearly melted away in the course of my reading about *la grande Rachel*, sometimes called simply *La Grande*. Which is not to imply that the difference between us has collapsed or even diminished. On the contrary. Said *à la française* (as the English refuse to say things), with a frog in the throat to start and a short "a," then an "sh" opening the stressed second syllable that closes with a deliciously light French "l," the name of the actress Rachel sounds nothing like my own name; to me, it has even begun to *look* different on a French page, where the upright Puritan rectitude of the letters softens somehow.

When I meet her in the reading room, the youthful British librarian allows herself one amused, assessing look—so-you-want-to-be-a-star—then proves friendly. Crackpot onomasticians and half-cocked genealogists are commonplace in her country, where it is also understood that the sun will never set on the labors of minorities working to whiten their kind. More to the point, perhaps, theater libraries attract assiduous fans of even bit players, as well as serious historians avid for all kinds of facts. My accent and clothes give her no clue as to which I might be. As she smilingly hands over the scrapbooks, I reflect that they order these matters differently in France.

In Paris I visit the archive where Rachel's tiny slipper is lovingly preserved. It strikes me that it is offered as evidence of her innate rank; I remember Byron's boasting to his mother that his small ears had been admired as signs of nobility by the Eastern tyrant Ali Pasha. But Byron was nobly born, while Rachel, as everyone who ever heard of her knows, was the daughter of Jewish peddlers from Alsace, and had no real claim to rank. No better claim than my own? The thought occurs to me, in France, uninvited, a grandiose, get-even hallucination induced by socio-linguistic and gender-based insecurities, and yes, standard-issue Jewish paranoia. Is the iron-haired French librarian hostile because she sees me as an imperialistic American intruder, or am I making her nervous by being so clearly (labeled as) a Jew? Do I only imagine they think that my (husband's) surname, not only Jewish but markedly American—with its "w" so troubling to the French—threatens to dim the luster of "Rachel"?

What difference is made by a name? What arbitrary or false connections can names make effectively true? Barthes coined the term "amphibology" to designate a word in which two separate meanings resonate at the same time. He distinguishes it from ambiguity or polysemy: "it is quite precisely amphibology, duplicity; the fantasy is not to hear everything (anything), it is to hear *something else.*" I don't mean my reader to hear my name in or behind the actress's. (I might have made the point by modeling my title page on the program of an American play about the actress: *"Rachel* [Pronounced Rashell]".) For me, the name works as a sign that she was different from me and from what I am able to imagine her to have been. It handily marks her strangeness and familiarity, as it begins to suggest what I think was important about her: her (feminine) gender, her (Jewish) genre, her appearance of singularity. I read the name as a sign of the paradoxical fact and fiction of unique personal identity.

WHEN I WAS A GIRL, a friend's father enjoyed singing out loud and strong, "Rachel, quand du Seigneur," when I came over after school. I assumed that Mr. Bloch had made the song up about me; I had never heard or heard of the aria or the opera it comes from—Halévy's *La Juive*—which, I later discovered, had its first performance in Paris the year before *la grande Rachel*'s debut. I still don't know whether or not Mr. Bloch had read Proust: the mistress of St. Loup, who begins as a cheap little prostitute and becomes a rival of the great actress Berma, is (archly) called *Rachel-quand-du-Seigneur.* Proust's reference to the historical tragedienne Rachel, whose Phèdre Sarah Bernhardt's was much compared to, is evasive and even ironic. If his novel has helped to preserve Rachel's memory, it has also managed to confuse the facts: *Rachel-quand-du-Seigneur* is not only the lesser actress but the younger one, the rivalrous successor who embitters the old greathearted actress's last years. While his first French readers would have caught the little joke, many latter-day Proustians have been misled to think that Rachel came after Bernhardt, the miraculous "Berma" of his boyhood.

In her autobiography, Bernhardt recalls that as a child she saw Rachel, who visited her convent school. "She went all over the convent and into the garden, and she had to sit down because she could not get her breath. They fetched something to bring her round, and she was so pale, oh, so pale! I was very sorry for her and Sister Appoline told me that what she did was killing her, for she was an actress." Sarah saw another little girl put her tongue out at Rachel, and resolved never to be an actress herself: "I did not want people to put out their tongues at me when I was grown up." Whether or not this early "memory" was a fact, Rachel and her fame were formative influences on Bernhardt's career and image. And in turn Bernhardt's image warped Rachel's: in her afterlife, it even began to approximate the shape of a character she never played, Marguérite Gautier of Dumas's *La Dame aux camélias* (1852), which Bernhardt performed with great éclat after Rachel's death.

With *Adrienne Lecouvreur* (1849), the popular playwrights Eugène Scribe and Ernest Legouvé first tailored the role of The Actress to Rachel's exact measurements; later, as players and playwrights and audiences, journalists and novelists, developed the image in the course of the nineteenth century, her particularity was elaborated and also blurred. To Bernhardt's fans, the later actress seemed to bring all the Rachel themes to more dramatic point. Half-Jewish and also from a shady background, she too lived theatrically, and made an even greater show of artistic temperament. She too amassed a fortune, and fought for independence with the Comédie-Française—and managed to found a theater of her own, as Rachel had not done. Like Rachel, she had many lovers (including a few men who had formerly loved Rachel); as Rachel's fame was famously threatened by the Italian Adelaide Ristori, Bernhardt's was menaced by Eleonora Duse; and in 1900, with her brilliant success in Rostand's *L'Aiglon*, Bernhardt even made her own triumphant identification with Napoleon, creating the role of the emperor's short-lived son, the Duke of Reichstadt. She toured and conquered Russia and America, as Rachel had done; like Rachel she chanted *La Marseillaise* and was acclaimed at home as Marianne, the symbol of France. Rachel had been insistently compared to a statue, and Sarah did her one better, exhibiting as a sculptor. As in Rachel's case there were anti-Semitic murmurs against her, for though Sarah was not so Jewish by half, it was the time of the Dreyfus affair. Like Rachel, Bernhardt provoked gossipy biographies and scandalous *romans à clef*; her physical attack, in 1883, on the author of *The Memoirs of Sarah Barnum*, her "friend" Marie Colombier, became part of her legend. Surely that story informed the "memory" of the American physician who, in an article for a magazine, "recalled" having seen Rachel fly at her sister's throat, in a New York hotel room, when she lost at cards. (Napoleon before her had been a famous sore loser at whist.)

Because she was a star Rachel was open for reinterpretation—and fictionalization—as ordinary people are not. Her single name continued to embrace images of other real and fictitious women, as it insisted on her specificity, and its own meanings. "What becomes a legend most?" went the advertising copy running under a photograph of a famous woman wearing a brand-name mink coat. Lillian Hellman, when she was photographed for the ad, is said to have initially misread the line as asking, "What kind of woman is most likely to become a legend?" A good question, to which the answer probably is, A woman who lends herself to being conflated with legends.

IT IS NOT CLEAR what name Jacques and Thérèse Félix gave their second daughter. When she was born in a roadside inn in Switzerland, they were peddlers so marginal, or so leery of the gentile authorities who wanted no part of them either, that they filed no official record of her birth. They themselves claimed to be uncertain of the exact date. It was not until after the quarrel between her father and the management of the Théâtre-Français, about the contract she had signed as a minor, that her age became a particularly vital statistic. Drawn up at the company's request, a certification of her birth was translated and filed with the Swiss consul in March 1840, duly inscribed with a name. One of Rachel's first biographers, Mme de B, whose own proud pseudonym claimed she was both married and aristocratic, crowed over the documentary proof—by documentary gap—of the characterlessness of actors, savoring the irony that "the great tragedienne of our age, she whose renown has been proclaimed in all Europe and confirmed in the New World, can not boast of that which is the patrimony of the humblest and poorest child of the people—an act that proves her identity!"

Most biographers think that her parents probably gave her a composite name, Elisa- or Elisabeth-Rachel. Three of her sisters, Sophie-Sarah the first-born, and Adélaïde-Lia and Mélanie-Dinah, were equipped with both a saint's name and an Old Testament name: Jews who have aspired to assimilation, or flirted with it, have often given their children this kind of scope or choice. On the other hand, the only boy in the family, Raphaël, born just after Rachel, and the sister born after him, Rébecca, had only one Old Testament name apiece. Some believe that the younger girl was called Rachel-Rébecca, and that the enterprising Elisa simply took one of her sister's names. "Elisa" is how she signed herself, when she wrote to her parents at nine or ten from the school where she was being trained as a performer—and sometimes, jokingly, "Pierrot."

When she went onstage she shucked her surname more or less for good. This invites being read as a meaningful act. One early commentator, recalling that Rachel and her sister were registered at school as "Mlles de Saint-Félix," characterizes the act of paring her name down as a proud assertion of Jewish identity: "Rachel did not accept a pseudonym that was given her; as soon as she was free, the name she chose to immortalize was her own name, the name of a daughter of Israel." By dropping her surname, Rachel seemed implicitly to embrace tragic identity, too. "Félix," Latin for happy, is a fairly common name among Jews, a translation of the Hebrew "Baruch," which means blessed. How better to signal the birth of a tragedienne than to cast it off? To make a stage name "real" is always to invite interpretation. Michael Rogin, arguing that Ronald Reagan found out who he was from the movies, points out that before he became an actor he was known by his nickname, "Dutch": Hollywood, which changes most actors' names, gave this one back his own, Rogin acerbly observes. The case of Rachel, part of whose name proved better for business than the whole, is equally suggestive.

The surname Félix was probably adopted by her father's family or conferred upon it by the edict of Napoleon I of 20 July 1808, which sought to integrate Jews into French society and make them subject to its authority by mandating that they take last names. Here as elsewhere, the best interests of the Jews were not Napoleon's only consideration in legitimizing them. A family name inscribes one into the social network of families, marks one as belonging to a group. Women who have refused to take their husbands' names, women and men who prefer to claim the suppressed surnames of their mothers, African-Americans who reject inherited "slave names"—all these recognize that bearing a family name marks one as owned. Refusing such a name, an individual signals independence and self-possession: so must have thought Rachel's contemporary, the photographer Félix Tournachon, who called himself simply and mysteriously "Nadar."

Creative artists have frequently chosen to mark their separation from the network of families by taking a name that is single, like a legendary character's or a king's or queen's. The most notable, perhaps, was the actor-playwright Molière; since him there have been a variety of one-named writers (Colette, Vercors) and performers (Mistinguette, Arletty, Miou-Miou, Fernandel, and, beyond France, Liberace, Cher, Madonna). To take such a name is to claim unusual personal freedom—a claim also staked by those who make a very different move. Celebrating the self-naming of Honoré *de* Balzac, who made his social pretensions more real with a homemade aristocratic *particule*, Stefan Zweig wrote that poetry had triumphed over history. But poetry—and language more generally—has its own constraints. A solitary *prénom*—the French term is especially useful in Rachel's story, as it avoids the awkwardness of "Christian name"—is suggestive in its own right. The performing heroine of *Corinne* goes by one name only: her "last name was not known; her first work [was] signed only Corinne." Before he even sees her, the morose Englishman Lord Nelvil finds his curiosity piqued by "the combination of mystery and public notice—this woman everyone discussed without even knowing her real name." He will fall in love with her. Writing about fiction, Roland Barthes asserts that "what is proper to narrative is not action but character as Proper Name."

THE FIFTEEN-YEAR-OLD actress went onstage as Rachel *tout court* for the first time at the Théâtre du Gymnase, one of the boulevard theaters, in a melodrama that had been written expressly for her. It was 1836—one year after the premiere of *La Juive;* the aria "Rachel, quand du Seigneur" was all the rage in Paris. The name that evoked the eponymous tragic Jewess of the opera—who by the way turns out to have been a Christian by birth—marked the new actress as a Jewess, marked her also perhaps as a little bit fictional, stagy, no more genuinely what she called herself than an actress was expected to be. More generally, it recalled the Hebrew Bible in which Rachel is the name of Jacob's second, more beloved and more beautiful wife (her tomb in Palestine had been a shrine for Jewish pilgrims for centuries). The name also occurs in a verse in the Book of Jeremiah about Rachel weeping for her children (the ship that picks up the orphaned survivors at the end of Melville's *Moby-Dick* is called the *Rachel*). Of the four mothers of Israel—Sarah, Rebecca, Leah, and Rachel—the last is an archetype of maternal woman in medieval Christianity, probably because of the prophet's verse. The Old Testament Rachel was seen by medieval Christians as a prototype of Mary. For the romantics, certainly, her Jewishness remained important: in Edgar Quinet's play *Abasvérus* (1833), based on the legend of the Wandering Jew, *"l'ange Rachel"* looks down from heaven and takes pity on the Jew who refused Christ comfort on the way to Calvary, and she is condemned to share the torment of his eternal life, comforting him.

In mid-nineteenth-century Paris, as a dark-eyed young actress brought it forward, the particular symbolic resonances of the name were probably less important than the sense of its having all that extra weight: "Rachel" signified legendary, literary, tragic Jewish Woman. Several Jewish actresses bore only *prénoms*, like hers—her contemporaries Mlle Judith, Mlle Nathalie, and eventually, if only colloquially, "the divine Sarah"—names that stood out in a Catholic country where saints' names were the norm. After Rachel, women like her would be seen as a type in France; someone thin, dark, Jewish, nervous, passionate, serious, and maybe a little desperate might be called *une vraie Rachel.*

The Greeks called all nouns "names." How different are "proper" names from ordinary, not-improper ones? What difference does a name make to its bearer? Nicole Toussaint du Wast's biography of the actress begins, "Rachel, there is something of Racine in the name borne by one of the nineteenth century's greatest tragediennes." The name, she fancifully ventures, suggests a princess whose family roots *("racines")* are deep in a legendary past—but in fact, Toussaint du Wast concludes, "Tout autre est la réalité." Her point is that Rachel was no poet's creation but a real woman, no princess but a poor man's daughter— in other words, that the name seems to say who she is but doesn't.

La grande Rachel herself liked to invoke her name and play with it. From America, she wrote home triumphantly and a little plaintively that she had carried her name as far as she could; earlier, she had professed that her "most cherished wish is to leave a great name in the theater, and a fine and *honorable* fortune to my parents." She savored her uncommonness, anticipated her place in history, insisted on the personal uniqueness expressed by her single name. Her great name in the figurative sense—her fame—has meant much to those of her biographers who like to contrast the chaos and obscurity of her origins with the fact that she came to be famous: "If Rachel's life remains widely unknown, in its details, in spite of the many biographies devoted to her, her name has retained all of its meaning and greatness. It evokes a talent that has never again been equalled. The name of Rachel also embodies the memory of a prodigious and moving life, is the image of the most extraordinary destiny."

One of several crowns given Rachel in her heyday was studded with precious and semiprecious stones—*R*uby, *A*methyst, *C*ornelian, *H*ematite, *E*merald, *L*apis lazuli—arranged so that the first letters of the words that name them—and the roles of *R*oxane, *A*ménaïde, *C*amille, *H*ermione, *E*milie, *L*aodice—spell "Rachel." A sign that these six fictitious characters epitomized or composed her, or that all of them were subsumed in her uniqueness? The paradox is at the heart of the actor's enterprise, and challenges the biographer.

MOST BIOGRAPHIES of women are lives of actresses; some are written by actresses. The title of a book by Edwige Feuillère about one of her great predecessors—*Moi, La Clairon* (1984)—plays on the shared profession of the writer and her subject: the first-person pronoun makes an implicit connection. Under the pen name "March Cost," an English actress named Margaret Mackie Robinson produced an "autobiography" of Rachel written in the first person, *I, Rachel* (1957). What doubled distortions result when actresses play in print at being other actresses?

I DELIBERATELY use the word "actress" rather than "actor," the term that many women players prefer: I like the fact that it marks the importance of gender. The power Rachel exerted on her audiences had a strong erotic component, and the question of whether she matched (various) dominant images of Woman charged the air around her. Her sex was critically important in making her seem "other"—but not, I think, more important than her distinctive "race" and social class. The daughter of homeless, despised wanderers belonged to something more marginal than an underclass; the glamorous star who dined with makers of opinion enjoyed real power in the world as well as onstage. The interplay of gender, race, and class informed Rachel's life and people's perception of her. As a "public woman" bare to the gaze of men she was an object of erotic interest, but it is significant that women were important among those who were engaged by her—Charlotte Brontë, for one, and Queen Victoria. Delphine de Girardin wrote Rachel a *Cléopâtre* in which the queen takes slaves to bed, then has them killed, like the heroine of Dumas's melodrama *La Tour de Nesle*. Giggling over the story that Rachel had taken issue with the playwright's choice of the ordinary name "Antoine" for Cleopatra's lover, *le tout Paris* took time also to whisper that the actress was the lover of regal Mme de Girardin.

It is too easy to be too explicit about the erotics of theatrical performance, and the ways luxurious dreams of changing selves and lives, of being glamorously other, are gendered fantasies and fantasies of changing gender. In the theater, as many people have written, gender itself seems to be a role. "Many homosexuals are drawn to actresses," write Sarah Bernhardt's most recent biographers, noting that Sarah was "a friend of some of the best-known homosexuals of the day." (The homosexual Marquis de Custine was Rachel's close friend.) Gold and Fizdale speculate that male homosexuals envy the power of actresses to attract men, also "their stylish indifference to convention, and their open promiscuity." But it is more complex than that. Theatrical "self-fashioning," to borrow Stephen Greenblatt's influential term, is a central concern of contemporary "queer theory." Experiencing the art of great performers, thinking of what it must be like to be them, is a kind of imaginary dressing-up that makes one dream of more wonderful radical changes. "I am jealous of the life of great artists: the enjoyment of money, of art, of opulence—it is all theirs," wrote the young Flaubert. "If I could have been simply a beautiful woman dancer—or a violinist; how I should have wept, sighed, loved, sobbed."

A FEW MONTHS AFTER Rachel's death, her family held a public auction of her effects. In the last months of her life, Rachel had anticipated them: in a contract signed on 1 September 1857, she had agreed to send her secretary and business agent, M. Bellevaut, to star-struck, dollar-rich America, to sell by public lottery—one hundred thousand tickets at a dollar apiece—"the diamonds, the silver, and the costumes belonging to Mlle Rachel," including a "river" of thirty-two diamonds, a pearl collar with a diamond and emerald clasp, a vermeil Russian goblet, an embroidered Turkish belt, and a knife, fork, and spoon also in vermeil. But there were laws against such sales in America, and poor Bellevaut was obliged to return home dollarless to Paris after Rachel was dead. Her survivors held their sale in April 1858: of dresses and costumes and silk underskirts; lengths of fabric and lace; one hundred pairs of new gloves; a coffer in malachite and gilded bronze presented by the empress of Russia; four Etruscan vases; more than thirteen hundred bottles of wine; tables, chairs, coffee urns, bracelets and rings and earrings both real and for the stage; an Abyssinian mandolin; the famous battered guitar. There were portraits of Mlle Clairon and Adrienne Lecouvreur; a statuette of Melpomene; copies of the Bible and the Koran, Homer and Byron, the works of Molière and Corneille and Racine and Eugène Sue and Charles Nodier, de Staël's *Corinne* and eleven volumes of George Sand, and—listed in the advertisement under the category *armes*—a revolver and a variety of knives, daggers, and sabers. The things were on view in the Place Royale apartment for several days, and Edmond and Jules de Goncourt, boulevardiers and lovers of the theater and of gossip, queued up to gape along with the masses. They set down what they saw in their journal:

> All the dead woman's old rags—old rags of a woman, of a queen: evening gowns in white satin, Athalie's robes, all the relics of her body, all the costumes of her glory, hung now in heaps as if on the walls of the morgue, looking like ghostly envelopes, clothes from a dream stilled and deadened by the first light of day.
>
> A few women, vendors of these gorgeous, rusty second-hand stuffs, move along, fingering Camille's tunic, seeking out the rent made by her brother's sword.
>
> "Move along, ladies and gentlemen," barks the seller as he prods the shoulders of the dazed crowd milling about. . . . Here is a bedroom, a bed made of black wood with blue silk curtains, and strewn about the room bits of lace, flounces from England, linens from Belgium, handkerchiefs from Valenciennes, all that careful work of a spider's servitude. An old woman sits at the bedside, yellow-faced, bright-eyed, greedy and Jewish, brooding over the lacework. "Move along," says the voice.

E tutto, all that Rachel left behind: a few old rags, diamonds, jewelry, books half-bound in calfskin, and bits of lace; a courtesan's legacy.

The sad clutter of real objects laid out in April light exposed the pathos that underlay the glamour, characterized *La Grande* as just another cheap item, a commodity exhibited to a gaping crowd. Her effects defined the *reine de théâtre* as a courtesan, to be used even after her death for someone else's pleasure and profit. Her family's hustling of even her intimate clothing was an insult to taste, art, privacy, reflection, feeling; it made her pathetic, reduced everything about her to a show, proved that her substance had been only an illusion. When Edmond de Goncourt transcribed the passage word for word from his journal into his 1882 novel about an actress, *La Faustin*, he blurred a line between history and fiction that had never been clear. Goncourt's literal "realism" served to anchor the myth of the *femme artiste* in history: but in the novel, the pathetic, dismissive "facts" about the dead actress prove she had only been illusory.

The *femme artiste* is a Jewess in an earlier novel Goncourt wrote together with his brother, *Manette Salomon* (1867). Manette is not an actress but a beautiful artists' model, whose greedy impoverished mother began putting her out for hire when she was just a child (as many poor Jewish and Italian immigrants were doing in Paris). The young painter who falls desperately in love with her sees her as the embodiment of art; he claims her as his own and forbids her to model for his friends. Deprived of her métier, Manette grows melancholy; pathetically, she poses for herself before a mirror at home. She is an artist in her way, and in her way authentically in love with art. But loving herself is a lamentable perversion. Women, who embody the artist's ideal, cannot themselves be artists, the Goncourts show; and Manette is not only not an artist, but not much of a human being. Beneath her beauty (it runs to fat) she is unregenerately the vulgar Jew, who combines petit-bourgeois values with Asiatic squalor. At the end of the novel, her large Jewish family—muttering men and conspiratorial women—move into the lovers' ménage. The hapless painter, thoroughly trapped, is finished, and his friends shake their heads over his squandered gifts.

In the later Goncourt novel, the protagonist is the *femme artiste* herself. Her stage name, La Faustin (her real name is Juliette), makes it clear that *her* soul is the one at stake. (The tragedy Musset began to write for Rachel was called *Faustine*.) La Faustin is first seen passionately studying and rehearsing the role of Phèdre, carefully following direction, working so seriously

that she goes to consult an old Greek scholar about Euripides. Her aim—
Bernhardt's—is to equal the great Rachel. Possessed by the role of Phèdre,
she becomes possessed, against her will, by lust, as Phèdre was. Of course the
novel has a sexual plot, provided by the actress's grand passion for Lord
Annandale, whose unexpected return to Paris causes her to jilt a man who
thereupon kills himself—causing her no guilt at all. This lord is a gloomy
and father-fixated Englishman unmistakably descended from Lord Nelvil, the
dour beloved of de Staël's *Corinne*, but Annandale's devotion to an old homosexual friend, who comes to live with him and La Faustin, gives his
character a new decadent fillip. For love of the rich dull lord, the actress
proposes to leave the stage and live in retirement with him in the country,
away from the theater and her friends. To show him that she is resolved to
repudiate her career for love of him, she takes him with her to see the display
of a dead tragedienne's pathetic effects.

When Marguérite Gautier, in *La Dame aux camélias*, proposes to her
lover that they leave the gay life of Paris for a simpler world, circumstances
prevent her from living out her hopeful dream of a purified, pastoralized self.
In the case of La Faustin, her own bad dreams undo her: in the most hideous
one, she sees her brains as a salad being tossed by a disembodied plaster
hand. One night in the country she gets up and in her sleep recites a speech
of Hermione's from Racine's *Andromaque*; when her lover awakens her, she
collapses into his arms, sobbing out her desire to forget the tragedienne in
the loving woman. But she cannot love, which is her doom, and his. The
climax of the novel and the ultimate revelation of the character of La Faustin
come when Annandale is mysteriously seized by an illness that permanently
twists his face into a sardonic rictus. Grieving at his bedside, poor Juliette
feels a terrible compulsion to mimic his ghastly expression, and store it for
later use.

Her impulse is an artist's, an actor's. Talma had confessed (a bit shame-
facedly) that his detachment extended beyond the stage: "I scarcely dare
admit," the actor wrote, "that even in a circumstance in my life when I felt
a deep sadness, the passion for the theater was so strong in me that, while
wracked by acute grief, weeping real tears, I in spite of myself made a quick
and fleeting assessment of the change in my voice, which underwent a certain
spasmodic intonation as it was constricted by sobs; and, I say this with some
shame, I automatically thought of using this when I needed it; and in fact
such lessons derived from my own life experiences have often proved quite
useful to me." But such detached observations of oneself are of a different

order than battening on the pain of another person; and different things are expected of men and women, in the realms of demonstrativeness and sympathy. Rachel was notorious for having studied—so as to copy—the collapse of a man in pain. Goncourt's La Faustin embodies the fiercest of misogynist fears. Not only does she copy the expression of the dying man, but she goes to the mirror to measure how well she has done so! At that revealing moment Lord Annandale opens his dying eyes. "Turn out that woman!" he says, twice, in a terrible voice, *in English*, and expires.

The *femme artiste* as Goncourt describes her is incapable of love. She is a monster, a temptress whose sexual allure is partly a function of class—and of crossing classes. A daughter of the people, she is more natural than bourgeois women: "La Faustin had about her the pungent distinctive flavor of a girl of the people, to whom she still belonged, whose coarse crude spicy foods she still preferred." On the other hand, she recalls women of the upper classes: "the duchess alternates with the *grisette.*" In fact she is neither natural nor in any way social, being a creature of the stage and a theatrical city, "the great Parisian courtesan, who gives the most perfect amorous pleasures on earth." The thoroughly artificial La Faustin is a representation of Sarah Bernhardt, of Rachel, of Woman; her evocative half-feminized name insists she is no one in particular, deflecting the charge that Goncourt's is a *chronique scandaleuse.* A novelist, Goncourt disingenuously writes, is "a historian of people who have no history": the distinction reminds the reader of the difference between public and secret history, and the different truths told by books that make revelations soberer historians conceal, or avoid. A similar claim introduces a novel that responds in kind to Goncourt's, the 1884 *roman à clef* by Arsène Houssaye that looks back through Sarah Bernhardt, and the *chroniques scandaleuses* she had inspired, to Rachel. Coyly, it is entitled *La Comédienne.*

Houssaye had been the director of the Théâtre-Français in Rachel's last years: the actress's influence with Louis-Napoleon got him the job, he claimed. In his youth he figured in a popular caricature of the young Rachel, which shows her standing sullen in her toga between two hatted, black-suited nineteenth-century men. In addition to her costume, the girl's identifying features are the large egg-shaped head balanced on a tiny body, dark lowering brows, and the anxious, slightly cross-eyed look that shows up even in flattering pictures of Rachel. She is worried but detached from her associates, engaged with neither the man who hustles her off nor the one bemusedly watching—both easily recognizable, in their time, as the rich impresario and

Rachel with Dr. Louis
Véron and Arsène
Houssaye, from a
contemporary caricature

publisher Dr. Louis Véron and Houssaye. The scene is a variant on, or parody of, the traditional Judgment of Paris, in which a man deliberates before choosing between allegorical female figures. Here the picture of a mind divided is paradoxically inverted. Although the sole woman between rival men is still the prize, and she does not so much choose as allow herself to be chosen, the *male* figures in their modern dress are the pointedly allegorical ones. Fat ugly Véron buttoned into his dark suit, tightly lidded by his stovepipe hat, clearly stands for Commerce; he hustles Rachel away while dapper Houssaye looks on, curious but negligent, leaning on a walking stick entwined by flowering vines, grazed upon by butterflies—a proleptic Whistlerian or Wildean aesthete representing Art.

Houssaye would live well into Wilde's time. Of all Rachel's imaginary and *soi-disant* fathers—playwrights and publicists, teachers and managers, critics and lovers—he is the most engaging. As a very old man, recalling—in his six-volume *Confessions* (1885–91)—the literary-theatrical fashionable Paris he had known, he apologized for his garrulousness, and likened himself, in a charming preface, to a guest who stays too late at a party in the hope of getting off a last really good story. The hint is helpful: fidelity to historical fact is not his chief concern. It obviously was not when he wrote his *roman à clef* about the celebrated actress "Esther Bonheur." The tone of semi-fiction and innuendo is set from the title, *La Comédienne* being both an inclusive term for "actress" and the opposite of *tragédienne*.

Houssaye's plot skips from one bit of familiar anecdote in the Rachel legend to another. He tells the story of Esther, triumphant, coming off the stage with her arms full of bouquets, and meeting the man who had once advised her to go back to selling flowers: she announces airily that she is about to take his advice. (Rachel herself had retailed a version of this story as early as 1845, to a journalist in Lyons, in a letter.) He repeats the tale that when her grammar was corrected, Rachel retorted that women like her made and unmade grammar. He also dishes out the (true) story of her generous love for her younger sister, for whom she bought and furnished a house she presented on the occasion of Rébecca's successful stage debut. Obeying but underplaying the convention that requires a heroine to have a single overwhelming true passion for a man, Houssaye also manages to indicate that Esther/Rachel had abundant other lovers, not neglecting the gossip that one or more of them were women. The novel is laced with famous names (Hugo, Véron, Janin, Samson), and broadly hints at others (Prince Napoléowski). The principals are more and less identifiable beneath their half-masks; a few of the main characters are teasing composites of several people the reader is meant to recognize. There are quotations from letters Rachel sent Houssaye (some included in a chapter entitled "Les Légendes"), and well-known remarks of other named celebrities (like George Sand) who knew her. "Esther" is quoted as having said to the writer, "Should the writers of scandalous tales one day wish to distort my life story, you tell it in all its simplicity; you know all too well that I wasn't raised at the Sacré-Coeur, and that the girls who were are no better than I am, as I have wronged only myself, while many of those young ladies marry a man only to betray him." She is as good as or better than good women: her heart is better than her upbringing was. For this is a scandalous tale written *for* Rachel. In a footnote Houssaye quotes Théodore de Banville, who wrote that Rachel's "most remarkable incarnation was neither Hermione, Phèdre, nor Tisbe, it was that masterpiece worthy of Gavarni or Balzac: Rachel the Parisienne." The novelist adds,

"Rachel, at her whim, could cover herself in jewels or dress in a two-bit wrap: she was always highly distinguished, regally in command and gracious, superior to all God's creatures, that is to say, a Parisian lady!" The snow-balling illogic of sexual enthusiasm, civic pride, male arrogance, and romantic excess recalls Goncourt and escapes analysis. But there is a point here, about the distinction with which Rachel fit into, carried off, whatever garments and ornaments were available—the sense she gave of making them part of herself.

STARS ATTRACT BIOGRAPHERS for obvious reasons: "made" by play-wrights and critics, they fall as if naturally into other writers' hands. ("I owe Ken a lot," Laurence Olivier is said to have protested when Tynan sought to write his life story, "but not my life.") Is it simply that the player who struts and frets her hour upon the stage is a compelling image of mortality? Or do we flatter ourselves when we see a great star's meteoric rise and fall as anything like our own? Are our problems in knowing who we are reflected in the performer's demand to be admired, her dependence on the recognition of other people and their applause? What is the connection between the charged exchange of emotion and identity that links actors and spectators and the felt mystery of being a separate person? Adam Smith wrote long ago that we have to pay actors well for doing what we ourselves wouldn't do for any amount of money: are they aspects of ourselves we admire or abjure, or both?

Gossip, *chroniques scandaleuses*, representations of the private life of an actress are responses to her erotic appeal. In Rachel's case, they were also a way of putting her in her place—insisting on her woman's nature, making the point that her "male talent" was not natural. Jenny Lind was called the Swedish Nightingale because her singing seemed effortless and instinctive; Heinrich Heine satirically imagined Pauline Viardot as natural to the point of exoticism, "especially when she opens wide her large mouth with its dazzling white teeth, and smiles with such savage sweetness and delightful ferocity, you feel as though the monstrous plants and animals of India or Africa were about to appear before your eyes, as though giant palms fes-tooned with thousands of blossoming lianas were shooting up—and you would not be surprised if a leopard or a giraffe, or even a herd of young elephants were to stampede across the stage." When George Sand describes watching Marie Dorval, she extols the performer's art as basic and immediate and physical; the spectator-writer, in contrast, is a (male) Sisyphus torn by "a relentless struggle between desire and impotence," dry and cold and blocked. In contrast to Sand's "poor poet" in agonies of self-doubt and self-consciousness, the actress is graceful, spontaneous; her body, her instrument, reveals her soul transparently—and captivates, reflects, reveals the onlooker's. Here is Sand:

> If, when I take my seat here, when I throw myself on these theater benches, all oppressed by the violence of my pain, burning with fever, my brain aching and heavy, my marble-cold lips smarting with bitterness, tears refusing to flow in my arid eyes, if this woman with her wasp waist, her carefree step, her sad, penetrating look, appears on the stage . . . [it] seems to me that I am watching my own soul, that my soul has dressed up in this pale and sad and beautiful shape to show itself to me, to reveal itself to me and to humanity.

Marie Dorval, the real actress Sand describes here, was the epitome of art-lessness, naturalness, femininity: Gautier wrote that when she performed, "It was no longer art, it was nature itself, it was the essence of maternity distilled in one single woman." In sharp contrast, Rachel was imagined as an avatar of austere, literary art. Hers was the kind of glamour which suggests that word's historical connections with "grammar"—the spells of witches, the magic power of saying certain words. Spotting her one day when she was sitting at her mother's side in a carriage crossing the Seine, engrossed in a book and oblivious to the world, Alfred de Musset marveled at the fact that audiences who cheered Pauline Viardot should also applaud the pale and otherworldly Rachel.

Romantic women performers like Taglioni, Dorval, and Viardot were praised for expressing with their bodies something beyond and more basic than words. Rachel, in contrast, spoke Racine's rhymed lines as if they were her own thoughts; she was *his* voice, some writers said. Representing Roxane, Aménaïde, Camille, and the rest, she also stood more generally for literari-ness, was identified as woman rarely are with language. One biographer has called her the only actor responsible for a literary revolution. The Comédie-Française had given the poet-playwrights of the seventeenth century a stra-tegic place in French culture, by making them central to the living repertoire of the national theater; in the mid-nineteenth century, when Paris seemed to be the center of Western civilization, Rachel reaffirmed the aesthetic value of Corneille's and Racine's works. Reviving them at a time when neither classical Greek tragedy nor the French courtier-playwrights' versions of it spoke directly to what was on living people's minds, she reinforced the "clas-sic" status of the plays, established their place in a canon of European high culture rather as her contemporary (and coreligionist) Felix Mendelssohn helped establish the music of Bach.

TRAGEDY, according to Aristotle the highest literary form, lent her its dignity and authority; representing Tragedy, Rachel identified herself, an actress and a woman and a Jew, with High Art and Genius, creating a disquieting, threatening persona. Misogyny and anti-Semitism fueled hostile criticism of both her play and her character. The two were seen as one by journalists who dug what pay dirt they could from the subject of the celebrity. As early as 1839, Parisian audiences were advised, "Do you know what you have to do to assure that Mlle Rachel will be grateful for your admiration? Go to the theater with your pockets full. Toss flowers to the other actresses, but throw Rachel your wallet. If you lay at her feet coins up to her ankles, if you make the gold shine in those eyes that are too hard to weep, you will give her the emotion and the tenderness she lacks." Rachel's greed and vulgarity were insisted on. The reading public savored stories that she planned to set up her sister in her own bed one night, in order to trick an unwitting lover who had annoyed her; about the showy pineapple she bought from Fauchon's gourmet shop, used as a centerpiece for a dinner party, and returned uncut the next day, demanding her money back; about the host who said she could have the silver epergne she admired, and offered his carriage and servants when she moved to take it right away, cautioning only that *those* must be brought back. As gossip proliferated, so did people who were eager to make a profit by writing it down.

The first full-scale biography published after Rachel's death, by one Madame de Barréra, was anti-romantic, anti-republican, casually anti-Semitic, and moralistic and envious above all. The biographer begins by gratefully marvelling that the high art of tragedy had been revived by "the hand of a child," and harps throughout on the congenital rapacity and lack of patriotism of the actress and her family. Rounding up the usual phrases, she insists of Rachel that "her idol was gold," and observes that she turned down the offer of a salary equal to "the amount paid to Monsieur Guizot to govern the most ungovernable nation on earth!" Rachel was "a thorough cosmopolitan," she writes with distaste; she by the way describes her as deformed by a protuberant breastbone like a chicken's. In performance, writes Mme de B., Rachel resembled "a viper standing erect on its tail" (in Thomas Corneille's *Ariane).* It was this biography, which he read the summer after Rachel's death, that inspired the three reverent sonnets in which Matthew

Arnold apotheosizes the actress as at once a tragic victim and a transcendent symbol of Art.

Mme de B. was concerned to reduce Rachel to ordinariness or worse. The actress's intimates had more complicated goals and motives. The squabbles of those who had known and sought to own her motivated many of the early books about her, notably Jules Janin's *Rachel et la tragédie* (1858), which recycled his reviews and insisted on their importance in her career, and Samson's rejoinder, *Lettre à M. Jules Janin* (1859). The marvellous child had indeed been gifted, Samson wrote, but she would have got nowhere, been no one, without him. In an effort to offset the inevitable gossip that was invited by this claim, Samson's widow wrote her version of the relationship, which was not published until 1898, reiterating her husband's claim of his importance to Rachel, insisting on the purity of his connection with his pupil, and suggesting that she herself had a hand in some important things—that Rachel's stage name, for instance, had been *her* idea. As many women writers about Rachel would do to blame or praise her, Mme Samson underscored her subject's unwomanly will to fame. Recalling a conversation with Rachel and another of her husband's students, she—who had herself given up a stage career for marriage—remembers Rachel protesting, "Renouncing the theater would be renouncing life itself!" Shocked Mme Samson could never forget what the young woman said: "Say what you will of love and marriage, nothing takes the place of glory."

In the last three decades of the nineteenth century, while Sarah Bernhardt dominated the theatrical scene, nostalgia moved garrulous old men to recall the wonderful earlier actress who seemed to incarnate their own lost youth; meanwhile new authorities purveyed their versions of the facts. The prominent drama critic Francisque Sarcey, for instance, spoke in London in 1879 about the lean years of the Comédie-Française, during the July Monarchy.

> Rachel alone could draw receipts in those days. It was the great Rachel. But Rachel cost the theater more than she ever drew, and she did more harm to art than she rendered it service. . . . The nights on which she played the receipts amounted to ten thousand francs, the whole of which went into her pocket. The next night the theater was empty. Rachel, moreover, must be blamed for having imparted a factitious life to tragedy and for encouraging her admirers to struggle against the advent of a new art. She obstinately confined herself

to a dozen parts, in which she displayed incomparable power, and left imperishable memories. She did not lend the assistance of her genius to any of the contemporary poets, or, if she did so, it was with regret, and without decisive success.

Partisans of the state theater had long invoked variants of those complaints: her lack of team spirit, an offense against the communal life of actors; in general, the evidence (her loyalty to her family only made it more compelling) that she was out for herself, a loner. The fact that she had allied herself with the magisterial dead, rather than contemporary artists, had always rankled even while her narrowness had intensified the sense that she was "incomparable" in a high art France considered distinctively its own.

As Bernhardt and other artists continued to recall her image, Rachel was now idealized, then reduced to one or another of the things she stood for. Guy de Maupassant invoked her obliquely in a story, "Mademoiselle Fifi" (1882), about a prostitute called Rachel who murders a German officer, proving herself a French patriot in spite of being a Jew: in a final paragraph, the narrator makes the familiar claim that she was really a better woman than the bourgeoisie who scorned her. In 1883, Oscar Wilde, visiting Paris, sent his card to Edmond, the surviving Goncourt brother, expressing his esteem for the author of *La Faustin*, which would influence his portrayal of Sibyl Vane in *The Picture of Dorian Gray* (1890). Texts produce other texts, get translated, re-presented. The murder in "Mademoiselle Fifi" was the subject of a painting by Ernest-Jean Delahaye that was exhibited in the Salon of 1898. Four years later, *Adriana Lecouvreur*, the opera by Cilea and Colautti, had its premiere in Milan: if the program notes did not recall, as they tend to do now, that Rachel had played Adrienne, and wept for herself while rehearsing Adrienne's death scene, that was because there still were people alive who could tell that story.

Biographies of the dead depend on documents, usually letters. From the handsome volume of Rachel's correspondence that was published in 1882, the editor, Edmond Poinsot (who signed himself Georges d'Heylli), took pains to banish all hints of scandal—for the greater glory of Tragedy and the Comédie-Française (and out of regard for Lia and Dinah Félix, who were still alive). He arranged choice bits of Rachel's voluminous correspondence to portray an energetic worker and a sometimes caustic wit; he emphasized the pathetic, tragic sufferer. In 1910 the "discovery" of new love letters produced a spate of biographies, the most sympathetic being *La Vie sentimentale de Rachel d'après des lettres inédites* by Valentine Thomson, the great-granddaughter of the lawyer Adolphe Crémieux. Thomson's Rachel, largely derived from letters the actress wrote to a lover with whom she planned a simple life in the country, is a loving, suffering, sympathetic woman. "Cold impartiality is not absolutely necessary," the biographer wrote in defense of her own sympathetic method. "On the contrary, isn't indulgence required, in making judgments of an already distant past? And shouldn't we allow the charm that seduced all the tragedienne's contemporaries to act on us, so we may know her better?" The same year Thomson's book was published, *Rachel et son temps*, by A. de Faucigny-Lucinge, also appeared. It emphasized Rachel the avatar of classicism and the awesome star—one of those "comets which have their own laws; the place they come from, the place they go to, everything, is strange, in their bizarre, tremendous, tormented destiny." As if to correct the feminine emphasis, Hector Fleischmann, the author of a biography of Mlle George entitled *Maîtresse de Napoléon*, produced his scandalmongering *Rachel intime* (1910), which reprinted many of the scurrilous caricatures that attacked Rachel in her time, and resurrected the most salacious lost gossip. Fleischmann claimed to reveal the base facts behind the noble appearance: among his juicy "revelations" was the Napoleonic menu of the dinner Rachel gave for Alexandre Walewski, shamelessly borrowed from Houssaye's novel, in which "Esther" serves "Comte Napoléowski" "Saucisson à l'ail de Toulon, Omelette au Jambon de Mayence, Andouilles à la Bonaparte, Poulet à la Marengo, Bombe Glacée à la Moscowa." The brandy-and-cigars tone is like Goncourt's and Houssaye's, the guiding premise that the life of the actress—excessive, theatrical, and implausible—by its nature invites and deserves embroidery.

In England, Francis Gribble put together a moralizing spin-off of Fleischmann, the disapproving *Rachel: Her Stage Life and Her Real Life* (1911), which deplores the great actress's offstage behavior; it is notable mostly for Virginia Woolf's rejection, in a book review, of its title and point of view. Woolf's claim that Rachel lived fully and truly and well in her imagination is a vigorous feminist variant on Wilde's epigram that "the only real people are the people who never existed." As Woolf understood, the sexual emphasis of Rachel's biographers calls out for a corrective insistence on her work: Henry James began to make it in *The Tragic Muse*, in which the old actress Mme Carré speaks of Rachel as "a drudge" who labored tirelessly at her art. But biographers continued to stress her sexual life. The American Nina (Mrs. Arthur) Kennard had managed loftily, in an 1886 book for a series called "Representative Women," to shift the emphasis slightly—from the erotic to the maternal. She gave pride of place, in her conclusion, to a letter the actress wrote to her son: "Come into my heart, dear little one, and find there all

the tenderness of which there is an unlimited supply for my sons. It is riches
without end that God gives mothers who love their children."

In a 1928 biography written for a series with a similar title, the English
critic James Agate predictably sank the doting mother. Agate pronounced
Rachel "first a great Jewess, second a great actress, and third a great lover,"
whose "great career may be used to point whichever of two morals one
prefers: either that abnormality in one direction must be balanced by abnormality in another, or that men and women are not made in one piece." The
tongue is somewhere near the cheek; the tone is arch and fey and pointedly
insouciant—and, like every biographer's, proprietary. Agate, born in 1877,
reached back through Bernhardt (whom his actress sister May had known)
to Rachel: he could "remember my father taking me to see Sarah Bernhardt,
in, I think, *Frou-Frou*. I remember, that while the tears were still running
down his face, he told me that Rachel was a greater actress." In filial pride,
he extends Diderot's paradox—that the actor who feels least performs most
effectively—across the proscenium arch, writing that his father's "detachment
proved him to have been a dramatic critic without portfolio." The son took
up the critic's portfolio in earnest, and by the way the cult of Rachel, and
pursued his obsession with the kind of fervent detachment he attributed to
his father—and to her. He went so far as to amuse himself by reconstructing
Rachel's London debut in honor of its centennial.

The salient, politically charged issue among her French biographers in
the years after the Dreyfus affair was, How French was Rachel? It was debated in sober academic tones. André Bellessort's meditation on Rachel and
tragedy (1929) insists on the paradox of the ignorant, vulgar, but supremely
gifted Jewess who revived the noble plays; Louis Barthou's respectful *Rachel*
(1926) is tactful about the relation of legend and history. It begins, "Il y avait
une fois une petite juive," and concludes by echoing and correcting itself: "Il
y avait une fois une grande tragédienne." Is this to be read as a claim that
legend can become history, or a confession of the writer's complicity in the
transformation? Or is it guileless rhetoric? In the mid-1930s, new threats and
fears in Europe created a new kind of partisan interest in the actress. Bernard
Falk's *Rachel the Immortal* (1936) put the emphasis on the woman of the
people (and the adorable playful child); Abraham Cahan's *Rachel* (1938), a
compilation of columns from his New York Yiddish newspaper, *The Jewish
Daily Forward*, claimed her as a heroine of the Jews.

The "discoveries" of letters and the publication of books about Rachel
inspired various stagings of her legend. In 1913, when a play about Rachel (by

Gustave Grillet) opened in Paris, it provoked a debate in the newspapers about whether its star was sufficiently ugly to play Rachel—illustrated with hideous portraits of the dead star and charming ones of the actresses who had been considered for the role. A four-act romantic drama very like Grillet's, *Rachel* by Carina Jordan, opened at the Knickerbocker Theatre on Broadway at Thirty-eighth Street in New York in December 1913. It ran for two weeks; both the star (Bertha Kalich of the Yiddish stage) and the subject were a little too foreign to please. "There has always been a tendency toward the historical play abroad," wrote the reviewer for *The Theatre, The Magazine for Playgoers*. "Those people live more in the past than we do." Nevertheless, over a decade later, the Belmont Theater in Los Angeles briefly housed a play about Rachel. The program concludes a brief synopsis of the "comedy-drama" thus: "Everything is taken away from her—even her jewels, and the one she loves." At least three other Rachel plays were planned or written in England and America: the playwright and critic William Archer considered producing "a story round that great name" for the American actress Elizabeth Robins. *La Guitare de Rachel*, a play by Maurice M. L. Savin, was published in Paris in 1964. Dead as alive, Rachel has remained intriguing as a character poised at a place where the commercial and vulgar and sordid aspects of the theater converge with emotional truths accessible only through a serious performer's art—"those more solid realities," as Proust called them, "*Phèdre* and the way in which Berma spoke her lines."

Scholarship emerged after the war, in the 1940s. Gabriel Laplane's *Lettres inédites* (1947), like d'Heylli's earlier volume of letters, took the form of a narrative, with commentaries by the editor splicing Rachel's own words. But it was more complete, printing new letters—notably, the vivid love letters between her and the playwright François Ponsard—without bowdlerizing them, and attempting to rescue Rachel from arguments about art and morality. In *Rachel en Amérique* (1957), Sylvie Chevalley painstakingly corrected the impression (cherished by the French) that Rachel's American tour was an utter financial disaster. Her recent fat biography of the actress, *Rachel: j'ai porté mon nom aussi loin que j'ai pu* (1989), presents a believable portrait of a gifted and ambitious woman. Chevalley seeks to emphasize the artist and de-mythicize Rachel. Before her, Joanna Richardson, in *Rachel* (1957), aimed explicitly "to disentangle her life from the legend." Richardson wrote that she wanted "to record it as completely as I can," believing that "if, in the process, fact resembles fiction, that is the fault of history." Richardson regretted that "Rachel was too well aware of the worth of publicity to fell the

298 — N° 3686   L'ILLUSTRATION   18 Octobre 1913

Rachel à vingt ans. — *D'après une lithographie.*   Collection J.-L. Croze.   Rachel à trente-six ans. — *Phot. E. Carjat.*

TROP BELLE POUR INCARNER RACHEL

Rachel est une des plus merveilleuses, sinon la plus merveilleuse, des interprètes tragiques qui ont illustré la scène française. A la seule force de son génie, la tragédie classique a dû se survivre en pleine période romantique, de lutter glorieusement contre le drame à la manière de Hugo. C'est à Rachel que les héroïnes classiques ont dû l'emporter sur les héroïnes du romantisme. De la vie de cette femme admirable, M. Grillet, un auteur dramatique ayant déjà fait ses preuves, a su tirer une œuvre pour le théâtre. Nous allions donc assister à une résurrection de Rachel. Animée par l'auteur, elle allait reparaître sur la scène un peu plus d'un demi-siècle après sa mort. La tentative ne manquait ni d'intérêt ni d'originalité. M. Antoine, l'ayant compris, accepta l'œuvre pour l'Odéon et l'annonça dans le programme de ses spectacles. Et voici que les tribulations commencèrent. A l'histoire de Rachel comédienne s'ajoute désormais l'histoire de *Rachel* œuvre dramatique.

D'abord la famille de l'actrice s'opposa à la représentation. C'était son droit. Le lustre qu'elle tenait du nom de Rachel lui suffisait. Elle ne voulait point y ajouter celui d'un spectacle dont son ancêtre ferait l'objet. L'auteur se débattit et tout s'arrangea assez vite. L'autorisation donnée, on s'occupa des répétitions, et naturellement de la distribution des rôles. A M¹¹ᵉ Gilda Darthy revint le périlleux honneur d'incarner Rachel. Puis, un beau jour, le rôle passa de M¹¹ᵉ Gilda Darthy à M¹¹ᵉ Séphora Mossé, premier prix de tragédie aux derniers concours du Conservatoire. Jusqu'ici rien que de banal. Il arrive fréquemment qu'un rôle change d'interprète. Mais où l'affaire prit de l'importance au point que l'Art y fut mis en cause dans ses principes mêmes, c'est au moment où fut révélée la cause de cette modification : M¹¹ᵉ Gilda Darthy est trop belle pour incarner Rachel ! Et l'on se révolte. Comment peut-on être trop belle pour évoquer celle qui fut une Phèdre si magnifique, une Monime si touchante, une Andromaque si sublime, une Esther, une Athalie qui ne seront peut-être jamais égalées.

Tout cela est vrai sans doute ; mais il ne faut pas confondre la personne de Rachel avec celle des héroïnes qu'elle a représentées. Celles-ci furent belles de l'impeccable beauté grecque. Du moins, les voyons-nous ainsi. Il n'en va pas de même pour Rachel qui était plutôt petite et mince, et dont le visage était fort irrégulier avec un front trop vaste, un bas de visage étréci, un nez long et fort. Toute sa beauté lui venait de son génie. Cela qui semble avoir peu d'importance en acquiert en réalité du fait que des gens existent encore qui applaudirent Rachel. M. Antoine vit en M¹¹ᵉ Séphora Mossé une interprète plus apte à représenter physiquement l'illustre tragédienne. Le talent des deux actrices n'est point en cause. Un simple coup d'œil sur les photographies de Rachel, de M¹¹ᵉ Gilda Darthy et de M¹¹ᵉ Séphora Mossé, montre clairement que celle-ci, au moyen de quelques artifices de coiffure et de maquillage peut, beaucoup plus aisément que sa camarade, évoquer la ressemblance de leur illustre devancière. Ajoutez à cela que sa stature se rapproche de celle du personnage qu'elle incarne, ce qui n'est pas le cas de M¹¹ᵉ Gilda Darthy, et vous aurez les raisons de convenance physique qui expliquent ce petit épisode de l'histoire anecdotique du théâtre contemporain.

Photographi'es H. Manuel.

M¹¹ᵉ Gilda Darthy, reconnue « trop belle » pour incarner Rachel.   M¹¹ᵉ Séphora Mossé, qui répète actuellement le rôle de Rachel.

"Too Beautiful to Play Rachel," page from *L'Illustration*, 15 October 1913

forest of legend that, fertilized by ignorance, by malice and design, rose about her in her own time." Unlike her, I am interested, above all, in how Rachel and her life were embedded in legends. I want to map that fantastic forest, to suggest that the interlocking branches of fact and fiction there cannot be disentangled.

For all the efforts of sober scholars, the romantic view of Rachel has hung on, inspiring *biographies romancées* more and less believable, suggesting as much about the writers as they do about their professed subject. The epiphenomenon attests to the continuing force, in the field, of illusions. On the dust jacket of March Cost's *I, Rachel* there is a photograph of the pseudonymous actress turned pseudo-biographer, decked out in the ladylike fashion of the 1950s: little hat with veil, white gloves, and a bunch of violets. Like Rachel, she looks away. Her book—evidently based on the curious series of passionate, agonized, enigmatic letters the young Rachel wrote to Samson in the summer of 1840—spins a tale of unrequited love between a powerful fatherly master and an apt girl pupil. It is the whispered story that the widow Samson tried so hard to squelch, retold with chaste British prurience.

Rachel was clearly a fantasized role for one actress-writer; was it something very different for those other biographers, women and men whose elaborate French names strike the Anglophone reader at least as comically antithetical to hers: A. de Faucigny-Lucinge (née Choiseul-Gouffier); J. Lucas-Dubreton; Martial-Piéchaud; Nicole Toussaint du Wast? In what sense are they closer, am I further, from what one journalist in the mid-nineteenth century called "la verité Rachel"? Did they imagine someone wonderfully like or unlike themselves? What are the consequences of the various distances between biographers and their chosen subjects? A pale shadow of the tensions of the theater, which link the spectator, the actor, and the role, informs the relation of the biographer and her subject. ("I thought her very pretty in London this year but she looked what Lady Ruthven called her 'a beautiful shadow' or more correctly to my idea a pale shadow," Effie Ruskin wrote of Rachel, whom she saw the same year as Charlotte Brontë did; Brontë also chose the image of a shadow—often used, by the Victorians, of a "fallen" woman—to describe her.)

Biography makes strange bedfellows. Rachel, who epitomized contradiction, has inspired lucubrations of very different types and tones. Parallel excerpts from two brief sketches will dramatize my point. At one extreme are the feminine, nineteenth-century accents of the American Sarah Josepha

Hale, who thus concluded, in Rachel's lifetime, a sketch in a dictionary of "Distinguished Women from the Creation to A.D. 1854":

> No doubt calumny has exaggerated the reports of Mademoiselle Rachel's amours; nor ought she to be judged by the standard of a Siddons, who was born and trained in a land where female chastity is required as the crowning grace of the actress. Still we do regret that a shadow has fallen on the fair fame of one who might have been, like Jenny Lind, a glory to her sex as well as to her profession. But let us record her good deeds. Mademoiselle Rachel is said to be very charitable to the poor. She has provided generously for her own family; educating her sisters and brothers, and never forgetting the humble condition from which she has risen. As a memorial of her street-minstrelsy, she religiously preserves her own guitar.

At the other end is an entry in a "biographical repertory" appended to an English edition of the Goncourt journals, which reads in part:

> Rachel possessed from childhood a particular genius for the declamation of classical French verse, a genius comparable say to that of certain Russian-Jewish boys for the violin. She was not beautiful; she was uniformly unfaithful to her lovers; she was notoriously avaricious; but she seems more than any other person to have been the cause of the revival of public appreciation of classical tragedy in the forties and fifties of the last century, when romanticism was still alive; and she became thus a kind of storm centre and great public figure. Anecdotes concerning her pullulate, but there is none that deals altogether kindly with her.

The actress, the woman, the foreign Jew inspire interlocking prejudices and odd assumptions of familiarity. The angle of vision and the climate of opinion powerfully affect images which in turn have powerful effects.

In a series of lectures he delivered in 1939–40, the actor Louis Jouvet invoked Rachel. Actors may be classified as either *pour* or *contre*, for or against, he argued. He offered Talma as the paradigm of the first kind, for whom audiences had an immediate affinity; the other kind, he said, was exemplified by Rachel, who fascinated by repelling. From here it is all too clear that, along with the habit of binary opposition, race (or what was problematically called race, in Europe in the 1930s) and gender figure in this belated professional assessment based only on hearsay: Jouvet spoke less than a decade after the German government ordered the demolition of a statue of the Jewish actress in Potsdam, which had been erected near the spot where she had performed for the King of Prussia in 1852. It should warn us that those complex interlocking factors which colored the experiences of hearing Rachel in the first place must charge any belated project of recalling her.

CHAPTER THREE

~

Origins

Men can do nothing without the make-believe of a beginning.
GEORGE ELIOT, *Daniel Deronda*

My parents are poor people, but we are of the ancient Jewish race.
I am a daughter of the Bible, because I am descended from Israel,
and because my father taught me how to read with the books of the
prophets and the patriarchs; I understand nothing of what is bourgeois and vulgar; I love summits.

"ESTHER," in Houssaye's *La Comédienne*

THERE ARE TWO KINDS of legends about Rachel. One is the tale of
miraculous birth; the other concerns the creation of a woman from mere
matter. In both, the creators are male.

The first, most fully elaborated story goes more or less like this:

*A pregnant woman, wretchedly poor and homeless, traveling in a strange
land, is turned away from inn after inn. Finally she is given shelter, and brought
to bed in a room ominously numbered 13 in a roadside hostel prophetically called
The Sun, near an obscure Swiss village named—ironically, it will seem—by a
mumble: Mumph. The baby's birth is not registered; her peddler husband packs
off mother and girl-child as soon as possible in the wagon that serves as their
shop and home. He is anxious to get back to business and/or to be on his way
out of hostile territory. The family—it includes another little girl of two—bumps
uneventfully across the rutted roads of Europe. One day the infant tumbles off*

the back of the wagon, and is returned to the parents by a passing peasant, a man of the people saving Rachel for France. (In other versions of the story, the bundled baby is rescued by Mouton, the faithful family dog.)

The children (in short order, there are several more) rattle around among the heterogeneous wares the parents sell. The dark eyes of the little girl born in the Swiss inn show flashes of what anyone looking on (but of course, there is no one to speak of) would recognize as signs of genius: she can find the right chords to strum on the guitar when her sister sings, and one day she surprises the family by reciting in a sort of chant, with astonishing fervor, the old Ballad of the Wandering Jew. Among themselves, the family speak a hideous bastard German dialect, but the gifted child's French is miraculously pure. (For French people, this is the most significant of all the portents.)

The father is by all accounts a rascal. (In Abraham Cahan's Yiddish biography of Rachel, he is said to have done some time in a small-town jail. The fact, if it is one, is hard to document; most biographers leave it out; is it fairer to suppress such an only possible truth, or to give space to what well might be calumny?) *He is shiftless, a tippler, depends on his wife, who mends the old clothes they sell, to do all the work for him. Can it be he who teaches the children to speak and play and sing? Who else is there? Does he also have the sophistication and intellectual wherewithal to teach them to recite alexandrines, and to harbor fantasies of success, assimilation, cultural legitimacy, comfort, and power?*

When the family settles eventually in a city, Lyons, he gets a job at a theater as a fireman: such people are very necessary, as the oil lights and the painted scenery and the crowds present a potentially perilous combination. The brute has a taste for drama (the theater has grown more violent and spectacular since the Revolution, over the years). He meets the actress Virginie Déjazet, who possibly (she has a heart of gold) invites him to look her up if he should come to Paris. Such things happen. He doesn't make much money, and (true to the customs of his kind, careless of their safety and education) he sends his older girls out on the streets to pick up what cash they can to support the mother and younger children at home. They are perhaps eight and ten; one singing and the other at the guitar, they frequent the cafés near the theaters—the brothels, some say—where the buxom blond good looks and flirtatious behavior of the elder attract the attention of idle loungers. Usually the dark, thin younger child strums the guitar as the blond one sings, but sometimes she recites in the strange, harsh, stirring voice that would later be described as a mélopée. A local woman, a good Christian, takes pity on the children, protects them, and often augments their small take at the end of the day, so as to forestall the father's beatings.

One day a kind stranger rescues the girls from poverty and their father and the cruising Don Juans of the taverns. Some cleaning up and minimal schooling in Paris, the capital of the nineteenth century, makes the younger sister's great destiny clear: Tragedy. At the national theater the best judges recognize a perfect classical actress, only fear that with her extraordinary (romantic) intensity she will too soon burn out. No one has seen her like before.

She is a metonymy, not a metaphor, of Tragedy. The dark eyes blaze with knowledge of terrible truth; suffering has left its mark on the pinched white face, the hollowed-out voice. But the child's head—not beautiful, with its protuberant forehead, and disproportionately large—is held with grace and majesty by her thin neck. The distinguished actress Mlle Mars admires the way she walks; Samson praises her more elliptically, less translatably: "admirable organisation théâtrale," admirably well organized for the theater, an admirable theatrical organism. The child from nowhere is recognized as the avatar of a nearly forgotten art in which inheres the lost glory of a once heroic nation.

IN THE MYTH of Rachel's miraculous birth, reminiscent though it is of older legends, the lineaments of her historical moment are legible. The story confirms both Napoleonic doctrine and Balzacian insight: that careers were open to talent, and that persons are only what they make themselves up, and out, to be. Also it serves to fill a material gap in evidence. Even today, obscure people like the Félixes leave few documentary traces.

For little people as for very great ones, personal history is implicated in world-historical forces. Rachel's peddler parents were children of peddlers, members of a class of poor Jews looked down upon by their own people as well as by the gentiles—the class from which the rich Gimbels and Guggenheims and Strausses sprang in the nineteenth century. There is a hierarchy even among peddlers, and in its terms the Félixes were not exactly the lowest of the low: only the more prosperous had wagons of their own, as they did. The lowliest walked with packs on their shoulders, leaving their houses at the beginning of the week and returning, when they could, for the Sabbath, sometimes walking the roads all summer, following the fairs. Peddlers with wagons could take their homes with them. In the way of business, such people often met up with actors, itinerants and hawkers like themselves. Secondhand clothes were bought and worn by most of the population of Europe then, but actors, who were required by theater managers to provide their own costumes, were especially good customers.

It is not clear how long the young Félixes had owned the vehicle—it was probably drawn by a mule—in which they were living and working in early 1821, when Rachel was born. Possibly they had bought it when they had made their not uncommon but still radical decision to move toward the cities of the west: it provided a convenient and economical means of travel. At the time their second daughter was born, they were doing business on the busy road between Basel and Zurich, in the canton of Aargau (in French, Argovie), near Aarau, in Switzerland, where they were welcomed by the isolated peasants of the region and feared by the local merchants who, jealous of their customers, had succeeded in having laws passed to prohibit giving Jews shelter. (In spite of such laws, Thérèse or Esther Félix managed to get the help of a midwife, as well as a room at the inn.) Their wagon was crammed with what humbler peddlers carried in their packs: old clothes and what used to be called "notions," needles and threads and fasteners for clothing, bolts of fabric, tanned animal skins, magnifying glasses, spectacles, scissors, umbrellas. Also stacks of pamphlets and chapbooks, the popular literature, or *bibliothèque bleue*, that never got into libraries or bookshops. Among such peddlers' books (*livres de colportage*) there well might have been a version—several, even—of the tale of the Wandering Jew. First written down in 1710, this medieval story is about a Jew (sometimes given the name Ahasvérus) who, for the crime of refusing comfort to Christ on the road to Calvary, is condemned to wander the earth eternally, like Cain. The tale appealed to the romantic imagination of a time when widespread immigration was changing the demographic face of Europe: like Cain, the Jew was an image of the *poète maudit*, an outcast from society, banished to solitariness for refusing brotherly love. (Later in the century, the painter Courbet, exploring social inequities, would draw on popular images of the Wandering Jew in his non-demonic form.) Dramatic versions of the story had been put on the boards in Paris in 1812 and appeared again in the 1830s. In the play *Ahasvérus* by Edgar Quinet, fragments of which were published in the *Revue des deux mondes* of 1 October 1833, Ahasvérus is comforted by the *ange Rachel*, who is doomed to share his wanderings. When in 1844 Eugène Sue's novel, *Le Juif errant*, was published, Paris gossips said the figure had been partly inspired by the real-life Jacques Félix: this intersection of fiction and history is only as factitious and ironic as the stranger-than-fiction fact that literally wandering Jews carried and sold to gentiles cheap printed versions of a story directed against the Jews. The often-told tale that Rachel first showed her talent by declaiming the ballad to her family has an anti-Semitic subtext: it is as if, by reciting, the Jewish actress authenticated it. Also it suggests that in some way the chapbooks bundled in the peddler's wagon along with the baby had generated the tragedienne, or begun to endow the biological accident of her birth with the signifying shape that literary language has.

SOME HISTORIANS of Jewish peddlers unblinkingly trace their origins to the nomadic life of the Middle East. A materialist view is more plausible. By the nineteenth century, peddling was a traditional way of life for European Jews, who in some countries were still forbidden to own land. The way of life was not only an affliction: the flexible hours and independence that peddling offered attracted people who wanted to remain on the margins of society and preserve, among other things, their religious freedom. Peddlers could carry their own kosher pots, and keep to the weekly rhythms of prayer and rest that Judaism mandated, as other workers among the gentiles could not. And peddlers had a quasi-religious function, too, as objects of charity. The arrival of a footsore peddler in a shtetl, of a Sabbath, was welcomed as a chance for the community to exercise the religious obligation of hospitality—as well as an opportunity to hear the latest news. On the other hand, a rebel Jew who balked at the rules and sequestration of the Jewish community might well look to the road for liberation (or temporary freedom) from the family creed. Peddlers were cosmopolitans. Though poor and marginal, they were not like those religious village Jews who were secluded from the Christian world and from secular knowledge, and afraid of the people they lived among. They were not unworldly, not naive. Since Shakespeare's gossipy Autolycus of *A Winter's Tale*, peddlers have been known as ragbags of information, and valued for their expertise about, for instance, currencies. Though he was not perhaps reliably grammatical, it is neither comical nor unlikely—although some biographers think it is—that Jacques Félix would have known enough of what might now be called business German to have people pay him to teach it in Lyons. The Félixes, then, must be imagined not as bearded and bewigged and Orthodox, but as an enterprising modern young couple attuned to their times, or eager to embrace modernity, when they left their parents behind and moved toward the Enlightenment and the cities of the west.

With the exemplary exception of Chevalley, however, most of Rachel's biographers call them by their Hebrew names, Jacob and Esther Chaya, in effect refusing to recognize them as French. (Mme de B. calls him Abraham, with what James Agate wittily characterized as "Christian inaccuracy.") The question of the actress's nationality confused a public already confused about Jews in general: "Mlle Rachel was born in Munf, in the canton of Aarau

(Switzerland), on March 24, 1820," one journalist wrote inaccurately in 1843. "Her mother, Esther Haya, is a Jewess; but, God be praised! Rachel is French by her father M. Félix of Metz. Like most Israelites, M. Félix was a common peddler who traveled from fair to fair with his large family." (Other journalists reported that the mother was from Bohemia, hinting at Gypsy ancestry.) Jews were in fact citizens of France, having been declared such—along with Protestants and actors—by a Revolutionary decree of 1791. And the Félixes' decision to take the road from Alsace suggests they were French by choice as well as by birth, French rather than Alsatian or German, or Jewish first of all. Jacques later said he had studied to be a rabbi, but probably only as a way of claiming (indefinite, untraceable) intellectual distinction; as her Jewish critics pointed out later, there was no protest from home when, on the solemn holiday of Yom Kippur, the young Rachel performed the role of Pauline in *Polyeucte*, who converts to Christianity. (When he was put on the spot about this, Jacques countered that his daughter belonged to the Comédie-Française and not to him, skirting the private matter of the family's religious observance to get to his favorite subject of debate.) In his memoir of Rachel, Védel, who was the director of the Théâtre-Français when Rachel was first hired there, recalls that forbidden meat was often on the family table.

The Félixes were swept westward on a huge wave of internal immigration. They went from Alsace to Besançon, Saint-Etienne, and then, for a few years before they settled in Paris, to Lyons, where the cloth industry was attracting many Jews from the east. They were pushed by the Jews who poured into France in flight from pogroms in Poland and Russia, and pulled by the promise of life in the capital, where people were beginning to practice what Guizot would soon be preaching, "Enrichissez-vous!" The wave they caught was one of several that were mixing populations and weakening the boundaries between classes. If their westward movement seems to signify their hopefulness, it was a sign of their concomitant helplessness that the family grew and stayed poor as they traveled. After Sophie-Sarah and Elisa-Rachel, who was born in February, 1821, came the only son, Raphaël, in 1826; in 1829, in Lyons, Rébecca was born. Adélaïde was born in 1830 at Saumur, on the very last, long-delayed leg of their journey to the capital, and Mélanie, the last child, in Paris in 1836.

The family arrived in the city in August of 1831, the year after the July Revolution had installed Louis-Philippe as King of the French. Paris was hot and unstable. They took up temporary, or tentative, residence in the crowded, noisome district of the Marais, where they knew people; they were lucky to live there, untouched by disease, through the great cholera epidemic of 1832.

Early biographers of Rachel insisted on the somber and romantic circumstance that the Félixes settled in an apartment opposite the Morgue (where the dead bodies were a favorite attraction, in those days, for bored Parisians and visiting tourists); some of Rachel's more class-conscious biographers have found it telling that for a time the family lived in a little street that had been named Passage Vérot-Dodat by two pretentious merchants of those plain names. Jacques chose or was obliged to go off traveling from time to time, leaving his wife to keep the old-clothes business going: the actress Mlle Judith, in her memoirs, suggests it was a woman's business, recalling that her mother and Rachel's were in the same line of work. One imagines these immigrants—strangers in the capital of their country—improvising their lives and future in a city full of elusive possibilities and unknown people, many of whom were also newcomers to the city, with a sense like theirs of excited dislocation.

IN *La Confession d'un enfant du siècle* (1836), Alfred de Musset described the "mal du siècle" of upper-class youths of his generation as an identity crisis that expressed and tried to forget itself in theatricality. The sons of fathers who had fought in the imperial wars felt themselves useless, he wrote—wanting in purpose, distinctiveness, conviction. *Malaise* and *anomie* found expression in masquerade. Without a style of their own, with and without a sense of humor or what would later be called bad faith, they borrowed the forms and fashions of other periods, betraying both their alienation from history and their preoccupation with it. He describes a kind of postmodernity *avant la lettre:*

> Our age has no impress of its own. We have impressed the seal of our time neither on our houses nor our gardens, nor on anything whatever. On the street you can see men who have their beards trimmed as in the time of Henri III, others who are clean-shaven, others who have their hair arranged to resemble the self-portrait of Raphael, others who look as if they lived in the time of Christ. The homes of the rich are cabinets of curiosities: the antique, the gothic, the Renaissance style, that of Louis XIII, all pell-mell. In short, we have every century except our own—a thing which has never been seen at any other epoch: eclecticism is our taste; we take everything we find, this thing for beauty, that for utility, another for its antiquity, still another for its very ugliness, so that we live surrounded by debris, as if the end of the world were near.

If the sense that glory had been lost forever with the empire caused Musset's generation to feel that the end was near, it also seemed to prove that anything was possible, and nothing reliably real. The extravagant young men of the generation of 1830—Théophile Gautier, Petrus Borel, Gérard de Nerval—protested theatrically against a world that seemed to them no more substantive or serious than a stage.

Meanwhile the theaters of Paris flourished, attracting people of all classes. Technology and cash were deployed to keep up with popular hunger and taste: huge sums were spent at the Opéra on increasingly spectacular special effects, including a lifelike volcano. The ballet *La Sylphide*, with the first tutus and decorations by Ciceri, was danced there in 1832. Dance and opera were the rage; the ballerinas Marie Taglioni and Fanny Elssler were passionately followed, compared, and contrasted by rival parties of fans, as were the divas Malibran and Pasta. Arguing that one stood for Art, the other for Nature, the fans worried and elaborated and further polarized the terms of the old debate, reinforcing, no matter what their position, the view of women performers as personified abstractions.

Napoleon's had been a hard act to follow, and—especially in retrospect—it had also been clearly an act. "Bonaparte, c'est l'homme," Alfred de Vigny wrote; "Napoléon, c'est le rôle." Crowning himself in Notre Dame, later having himself painted in the act, and also portrayed in the regalia of a Sun King, the emperor aped the ancien régime he had begun by rejecting. Musset went so far as to see him as a self-parodist: "the last flicker of the lamp of despotism, he both destroyed and parodied kings." Among the parodic ambiguities of the revolution of 1830, which replaced one king with another, was a resurgence of Bonapartist feeling, which as if to memorialize the dead emperor's favorite art took a theatrical form. Napoleon plays were popular during the first years of the reign of Louis-Philippe; the nation that had just rejected the Restoration was eager to idealize the fallen hero. Martin Meisel, describing how history merged with spectacle in the period, cites Alexandre Dumas's recollection that the new regime had barely settled into place when several directors of theaters approached him for a Napoleon play. Dumas waited for the new king's permission to write one, and by the time he began to write without it, he recalled, "six theaters were putting on their Napoleon plays, and I, I was still waiting." Jules Janin commented mischievously on the vogue for plays about Napoleon, writing that "one wondered who in fact reigned, Bonaparte or Louis-Philippe." But the effect of so many Bonapartes was not altogether to praise the lost leader: Virginie Déjazet, playing Napoleon *en travesti*, tested the line between mimicry and mockery. As well as nostalgia for lost glory, the rage for Napoleon plays reflected the sense that there was a problem in imagining the place of the heroic in history: Musset suggests as much with his chaotic, Shakespearean, romantic tragedy *Lorenzaccio* (1834), which did not get produced until 1896, when Sarah Bernhardt triumphed in the title role.

The mix of nostalgia for a lost heroic ideal and enthusiasm for ambiguous mock heroics helped inspire the unprecedented vogue for stars. Dancers and singers and actors peopled a dense demimonde in Paris, and fascinated the great world. The great stars of the time were original performers who made egregiously theatrical, semifictional projections of themselves: the mime Deburau, who transformed the white-faced Harlequin of *commedia dell'arte* into his own unique persona, a gracefully expressive mute; Frédérick Lemaître, who on the basis of a rudimentary role in a mediocre play created the memorable figure of the raffish Frenchman-in-the-street, Robert Macaire. Lemaître and Deburau were admired as romantic geniuses able to express with a look or a gesture what words could not say. The success of these innovative performers, and of Marie Dorval, suggests how extraordinary Rachel had to have been to make old-fashioned rhymed tragedy riveting. On the other hand, the other stars of the time did whet the appetite that she would help to satisfy. As cartoonists appropriated the figures of Macaire and Deburau, and images of the actors embarked on lives independent of the men who created them, they delighted a public that wanted a hero and suspected there was no such thing—suspected that the age, as Byron put it in his mock epic, *Don Juan*, could not produce a true one. A female hero would neatly pose the problem.

History merged in a timely way with theatricality: the Boulevard du Temple in Paris, called the "Boulevard du Crime" because of the bloody melodramas performed in the many theaters there, was chosen for an 1835 attack on Louis-Philippe's life. The bomb that went off there was spectacular, if ineffective, and it provoked another street show. Even more than his enemies, the king required an audience: Michel Foucault, in his analysis of how power and spectacle interact, recalls the staging of the punishment of the assassin Fieschi, who was sentenced to be taken, in November, "to the place of execution wearing a shirt, barefoot, his head covered with a black veil; . . . exhibited upon a scaffold while an usher [read] the sentence to the people, and . . . immediately executed."

The streets of Paris produced, along with more and less solemn spectacles, the casual walker in the city, or *flâneur*, who mused on life as masquerade while poor *saltimbanques*—acrobats, jugglers, street singers, fire-eaters,

clowns—competed for their attention with modish young people extravagantly costumed, and peddlers with pushcarts hawking their wares. (In a
powerful series of watercolors and paintings made rather later, Daumier presented the *saltimbanques* as tragic clowns who epitomized the misery of the
urban poor; in 1849 they were driven from the streets, when the government
decided they were agents of subversion.) Contemporary caricatures of theater
audiences suggest the prevailing sense that spectatorship verged on performance: Marcel Carné evokes the scene in his 1945 film, *Les Enfants du
paradis*. Salesmen hovered near the queues outside the theaters, where the
crowds were eager to be distracted as they waited, and to buy opera glasses
and umbrellas, and the scripts of the new plays. It was by collecting the rights
to sell those plays that Michel Lévy augmented his father's pushcart business
into Calmann-Lévy, the publishing house that would become a monument
of the cultural establishment, publishers of Dumas, Flaubert, and George
Sand. The Lévy family had come from the same part of the world and the
same social class as the Félixes; young Michel went to school with Raphaël
Félix, auditioned and was accepted at the Conservatoire, and was probably
instrumental in bringing Rachel to the attention of the management of the
Théâtre-Français.

In 1840, there were approximately nine thousand Jews in Paris, three times
as many as there had been in 1808; their number would quadruple by 1880.
It was a small but tightly organized and visible population. Napoleon's appointment, in 1809, of the Jewish Consistory, a state-sanctioned center of self-
government, had done much to legitimize and to encourage a Jewish presence
in France. In January 1831, an act of the July Monarchy had "put Judaism on
the state payroll," in one historian's phrase, stipulating that rabbis, like priests,
were to be paid by France. Phyllis Cohen Albert writes that "when the
consistory system was established . . . the total French Jewish population was
approximately 47,000. During the next twenty-five years, under Napoleon
and the Bourbon Restoration, it increased rapidly to a total of about 70,000
in 1831. . . . By 1861 it reached 96,000." The general aim of the Jewish community of Paris was to retain religious identity while attaining social assimilation. In the school the consistory established for the likes of Raphaël Félix
and Michel Lévy, to which new immigrants to Paris were enjoined to send
their boys, pupils were not allowed to speak Yiddish. Frenchness, integration,
was the aim. It may seem somewhat paradoxical now that racial pride was
harnessed toward this end.

By the third decade of the century, Jews had gained distinction in law, medicine, the army, science, literature, the embassies, and the new railroads. Some of them were members of Sephardic families that had fled Spain during the Inquisition, and had been long resident in France. Adolphe Crémieux, whose great-niece was to be the mother of Marcel Proust, was one of that elite group. Descended from a family of republican merchants, Crémieux became a lawyer and gained national recognition during the Restoration by his skill at political trials, especially an effective defense of two youths accused of singing the revolutionary anthem, *La Marseillaise.* He settled in Paris in 1830 and was soon elected to the consistory, of which he became president from 1843 to 1845. He was twice a minister of the state, and a member of the French senate until his death in 1880. The lawyer whom Jacques Félix hired to defend his daughter's interests against the Théâtre-Français was her "Papa Crémieux," who wrote rough drafts of Rachel's letters, at her request, to people she wanted to impress—she hoped people would think she was another Madame de Sevigné, she astonishingly said. Of greater general historical importance were Crémieux's successful efforts to defend his people in France and abroad. In 1839 he argued against a law that required Jews to take a special oath in court; it was repealed in 1846. In 1840, he journeyed to Damascus along with Moses Montefiore, to defend a Jew accused of ritual murder. The mid-nineteenth-century career of Crémieux illustrates both the successful integration of Jews in France and the nascent sense of a Jewish identity that transcended national borders. For his achievement as a Jew and a Frenchman, he is remembered as having "rehabilitated the Jew in Europe."

A cultured man and a zealous patron of the arts, Crémieux was the cordial host of writers and artists. Delighted by the idea of a Jewish queen of tragedy, he invited the young Rachel to become an intimate of his family, among whom she picked up shreds of education and some notion of respectable life: people enjoyed the story that the lawyer had defined the word "firmament" for the ignorant child, and the other one that—amazed that she knew only her own lines—he had explained the various plots of the classical plays to her, including, with quite unnecessary delicacy, that of *Phèdre.* Perhaps sloppy habits of expression she had caught on the street account for Rachel's signing some of her letters to Crémieux "Yours, body and soul"; she maintained that he was the only man who had never made her a proposition.

Emile Péreire, like Crémieux a member of an old Sephardic family, opened the Paris–Saint-Germain railroad in 1835; newer Jewish arrivals were also thriving in the Paris of the 1830s. The Rothschilds and the Foulds gained importance in finance; Halévy and Meyerbeer were conspicuous in the arts.

These representatives of their people delighted ordinary Jews as proof of the witlessness of their enemies, and promise of their own ultimate success. The impoverished *juiverie* that filled the cheap seats—the *paradis*—to applaud Rachel wanted France to have a Jewish *reine de théâtre*, and wanted to have a hand in her fame; so did her wealthy and prominent coreligionists, who loaned her their jewels when she appeared in the role of the avenging Jewish heroine Judith.

Jews were turning up, increasingly, on both sides of the footlights in the theaters. Eager to get on, enterprising and adaptable, socially marginal and used to improvising, they had, both their friends and enemies argued, a special affinity for the stage. Like Jews, actors were not respectable: in France they were denied Christian marriage and burial. Implicitly, the theater invited Jews. Their importance there has been variously interpreted and reinterpreted: one historian of French Jewry protests, for example, that "the remark in Proust's great novel about a dramatic producer who changed his name to Samuel so that he might be more successful was not an antisemitic gibe, but a bow to the prominence of the Jews in the theaters." Jewish actresses and models were in fashion in the 1830s and 1840s; Jewish parents who see their daughters as salable commodities are a staple of nineteenth-century fiction.

The stereotype of the Jew who confuses his ducats and his daughter easily embraced Jacques Félix, who aimed unapologetically to get what he could from Rachel. He was perhaps distinctive in desiring cultural legitimacy as well as money. As careful of her image as a Hollywood agent, he indignantly refused, for example, to allow her to play the role of "une mulâtresse," in a play about the Haitian revolution by Lamartine. He had more imagination than most men, according to Julie Bernat, Mlle Judith of the Comédie-Française, who recalled in her memoir that when she was a child living in the same Paris neighborhood as the Félixes, Jacques enlisted her into the performing group he hoped to make of his young children, having been inspired after some visiting Italian child actors, the Castelli Troupe, were acclaimed at the Salle Ventadour. He fed the children mostly on potatoes, she remembered, and worked them very hard; she also claimed that he tried to molest her sexually—hardly the only negative thing that was said about him, but the only one of this kind. Dictating her memoirs in advanced old age, after a career of rivalry with Rachel, she remembered her colleague's father as an immoral man who made his wife work for him, and an exigent, excellent teacher.

A radically sanitized and idealized version of Félix figures in Benjamin Disraeli's novel *Tancred* (1847). Baroni is the benign and enterprising patriarch of a family of wandering Italian Jewish acrobats. Poor players, they are (like the Disraelis, and unlike the Félixes) Sephardic, more exotic and cultivated than ordinary East European Jews. They belong to a spiritual aristocracy of artists as well. Baroni's adolescent daughter Josephine is already set apart from the others—they all are gifted—by the solemn foreknowledge that she will be, one day, the "glory of the French stage; without any question the most admirable tragic actress since Clairon." Destiny has chosen her to awaken "the spirit of French tragedy . . . from the imperial couch on which it had long slumbered." Her art is instinctive and innate; her father, acceding to its force, says, "I let her do this to please herself." The story of the Baronis is a strangely unmotivated pastoral interlude in a novel about a young Englishman's pilgrimage to Palestine in search of a purer original Christianity. It is told to the hero by the rich, powerful, cosmopolitan Jew Sidonia, partly so as to illustrate his belief that "All is race; there is no other truth." In Disraeli's earlier novel, *Coningsby* (1844), this same philosophical Sidonia argued that musical Jews are the purest example of the unpolluted Caucasian race:

> The ear, the voice, the fancy teeming with combinations, the imagination fervent with picture and emotion, that came from Caucasus, and which we have preserved unpolluted, have endowed us with almost the exclusive privilege of MUSIC; that science of harmonious sounds, which the ancients recognised as most divine, and deified in the person of their most beautiful creation. . . . [W]ere I to enter into the history of the lords of melody, you would find it the annals of Hebrew genius. But at this moment even, musical Europe is ours. There is not a company of singers, not an orchestra in a single capital, that is not crowded with our children under the feigned names which they adopt to conciliate the dark aversion which your posterity will some day disclaim with shame and disgust. Almost every great composer, skilled musician, almost every voice that ravishes you with its transporting strains, springs from our tribes. The catalogue is too vast to enumerate: too illustrious to dwell for a moment on secondary names, however eminent. Enough for us that the three great creative minds to whose exquisite inventions all nations at this moment yield, Rossini, Meyerbeer, Mendelssohn, are of Hebrew race; and little do your men of fashion, your muscadins of Paris, and your dandies of London, as they thrill into raptures at

the notes of a Pasta or a Grisi, little do they suspect that they are offering their homage to "the sweet singers of Israel!"

Sidonia is smug and even spiteful as he contemplates the success of Jewish performers in a Jew-hating society. His Baroni story seems to be motivated by a related impulse: to claim Rachel for the Jews, which also seems to be Disraeli's motive. Framed as a little history separate from events chronicled by the novel, the portrait of the wandering players is set apart like Brontë's sketch of Vashti in *Villette*. The Baronis seem to exist on a different ontological level, in an ideal pastoral world—though they are linked to the wider world through Sidonia, who enjoys mysterious international influence (and transcends *Tancred*, turning up as he does in another Disraeli novel).

At least one early reader wondered who the Baronis of *Tancred* were actually based on. "Did you not think the picture of the Baroni family interesting?" Mary Ann Evans wrote to a friend in 1848. "I should like to know who are the originals." The woman who would become George Eliot judged *Tancred* the least of Disraeli's trilogy, "very 'thin' and inferior" to *Coningsby* and *Sybil*. She added that Sidonia's philosophy repelled her: "Everything *specifically* Jewish is of a low grade," she declared. In her last novel, she would counter Disraeli's picture of Baroni, and utterly revise her view of Jews. Two of the minor characters in *Daniel Deronda* (1876) are Jewish women performers with significant fathers. Mirah Lapidoth, who marries the hero at the end, is a poor and gentle girl with a sweet voice, the daughter of a rascally hanger-on of fairs and theaters who steals her from his pious wife and schemes, at one point, to sell her to a rich, lascivious gentile. She suggests Rachel less urgently than another character in the novel, the hero's imperious mother, a successful diva. In her youth, Leonora Charisi rebelled against her good Jewish father, who forbade her to go onstage; as a middle-aged woman, she is tormented by remorse for having done so. In contrast, Mirah manages to escape her bad father, and will thrive (and leave the stage, which she hates). Together, and braided with the story of the English heroine Gwendolen Harleth, these women's stories evoke the legends about Rachel and her father; they elaborate George Eliot's complex, conflicted attitudes toward daughterly and womanly duty and guilt, and her fears of the killing possibilities of an artist-woman who acts out her own will, desires, and genius.

According to Rachel's biographers, the real Jacques Félix was closer to Eliot's rascally Lapidoth than to either Disraeli's benign Baroni or her own holy Charisi: sharp-witted, hardheaded, selfish, and vulgar. They write his

lines in the accent Balzac gave the rich Jewish Baron de Nucingen; they insist
that his greed drove the greatest wage-earner in the family to her early grave.
Many nevertheless acknowledge his talent and acumen. In his memoir of
Rachel, Védel of the Comédie-Française repeats the well-circulated funny
story of the father saying, absurdly, "That was some good 'Rome' she gave
me today," after his daughter's rendition of Camille's great high-minded tirade. Védel observes that, for all his ridiculous half-German, half-French
pronunciation, the man had taste, and a perfect understanding of poetry.
Heinrich Heine saw the conjunction of Félix and high tragedy as irremediably
ridiculous: "Père Rachel preens himself with the success of his daughter," he
wrote, reporting on the cultural scene in Paris. "There he stands, in the stalls
of the Théâtre-Français—an old Jew—and thinks that *he* is Iphigenia or An-
dromache, that it is *his* declamation that has moved all hearts; and when the
audience applauds, he blushes and bows." The figure of Félix lends itself to
caricature, exemplifying as it does two related stereotypes: the parasitical
stage parent and the Jew showman. As usual, racial prejudices reinforce antitheatrical ones: Clara Schumann's father, who exploited her as Félix exploited his daughter, was never so generally condemned. Rachel's biographers
take a more sardonic version of the satiric tone Thackeray takes in *Pendennis*,
when he draws the drunken, feckless Irish father of the actress who calls
herself, mellifluously, Emily Fotheringay, but is really just plain, lower-class
Miss Costigan. Dickens, in an essay, more gently characterized the indigenous
London variant on the stage father. He calls him a "gaslight fairy," a man
"principally employed in lurking about a public house, and waylaying the
theatrical profession for two-pence wherewith to purchase a glass of ale,"
who lives off his daughter's blind loyalty: "Miss Fairy never relinquishes the
belief that that incorrigible old Fairy, the father, is a wonderful man! . . . She
has grown up in this conviction, will never correct it, will die in it." By her
side her father, a failed or would-be actor, proves that fairies, although they
seem to be such from seats in the audience, are not in fact real; to focus on
him is to begin to debunk his daughter, whose charming, stupid devotion to
him begins to suggest her own serious limitations. Together, daughter and
father pose the problem the theater sets by being a mixture of art and commerce, "high" and "low." In Oscar Wilde's *The Picture of Dorian Gray*, the
greasy Jewish manager of otherwise fatherless Sibyl Vane serves similarly as
both a foil to her magic and a hint that the theater is a business. The magic
of the theater, on the other hand, can make even Jews into something else:
in *Tancred*, the *pièce de résistance* of the tumbler-patriarch Baroni and his

children is a *tableau vivant* in which the whole family arranges itself, as if turned to stone, to mime familiar Christian religious paintings.

Was Jacques Félix maligned by his enemies? Might he not have been a cultured man in fact, for all his accent? Hard to say; and hard, even, to debate the question without calling on and falling into stereotypes. Here is a recent letter to a newspaper, objecting to a "needlessly unkind" characterization of a dead movie magnate as a vulgarian: "The first time I saw Sam Spiegel, in 1941 or '42, he was in a barber chair reading 'Swann's Way,' in the Modern Library Edition, while his hair was being cut. . . . He was a man of culture, a master of languages, a man of true, broad understanding and sensitivity."

C O M I N G   T O   F A M E in the Paris of Halévy's *La Juive*, at a moment when Shakespeare and Scott were especially admired in France, Rachel and her father might have been generated by literary stereotype—Jessica and Shylock, Rebecca and Isaac of York. A French variation on the couple occurs in Balzac's *Le Cousin Pons* (1847), where miserly "Magus the collector" has a daughter, "a beautiful girl, like all Jewesses who incarnate the Asian type in all its purity and nobility." Magus is a "monomaniac," one of those "strange figures so devoted to their particular religion" that you see in the city, "a Jew with a three-million treasure around him," who is "one of the finest spectacles the human race can offer." With pointed irony, the narrator remarks, "Our great actor, Frédérick Lemaître, superb as he is, cannot rise to poetry like this." The Jewish father and his lovely daughter, offered as specimens to ponder, are art objects with very different, indeed opposite, provenances, the man being a creature of the crowded, European city of commercial exchange and real actors, and the young woman a representative of a remote idealized East—a Jew of the Bible, not the Bourse. The father at her side sets off her sexuality the way a eunuch in a harem does—also sets her up as a commodity.

"He is the Wandering Jew, and I am his four sous," Rachel supposedly said of her brother Raphaël, who eventually became her (rapacious) manager. But some of her critics insisted from the first on her own, independent, active greed. As early as March 1841, the *Courrier des théâtres* reported that poor old Félix had only accepted the role of heavy to save his daughter's image: "He's only a puppet, it's the *child* who's pulling the strings." Biographers like to tell how she sweated out the dull aftermath of a triumphant tour in Lyons because the gold crown she had been promised was not ready (she collected crowns, and gold as well, and had been assured that this gift from the city of her youth would be gratifyingly heavy). "Moi, je suis juive," Mlle Judith was supposed to have remarked complacently; "Rachel, c'est un juif." The epigram, useful for characterizing Rachel as unfeminine and unnatural, was much quoted. Insisting on Rachel's avariciousness, Hector Fleischmann pontificates, "Greed is only natural, in Père Félix; in Rachel, it's a vice." The star's partisans told different stories, about a childish love of beautiful objects that made her want whatever she saw, and give it away almost immediately. They said she held onto a new toy or jewel no more than four days. Without the good financial management of her father, Arsène Houssaye writes, she would have left nothing at all behind for her children and parents.

The benefit performances for other actors that Rachel appeared or refused to appear in, the ones she arranged for members of her immediate family, are cited by her admirers and her detractors to make opposite points. Sums she contributed to victims of floods and epidemics (too little? too showy?) are adduced as evidence that she was and was not both typical and perverse; the house she furnished for her sister Rébecca proves both her generosity and her Jewish allegiance to her own. People prefer their entertainers (the women especially) to be impulsive, even demonic, rather than calculating. Admirers of Mrs. Siddons were horrified to hear she cared about box-office receipts. Men flatter themselves to think an actress gives herself involuntarily, or at least generously, and pay to entertain the illusion that the other side of the coin isn't there. Jonas Barish, observing that the Roman actor Roscius did not "play" for money, asks, "Why should it have been so much more unacceptable for actors to receive pay than for members of other callings? Why should the celebrated Roscius have felt it necessary to decline all reward for his performances? Would he have done so if society had not made it seem ignoble for actors to be remunerated for their work?" In Rome, he notes, love of actors and contempt for them became allied: "The gradually eroding link between religion and theater was to turn the theater, a source of pleasure, adrift from its moorings in morality, and thereby inspire a guilt such that the Romans, recoiling from their own pleasures, came to persecute the purveyors of them even as their addiction to them intensified."

LIKE HER FATHER, Rachel's energetic older sister Sarah is often invoked as the tellingly vulgar counterpart of Rachel. "My crazy sister," Rachel called her, and paid her debts. Sarah won renown as a compliant *amoureuse* rather than an exigent one, a *soupeuse vaillante* or party girl who moved merrily from lover to lover. The tragedienne was often embarrassed by her elder, whom she roundly rebuked by mail for bad behavior (during the years with

Walewski, she wrote at least one note to herself vowing to be nicer to Sarah). A particularly severe but poignant lecture was provoked by a letter from Rébecca that described a terrible scene at home. "My dear Sarah, it is time to change your character," Rachel writes, declaring she can no longer tolerate her family's behavior. "I am humiliated to see my family go on this way, so much that I ask if God was not wrong in taking us out of the filth in which we were all living before my entry upon a dramatic career. . . . You are none of you worthy of the happiness which God has poured out among us these past ten years. . . . Is there any family where there is less heart than among us?" She ends by observing there's nothing filthier than Sarah's filthy mouth, adding "the advice of a sincere friend," evidently apropos of Sarah's treatment of Rébecca: to bend in the world, where one does have need of others, or at least not to repay them with injuries.

Bold Sarah rushed out to meet the world head-on, playing the fool in early life, even going to jail at one point when a lover left her behind to pay the hotel bill. Her more clever younger sister, subtler and more gifted, outshone her. But in the end Sarah proved to be more sensible than not: in middle age, prefiguring the career move of many shrewd actresses today, she put her name on a product called "Eaux des Fées" or "Eau Sarah Félix"— "souveraine pour la régénération de la chevelure," according to the advertisement—and managed to make some money. (Evidently she lost it, but she continued enterprising: later, she opened an oyster farm in Normandy.) The two girls had started out together, first on the streets of Lyons and later in Paris: Sarah was acting in the little Théâtre du Panthéon where Rachel sold brochures and flowers (pursuing her studies, she primly told the men who asked what a girl like her was doing there). The sisters always remained close. Sarah accompanied Rachel to Egypt, where someone did a drawing of them in their barge on the Nile, nervous Rachel hard at work on her embroidery, buxom Sarah relaxed among the pillows. Sarah was as healthy as the day was long, Rachel reported home to their mother. "She glows, and she would make the sun pale if she looked back at it."

Talma's father had been a *valet de chambre*, but the fact hardly figures in his legend. In contrast, Rachel's emergence from the bosom of her unlikely, awful family was always crucial. Her gender and religion made the difference. Women are defined by their connections as men are not; also Rachel flaunted her family. The early experience of poverty, the sense of being outside French society, kept her close to her parents and brother and sisters. Since she never married, and they were gifted and ambitious, too, all the Félixes surrounded her in the public eye: the Théâtre-Français turned into a synagogue, wits complained, when their powerful sister arranged for Raphaël and Rébecca Félix, Sarah and Lia and even the child Mélanie, to join her onstage. (All became variously successful, independently.) While some were astonished by the family talent, most commentators could look no further than the marvellous fact that Rachel, with such parents and such a crowd of relatives, became or seemed to become the rare creature she was.

There are very few anecdotes about Rachel's mother, as there are only a few about her motherhood: patriarchal legend must have it that she was produced either by a miracle or by a man. Clothes figure in all the stories about the old-clothes woman, who supposedly made Rachel a hat fashioned from ill-assorted scraps of fabric—her only hat, made to serve in all seasons— when she was admitted to the Conservatoire and given a pass to the Théâtre-Français. Mme Félix is said to have piled extra petticoats on the child when she went to her first interview with Samson, then unabashedly pulled them off when he complained she was too fat. After her first triumphant tour of England, the star supposedly came home and draped a rich paisley shawl, the gift of a duchess, on her mother's humble shoulders. While they retain a remnant of Thérèse Félix's historical reality, the stories about her also imply she was immaterial: a sloppy housekeeper who relegated the cooking and marketing and the younger children to the care of Rachel, while Sarah cavorted with boyfriends. A vulgarian peasant mother is easily summoned up by the structure of legends like Rachel's; in fact, Rachel found Thérèse sufficiently *sortable* to take her along as a chaperone in her first years of fame.

A jolly early letter from Rachel to her mother, planning a picnic, and another written on tour from Poland, about the East European food that reminds her of her mother's cooking, suggest a certain coziness between mother and daughter. But Rachel's letters to her father are more frank and fluent: it is to him that she confides details about her health (including her monthly periods), always urging him to assure the mother that all is well. Mme Félix was overly anxious about her daughter's health, possibly because she depended on her daughter's earnings. Papa is lovable, writes Rachel to Sarah in the 1850s, and she is not at all surprised their younger sisters prefer his company to that of Mama, whose character is so grasping and self-interested. When Rachel was away on tour Mme Félix went to pick up her salary at the Théâtre-Français, and Rachel sought to please her from afar with gifts and flattery, insisting, in a letter from America, that she hire (at her daughter's expense) a carriage for the four winter months, in order to travel in a style befitting the mother of a *grande tragédienne*—and visit her grandchildren when she pleased. Charming with little jokes and intimacies was the tragedienne's style: letters written around the same time to her business agent suggest Rachel preferred to keep her boys from leaving school to visit the Félixes—possibly to keep them at their work (they were not great students), but perhaps also (she was ambitious for them, socially, and had had both of them baptized) in order to protect them from the ancestral "filth" she herself always managed to navigate and even to exploit so brilliantly. There may be some truth to the story Victor Hugo tells of how Mme Félix deliberately degraded the three-year-old grandson of Napoleon, dressing him in rags and training him to make sassy remarks about his father and his mother's rivals.

The Félixes survived their daughter and ended their lives in respectable dignity on the estate Rachel had bought them, in the village of Montmorency.

ONLY A RIVAL FATHER can efface the ignoble family central to the legend of miraculous birth, and make the story of Rachel's achievement realistic and plausible—turn it, that is, into another exemplum of patriarchy, the tale of a goddess not born of woman but made by a man. The story that Lana Turner was discovered as she sat on a stool at Schwab's soda fountain in Hollywood was anticipated by the various legends about Rachel. In the most familiar version, Victor Hugo notices the starved little girl, too young to understand a dirty word, reciting scabrous verses to a crowd of leering men on the Place Royale; he pauses, sadly shakes his sage's head, then thrusts some pure poems of his own, with a gold coin, into her thin hand. As he walks away the child stares after him, eyes shining, unable to understand why her less perceptive sister cannot see the halo round his head.

There is an embarrassment of candidates for the role of Rachel's true father, the Christian who—like the father of the heroine of La Juive—is revealed at the end to be the legitimate source of her imaginative superiority. In the actress's case it is no lost "real" father who turns up surprisingly to disclose a secret origin, but the Pygmalion whose efforts transformed her into an object of art. Rachel played up to various would-be Pygmalions, quickly catching on to what men could do for her, saying what was needful to get their help. In January 1839, for instance, the eighteen-year-old actress writes prettily to the literary Marquis de Custine, assuring him she has taken his suggestion about the way to deliver a verse of Roxane's, and begging him to return her letter after correcting all the errors in it (he evidently did). Men like Custine and Crémieux facilitated the career of Rachel as significantly as the men who assisted her professionally: the music master Etienne Choron, her first teacher; the actor Saint-Aulaire, who ran the little theater where she first studied acting and publicly performed; Delestre-Poirson, who made possible her Paris debut at the Théâtre du Gymnase, and amiably released her from her contract when she decided to return to the Comédie-Française; and the several more self-important others who asserted their claims to her fame more flagrantly.

The thing to remember about Pygmalion's story is that it is not Galatea's. It is a myth about a man whose ideal becomes real in a beautiful woman's form. As interpreted by nineteenth-century artists, the dream is intensely erotic: a painting by Gérôme catches the charged magic moment when the statue on the pedestal stirs into flesh as the sculptor yearns breathlessly toward her. But when Shaw conceived his barely sexed Henry Higgins, who turns a vulgar little flower-seller into a lady worthy of bouquets, he made another important point about Pygmalion: women are not his main interest. The story of the sculptor whose statue becomes real is an alternative kind of creation myth, in which man, not God or woman, makes life. Pygmalion is an artist—a craftsman—so skillful that the work he produces is in effect natural, like the grapes of the Greek painter who fooled the birds. The story of Pygmalion gained new retaliatory resonances as the age of mechanical reproduction began, and the romantic myth of the creator became problematic. As cheap engravings of paintings, plaster replicas of statues, caricatures and photographs began to change the way people looked at artists and art, the audiences that applauded volcanoes at the Opéra trembled on the cusp of modernity: they were thrilled by the patently fake and stagy and at the same time stirred by the idea that creative genius might make mere matter quicken into life.

The number of Pygmalions who figured in Rachel's career suggests the appeal the legend had in her time, proves the fertility of the legend-making faculty, and indicates how much a talent like hers could promise in the 1830s. The financial, social, political, and cultural importance of the theater is suggested by the range of those who are said to have "discovered" her and trained her, and those who sought to influence or use or control her. Individually and as a group, these men reflect the forces that came together in her self-contradictory image. In her story, they become legendary themselves, representations of the opposing forces she figured. On the question of whether the young actress was to be seen as an artist or an artifact, a thinking being or a mere commodity, they fall out somewhat surprisingly.

Obscure talents, like remote countries, are "discovered" by those who

seek to exploit them. It was not of course true that no one had seen her
before Rachel was found playing the guitar as her sister sang on the streets
of Lyons (not the Place Royale in Paris) by a musician. But Etienne Choron
had in mind a use for her. He was a kindly Parisian with an interest in
education: his system for teaching reading and writing at the same time,
which presumably made the nine-year-old Rachel literate (supposing her parents had not done so), continued in use, in France, for decades after his
death. He was passionately committed to early music written for church
choirs. It was not a fashionable art in the years after the Restoration, and
the school in which he trained promising boys and girls to sing together lost
its government support as a result of anti-Catholic feeling attendant on the
revolution of 1830. Choron continued to run the school at his own expense,
continuing also to scout for young talent. The little girls on the Lyons street
appealed to his ear—the two girls probably sang together, the dark one har-
monizing with the blonde's sweeter and higher voice—and he went home
with them to meet their father, who agreed to enroll them in Choron's
school. The commitment might have encouraged the family's move to the
capital: at the time the men met, Félix was sick in bed, out of work, and
discouraged.

In Paris, in September 1831, a month after the family arrived, the girls
were signed up at school, unaccountably as "Mesdemoiselles de Saint-Félix."
The institution was residential. The parents traveled at least part of the time
while the girls were studying there: in a postscript to a letter that Rachel
wrote to her parents, Choron asked the Félixes to look around for a young
tenor for him (indicating his commitment to his enterprise and his faith in
the Félixes' taste). His faith in their child soon proved to have been misplaced: Rachel was a good student, he told them, but her gifts were not for
singing. This chorus-master, unlike the music teacher Porpora in George
Sand's *Consuelo*, was not to be gratified by transforming a waif of the streets
into a brilliant solo singer like Pauline Viardot. Still, Rachel's vocal training,
what she learned from Choron about rhythm and ensemble work, and reverence for a traditional, solemn, spiritually uplifting art, prepared her for the
great career that was to come. She would always speak with respect of her
first teacher. There is a story that destiny or instinct impelled Choron's student to seize a tablecloth one day, and wrap it around her as if it were a
toga to signal the direction she could not but take. Something like that must
have helped the music master discover that her gift was for acting. And since
he was not unworldly, he was in a position to recommend a girl who could

not sing—it would be wrong to describe her as having no voice—to a friend
of his in Paris named Saint-Aulaire, an actor of the Comédie-Française who
like him had an interest in forming youthful talent.

The very existence of Saint-Aulaire's Théâtre Molière begins to suggest
the demand for new performers in Paris in the 1830s. The Opéra and the
Boulevard houses were voracious for young theatrical flesh; the number of
theaters and the volume of business they had, the possibilities for fame and
fortune that were available only there, attracted ambitious and talented people who wanted to escape from the growing ranks of the wretched urban
poor. Girls ran away from hopeless homes to become *rats* of the *corps de
ballet*, prepared to suffer at the whim of tyrannical directors and possibly to
be noticed by the manager or by one of the black-hatted pleasure-seekers,
depicted (later) by Degas and Manet, who prowled the corridors backstage.
Poor parents sometimes exploited and colluded with dependent, ambitious
children. The theater was a hard and risky business, in which few made real
money and fewer enjoyed dignity. Actors and actresses were expected to
submit utterly to their employers: historically, the managers of the theaters
of the fairs had been entitled to fine and even jail misbehaving performers.
But students who were accepted at the Conservatoire might hope to have a
chance to become, eventually, *comédiens français*, who enjoyed some measure
of the national company's dignity and (should they become *sociétaires)* voting
rights and a stipulated percentage of the profits. A new government order,
motivated by concern over the state theater's decline, directed the Comédie-
Française to hold auditions in the fall of 1836.

The actors at Saint-Aulaire's Théâtre Molière would have been among
the first to hear about these auditions. The shabby outpost of the Théâtre-
Française had two social functions: for a pittance, it entertained working-class
audiences, educating them in the French literary and dramatic tradition by
the way, and meanwhile it trained children of the poor who hoped to be
actors, and served them as a showcase. Rachel's brother's schoolmate Michel
Lévy was a member of Saint-Aulaire's company: like Rachel, he lived at home
and helped out his peddler parents, getting away to the theater only when
work permitted. At the Théâtre Molière, Rachel was introduced to the classical repertoire, and trained in the traditional high declamatory style. She
learned to speak her words and bear her body with the elegance and grace
perfected by late-Renaissance courtiers, who understood—as we still do—
that the surest markers of social class and personal taste are pronunciation
and posture. At an academy for aristocratic young ladies, another girl might
have been schooled quite similarly. In addition, Rachel acquired a skill: she

memorized the specific gestures and inflections that had been developed by the Comédie-Française to encode certain emotions and accompany particular verses in the classical repertoire. She emerged from Saint-Aulaire's workshop a different kind of person, confident of her ability to impersonate.

Some conservatives disapproved of Saint-Aulaire for being less rigorously prescriptive than he should have been. Védel's defense of him suggests he was (quietly) one of those advocates of more natural acting who, since Diderot and Talma, had sought to overthrow or undermine the faith in absolute fidelity to tradition. "Everything in the theater is only an illusion," Védel wrote, "everything depends on the character, the voice, the appearance of an individual, on something indescribable that leads a person in the direction of one genre rather than another. M. St.-Aulaire attempted to discover the dramatic instincts of his students, rather than impose them; correctly, he wanted the theatrical process to make those instincts evident." Saint-Aulaire's laissez-faire policy allowed the young Rachel to do comedy as well as tragedy, to take men's roles as well as women's—much has been made of this—but her natural bent for tragedy soon was clear. The American actor Edwin Forrest, passing through Paris in 1834, was struck by "that Jewish-looking girl" he saw at the little showcase theater; his description of Rachel strikingly anticipates most of the rhetorical figures that would be used to construct the star. In "that little bag of bones with the marble face and flaming eyes" he could see "demoniacal power." He predicted, "If she lives and does not burn out too soon, she will become something wonderful." When Védel, then the treasurer of the Théâtre-Français, came to the Théâtre Molière to see another actor one day, he was much struck by Rachel in the title role of *Andromaque.* Her intelligence, the purity of her diction, her naturalness in speaking Racine's lines impressed him: so did her puniness, the weirdness of her dignity. Like Edwin Forrest and nearly everyone else who wrote about Rachel, Védel was probably projecting his own uncomfortable self-division onto her when he traced her unusual power to the force of irreconcilable opposites: "I was unable to reconcile that fragile nature and that remarkable intelligence," he wrote. He urged the Comédie-Française to audition her, and she was admitted to the Conservatoire in October 1836. A small stipend of six hundred francs was allotted her.

Gratified by success, the young actress was soon pining for the applause of real audiences, the exhilaration of great roles. And the birth of the last Félix child, Mélanie, made her parents eager to have her work for money. Before Rachel had been given a role at the Théâtre-Français, she was successfully tempted to sign a contract with the directors of the Théâtre du

Gymnase: the lure of a real paying job, the flattery of a play written expressly for his daughter to star in, were hard for Jacques Félix to turn down. Later, people would interpret Rachel's early move to the Théâtre du Gymnase as symptomatic, observing that even in her youth she was easily deflected from service to France and high art by her appetites for money and applause. Gérard de Nerval wrote critically much later that far from being a miraculous born tragedienne, Rachel was merely an ambitious little boulevard actress who had willed herself to be something more.

Father and daughter signed with Delestre-Poirson of the Théâtre du Gymnase, who advertised the Paris debut of the actress Rachel, and the fifteen-year-old girl began rehearsing. The plot of the new play written for her by Paul Duport, *La Vendéenne*, adapts the story, from Sir Walter Scott's novel *The Heart of Midlothian*, of Jeanie Deans. In the novel, the heroine walks from Edinburgh to London to ask the king's mercy for her sister, who has been condemned to death for the crime of infanticide. In Duport's play the heroine is from the region of France that resisted the Revolution and remained loyal to the king even after Napoleon came to power; her father has been condemned for taking part in the legitimist uprising in the Vendée, and she walks to Malmaison to plead for the clemency of the Empress Joséphine. Paul Duport's was one of fifteen staged versions of the Scott novel, and a variation on the popular Napoleon play designed to please legitimist and Bonapartist alike. It meant also to exploit Rachel's youth, starved pallor, and fervor—and it began to elaborate her legend. It was easy to believe in this girl's dutiful daughterliness, and her fierce fidelity to a private vision of the Virgin Mary, who appears to the Vendéenne and directs her to go to Paris to save her father—as Rachel had done, people would say, looking back.

> *Suddenly she moves toward me*
> *And with a finger seems to point*
> *To a huge and unknown city*
> *Only one sole word she breathes:*
> *"Paris!" whereupon she adds,*
> *As if in answer to my prayer,*
> *"Go alone on foot, for there*
> *You will save your father's life."*

Most people had only moderate praise for the new actress in *La Vendéenne*, including the fluent Jules Janin, who had become theater critic of the *Journal des débats* in 1836. In the opinion of the self-styled "prince of critics," as he fatuously called himself, "the child would never be acclaimed as a prodigy." (Janin, who made a career of Rachel as he helped make her a star, would use up a good deal of ink in an effort to drown this assertion.)

Nevertheless, *La Vendéenne* had a decent run. It was followed by *Le Mariage de raison*, in which Rachel attempted to re-create a role recently played by a deft comic actress with a high feminine voice and healthy good looks. She was unsuccessful. Delestre-Poirson agreed to let her break her contract, and she set about to seek readmission to the Conservatoire. Was it because she saw she had no gift for comedy that the hope of doing tragedy returned with force? Because she was—Samson would say it—intelligent enough to know how little she knew? She wrote to Védel, who had first admired her, appealing for his help; when he made no reply she turned directly to Samson, who had been one of her three teachers at the Conservatoire. He agreed to take her on as a private student to prepare her to return to the Comédie.

IN A SPLENDID PHOTOGRAPH by Carjat, Joseph-Isidore Samson looks almost like a bronze. The face is clever and benign, with shrewd eyes and a wide mouth—also a little weary. If he is not quite an absolute bourgeois, with his tie askew and his perceptible rumple, he is clearly a man of substance and decisiveness, definitely proud of himself, and more than a bit of a ham. He and his wife had three daughters and a son, an apartment near the Théâtre-Français, and a house in the country. The *maître* took no money from Rachel for his lessons, but did demand a small sum from Jacques Félix to pay the governess of his daughters, whose lessons Rachel shared. It was said that in the Samsons' *foyer* she acquired the basics of those elegant manners that would carry her in triumph through the palaces of kings; more likely, she learned them as Samson spoke the lines of princes, rehearsing her. During the summer of 1837, she studied as much as she could with her teacher, sometimes spending weekends with his family in the country; but she lived with her parents still, practicing the role of Hermione in the cramped quarters under the roof, scraping a carrot for the family stew—brandishing it in the face of an imaginary Pyrrhus, legend goes, then ferociously chopping it up into pieces with great glee, the carrot having become the faithless lover. She had to wait for her single dress to dry, she wrote Mme Samson, in a note asking to be excused for tardiness. Samson was as enthusiastic and as tireless as his pupil: he was committed to the Comédie-Française and its repertoire, proud of his art of teaching acting, excited—as Choron and Saint-

The actor Joseph-
Isidore Samson,
from a photograph
by Carjat

Aulaire had been—by the possibility of grooming a star, above all thrilled by
his new pupil's aptness. Biographers like to say he set about his work on her
as if on a block of marble.

Racine had carefully schooled La Champmeslé, his star and mistress,
going so far as to note on her scripts the precise inflections she was to use.
(After his death, they said, her acting deteriorated.) When Rachel performed
in works by living playwrights, the writer would direct her. Samson saw
himself as a surrogate for the dead poet-playwrights who would have shown
her how to render their lines. Others saw it differently. Gossip was rife:
gossips know that characters, like plots, repeat themselves. A century before
Rachel, the adolescent Adrienne Lecouvreur had been similarly spotted and
trained by Marc-Antoine Legrand, an actor who, like Samson, was said to
have been better as a teacher than as a player; Adrienne presumably became

his mistress in exchange for training. Even if we grant that Samson's virtue was as unimpeachable as he and his wife maintained, there were no doubt erotic forces at work as the older man instructed the girl in the art of playing a woman, praised and criticized her, awakened in her an appetite for his full attention that he could or would not always satisfy. Inevitably, there was rivalry between the possessive feelings of the militantly respectable Samsons (actors who, after all, had to insist on their own dignity) and the raffish, ambitious Félixes; but surely the parents were not altogether distressed to have their daughter thus promisingly taken up. Characteristically, Rachel played off one set of parents against the other, telling Samson that as a father of well-brought-up daughters he of course understood what she owed her parents. "I will always say everywhere that if I am something today, I owe it to you," she assures him, after he and her father (negotiating for her) have quarreled.

In February 1838, Samson persuaded Védel, now the director of the Théâtre-Français, to hear Rachel in his living room. Védel was impressed. Early in March she was given a free pass for the theater, and in April she (and her father—she was still a minor) signed a contract: at a salary of four thousand francs per year, the Comédie-Française engaged her as a *pensionnaire*. The wrangles over whom she belonged to now began in earnest, and they would become more impassioned as the stakes very quickly got higher and higher.

SAMSON'S PROPRIETARY feelings about Rachel were expressed in a cautionary didactic letter he wrote and published when she first became the toast of Paris. In clumsy rhymed couplets, he laid out the principles of the art of acting as he saw them, and warned against the recitations at private parties that would debase her art and ruin her health. In a suggestive confusion of biblical imagery, he warned against worshiping and being worshiped as the golden calf. The admonition was aimed at the public as well as at Rachel: Samson (and his wife) were not only contemptuous but fearful of the praise of the ignorant. They knew that the quality of an audience could affect a performance—and perhaps a career. The Samsons were Parisians, elitists, proud to be "of the Comédie-Française": passing through Brussels, Mme Samson was seriously distressed, once, by the sight of a farmer's cart drawn up in front of a theater where Rachel was performing. More narrowly, it was an article of Samson's artistic creed that the space of performance affected an actor's relation to a role. In the intimacy of home, he wrote, an actor might (to his loss) lose himself and feel he had become the character he played: the *optique du théâtre* required an art and a calculation that maintained the requisite balance.

Decades later, when Sarah Bernhardt recalled the different approaches of her various professors at the Conservatoire, she described Provost's as "broad," Regnier's as "true," and Samson's as "precise." In Samson's view, there was a correct way of rendering not only each role but each word. Rachel, he argued, had needed his teaching: how else would a girl like her, no matter how talented, know what to do with the great roles? He articulated his eighteenth-century aesthetic most emphatically in a public "letter" (this time in prose) to Jules Janin, written in response to the publication of *Rachel et la tragédie* shortly after the actress's death. Infuriated by Janin's breezy dismissal of him as a teacher whom Rachel had soon sent on his way, and determined that a man he despised should not have the definitive word about either her or himself, Samson documented his own sustained importance in her life and art, then went on to argue that she could not have done without him. Acceptance of the playwright's authority is the ground of his argument. How should an actor know what to do with a text when its author is dead? he asks. The age of creative directors was far in the future: Samson argued that it was the pride of the Comédie-Française to preserve and to honor Racine's instructions to La Champmeslé. Rachel, he observed, had had no models: when she started out, Mlles Raucourt, Maillart, and Duchesnois were already dead, and Mlle George had turned to the modern repertoire. He himself had performed the function of a necessary intermediary: one of Rachel's most admired effects had come down to her through him from the great Mlle Clairon, who had been dead for years.

But of course, how was a Janin to comprehend such matters? He was nothing but a cheap journalist, a mere phrasemaker. He knew nothing of art or technique; his own work lacked consistency, he had no memory, no powers of observation or discrimination, no seriousness, no respect for even his own words, which he himself freely contradicted. He had no theory, no ideas, only phrases that made no sense. The man of a hundred voices, as Janin called himself, was a pen, not a man! Samson, the representative of Racine, lambasted Janin for pandering to the mindless masses, and for being as ignorant as they. For only ignorance could explain his belief that Rachel's genius was absolutely spontaneous, purely inspired. The art of acting is to make the public believe that the deliberate and studied is spontaneous and accidental: Rachel had fooled the poor critic. The niceties of her art were lost on him; altogether, she had taken him in. Janin had made much of her ignorance; Samson protested that she knew a great deal, not that she had

The critic Jules Janin,
from a photograph

had a classical education but that she had been educated in her art. Her perceptions were unusually quick, her taste and her ear very delicate, she had a *nature d'élite*—but at sixteen she had needed (and afterward she continued to need) someone to help her interpret the difficult words of the finest poets. For an actor is an interpreter, not a creator, he insisted. (Years later, his wife assembled clear evidence from her letters that Rachel continued to depend on Samson's counsel and coaching well into the 1840s.)

The argument between Samson and Janin was between an Enlightenment aesthetic and a Romantic one. Janin had lauded Rachel as an inspired *pythonisse*, a Danaän vessel miraculously filled with divine afflatus; Samson defended her as a deliberate and conscious artist. He valued technique and above all control, believing that the best actor kept a part of himself in reserve, and submitting anecdotes that proved Rachel had done that. When Talma, Samson's ideal and mentor, had courteously rejected (as only a philosopher's) Diderot's proposal that the best actor is one who feels least, he had offered (with a practicing artist's authority) a less mischievous formulation that did not altogether contradict its basic premises. An actor is an artist, Talma believed, precisely because he can watch and gauge his own performance, keep the distance from the character he represents that allows him to shape it. On the days he threw himself into his part and exhausted himself on the stage, he confessed, he was not very good. Samson insisted in the same vein that the famous evening when Rachel collapsed after playing Camille was not at all evidence of her genius: she just had an unfortunate taste for applause, became overexcited by it that night, and lost herself. Samson made the point haughtily early on in his diatribe: he was responsible for Rachel's art, and Janin for her fame. When one weighed art in the balance against celebrity, money, applause—when he did—there was no question which mattered more. The mandarin actor's contempt for the general audience and the critic's contempt for the mere player have survived the battle of classic vs. romantic.

To attack Janin, Samson mockingly used the image of Columbus, not Pygmalion. "She's my discovery, my creation," he mimics Janin as saying. But what of Saint-Aulaire, he asks, and Delestre-Poirson, and Védel, and the comédiens-français, and the audiences who applauded her for three months before Janin even saw her? (Not to mention her teacher.) "Voilà bien des Christophe Colomb, qu'en dîtes-vous, Monsieur?" His choice of image nearly concedes the embattled point, that Rachel was a creature of nature and not a creation of art, that (as Védel claimed) all her gifts were instinctive, God-given. But the lines were delicately drawn, from his eighteenth-century perspective: nature and art were friendly collaborators; Rachel had come to him admirably equipped to be a great tragedienne and he had instructed her. Janin's more romantic aesthetic required the dramatically ungrammatical and ignorant waif, ridiculous offstage but noble in action, miraculously transformed by Art's power, Tragedy's, Racine's, his own. For Janin as for Samson, the word was everything: the teacher claimed he had had to explain Racine to Rachel, the journalist that the immortal poet's soul informed hers.

A THIRD MAN, another candidate for Rachel's Pygmalion, altered the literary terms of the struggle. For Rachel's more naive biographers Dr. Louis Véron is a monster, a powerful middle-aged man who first seduces the am-

bitious teenager by promising to make her career, and later on ruins her
reputation for Attic chasteness—the phrase is Musset's—by reading aloud to
his friends some compromising letters in his possession (it is unclear who
wrote them to whom). The caricaturists of his time delighted in his grotesque
fatness, sparse hair, gross features, and the neck scarred by scrofula which he
hid in enormous cravats, prompting one joker to address a letter to "Dr.
Louis Véron, Dans Sa Cravate, Paris." (The letter, like one addressed to
"Mr. Barnum, America," is supposed to have been delivered.) Daumier's big-
bellied, naked Véron as St. Sebastian is the most widely known send-up of
the powerful Parisian, but few books on Rachel have not reprinted the drawing of the tragedienne in her toga between the sinister man of commerce
and the aesthete Arsène Houssaye. You made her a star but I made her an
artist, Samson insisted to Janin, conceding to the journalist a (lesser) role in
her story: who could deny that the performing artist needs a public? With
Véron a third figure is introduced, an agent to manipulate public opinion, a
man whose covert operations, deliberately undertaken for the purpose, give
an actress the cachet a critic can praise and puff. At the time, the modern
figure seemed sinister; the idea of a free press and an enthusiastic voluble
journalist as midwives for genius is still more attractive than the notion of a
commercial-minded middleman.

It was therefore easy for Janin to present himself—and be remembered—
as the man who rolled into the Théâtre-Français on a hot August evening to
be astonished by the young Rachel, when in fact Véron was the one who
first appreciated how rare she was. It was he who, in June 1838, began to
whisper in the ears of *le tout Paris*—that is, the twelve or fifteen hundred
Parisians who made public opinion, all of whom he personally knew—that
a phenomenal new actress had appeared. "Have you seen Rachel?" he
recalled saying throughout the summer of 1838, in lieu of "Good day." Rachel
was his "new religion," he wrote, adding (slightly shifting the metaphor) that
before he intervened she had been preaching in the desert at the Théâtre-
Français. He had been one of the five people seated in the orchestra on 12
June, the evening she made her debut, and he had recognized that "Racine
and Corneille were living among us once more, as in the great century of
Louis XIV," he remembered. (The idea of the splendor of the past, revived,
appealed to the self-styled *bourgeois de Paris*, whose nostalgia was characteristic of the Bourgeois Monarchy: a few years later, the twenty-one-year-old
Flaubert went home after seeing Rachel in Rouen and wrote in his notebook,
with a quite different emphasis, "She makes Corneille and Racine into contemporary geniuses, full of immediacy.") Janin had been out of town in June,

traveling in Italy; he took his seat at the Théâtre-Français in mid-August not because he was glad to be home and eager to cool off on a hot evening with dull familiar pleasures (as he wrote), but because he had heard, through Véron, about Rachel.

DR. VÉRON is always given his honorific, although he never finished his medical studies or practiced as a physician, and was important in medical circles only as the marketer—he made a fortune—of a patent medicine invented by a colleague of his who had died. (Like Sarah Félix, he was before his time in making money by packaging nostrums.) A great maker of opinion and artistic careers, he was called, by one wit, "the Mercury of intellectual materialism." In 1829, he founded *La Revue de Paris*, which published Dumas, Balzac, and George Sand; in 1831 he became the director of the Opéra, where he produced *La Juive, Robert le diable, Les Huguenots,* and ballets featuring Taglioni and Elssler; later, the political journal *Le Constitutionnel* came into his hands. But because his modern professions, of producer and impresario and publisher, were not yet recognized as categories in which a man might be said to have distinguished himself, Véron was made a Chevalier of the Legion of Honor as a doctor. He boasted that he had drunk champagne and been asked by the government for his advice every day of his life, and slept with every woman he ever wanted. Delacroix, in 1849, noted that Véron "lives in amazing luxury; great apartments hung with magnificent brocade, including the ceilings . . . superb silver and an orchestra playing during dinner." Fond of wielding power behind the scenes, fascinated by power of all kinds, Véron left indelible images of Rachel: not only of the tragedienne ("that strange physiognomy, that fiery gaze, that spindly body, that voice of such intelligence") but also, most compellingly, of a charming and clever woman. Summing up his assessment of her career, he pointed out "how much study, strength, and seductiveness, I want almost to say how much political savvy, Mlle Rachel needed in order to maintain her brilliant popular reputation over the long period of sixteen years." In an extraordinary view of the private woman, the pragmatic doctor compared Rachel to the powerful minister Adolphe Thiers, who like her had been his antagonist and his friend. If there is some ambivalence in the description, it is nevertheless remarkable in the annals of rhapsodies about actresses. This is no object of the male gaze, no pawn or slave to passion, no doomed or driven tragedienne, no man's Galatea. Of Thiers and Rachel, Véron writes that "they had the same sharpness of vision, the same commitment to the goal they had in mind, the same ingenious ruses, the same calculated seductions, the same wealth of expedients, the same philosophical tolerance that seeks neither vengeance nor hatred, and is ready to negotiate. . . . I would estimate that, having a loftiness of spirit almost equivalent to an education, Mlle Rachel, in ordinary conversation, displays as much wit, judgment, common sense, and unexpected, pointed insights as the great orator and statesman of the July Monarchy. The art of oratory (by which I don't mean eloquence) and the art of the stage demand almost the same talents, the same tricks—the same make-up, almost." Mocking the politician is more than half of Véron's point, but the comparison that belittles Thiers dignifies Rachel. He was as false-faced as an actress; she was as astute and insightful as he. This is far from the standard stereotype of the cold, heartless woman, empty of everything but ambition— or of a little actress formed and promoted by a clever man. Véron's Rachel is charming and worldly, calculating and manipulative, understood to be using her considerable wits and talents fairly to get what she wants—which is not really very different from what "great" men want, and get.

Janin's quarrel with Samson over Rachel was about her authenticity; Véron's Rachel adds a disturbing modern dimension to the discussion. She is like a great man, as he sees her—an intelligent professional, consciously and deliberately excelling at her métier, and managing her career. Like all visions of Rachel, it is legibly a projection—of the man of the world and fortune-maker, disparaged in the English papers as "the old lozenge-maker," without whom "Rachel might have lain buried like a truffle, for want of the judicious pig's snout to disinter and give its fragrance to the world." But it makes one wonder. What if he didn't seduce and exploit the young tragedienne (who had had at least one lover before him)? Might Melpomene, the Tragic Muse, have embraced Dr. Véron not because he forced or bribed her but because he was her sort, during that first summer when she set about to make it in the world?

In his memoir, the *bourgeois de Paris* follows up the discreetly told tale of how he saw Rachel in the theater and made her famous. He gave a lavish party for her at his magnificent house on the rue Taitbout in the fall of 1838, where his discovery gratified her host as the gracious star of the evening, a credit to her patron's taste (tastefully, he does not hint he was her lover). She had none of the gloom of the tragedienne about her, he recalls (how Samson would quiver in fury!); she danced and talked and charmed everyone. In his worldly way, Véron reasons that this talent was logical and necessary for an actress, who needed, after all, to affect the poor sitting in the *paradis* as well

as the rich in their boxes. "Like Célimène, Mlle Rachel has the policy of
pleasing everyone," he reflects, invoking the clever, hypocritical young widow
who drove Molière's misanthrope mad by her promiscuous charm. (Later,
Rachel would have great success in England in the role of Célimène, but
would fail in the role in Paris: it is hard to know whether it was because she
fell short of Mlle Mars, who had been brilliant in the part, or because Paris
was invested in the idea of a *grande tragédienne* unfit for comedy. Her performance in 1853 as the heroine of Delphine de Girardin's *Lady Tartuffe*, a
latter-day Célimène, was effective in the manner of a *chronique scandaleuse:*
much more venomous, less engaging and girlish, than Molière's Célimène,
Virginie de Blossac was understood by the knowing to be a compound of
Rachel and the clever playwright, as well as some well-known Parisian ladies
the latter said she meant to satirize.)

Véron, a connoisseur of power, admired the way Rachel deployed hers.
He describes the actress offstage, surrounded by powerful men, as more a
salonnière than a courtesan. Though she herself said she was a better hand
at other people's verse than at prose of her own, he sketches a brilliant
conversationalist: "I have often had the pleasure of having Rachel at my table
alongside the distinguished men of our time: Count Molé; General Changarnier; Achille Fould; the Duke of Soto-Mayor, the Spanish Ambassador;
Sainte-Beuve; Eugène Delacroix; Meyerbeer; Auber; Halévy; etc. etc. With
the most natural air, the young artist showed herself to be a great lady, with
all the qualities of mind necessary to charm even superior men—the rare
qualities especially characteristic of those women of the last century whose
salons were enlivened by the regular attendance of the most splendid names."
Delacroix corroborates this picture. Although he noted in his journal that
some of Rachel's performances were not as good as others, he also observed,
after a dinner at Véron's, that "Rachel is exceedingly witty, very fine in every
way. It would have been extraordinarily difficult for any man, born and
brought up as she was, to become what she now is quite *naturally.*" Rachel
herself professed to agree that nature and society treated men and women
differently. In a letter to Raphaël, who was still a boy at school, she urged
him in a big-sisterly spirit to study hard so that he might be recognized as
an *homme d'esprit*. Things are different, she says, for a woman, whose natural
curiosity and powers of retention make education quite unnecessary: "A
woman," she wrote, "can arrive at an honorable, esteemed, and suitable
position, without quite possessing that polish society properly calls education.
How can that be, you ask? A woman loses none of her charm in being

reserved in manner and language. On the contrary: a woman responds, she doesn't ask questions; she never opens a discussion, only listens. Her natural coquetry makes her wish to learn, she retains what she hears, and so without having had any solid foundation, she nevertheless acquires a polish that can pass for education." People said she knew only her own lines, but she seems to have been aware of the whole scene.

~

CHAPTER FOUR

Playing Rachel

Oh my sweet Racine, it is in your masterpieces that I recognize the heart of woman! I shape my own to your noble poetry. If the lyre of my soul does not always weep with your harmonies divine, it is because admiration leaves my whole being in ecstasy.

RACHEL, 1851, in a copy of Racine's *Works*

So you see, tragediennes are comediennes, after all!

MLLE GEORGE, tragedienne, to Victor Hugo

THEATRICAL ILLUSION IS the basis of an actor's social reality, what status, wealth, and power he or she enjoys in the offstage world. Surely it helps construct character as well—notions of what character is, therefore characters to fit them. By embodying storied women on the stage, acting out the roles of Tragedy's Muse and victim, Rachel took on increments of meaning for herself. She assumed the severity and scorn of Camille and Hermione, the guilt of Phèdre; she borrowed the solemn dignity and high moral seriousness that she helped persuade the nineteenth-century public to attribute to Racine's and Corneille's plays. She glowed with the aura of the opposing aesthetic ideals that she seemed to exemplify, and the general idea of Art and of abstraction. Acting brought her fame; she became a star. The creature of a script and a dramatic tradition; of a moment, an occasion, a stage and a costume; of a culture's *idées fixes*, obsessions, and modes of representation; of the psychosocial structures that connect performing women and paying au-

diences—she was also palpably herself, right there. Her fans were fascinated
by the mystery of Rachel's private, secret self, the question of how much of
her was real.

1. Young Princess

"High tragedy," Napoleon is said to have remarked in a philosophical mood
one day at Saint-Cloud, "is the school of great men. It is the duty of rulers
to encourage and cultivate it. One does not have to be a poet to be a judge
of it; one has only to understand men and things as they are, to be acquainted
with power, to be a statesman. Tragedy sets the soul aflame, elevates the
spirit, can and must create heroes. France, therefore, owes no small measure
of its history of glorious actions to Corneille. Yes, gentlemen, if he were alive
today, I would make him a prince." With all but the last, Louis XIV would
have agreed. Why else had the Sun King established the Comédie-Française
in 1680, pledged to underwrite it, and charged it with the duty of preserving
the French cultural heritage? Louis was quite as clever as Napoleon would
be about the politics of performance and display; the heroes of Corneille and
Racine were models for the theatrical court he directed and starred in. And
his creation, the state theater, would redound to the country's glory for
generations.

The permeability of the "fourth wall" of the stage can have an important
political function. Theaters may direct, encapsulate, drain off energies that
threaten the social order, or inflame and exacerbate them. The role of the
popular theaters of the fairs and the streets in France, before and between
revolutions, has been debated by social historians; as for the role of the
"legitimate" stage, Napoleon's view is the decisive one.

If it cannot be credited with breeding up a martial race of Corneillian
heroes, the Théâtre-Français has successfully sustained, over the centuries, an
idea of French cultural coherence, and the supporting idea that elegance,
reasoned high-mindedness, artfulness, and exigence are characteristically
French. It has helped to shape France's self-image and dazzle foreigners.
Goethe, Matthew Arnold, Henry James, and George Bernard Shaw were
among the many who envied France a theater dedicated to national and
aesthetic purposes that transcend mere commercial interests; England would
undertake to match it only in the twentieth century. The national theater
was a source of French cultural and linguistic pride: in the nineteenth century,

it served as the ideological underpinning of the nation's colonialist *mission civilisatrice*—distinguishing France's cultural obligation from England's drearier "white man's burden."

THE TRAGEDIES that provided the state theater's repertoire, along with Molière's comedies, were neoclassical—for the most part, adaptations of Greek and Roman plays, or dramatizations of stories from ancient history. Obedient to rules of art that had been articulated by Aristotle and Horace, and reaffirmed by their contemporary Boileau, the Renaissance poet-playwrights paid homage to the ancients by their work. Claiming the legacy of the past, they appropriated it, and the cultural authority of antiquity, for themselves, their king, and their country. Neoclassicism has an equivocal relation to history. On the one hand it defies the passage of time, looking to the past for the matter and the rules of "eternal" art; on the other, it holds the mirror up to time passing. Re-creations of the past make us believe that deeds worthy of applause can be performed today, but they also chasten by reminding us of once powerful peoples now defeated and dissolved. Revived, the past is rewritten into time—and the present subtly revises it. A "classical" ideal can only be imagined in the terms at hand at the moment. What can a classical tradition come to but a succession of classicisms?

In France at the turbulent turn of the eighteenth century, as a revolution overturned a monarchy and an empire succeeded a republic, history dramatically inflected changing visions of ancient Greece and Rome. By the time Alfred de Musset declared that Rachel was Tragedy—just before or just after his putative short term as her lover—a series of national calamities had revised ideas of what tragedy might be. In the 1830s, 1840s, and 1850s, literary men and politicians of different political persuasions—Louis Blanc, Etienne Cabet, Alphonse de Lamartine, Jules Michelet, Edgar Quinet, Alexis de Tocqueville, Adolphe Thiers—rewrote, in many volumes, the history of France, seeking to find and fix revolution's meaning and its ends. Meanwhile history moved on toward yet another revolution, illustrating one or another proverbial truth about change and repetition. "Hegel remarks somewhere that all facts and personages of great importance in world history occur, as it were, twice," Karl Marx began his book about the events of 1848–51. "He forgot to add: the first time as tragedy, the second as farce." In the late 1830s, when Rachel revived the classical tragic repertoire that Talma before her had reinflected to suit a time of revolution, she already seemed a disturbing sign—among many—of history ambiguously or ambivalently reversing or repeating itself.

The nineteenth-century cult of classicism began with respect for pre-

Christian learning and the Roman republic, among Enlightenment philoso-
phers and radicals, and peaked when Napoleon took the Emperor Augustus
as his model. The growth of schooling, the development of scholarship, encouraged admiration for the culture of the past. The Greeks and Romans
were sought out as models, acknowledged as the sources of French civilization, also looked to for an escape from the present. But the present inescap-
ably informs and colors ideas of the past—had done so even in the
Renaissance. And notions of classicism are complicated as succeeding generations interpret them. In Gérard de Nerval's view, the poets of the seventeenth century were less Greek than decadently Roman: Racine's *Phèdre*, he
alleged, owed more to Seneca's version of the play than it did to the *Hippolytus* of Euripides. Heinrich Heine argued, tongue in cheek perhaps, that
Corneille and Racine were not earnest neoclassicists at all but parodists, who
were elaborating a witty conceit when they put the elegant periphrases and
polite formulas of late Renaissance courtiers into the mouths of ancient Romans and Greeks. Schlegel was wrong, Heine argued, in reading Racine as a
poor imitation of Euripides; he missed "the infinite grace, the sweet jest, the
profound charm that derived from Racine's dressing his modern French heroes
in ancient costumes and thus adding to the fascination of a modern passion the
interesting element of a brilliant masquerade." This probably sheds more useful
light on history-minded, mask-ridden nineteenth-century Paris than it does on
seventeenth-century Versailles; certainly it illuminates the figure of Heine's contemporary Rachel. Reviving Racine after Talma, she revived multiple pasts and
superimposed them on one another: an idealized Greco-Roman world that
seemed nearly legendary, and the differently, dubiously glorious periods of the
ancien régime and Napoleon. And by figuring high tragedy and heroism in
female form, she subtly redefined and undercut them.

Although the classic French repertoire is unparalleled in tragic roles for
women, and although actresses worked on the French stage long before women
came on the boards in England, France had never had an awe-inspiring tragedienne like Mrs. Siddons. La Champmeslé had been acknowledged as Racine's best interpreter; the brilliance and pathos of the eighteenth-century
actress Adrienne Lecouvreur had been widely admired and appreciated. But
France, which loved its tender Adrienne, was inclined to jeer at more commanding tragic actresses. A caricaturist of the First Empire portrayed Mlles
Duchesnois and George as robust viragoes disputing the crown of tragedy
with muscular contortions and whirling drapery, as they gestured histrioni-
cally around a sacrificial fire suggestively crawling with snakes, for an audience of geese and turkeys. In the early decades of the nineteenth century,

beautifully controlled Mlle Mars was admired for her charm and wit, polish and skill—in other words, as the model of an elegant woman. But all that hardly added up to genius. Jules Janin pointed to the visit of the Shakespearean actress Harriet Smithson to Paris in 1827 as the moment that the French understood an actress could be taken seriously, and began to want a great tragedienne of their own. A member of the English troupe—it included Kean and Kemble—that had moved Stendhal to praise Shakespeare over Racine, Smithson gave a thrilling rendition of Ophelia out of control. Stage madness had never been so convincing or attractive before, and ladies' heads dressed à la Smithson, stuck with bits of straw, were all the rage in Paris. The young Rachel was said to be reminiscent of her violence and her pathos—and also reminiscent of the very different, majestic Mrs. Siddons. As Talma had before her, she stood for France partly by reminding people of England.

FRANÇOIS-JOSEPH TALMA, the remarkable tragic actor who was the favorite and friend of Napoleon, had become a star in one spectacular move, in the revolutionary year 1789. Cast in a minor role in *Brutus*, a proto-republican tragedy by Voltaire, he appeared onstage clad in a toga, with his bare feet in sandals, and his hair cut short and left unpowdered. By that startling sartorial gesture Talma claimed the national theater for the people, and all eyes for himself. The costumes actors had traditionally worn identified "high" tragedy with a social elite: the Greeks and Romans as the Renaissance poet-playwrights imagined them wore silk knee-breeches, ruffled shirts, and embroidered coats. In a period when actors were expected to supply their own costumes, these outfits were usually handed down by courtiers to their servants, the players, who by wearing them in effect claimed a semblance, at least, of eternity for the court. Talma's plain republican cloth proved that change was possible, and in context it encouraged thoughts of wider, deeper changes. His revolutionary act of revisionary dressing was made independently: the other actors were as surprised as the audience was by the costume he had concocted with his friend the painter David (who was soon making mantles on the same model for the senators of the new republic). Of Talma in his toga, the actress Mlle Contat is supposed to have said in the wings, with a giggle, "He looks like a statue!" Everyone repeated the *mot*, but not at Talma's expense: the charismatic actor was not a man to be laughed at.

Talma's implicit call for a more natural, historically accurate style was based on new ideas he had gathered in the London theaters, where as a young man he had seen the actors John Philip Kemble and Charles Macklin in costumes based on drawings of art and artifacts newly uncovered by the

Portrait of Rachel, or *La Tragédie,* by Jean-Léon Gérôme, 1859; Salon of 1861

François-Joseph Talma in the Role of Nero, by Eugène Delacroix, 1853

Rachel, by Edouard Dubufe, 1850

La Sybille au rameau d'or (*The Cumaean Sybil*), by
Eugène Delacroix, 1838(?); Salon of 1845

Mlle Rachel, by William Etty, 1840

Contemporary lithographs of Rachel's costumes

: Rachel and the company of the Théâtre-Français, watercolor by Henry de Montaut
BOTTOM: Contemporary caricatures of Rachel

La Tragédie, by Eugène Emmanuel Amaury-Duval, Salon of 1855

excavations at Pompeii. Although classicism had strong associations with courts, the political implications for France, at the moment, were clear: the show of plainness was an unmistakable warning of populist, revolutionary changes. The applause for Talma in his toga echoed the excitement in the state theater of five years earlier, when Beaumarchais's *Le Mariage de Figaro* (1784) had been heard as a trumpet call to revolution. It was a sign of the rapidly altering times that a common actor, rather than a literary man like Beaumarchais, should now be the one making the call for change.

Mutely asserting that the past had been different from the present, Talma's costume hinted at what the future could be. By his gesture he cast his vote for a socially responsible theater involved in national political life as "high" courtly dramas no longer could be. He was applauded for the ideas he represented, also for himself; he was understood as an inspiring model of individualism. Among other things, Talma changed the view of his profession. For the first time in France, the actor was recognized as an artist—a romantic creator—rather than a mere interpreter. Talma's silent declaration of independence shifted the emphasis from the company to the individual star, from repetition to re-creation, from imitation to performative action. An Anglophile, he admired the English verbs by which an actor could be said "to perform tragedy" or "to act a part," rather than, as in French, either to play *(jouer)* or speak *(dire)* tragedy. In his book on acting, he differed gently with Diderot, claiming the authority of experience, and stressing process: an actor, he wrote, was not so much detached as divided. Talma's intelligence and artistic brilliance were transformative. When he performed, one theater historian writes, "*Britannicus* and *Brutus* ceased to belong to a world of reference dominated by the court and the ancien régime, and became historical and deeply political tragic dramas. By his reappropriation of classic authors, Talma 'invented' the national theater that the *philosophes* had so long wished for." In the act he enhanced the status of the actor and made himself a symbol of the nation.

Talma's subsequent history proved him to be politically capable offstage as well as on. He shrewdly navigated the shoals of the 1790s, surviving the threats and political schisms that afflicted the Comédie-Française. His personal popularity prevailed in spite of the fact that bloody spectacles in the streets made stage tragedy look pale, and melodrama and romantic drama mimed the "mode of excess" prevailing in real life, where there were spectacular executions on the Place de la Révolution, and, later on, huge and expensive communal rituals in which the republic celebrated itself. Offstage, Talma was both romantically and classically theatrical, a star who received his friends at home dressed as an ancient Roman, and gave his twin sons ostentatiously double names, one Christian and one pagan (Roman, that is, and therefore republican): Henri-Castor and Charles-Pollux. His style might have been deliberately calculated to match Napoleon's taste—if it did not form it.

Commenting on Napoleon's remark that high tragedy is the school of great men, Sainte-Beuve pointed out that when he made it the emperor had seen not merely Corneille, but Corneille as performed by Talma. Napoleon's severe, exclusive taste for classical tragedy was sharpened, if not created, by a single actor's art. Like Nero before him, the emperor was a theater buff: the statuesque Mlle George had been his mistress (she was later Jules Janin's), and among his more effective moments, during the siege of Moscow, were the ones he spent revising the administrative structure of the Comédie-Française. After he seized absolute power it was Talma, they said, who instructed him in imperial bearing. In at least one instance, the actor even had an effect on imperial policy: his performance as King Assuérus, the monarch who repudiates the enemy of the Jews in Racine's *Esther*, is supposed to have moved Napoleon to rethink the position of French Jews and eventually to accord them further rights. In return the emperor gave Talma the benefit of his experience. When the actor undertook the role of Néron in *Britannicus*, the tyrant contributed his insider's insight: "I would like to see you make fewer gestures," said Napoleon; "natures like these aren't so expansive; they are the more powerful for being restrained."

Having embellished, shared, and borrowed the emperor's aura, Talma survived to unnerve Restoration audiences by recalling the lost leader. But after he died, in 1826, tragedy seemed dead as well, unthinkable without him. The Théâtre-Français had become a shrine of an old religion populated by ghosts, its critics said, a gathering place for peevish legitimists who lamented the new order. And then, late in the decade of ambiguously nostalgic Napoleon plays that followed, a slender and very young woman revived Talma's memory. His mantle fell, or was disposed by the guiding spirit of romantic irony, onto Rachel's shoulders.

RACHEL MADE HER DEBUT at the Théâtre-Français on 12 June 1838 as Camille in Corneille's *Horace*. Chafing at the bit of apprenticeship, longing for the applause she had tasted at the Théâtre Molière and briefly at the Théâtre du Gymnase, thoroughly rehearsed in anticipation of her moment, she was ready for the role and the date as soon as he named them, Védel later recalled. For his part, he was willing to take a chance on a beginner in an extra-slow summer season. In 1830, it had been important for Victor Hugo and his followers to stage the Battle of *Hernani* in the house on the rue de Richelieu: the victory of romantic drama over classicism, its acknowledged supremacy in France, could only be achieved in that place. Eight years later, partly as a result of the Battle, no one expected more surprises there. The popular theaters of the boulevards were flourishing; the Théâtre-Français had declined into a preserve for an endangered elite art. It could not compete with action-packed historical dramas by Dumas *père*, and lurid melodramas by Pixérécourt and his followers. The bloody-minded excitements of the Boulevard du Crime, the easy pleasures of song, dance, and spectacle at the Opéra, the titillating amusement of domestic farces, the compelling physical presence of Frédérick Lemaître and his partner, Marie Dorval, made the *bienséances* seem silly, the rhymed tragedies stiff, slow, cold, and wordy; the large and eager theatergoing public found Corneille's legalistic arguments and Racine's moral urgencies artificial, irrelevant, and taxing. Revenues at the state theater continued to decline: the government-sponsored effort to find new young actors who might prove to be drawing cards seemed doomed. For although Talma's influence had changed the actors' costumes, his "natural acting" had had small effect on the tradition of declamation and bombast. The *sociétaires* of the Théâtre-Français continued faithful to the standard repertoire of postures, gestures, and inflections. They could not but seem wooden to fans of expressive Marie Dorval and brilliant Lemaître, called "the Talma of the boulevards." Dorval and Lemaître melted into their roles, expressed their feelings with their bodies: the romantic desideratum, for actors, was transcending, not transmitting, language. Furthermore, while the Théâtre-Français still could claim a few stars who glittered in the old artificial way, like Mlle Mars, they were aging; in a politicized cultural climate that polarized styles and generations, the state theater, which could not muster the money to match the salary Lemaître commanded elsewhere, seemed well on the way to becoming a museum.

RACHEL CHANGED THAT. During the hot summer months of 1838 she performed the roles of the high-minded, strong-willed *jeunes princesses* of the classical repertoire: Corneille's Camille, Hermione in Racine's *Andromaque*, Aménaïde in Voltaire's *Tancrède*, and Eriphile in Racine's *Iphigénie en Aulide*. She memorized hundreds of lines of rhymed poetry, perfected innumerable subtle inflections and gestures, acted her heart out. Audiences were small at first. Jules Janin did not hear her until 4 September; it was only after his two rave reviews in the *Journal des débats*, of 10 and 24 September, that box-office receipts mounted very dramatically, from eight hundred francs a night to more than three thousand, and then to an astounding six thousand on 19 October. Once set, the pattern was permanent: when Rachel performed—and only then—the house was full. She saved the Théâtre-Français, which had been collecting only four or five hundred francs a night, and she made it depend on her.

The young actress studied her lines in the tiny dressing room under the roof that had been assigned her (she moved her things in herself), repeated them in her continuing lessons with Samson, said them over in the squalor of the Félix apartment, as she scraped the carrots for the stew. We can only conjecture about the effect, on her otherwise untrained mind, of the old-fashioned language, the rhythmic, symmetrical rhymed alexandrines, the elaborate phrasing, the moral and aesthetic values of another age. Getting her lines by heart, did she take them to heart as well—and the ideals between the lines, of high-mindedness and high artifice? Samson initiated her into the structured mysteries of the Théâtre-Français: he showed her how to mime the inflections of Mlle Clairon, whom Diderot had praised for staying separate from the passions she rendered. The standard of self-control that the *philosophe* had ascribed to the very best actors, in his *Paradoxe sur le comédien*, was not the least lofty of her goals. To enter the acting profession where and when Rachel did was to give over part of oneself, and retain the rest. The required psychological gymnastics would have marked a very young woman for life, as well as for the stage. Samson surely urged on her a reverence for the weight of the words she spoke, taught her to respect the authority vested not only in them but in the actor who delivered them on the stage of the state theater. To take herself seriously. Did she persuade herself, along with her public, that she was a heroic Camille, a scornful Hermione? How do actors carry their audiences with them if not on the strength of their belief in their imagined selves?

S H E   P U T   S H A K E S P E A R E in Racine, they would say—was at once wild and regular, astoundingly natural and elegantly artful, an original genius perfectly faithful to tradition. The force of rules, rhymes, and regularities served to set off her emotional intensity, to contain, constrain, compress, and thus to increase it. The very orthodoxy of her repertoire underscored the sense of her newness; speaking line after line, couplet after couplet, putting antithesis upon antithesis, she pushed to the limits of the rules of art, and by doing so proved their truth. If the elevated persons she played were on the one hand palpably discrepant with the very young, pale, and plain-faced girl, on the other they fit her like a second skin, or a life-mask. She had appeared to be miming her own personal circumstances at the Gymnase, playing the poor girl from the Vendée who walks to Paris to save her father; she played as real an aspect of herself now, as Camille, the Roman maiden who bravely defends her high ideal of personal integrity. Standing up alone for Corneille, assuming the grand manner and making it thrilling once more, she seemed to chasten the corrupted taste of the Boulevard du Crime, and to stand for France at its noblest. Engravings of the proud and rigid young woman in her toga reveal how well it suited her. The actor Edmond Got wrote wickedly that no matter what the script was, Camille was the only role she ever played.

The heroine of the baroque tragedy *Horace* (sometimes called *Les Horaces)* is nothing like the more popular theatrical "Camille," Marguérite Gautier, the tubercular *dame aux camélias* of the 1852 play by Dumas *fils* that Sarah Bernhardt was to make so famous. The most interesting character in Corneille's play is a virgin who speaks up for the personal life against the state. The story of her struggle with her family, based on an anecdote told by Livy and Plutarch, is most familiar today outside France as the situation depicted in David's painting *The Oath of the Horatii* (1785). During the bicentennial celebration of the French Revolution, in 1989, it served as a forceful image of fraternal solidarity and, by the way, a representation of exclusionary maleness. It portrays three helmeted, hard-limbed heroes accepting the blessing of their father, joining their swords as one in bright sunlight in the center of the canvas, while off to the right, in the shade of a portico, their women mourn, collapsed together. David borrowed more than its classical subject from Corneille's 1640 heroic tragedy, notably the tensions between public and private virtue, and violence and cold control. He follows Corneille also in coding public and private as male and female. But he makes a very significant change in focus: in the play, only one glorious brother is a speaking character, and one of the gracefully draped women in the heap to one side is his chief antagonist.

The conflict in the story of the brothers Horace, who are obliged to fight for Rome, is between allegiance to the state and to the family. The champions of rebellious Alba, the brothers Curiace, are connected to the Horaces through their women: a daughter of the Curiaces is one brother's wife, and Camille, the daughter of Old Horace, is engaged to a young Curiace. As the play begins, she and her sister-in-law Sabine implore the men not to fight, while the father urges his sons to defend Rome and pursue glory. The patriarch wins. In the ensuing battle—which, following the precepts of the Roman poet also named Horace, takes place offstage—two Horaces and

Rachel in her toga, engraving after a portrait by Edwin D. Smith, 1841

all three Curiace brothers are killed. When, in Act IV, the surviving Horace returns home victorious and describes the battle, he meets the scathing scorn of his sister; in the most famous speech in the play, she reviles not only the man acclaimed as the hero of the state but Rome itself.

> *Rome, l'unique objet de mon ressentiment!*
> *Rome, à qui vient ton bras d'immoler mon amant!*
> *Rome qui t'a vu naître, et que ton coeur adore!*
> *Rome enfin que je hais parce qu'elle t'honore!*

> Rome, the sole target of my burning pain!
> Rome, for whose sake my darling you've just slain!
> Rome, who engendered you, whom you adore!
> Rome, whom for honoring you I now abhor!

Rome's defender turns on Camille and she flees; he pursues and murders her.

Horace's sister is hardly a revolutionary or even a rebel: her first arguments against war, and for the holiness of the heart's affections, are couched in the rhetoric of monarchy and patriarchy. She thinks the will of the gods is made manifest in the bosom of kings, rather than the voice of the people; she believes that her brother's wife owes no allegiance to her family of origin, and that she herself, being promised but not yet given by her father, hangs suspended between the warring parties. When she argues that she loves Curiace more than her sister-in-law Sabine loves Horace, she explains that the passion her father has sanctioned is no tyrant but a legitimate king: Corneille plays on a standard poetic vocabulary of periphrasis, in which love is always referred to as a flame and the lover as a tyrant. Only after her two brothers are reported dead and her father alleges that their glory repays him for the loss does she begin to see the patriot-patriarch as the enemy of the personal relations she values, and therefore as her enemy. Doubting the authority of Old Horace brings her logically to question the state's. She insults the masters of the civilized world as tigers, brutes, and barbarians, and imagines Rome's enemies rising up against the fatherland, and Rome turning—as Rome's daughter Camille has done—against itself.

> *Puissent tous ses voisins ensemble conjurés*
> *Saper ses fondements encor mal assurés,*
> *Et si ce n'est assez de toute l'Italie,*
> *Que l'Orient contre elle à l'Occident s'allie,*

Que cent peuples unis des bouts de l'univers
Passent pour la détruire et les monts et les mers,
Qu'elle-même sur soi renverse ses murailles,
Et de ses propres mains déchire ses entrailles!

May all her neighbors in a grand alliance
Sap her foundations as they hurl defiance!
And if all Italy prove insufficient,
May Occident ally itself with Orient;
May a hundred peoples from the ends of the world
Cross mountains, seas, to crush her, flags unfurled!
May she herself crash down her ramparts stout,
And with her own hand tear her bowels out!

Adrienne Lecouvreur had played Camille as a pathetic creature maddened by her losses; Rachel was different, a threatening, avenging fury. Mme Samson (disapprovingly) recalled that she was unwilling to give up a crowd-pleasing spasm of horror she had improvised as Camille hears her brother describe her lover's death at his hand: the innovation, the little rebellion against Samson's authority, is further evidence that she made the role her own. As her *tirade* develops, Camille grows from a wounded, angry young woman to a prophet of disaster and finally a monster of destructive, ambitious egotism. (Rachel grew to Homeric proportions onstage, Janin wrote.) She imagines herself as the cause and the spectator of Rome's fall, imagines dying, in ecstasy, of the pleasure she has brought herself:

Puissé-je de mes yeux y voir tomber ce foudre,
Voir ses maisons en cendre, et tes lauriers en poudre,
Voir le dernier Romain à son dernier soupir,
Moi seule en être cause, et mourir de plaisir!

May I, with my eyes, see Heaven's lightning flash,
Her mansions dust, your laurels turned to ash,
See the last Roman breathe out his last sigh,
Myself, sole cause of all, ecstatic die! (IV, 5)

It is a vision of the self transcendent—and a fit of self-destroying despair. The Russian critic Pavel Vasil'evich Annenkov, who would see Rachel's Camille in St. Petersburg in 1853–54, found the whole scene "practically unendurable," from Camille's spasm, when she learns of her lover's death, through her ringing monologue, which was so beautifully integrated in the action as to be no longer the set piece earlier actors had made it. He wrote that "it is impossible to differentiate the couplets, feelings, nuances in her and present their significance out of context; everything originates in and flows with the fiery rush of passions which tears to pieces all moral barriers and pours forth as a hideous phenomenon of the human soul. One might simply mention the plainest, positively savage pleasure of Rachel, when she disgraces Horace's laurels, tramples all his beliefs under foot, mocks what he holds holy. She no longer cares about her words, her predicament, herself. Her face is distorted, her mouth agape as if from a bloody flux, her very tongue, it seems, parched, and her voice sometimes alters, breaks and turns into a strident shriek—a startling effect which completes the ghastly picture of frenzy and self-oblivion which you see before you. The sword of the enraged Horace encounters a she-wolf even then, as with the last word of the monologue she trembles and collects herself for a new vengeance."

Rising against Rome, Corneille's Camille transcends not only her woman's place but her humanity. Killed by the sword of a hero whom she taunts to match her crime for crime, she suffers the suggestively sexual, heroically martial death that is the fate of virgins in Greek tragedy. In the play's last act, Corneille spells out its moral: that patriotic virtue justifies and may fairly require the murder of even a sister who is an enemy of the state. In Act V, the wise king, who refers to himself as a demigod, is supposed to come onstage to render justice, and Old Horace advises his son that a king's words and not a stupid people's make a man a hero:

> *Horace, ne crois pas que le peuple stupide*
> *Soit le maître absolu d'un rénom bien solide,*
>
> . . . .
>
> *C'est aux rois, c'est aux grands, c'est aux*
> *   esprits bien faits,*
> *À voir la vertu pleine en ses moindres effets,*
> *C'est d'eux seuls qu'on reçoit la véritable*
> *   gloire;*
> *Seuls des vrais héros assurent la mémoire.*

> Horatius, do not think that the foolish mob
> Are arbiters of a renown that's sure:
>
> . . . .

It is for kings, for great men of sound judgment,
To weigh up probity in all its aspects;
It is from them alone that springs true fame;
And they alone assure a hero's name. (V, 3)

But the distinction Corneille drew in 1640, between a stupid populace and a wise absolute monarch, would have sounded problematic two hundred years later. So did the ruling about who has the right to confer and to receive true glory—and perhaps also the very definition of glory itself. By 1838, struggles for power and influence among legitimists, Bonapartists, Orléanists, and various factions of the bourgeoisie had made it hard to delimit and define *les esprits bien faits*. The lessons of history and the new machinery for creating and marketing fame were changing ideas about true, eternal glory. When Rachel played Camille, the last act of *Horace* was cut. Purists protested the mutilation of the text, but the curtain fell after the heroine's *tirade* and her death.

The *bienséances* required that violent deaths take place offstage, but the playwright's stage directions were ignored in the mid-nineteenth century. Annenkov describes an extraordinary climax: "Struck by her brother's hand, Rachel emits a howl, falls silent and to the ground. Simultaneously the curtain descends, but for a long time afterward you cannot recover and collect your thoughts and feelings, scattered, so to speak, in all directions by this cruel and incredible scene."

JANIN'S REVIEWS in the *Journal des débats*—there were two, but he later would cultivate the legend that he had made her a star overnight—hailed Rachel as the actress of the moment. She was introduced as an ideal of the status quo ante, an avatar of true, legitimate art. Janin's rhetoric was reactionary: he rejoiced that noble sentiments and chaste true love—forgotten among nameless, violent modern barbarisms—had at last found a voice. The man of the world marvelled that such excitement could be generated in the Théâtre-Français, of all places; the patriot celebrated Rachel, with a fine dramatic sense of his own national importance, as the herald of a new kind of revolution—the return of the nation's identity, its aesthetic standards and moral values. "Be it known," the critic intoned, "that at this very moment there exists at the Théâtre-Français—I repeat, the *Théâtre-Français*—an unexpected triumph, one of those lucky victories of which a nation like ours can be rightly proud. We have happily escaped from endless barbarisms, and been returned to honest feeling, proud language, chaste and refined love.

What a joy for an intelligent nation to find itself suddenly brought back to the masterpieces that have been wrongly neglected for so long. Praise be to ye gods and goddesses, who have indulgently granted immortality to these great works of art!" That the actress herself was only "an ignorant little girl, without art, without polish, fallen into the midst of old tragedy" made her genius the more authentic: her sense of tragedy was inborn, not acquired, Janin argued. Her humble origin made the triumph of high culture the more absolute, to his mind: that Tragedy could transform and exalt the likes of Rachel attested to its power. On the other hand, "she was born in the realms of poetry," he raved with mounting illogic; "she knows its geography; she unveils all its mysteries. The actors who perform alongside her are stunned by her daring; tragedy itself grows hopeful; the audience, moved and charmed, lend enchanted and delighted ears to that divine poetic language of which we have been deprived since the death of Talma; full of superb pride, the crowd abandons itself to these all-powerful great poets, to the honor of France, to the pride of the human spirit."

Like Talma, Rachel invested Racine's lapidary verses with a natural fire that people called Shakespearean, and like that earlier actor and symbol of France she was compared to English actors. Most frequently, she was likened to the romantic Edmund Kean, who had been fixed in the French mind as a new kind of actor-hero by *Kean*, Dumas's 1836 play. (Sartre would adapt it more than a century later.) Kean was dark-haired and pale, small, nervous, intense, like Rachel; watching him, Coleridge wrote, was like reading Shakespeare by flashes of lightning. When, as Othello, he quieted the quarreling swordsmen, he seemed to the poet John Keats to embody the authority of beautiful language, the supreme power of speech: "We feel that his throat had commanded where swords were thick as reeds," the young poet wrote. Kean was famous for his feverish, exhausting performances, and for ruinous offstage binges—he was the actor as self-destructive genius. Rachel, like Kean, seemed to consume herself in performance; her most influential English critic, G. H. Lewes, would write that she was as a woman what Kean was as a man, "the panther of the stage" to his lion. The pairing, the contrast, the animal imagery slipped as if naturally into the strongly polarized field where accepted ideas about England and France, romantic and classical, male and female, informed one another and structured people's thinking; the opposition, and the similarity, acknowledged Rachel as a significant player in the field. Kean had become a star by dramatizing himself, appealing to the self-reflexive imagination that made a star of the Noble Poet Byron—"the grand Napoleon of the realms of rhyme," as he had put it himself. The flexible concept of romantic heroism continued to produce images of remarkable human beings that were ambiguous, self-conscious, even parodic.

It was apropos of Talma that Germaine de Staël had declared that an actor is the second author of his roles. Rachel effectively rewrote Corneille by being who she was: by her strangely rough voice, her flashing eyes, her spectral look, her feverishness. As the unnerving immediacy of her presence in the theater gave the lie to rigid, regular alexandrines, Janin's characterization of the actress as a waif of the city streets, and his vivid reports of Rachel's offstage lapses in grammar, undercut the image she presented of literariness and high culture. By lopping off Act V of *Horace*, the Comédie-Française implicitly acknowledged that people came to see the star more than the play—and also, perhaps, that the play could not altogether contain her. When the peddler's daughter voiced Camille's imprecation against Rome, she might be heard as speaking in the name of the oppressed and powerless. The spirit astonishingly housed in the fragile body, her affecting aloneness on the stage, the awesome force of her voice, represented a timely version of heroism more compelling than the image of an all-powerful wise king, or of the hard bodies of heroes fraternally welded together, or even of the splendid Talma. This young woman was a vulnerable human being beset by the brute force, the crude realities, the impurities and confusions of flesh and practical politics against which she has the spiritual force and grandeur to rise up. As Rachel interpreted her, Camille seemed to be propelled beyond the Corneillian conflict between public and private virtue into an empyrean of triumphant, transcendent, romantic self-assertion. When her voice broke at the end of her tirade, one could feel the force of the divine inspiration that threatened to shatter its vessel. The actress made a subtle innovation in her harangue against Rome: at the end of each line, she raised her voice as if to question— contemptuously—Rome's power and glory. Was Rome the sole object of her hatred? Was Rachel-Camille daring to question her lines? Did she—though letter-perfect—manage to alter their meaning by the way she inflected them? Was this arrogant unbeautiful girl, a daughter of the Orient she exhorted to rise against Rome, playing Camille quite straight?

LIKENESSES of the new young star, dressed for the stage in a chaste white toga or for the street in black, suggest Camille's dignity and her hardness. She glares out from Charpentier's portrait, which was engraved and widely reprinted: her hair, parted in the center as in the ancient Greek tragic mask for the virtuous virgin, is skinned back to reveal knobby little ears. She is

Engraving of Rachel after a portrait by Auguste Charpentier
exhibited at the Salon of 1840

plain, in her decorous velvet trimmed with lace, and ferocious. There is
suppressed energy in the strenuous turn of the neck and the hands clasped
tight against the body; dark defiance smolders in the uneven sidelong stare.
On her, the matching coral brooch and earrings—civilized, fashionable ornaments—look like teeth. Rachel was almost perversely non-carnal: "On n'a
pas de sexe en la voyant," wrote the correspondent of the *Journal de Rheims*
in 1839. Janin called her a sword of gold in a sheath of clay: the metaphor
begins to suggest the threat she posed, the violent fantasies that underlay the
awe of what they called her male talent. In Delphine de Girardin's *Judith*,
the journalist's image entered the playwright's text, the heroine's own dia-
logue: Rachel, as the murderess of Holofernes, called herself the sword of
God. It was not merely that her body and deep voice seemed unfeminine;

what was disturbing was Camille's intelligence and self-respect, her independence, self-possession—above all, perhaps, the strong-minded girl's scorn and
disdain for martial heroes.

R ACHEL WAS ACCLAIMED as a priestess of aesthetic exigence, a princess
of the spirit, therefore a true aristocrat. Samson would recall that she had
the hands and feet of a duchess. Delphine de Girardin, in one of the newsy
"Chroniques parisiennes" she signed "Vicomte de Launay" in her husband's
newspaper, *La Presse,* praised the peddler's daughter's "natural rank" and
went on to explain what she meant in a heady mixture of elitist and democratic protestations: "The high rank of an actress! . . . No, her high rank as
an individual. For each of us is in some way given at birth an *individual rank*
that must be recognized, and leads us down or up in the world. While our
positions in life are imposed on us by society, we also all have ranks bestowed
by nature, and nothing is stranger to observe, in our lives, than this often
dangerous struggle between social condition and what we may call *native*
or *natural rank.*" In his memoir of Rachel, Védel cites Sainte-Beuve on her
natural charm and distinction: "It's an accident, my dear man, one of those
natures that knows at birth what so many others never can acquire." Another
contemporary defined her distinction in Napoleonic terms, calling her one of
"those privileged by destiny, those noble natures who carry upon their majestic brows, their dignified tones and gracious gestures, the indelible titles of
that feudal system designed by Providence, of which God is the suzerain."
(The image by the way recalls the Wandering Jew, with the mark, like Cain's,
on his forehead.)

Native, innate, or natural rank was an idea whose time had come at the
midpoint of the Bourgeois Monarchy when, although the old order had
collapsed more than once, its categories still prevailed. The concept had
developed logically from the notion of natural man, which intersected with
the ideal of meritocracy developed in the Napoleonic period. It was at once
aristocratic and democratic. The remarkable individual—Napoleon, Talma,
Byron, the Regency dandy Beau Brummell—was admired as an embodiment
of extraordinary selfhood that transcended traditional class boundaries. It was
on the one hand natural, inborn; and on the other hand it was attainable,
the basis of an aristocracy that qualified new members might enter, regardless
of birth. A young man from the provinces making himself over as Lucien de
Rubempré attested to the truth that rank was innate. So did a tragedy queen
from the lowest social class. The idea of natural rank is explored in many of
the novel heroines made in Rachel's image, for example the Goncourts' Ma-

nette Salomon, the artists' model who "had those qualities which lift some low-born people above the rabble." The Goncourts explain that Manette "was born with the mark of pure blood, the quality of rarity and elegance, those personal characteristics which in defiance of accidents of race and fortune distinguish the aristocrats among women, those who belong among first-class people—marks of innate distinction." Images of women like Manette were compulsively constructed and analyzed in order to contest prevailing notions of distinction—or, more often, merely, titillatingly, to play with them.

IN GRATITUDE for the audiences and profits she brought them, the *sociétaires* of the Comédie-Française crowned Rachel, in 1839, with a wreath of gold laurel leaves like one the company had once bestowed on Talma, each leaf inscribed with the name of one of the heroines she played. Wreaths of flowers *(couronnes)* were conventionally given to actresses in Rachel's time—flung to them, sometimes, as they performed. (Gautier complained that the practice of buying flowers to bring to the theater for the purpose had emptied a once spontaneous gesture of meaning.) In 1843, when Rachel was on tour in Marseilles, such a crown came flying at her in the middle of a great scene in Racine's *Bajazet*. Remaining in character as Roxane, she ignored it, in spite of the cries from the audience, "The crown! the crown!" The inferior actress playing opposite her, Rachel scornfully wrote to Mme de Girardin, "playing to the public instead of staying in character, picks up the crown and gives it to me. Outraged by so vulgar an interruption, I take the unfortunate crown and abruptly fling it aside, so as to continue Roxane. Fortune favors the bold: there was never stronger proof of this axiom; three salvos of applause greeted my instinctive move." The gesture was true to both Roxane's imperious character and a tragedienne's dignity, evidence of Rachel's absorption in her great role, her respect for Racine's high art and her own.

"Mlle Rachel est un principe," her detractors claimed—nothing but a banner for reactionaries to mass behind. Following Janin, the critics applauded the new queen of tragedy in a jumble of legitimist and radical rhetoric. "The Comédie-Française is rejuvenated," one critic wrote in 1838, "with that irresistible ease characteristic of legitimate revolutions." Another extolled her as "a queen among actors," comparing her to Adrienne Lecouvreur, "that illustrious actress who sought to revolutionize the art of the drama at the beginning of the eighteenth century." He concluded, "Mlle Rachel has brought that revolution about in our time." Louis-Philippe, the so-called Citizen King, honored the new star with a visit to the theater to see her play Emilie in *Cinna*, Corneille's play about a conspiracy against the Roman Emperor Augustus. The King of the French, as he styled himself, congratulated her for bringing back the great days of French tragedy; heavily, he apologized that the press of business prevented him from coming often to the theater. She was charming, but notably made the error of calling the king *monsieur*, not *sire*—not out of ignorance, she explained later, but because she was in the habit of addressing emperors (Augustus, for instance, in *Cinna*). Many on the left had been critical of Rachel's too contemptuous pronunciation of *le peuple*, in a crucial political speech in the play, but everyone enjoyed the anecdote about the sharp little actress pulling rank on the dull old king. And her point was good: a uniform honorific—*monsieur* nearly as much as "citizen"—effects a measure of leveling.

To show its commitment to the arts and to the past, the Citizen King's government presented Rachel with a library of the classics. Bourgeois society, eager to parade its elite tastes, embraced, enveloped, and claimed her. The class that had profited most from the revolution of 1830 was hostile to romanticism, especially in the theater, therefore hospitable to Rachel. And the Catholic aristocracy of course valued what she stood for, Racine and Port-Royal. Careful parents allowed her to dance alongside their daughters in the Faubourg Saint-Germain—"not only society women but young ladies of the highest rank aspire to the friendship of a woman of the theater," Sainte-Beuve observed. At evening parties, in her white dress, Rachel traded on Camille's high moral tone and sexual purity, and Hermione's proud disdain for a faithless lover. Her Hermione soon became a favorite: thrillingly, she acted out "passions so profound that their depths can only be glimpsed through a smile of irony," one critic wrote, "restrained melancholies that look inside themselves, analyze their own despair." If, as people said, her Jewish audiences especially identified with Rachel's scorned and scornful Hermione, Christian fans were awed by the Jewess's unexpectedly pure elegance and grace. They praised "this young girl, this poetic Rachel, who wears upon her brow a halo of purity, the loveliest adornment of a woman, just as, in the evening, she wears a diadem, the most splendid ornament of a queen." The Racinian aura of loftiness provided the ground for an extraordinary reputation for sexual virtue, the memory or residue of which, even after Rachel's "fall" into scandal, lent the unmarried actress unprecedented dignity.

In France, a reputation for wit did not—as it would have done in England—make a woman's morals automatically suspect. On the contrary: Rachel's sallies were delightedly repeated as proof of her spirit and self-possession, her *salonnière*'s charm. Everyone talked about the scornful reply she made

Rachel in 1842, from a
contemporary lithograph

when a man of rank proposed to marry her: Marquise indeed, she had
snorted, when she could be a princess every evening! (That the suitor to hand
was the homosexual Marquis de Custine seemed beside the point.) Mme
Récamier invited Rachel to her Catholic salon at l'Abbaye aux Bois, where
(people said) schemes for her conversion were hatching, and she was introduced to the aged Chateaubriand, the hostess's longtime lover. Gallantly, the
author of *Mémoires d'outre-tombe* told Rachel that her arrival on the scene
increased his reluctance to die; some men never die, she replied as gallantly.
It was at l'Abbaye aux Bois that she was asked to perform, before an arch-
bishop, the speech in Corneille's *Polyeucte* in which the newly converted
Pauline declares her faith with a dramatic, "Je crois." She demurred and
pointedly chose one of the Jewish queen's speeches from Racine's *Esther*
instead. Diffidence, or defiance? When the prelate pressed her hand on part-
ing, and murmured that one surely had to believe the words one uttered in
order to speak them as she had, she replied very ambiguously, "Je crois"—
which is to say either, in Pauline's phrase, "I believe," or merely the conventional, formulaic "I believe so."

From the first glittering party for Rachel at Véron's large house on the

rue Taitbout, admirers had marvelled at her gaiety and charm, her wit and
self-possession. Not yet twenty, the daughter of people of no substance or
consequence, she moved easily in the most elegant salons, notably not dazzled. Shrewd and watchful, the studious child was centered by her commitment to her art. "People invite me on all sides, baronesses, duchesses, counts,
and if I accepted all these invitations, I would never have time to open a
book," she wrote her sister Sarah in her early years of fame. "The only
society appropriate for an artist is her roles, not these pretty ladies and
gentlemen who pay you flattering compliments at their parties, and trash
you and tear you apart once you've left." (They've offered her eighteen
thousand francs for sixteen performances at Bordeaux and Lyons, she adds
complacently.)

The theater had taught her to play the lady, and to know pretense when
she saw it; success had taught her to think well of herself. Her hostesses
found her self-confidence disturbing: Was it that easy for a vulgar little Jewish
actress to assume the appearance of a young woman of good family, to look
and act like the real thing? A hundred years later, another French actress
speculated (along lines that must have presented themselves to people of
Rachel's time) that Rachel's poise had its roots in her distance, and constituted
a kind of mockery. Because she was an outsider, Béatrix Dussane conjectured
in the 1940s, Rachel was able to take less than seriously the conventions true
Frenchmen respected, and therefore had no trouble imitating and exploiting
them so as to pass in good society: she succeeded "precisely because she did
not believe in it, because she understood the amount of snobbery and imitation involved, because, beneath her show of respect for proper manners,
she remained a foreigner. A foreigner intent on pleasing in order to conquer
and dominate; a foreigner upon whom none of our conventions and hierarchies ever imposed themselves."

Diderot's paradox obtained offstage as well as on: Rachel was so good at
passing for a young girl of good family precisely because she kept a part of
herself apart. In effect, her play implied that manners, *ton*, Frenchness itself
might be acquired, that a foreigner could get herself up to be absolutely
comme il faut, as it were *plus française que les Françaises*, and breach the wall
of French high society and undermine it. Was Rachel laughing at her hosts
in the Faubourg Saint-Germain, observing and criticizing them as she would
criticize the English aristocracy when she wrote home from London that she
longed to "disenduke" herself? From Paris she wrote no telltale letters to her
family comparable to the sharp-eyed reports she would send home about the
barbaric table manners of upper-class Russians. She merely kept her mother

at her side as her chaperone—with whom, perhaps, she could chuckle over
the triumphs of the evening later on.

IN THE EXCLUSIVE SALONS she graced, Rachel was expected to entertain with excerpts from her tragedies, as Adrienne Lecouvreur had done
in the eighteenth century. But the world was further than it had been then
from the formal stage. In a modern, bourgeois context her recitations were
sometimes seen as implausible and even ridiculous. Samson was not the only
one to be distressed: Mérimée found her absurd and vulgar, declaiming Pauline's exalted periods between a piano and a tea-table, and George Sand was
disturbed by a discrepancy in scale. "Rachel, Rachel herself, breaking the last
cords of her admirable instrument in order to move all the waves of her
public, appeared up close to be a victim of epilepsy," she declared. Those
who most respected Rachel's art believed its proper place was the stage on
the rue de Richelieu, where her voice and gestures had been trained, and
where they would continue to be appreciated, evaluated, and further perfected by the trained eyes and ears of connoisseurs, for the sake of her own
development as well as for Art's sake. But the young Rachel wanted more
flattery and applause, more scope, more freedom and excitement, more money
and social recognition, than confinement to a single stage could give her. She
was brilliant in the roles of stern young heroines who were unhappy in their
affections, exiles in a strange land, solitaries in a hostile universe, reliant only
on their wit and strength of mind, on irony and paradox, to assert their
personal worth. Was she obliged to stick to the plot as well as the tenor of
the tragic scripts, and maintain not only the dignified bearing but the renun-
ciatory mode of a heroine by Racine?

A FEW MONTHS BEFORE her eighteenth birthday, in November 1838,
the Comédie showed off its new dark-eyed star in a gorgeous, expensive
production of Racine's *Bajazet*. The setting of the play is a Turkish seraglio;
in his preface, Racine had explained that he hoped the geographical remote-
ness would compensate for the fact that the story was contemporary. The
conquests and orientalist fantasies of the mid-nineteenth century had nar-
rowed the distance from the East: as Roxane, the wily, imperious, bloody-
minded mistress of a sultan, Rachel was a familiar figure, a dusky, demanding,
desirable woman out of fashionable paintings by Chassériau and Delacroix,
an image that flattered France for possessing its luxurious Eastern pleasure-
dome. But either the strength of her play or her initial awkwardness in the
role—it is hard to tell which—proved at first to be disturbing.

Rachel in the costume of Roxane, after a painting by Devéria, 1840

Her elaborate costume altered the image of chaste Camille. She wore red velvet Turkish slippers with turned-up toes, embroidered in gold, on her fairy feet: above them, pantaloons billowed under a long skirt, an overskirt, and a sash—yards of fabric richly colored and trimmed. This Rachel was no starved waif, no spectral emblem of an ideal: the costume emphasized her womanly curves. Its sheer excess and the contrast with her usual chaste garb insisted on the fact of masquerade. Gold and gems clasped her arm, swagged across her chest, hung from her ears, and one jewel even fell, in an oriental fashion, from her turban onto the high pale forehead, still imposing but no longer seeming quite so severely intellectual or virginal. (It is hard to know exactly how to read the ethnic nuances of this costume: in Balzac's *Les Illusions perdues*, Mme de Bargeton is described as wearing "a Jewess's turban, enriched with an Eastern clasp.") The costume became her—and newly sexualized her. Long loose sleeves gave a flourish to the pointing finger by which Roxane seals the doom of the man who dares to turn her down. Rachel was formidable, enchanting, adorable.

Protective of the Grecian myth he had so heavily invested in, jealous of his power, eager to make news, Janin was obliged to object to the radical change. He damned the whole expensive production, and protested that the inexperienced Rachel was miscast as the doyenne of an oriental seraglio. One barely needed to read between the lines: the experience at issue was sexual, the implied threat was of exposure. Anticipating the wreck of a promising career, Jacques Félix urged his daughter to withdraw from the play. For the first time on record, Rachel openly disobeyed him. She responded superbly in Camille's tones, pulling herself together in daring defiance of her father—and counting on her convenient superfluity of fathers in the wings. She had played off Samson against Félix for some time; now, in a girlish note, she wrote to Védel, vowing to stay with the production, disingenuously explaining that when one liked people, one naturally wanted to please them. She went back into dogged rehearsals with Samson, and three days after the premiere repeated the role so brilliantly that Janin was forced to recant.

Alfred de Musset, who had nearly come to blows with the critic of the *Journal des débats* after his review, praised the "reprise de Bajazet" in the *Revue des deux mondes* of 1 December 1838. He attacked Janin for hearing sexual innuendoes in Roxane's speeches. When she speaks of the "charms" of her lover Bajazet, what could she have in mind, Musset asked, but "the beauty of features, the gracious manners, the sweetness of language, which a man as well as a woman can have?" Since when had *charmes* meant anything else?—except in Janin's mind, which was fit for a world of crude spectacles and newspapers. Used to vulgar plays and players, the critic was deaf to higher things. Janin's paragraphs were an insult to Racine as well as Rachel, Musset argued, suggesting that the purity of the one was surety for the other. Of Racine, he wrote, "How the poet would have blushed, only heaven knows, if someone had proposed an obscene interpretation of his verses! But what do you expect? In Racine's time, Robert Macaire didn't exist." The critic of a fallen world was effectively silenced by the poet, whose call to arms to defend the glory of the *patrimoine* brought Rachel more high-minded enthusiasts. After her second performance as Roxane, Védel wrote, Rachel might have said à la Louis XIV, "La tragédie, c'est moi."

The Comédie-Française duly gave her a legitimately royal role—inevitably, the Jewish queen, Esther. The move might have been predicted: the alternative would have been Bérénice, Racine's other Jewish heroine, who is considerably less pure (Rachel did not perform that role until 1844). *Esther,* more a dramatic poem than a play, was taken out of mothballs to be a vehicle for her. The first performance was pointedly set for the Jewish holiday of Purim, when the biblical Book of Esther is read in the synagogue. Purim, which is calculated according to the Jewish lunar calendar, fell unusually early in 1839, on 28 February—which the certificate prepared in 1840 would duly specify as the birthday of Rachel. While the chronology is suspicious, the relation of cause and effect is not quite as easy to define as it seems to be: very possibly, the Félixes dated events by the Jewish holidays, and remembered Rachel had been born around Purim. (This might be one reason why the month of her birth is sometimes given as March.) Probably, the theatrical event served to confirm a less than clear fact, corroborating if it did not quite create it.

The Feast of Esther celebrates the victory of the Jews over their enemies through the agency of a Jewish woman. Esther becomes a queen after winning a beauty contest held by King Ahasverus (no relation of the Wandering Jew, and denominated, in Racine's play, Assuérus). The king, who reigned from India even unto Ethiopia, has dismissed his old wife, Vashti, because of her proud independence: she stubbornly refused to show herself at a feast where he was entertaining his friends. Advised that no man in his kingdom will be master in his own house unless the woman is rebuked severely, Ahasverus sets about to find a new queen to replace her. Esther is Vashti's compliant opposite, a heroine—an instrument—of patriarchy. She is entered in the beauty contest by her pious guardian Mordecai, who intends to exploit her position at court; at first, she does not reveal her ancestry (or her Jewish name, Hadassah). When Mordecai learns of a plot to murder all the Jews, he directs Esther to invite the king to a feast in her quarters, where she reveals the plot, acknowledges her own Jewishness, and saves her people. Showing her beauty instead of concealing it, inviting and serving her husband instead of refusing his invitation, Esther is a traditional good woman. Vashti seems to be her rebellious opposite, but the structural similarities between their stories suggest a complex connection between them, to which Charlotte Brontë's choice of name for the Rachel figure in *Villette* perhaps begins to point. In Racine's play, Esther has neither a foil nor a shadow: Vashti is not even mentioned.

Rachel's performance got some cool reviews, but it was on the whole successful. The Jewish actress's appearance in a play in which a King (Assuérus) describes the Jews as unclean (*impure*) was calculated to compel the attention of the public. The so-called *juiverie* turned out in force, as expected, and Paris generally was fascinated by the curiosity. The exquisite ambivalence in the air, about a Jewish *reine de théâtre*, is suggested by a poem offered at the time as a "Bouquet à Mlle Rachel"—along with its attendant footnote. The poem celebrates the Jewess as a new Esther, idolized by the thousands of Christians of Paris; the note soberly points out the "fact" that Rachel had been circumcised in accordance with Hebrew ritual.

Janin was moved to create even more excitement, and draw attention to himself, by attacking again *ad feminam*, now from another angle. He insisted the "real" Rachel was insufficiently the lofty vestal to play Esther: he argued that she could not believably perform a role that had been conceived by Racine, the Catholic poet of Port-Royal, for one of the virgin schoolgirls at Mme de Maintenon's academy at Saint-Cyr. People thought of her as Camille, he insisted—and also as the greatest of her creations, the Parisienne Rachel, the creature out of Balzac or Gavarni! Debate about who Rachel really was, and what she stood for, and whether she had a claim to stand for anything, raged right alongside arguments about the quality of her art. Many insisted that the daughter of the dead was hardly an artist. The painter Courbet, for instance, had only contempt for the party of "Ingres, Mlle Rachel, and M. Scribe"—all three, presumably, bloodless. The resentful Dumas would also class her with Ingres, and mockingly relegate the two of them to a room apart from the salon where modern artists exhibited—the *salon des morts*. The charges that she was a mere creature or puppet of Samson's, and/or the creation of newspapers and claques, helped make the more general point that she was nothing but a mimic, nothing but hype, nothing in herself. In January 1840, at the height of her fame, the *Courrier du théâtre* mocked her as everything and therefore nothing, with its "example" of "Le Puff Rachel": "Genius, Goddess of Love, liberator of Racine, toast of the salons, the Théâtre-Français personified, the teacher of its actors, cosmopolitan tragedienne, idol of the Jews, spoiled child of the aristocracy, eighth wonder of the world, jewelry shop."

The ambivalences and alterations of public opinion did more than make Rachel's fame and her image: it informed her craft as well. It is hard to say in retrospect, and was hard to estimate at the time, whether her several failures were her fault or the crowd's. In either case, they kept the question of her genius open, and kept her a subject of debate. When she played Hermione before an unresponsive audience one evening in February 1840, she unaccountably lost her grip on her role. The *Journal des débats* reported that the unaccustomed coldness of the spectators chilled her and brought her up short. "She could not get used to the silence; she wished her gestures, her words, to have immediate effect; if not she hesitated, worried, forgot— not her role but the play she was in; so as to get the applause she needed, she called on all the exaggerations of dramatic art; where she should have shown irritation, she became enraged; where she had been great, she became swollen." A stage queen reigns at her people's sufferance; her only job is to subdue and conquer them every night.

2. FORTUNATE FALL

In Gautier's opinion—and he admired her—Rachel's success was not to be interpreted as a tribute to Corneille and Racine and Tragedy, or to the traditions of the Comédie-Française. It was, he insisted, an utterly modern phenomenon. She was the darling of a lazy nation that had been stupefied by opera and dance and music, and went to the theater now only for the spectacle. He wrote this in 1843, the year gaslight was installed in the Théâtre-Français, where a central chandelier, which glowed throughout the performances, allowed people to train their glasses on one another, or enjoy the newly brightened paintings on the walls—or glance languidly, if they chose to, at the stage, more softly illuminated by oil lamps, where Rachel in her tragedy toga stood framed and set apart. The poetry she so beautifully spoke was scarcely heard by her distracted audiences, Gautier maintained. The public dozed or chattered through the dull parts of the old plays, and only came to life to cheer vigorously, and hurl the bouquets they had bought for the purpose, in response to star turns. Her recitations of familiar and melodious *tirades* suited a modern taste for arias and for oddities, and for stars. Perfect as it was, he maintained, her diction contradicted the spirit of the smooth old regular alexandrines: "her delivery—precise, rigorous, staccato, *raging,* if I may put it that way—is at variance with the large periods, the elegant circumlocutions, the long enfolding phrases of classical poetry." He concluded that "the contrast itself is the source of her success."

The romantic taste for contrasts accounted also for her sexual appeal. Unfeminine and unyielding, Rachel was the womanly Marie Dorval's antithesis—was "beautiful, but not lovable," as G. H. Lewes wrote. It was a crux. In the middle of the nineteenth century, she raised "the whole issue of a woman's lovability." That phrase is the film critic Molly Haskell's, from a 1988 article about Meryl Streep, who, she writes, "brings to dramatic point something that has been nosing its way to the forefront of consciousness for some time." Rachel's "terrible beauty," as Lewes called it, first put the question of whether an actress's job is to be pleasing. (Bernhardt said she thought it was.) The pale waif with burning eyes, the self-contained young woman rigid with disdain and contempt, the serious classical actress engaged in something more exigent and difficult than simply and artlessly playing herself, unsettled unexamined assumptions about Woman's nature.

Only in her teens when she made her debut, Rachel grew literally as well as figuratively: she grew as the applause grew, Janin wrote. Sure of her strength, although always most confident when most rehearsed, she stuck to the classical repertoire, resisting criticisms of her "narrow" range and challenges to undertake romantic drama. But there were just so many roles of young princesses, and Alfred de Musset's passionate plea for modern tragedies for Rachel had not been answered (he himself attempted but didn't finish writing a play for her). Briefly, she undertook comedy at the Théâtre-Français, and failed as she had at the Gymnase: her Dorine in Molière's *Tartuffe,* in April 1839, was not a success. (Gautier, who insisted that an actor must be versatile, later on praised another of her attempts at comedy, which most critics considered a mere caprice.) She performed a vivid variation on the regal theme in December 1840, when she triumphed opposite Mlle Maxime as Queen Elizabeth in Lebrun's *Marie Stuart:* the great éclat attendant on the event was partly due to Janin, who had inflated Maxime's importance as an actress in order to exaggerate the rivalry. Having successfully toured the provinces—she played Rouen, Corneille's birthplace; Lyons, where she had been a child; and other cities—Rachel was ready to accept an invitation to England that was proffered by Benjamin Lumley of Her Majesty's Theatre in London—"M. l'Omelette," she liked to call him. Actors in England enjoyed considerably better salaries than their opposite numbers in Paris, especially those who were expected to draw nourishment from the cachet of the Théâtre-Français. Rachel would be paid the considerable sum of thirty-five hundred francs for five performances in May. In return she was able to pull off the star's economic magic trick: "she propped up the declining fortunes of Her Majesty's Theatre, and filled its deserted benches." Rachel's reception in England was unparalleled. And in France her conquest of the land of gentlemen and ladies—and its queen—was taken to be further proof of her innate rank.

She had appealed to the British imagination even before she arrived in London: as early as December 1840, an astonishing number of column-inches in the English papers were devoted to the Paris production of *Marie Stuart.* Filtered though it was by Schiller and Lebrun, the subject of rival British queens was particularly interesting to the subjects of the young Victoria. So was Rachel, who was just two years younger than the queen who had come to the throne in 1837. By the time the actress appeared at Her Majesty's Theatre in May 1841 she already had an English reputation and was seen as something like a qualified pretender to the English throne.

The audience that came to see her first performance was full of anticipation—so eager that it broke into premature applause for the first actress who walked onto the stage, who turned out to be a certain insignificant Mlle Larcher, in the title role. Had they not read on the posters that Rachel played Hermione and not the titular heroine, and understood that she was still in the wings? Had they any idea of what was being said on the stage? Embarrassed after discovering their error, people clapped all the harder when the idol of the hour did appear. For her part Rachel, always unsure of herself in new circumstances, was frightened at first by the serious English faces, and gratified by a welcome "which was only a mark of kindness, as they had yet to hear me." Watching the audience watch his daughter perform, Jacques Félix reported the "bizarre" transformation from cold and solemn silence to absolute attentiveness, animation, and more. He said he could see Rachel's emotions and expressions register on the bland British faces of the people who watched and listened to her: initial impassiveness dissolved, and pleasure, shrewdness, irony, vehemence, anger, fury followed one another in succession. Virtually unmediated by language, Rachel's appeal to the emotions was direct: in England she was unfailingly successful. Some years later, anticipating a tour of the secondary cities in Britain, she wrote mischievously to Mme Samson that "it will be highly amusing, as I have been assured that they don't at all understand the French language in the places where we'll be

playing." (The Glasgow papers duly advised ladies to go to the theater to
see Rachel, and learn more French, in an hour, than in a whole year of
lessons.) The alien, distancing formality of seventeenth-century tragedy, its
emphasis on aria-like *tirades*, the melodious rhythms and rhymes, the focus
on a tragic heroine, the incomprehensible words, were all pleasurable in
Britain, where operagoers had the habit of hearing tragic dramas sung in
foreign languages. After Rachel became the rage in London, her repertoire
quickly became fashionable too. Her fame came to qualify the national distaste for icy Racine: in 1843, posters in Birmingham advertised the performance of an English actress, Mrs. Foster, in "A Selection from Racine's
Tragedy of Bajazet, in the Original French, in Imitation of MADEMOI-
SELLE RACHEL."

   "Everybody here is now raving about her," Fanny Kemble wrote in June
1841, at the height of Rachel's first London season. The English actress had
heard Rachel declaim at a private party, and had also seen her play Hermione
at the St. James Theatre. "Her reply to Andromaque's appeal to her, in that
play, was one of the most perfect things I have ever seen on the stage," she
wrote. "The cold, cruel, acrid enjoyment of her rival's humiliation,—the
quiet, bitter, unmerciful exercise of the power of torture, was certainly, in its
keen incisiveness, quite incomparable. It is singular that so young a woman
should so especially excel in delineations and expressions of this order of
emotion, while in the utterance of tenderness, whether in love or sorrow, she
appears comparatively less successful." Scrupulously fair, Kemble judiciously
added that "Hermione and Emilie, in Corneille's 'Cinna,' are not characters
abounding in tenderness. Lady M—— saw her the other day in 'Marie Stuart,' and cried her eyes almost out, so she must have some pathetic power."
The question was critical. Like the question of her looks, and her sincerity,
it was about whether Rachel was, as they put it then, womanly (i.e., lovable).
In the course of the debate, antitheatrical and gender stereotypes intersected
with national ones to strengthen one another. The critic of *The Era*, review-
ing a performance of *Marie Stuart* that had been attended by Queen Victoria, condemned the French play as "unworthy her acknowledged talent,"
but praised "the great intellectual acumen and concentrated power of Mlle
Rachel." A month before, the reviewer had agreed with Fanny Kemble's
friend Lady M——: "We think, despite the French critics, that in passages of
tenderness, and not of terror, consists Mlle Rachel's forte."

   She was given a welcome fit for a queen when she first came to England.
Victoria invited her to dine and perform at Windsor Castle, where she was
duly dazzled by the splendor—it included a stuffed tiger from India—and the

Rachel as Hermione, photo illustration from Jules Janin's *Rachel et la tragédie*

honor. The queen presented her with a bracelet that people in France (mistakenly) said was engraved "Victoria à Rachel," one queen's tribute to another. ("Victoria Reine, à Mlle Rachel," was in fact the more conventional inscription.) But as Rachel reported to Mme Samson, the queen herself placed the bracelet on her arm: "My dear Mme Samson, if I did not succumb to my emotion, it was because I understood the obligations such a great honor imposed on me in the future." In London, the prominent actor Macready gave a party for her, and titled ladies vied with one another for her presence at their gatherings: she recited at the Countess of Jersey's, the Marchioness of Aylesbury's, and Countess Cadogan's. The clash of classes was wonderful to contemplate. Benjamin Lumley, the impresario, recalls in his memoirs that Rachel told him she was "greatly embarrassed by the conventions of the table, and the question that once arose in her mind, at a grand dinner, as to the proper use of the knife and fork in the consumption of asparagus, was infinitely embarrassing." The Paris papers reported gleefully that the old Duke of Wellington had escorted Rachel to dinner at one evening party, and later called to ask after her health, and advised her to bathe in "eau sale" (dirty water), meaning to recommend "eau salée" (salt water). The pulse of French national pride was quickened by the evidence of British impotence: Napoleon's conqueror fallen for Rachel, the hoary general at the twenty-year-old actress's feet, eager but unable to master her language. Smugly, the French savored the triumph, in England, of France's national literature and national theater, the triumph, *sub specie aeternitatis*, of France—which effectively reduced the sublunary event at Waterloo to dust, a passing show.

The year before Rachel's first appearance in London, the cultural event of the spring season there had been a series of lectures by Thomas Carlyle, "On Heroes, Hero-Worship, and the Heroic in History." Had Carlyle come before to show the way for her, or did he set up a fixed idea she would interrogate and unsettle? His six lectures had traced the emergence of the heroic ideal from the mists of time into history, through the agency of writer-heroes: The Hero as Prophet, Poet, Priest, and Man of Letters. The History of the World, Carlyle repeated, is the Biography of Great Men. He had begun, on 5 May 1840, with the subject of "The Hero as Divinity," and in the course of the month he went from Norse mythology to Napoleon ("The Hero as King")—"a great *ébauche*, a rude draught never completed, as indeed what great man is other?" But he insisted that the personal quality which distinguished such men was transcendence of history: "The Hero is he who lives in the inward sphere of things, in the True, Divine and Eternal, which exists always, unseen to most, under the Temporary, Trivial: his being is in that; he declares that abroad, by act or speech as it may be, in declaring himself abroad." The paradoxes attendant on a hero of modern times—the hero since Cervantes, since Fielding, since Byron—invited counter-concepts inflected by increasing irony: of the antihero and perhaps also of the actress-heroine, that ambiguous avatar and undercutter of the romantic Fatal Woman.

IN RETROSPECT, it seems ironic that Queen Victoria led her people in rapt response to Rachel, from the summer of the engraved bracelet on through the rest of the decade. In 1846, she wrote in her journal that "Mlle Rachel's wonderful impersonation of Phèdre excited the most unbounded enthusiasm from first to last," adding that although she found French tragedy "not pleasing and extremely unnatural," she thought "Mme Rachel's acting was very fine." (Victoria's use of "Mlle" and "Mme" indiscriminately is fairly standard, but possibly it is evidence that the queen might have got wind by then of whispers about Rachel's private life, and perhaps about the plot of *Phèdre* as well.) In London it soon became fashionable to have seen Rachel the year before, to be able to compare and contrast her performances. Professional critics competed in observing subtle changes, some despairing of the task of praising her year after year: "It becomes somewhat difficult for the dramatic critic to find fresh phrases in which he can commend the excellences of this great actress," wrote the man from the *Illustrated London News.* The *Times* reviewer suffered similar fatigue, confessing that "we really do not know whether there is really a change in Mademoiselle's performance, or whether it is the power of genius to give the air of novelty even to its repetitions."

At the St. James Theatre ("decidedly the worst ventilated in London") in the 1840s, one could see a number of French actresses—Mlles Déjazet and Plessy, and Mme Doche—and such wonders as Barnum's prodigies from the United States, the sisters Kate and Ellen Bateman, only eight and six years old, who recited the dialogues of Richard and Richmond, Macbeth and Lady Macbeth, Shylock and Portia. But Rachel, who appeared there yearly after her first season at Lumley's theater, seemed more than a mere entertainment to Victorians. "It is delightful to be popular on your side of the water, . . . for you all take things so intensely seriously," Sarah Bernhardt told an English reporter in 1894. They had been quite as serious fifty years earlier. Rachel inspired religious awe and earnest didactics in England. Her severe, violent tragic passions seemed to Anglo-Saxons to translate and disembody female ardor, transmuting it into safe, high-minded, and foreign poetic language. Macready praised "the intellectual variation of her sweet and classic features"; Emerson saw in her smile "a kind of universal intelligence." That she spoke in an archaic form of a language that you had to go to school to learn made her somehow intellectual. "No voluptuous sinner, she seems a victim of an irresistible fate. . . . There can be nothing less joyous than this love," *The Times* commented approvingly of her Phèdre in 1847. The grotesque, when it touched her, was interpreted as sublime. In Paris, the critics had jeered when a cat walked across the stage at a crucial moment in Mme de Girardin's *Judith;* in London a parallel incident was deemed "rather singular": "Mlle Rachel fainted away in the last act of 'Adrienne Lecouvreur.' Just at the moment she was receiving the poisoned bouquet, a dog introduced into the theatre began to bark, and the offended tragedienne tottered and fell. The shock upon her nerves, in a state of unusual excitement, was too much." The reporter did concede it was a matter for interpretation, adding, "Had this accident happened to a young actress, it would have been attributed to inexperience."

Deaf to the rumors about her scandalous sex life, English critics recommended Rachel with something like moral fervor: "Our readers must see Rachel; and not only see, not only hear her, but study her. It is a fine lesson." The difference between "the great mistress of the passions" and the ordinary run of actors inspired critical enthusiasm that drowned patriotic feelings: she had, in her stillness, "the severer style of high art," therefore was pleasing to "an intelligent and brilliant audience." Mid-Victorian admirers of Dickens and Thackeray—who had presumed on their readers' prejudice against Frenchwomen when they sketched murderous Mlle Hortense of *Bleak House* and the flighty mother of Becky Sharp—were fascinated by Rachel. As a lesson and a sign of art and intelligence, she posed an agonizing problem that complicated the standard binary oppositions of high and low, restraint and passion, virtue and vice, the schoolroom and the theater—in two words, England and France.

WHEN G. H. LEWES, writing about Rachel's performances in classical and modern drama, pronounced that "Phèdre is separated from Adrienne by a chasm as wide, deep, and impassable as that which separates Phidias from Tussaud," he neatly suggested some of the charged oppositions she focused for Victorians: between ancient and modern, elite and popular, deathless and morbid, male and female, hard and soft, the original and the copy. What he fudged was the always significant difference between the two rival nations. Invoking "Phidias," Lewes confounds Racine with Euripides, while with "Tussaud" he ranges (modern) Frenchness with the forces of darkness, against ancient Greece and (illogically, as Madame Tussaud's Wax Museum was in fact one of the tourist attractions of London) England. To the Victorians who idealized Greece, France was its worldly opposite. The shallowness and display of the ancien régime, the succession of fearful events since 1789, the amenities and luxuries of Parisian life, made the British equally nervous; France stood for radical democratic politics, vice and violence, sexuality and shallowness, and it was hard to tell which was worst. In Mary Wollstonecraft's posthumous political novel, *Maria* (1798), a trial judge rebukes the heroine in divorce court by saying, "We did not want French principles in public or private life—and, if women were allowed to plead their feelings, as an excuse or palliation of infidelity, it was opening a floodgate for immorality." From the English point of view, "French principles" was an oxymoron.

Frenchwomen haunt the margins of Victorian novels about virtuous heroines. On the other hand, since the eighteenth century, middle-class young ladies in England had been required to learn French: Becky Sharp is accepted at her London school because she can help to teach the language. It was one of the standard accomplishments expected of so-called elegant females: Charlotte Brontë, when she decided to open a school together with her sisters, went off to Brussels to improve her French. But at least since bluff young King Harry wooed his queen in Shakespeare's play, French has been laughed at by English writers as effeminate and absurdly fancy. In Thackeray's *Pendennis* (1848–50), the French phrases and phony French name of Blanche Amory (who was originally plain Betsy) are clear signs of her shallowness. (The affectation of Anglicisms by Odette de Crécy in *Du Côté de chez Swann* indicates a matching dynamic on the other side of the Channel.) French was the language of hypocrisy for the Victorians: the first of the merely modern languages seemed the flashy opposite of the honest ancient ones. In Disraeli's *Coningsby,* the hero's pragmatic businessman grandfather shows how cynical he is when he counsels the young man not to study the classics at the expense of French:

> A classical education, he said, was a very admirable thing, and one which all gentlemen should enjoy; but Coningsby would find some day that there were two educations, one which his position required, and another which was demanded by the world. "French, my dear Harry," he continued, "is the key to this second education. In a couple of years or so you will enter the world; it is a different thing to what you read about. It is a masquerade; a motley, sparkling multitude, in which you may mark all forms and colours, and listen

to all sentiments and opinions; but where all you see and hear has only one object, plunder. When you get into this crowd you will find that Greek and Latin are not so much diffused as you imagine. I was glad to hear you speaking French yesterday. Study your accent. There are a good many foreigners here with whom you may try your wing a little; don't talk to any of them too much."

French was the language of dangerous foreigners, of pretense and parties, of falsification, (shady) business, and very questionable pleasure. France was feminine and effeminate: the French count who turns out to be a cook in *Pendennis* is the descendant of many a dressy Frenchified rake in a Restoration play. In his letters to the English papers from France, Thackeray is always ready to express disgust for cold damp alien foods like frogs' legs and snails, and praise of the roast beef and foaming ale of home and England. Nations share the shortsighted views of people whose nearest friends and relations seem their only really threatening rivals, and distinctions between self and other lend themselves to infection by gender prejudices. If England is to be plain and frank and male, France must be artificial, effeminate, perverse.

Frenchwomen were fascinating, of course, to the normal (English) male, but also foolishly and unreasonably vain, stingy, false, selfish, and self-indulgently theatrical to the point of madness and murderousness. One of the first of the line in fiction is the eponymous heroine of Daniel Defoe's *Roxana* (1724), a Huguenot refugee who gets the only name we know her by when, as she dances in Turkish costume, a man in the audience cries out, "Roxana, Roxana, by ———!" Roxana, like the heroine of that name in Racine's *Bajazet*, becomes a murderess. In Mary Elizabeth Braddon's popular novel *Lady Audley's Secret* (1862), the heroine—who has inherited insanity from her mother—is actress enough to assume an artificial identity. When she is finally incarcerated in a Continental madhouse, at the novel's end, and violently hisses out her real feelings of hatred, she reminds the man who watches her of Mlle Mars. (Braddon's sensational novel—the work of a former actress—was very successful as a play.) French actresses in the dominant tradition of moral English fiction usually turn up in connection with a man's misspent youth (but the grandfather in *Coningsby* is in his dotage when he is preyed upon by a couple of gold-digging actresses from the Comédie-Française). The dead mother of the child Adèle in *Jane Eyre* (1847) is a case in point. The sad brief tale of faithless, silly, dependent, French Céline Varens is a foil to the stern and virtuous English heroine's life story; Céline is a mere episode in the history of Rochester, whereas Jane—his true love—is the sub-

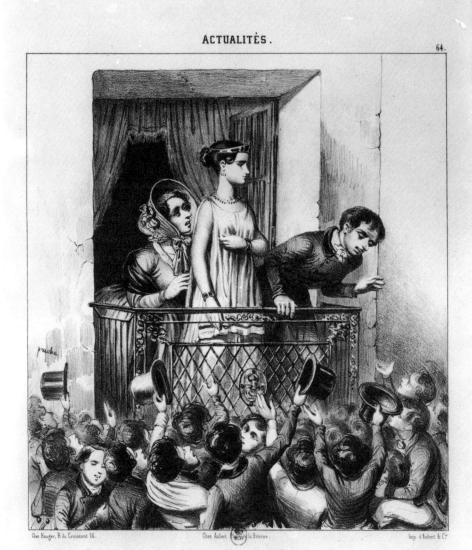

ACTUALITÉS.

64.

Peuple d'Albion !! nous sommes infiniment touchés de l'accueil bienveillant !...... que .... qui .... enfin voila! mais tout cela n'est pas une raison pour nous embêter a l'exces ! je vous ai deja dit que vous étiez tres admirateurs du talent ! ainsi, payez ! et restez tranquille ! sans quoi il y a des gens qui penseront que tout cet enthousiasme là n'est qu'une charge !!

"People of England!" Rachel being hawked to the British by her family, from a caricature by Pruche, 1841

ject of a proud "autobiography," the very writing of which proves that she is in charge of her own life.

More sinister than Céline is the French actress in George Eliot's *Middlemarch* (1871–72), who figures in the early career of the physician Tertius Lydgate. As a medical student in Paris in the 1820s, Lydgate falls in love with a sultry actress of melodramas and goes repeatedly to see her perform. Her husband is an actor who performs opposite her, and one night, in the course of a scene, she actually stabs him. He dies. Acquitted by the predictably lax French authorities, Laure goes off to live in the country, where Lydgate repairs to adore his bovine beauty. In their final interview, she relieves him of the notion of her innocence. *"I meant to do it,"* she insists about the murder. By way of explanation she tells him her husband annoyed her, wanted to live in the city while she preferred the country; she adds that her impulse "came to me in the play."

Since Jane Austen's *Mansfield Park* (1814), English novelists have explored the charge that acting is injurious to the character, first of all because the roles of "bad" characters are contaminating, secondly because assuming any character at all that is not one's own encourages a softness and malleability of the self and leads by easy degrees to mortal sin. Fanny Price, Austen's heroine, virtuously opposes her cousins' project of putting on a play. (The young people who attempt amateur theatricals in a house in the country are portrayed more sympathetically in Goethe's *Elective Affinities* [1809], and certainly in Gautier's *Mademoiselle de Maupin* [1835].) George Eliot's Lydgate is morally weak, being overly susceptible to theatricality. His self-destroying taste for women who seem decorative and are worse leads him to marry Rosamond Vincy, whose artificiality finally destroys him. Eliot continued to mull over the fatal attractions of theatrical women and the slide from moral malleability to hardness and murder in her last novel. Early on in *Daniel Deronda*, Gwendolen Harleth turns rigid in fear when she suddenly sees a picture of a "dead face" and a "female figure fleeing" while she performs in a *tableau vivant*. At the end of her sad story, she sits motionless, frozen, unable and unwilling to act as her hated husband drowns before her eyes. Gwendolen has been born and brought up to shine in a society that overvalues appearances, and her success there makes her think she can be a professional actress; dissuaded when she is told she should have started studying the art of acting long before, she sells herself in the socially sanctioned way, by marrying for money. Like Laure and like Rosamond, she effectively kills a man, refusing to throw the dying Grandcourt a rope. "I saw my wish outside me," is how she explains her (in)action, echoing Laure.

. . .

TO THE ENGLISH, at first, the threat of murderousness that Rachel posed seemed strictly, therefore safely, classical. Onstage she did not commit murder, imaginary or real, like a Laure in a melodrama. Rather, in accordance with the courtly *bienséances*, the violence she engaged in took place behind the scenes—and evidently, excitingly, in her mind. She was reputedly chaste; Roxane's graceful little hand seemed clean enough for the English actress Helen Faucit, who was praised by George Eliot as a model of female virtue, to beg for a cast of it in 1840. Later, in response to gossip, Miss Faucit backed away: as the respectable wife of Sir Theodore Martin, she could visit a "fallen" Rachel no more than she could be visited by George Eliot, who defied Victorian convention by living with G. H. Lewes without being married to him.

Miss Faucit is the exception that proves the rule often enviously cited in France, that it was easier for actresses to cross over into respectability in England. In general, in both countries, the line between the great world and the demimonde was firm: in both France and England, the theater was a counter-world where many bourgeois conventions were inverted. Plays and novels abundantly dramatize the contrasts between the theatrical and "real" worlds, and their interesting points of intersection: in novels as different as Balzac's *La Cousine Bette* (1846) and Charles Reade's *Peg Woffington* (1853), encounters between virtuous wives and shady, imperious theater queens with hearts of gold exploit the depth of the divide, the strength of the clichés about the difference, the reliable drama inherent in challenging it. In fact, the world of the theater was in some respects better than any other one for women, and not necessarily a moral abyss. Women of the theater could assume positions of management, as the Béjart women in France and Madame Vestris in England did. For all their comparative raffishness, theater people often led family lives in a separate sphere of unimpeachable respectability: in *Hard Times*, Dickens sympathetically portrays the devoted husbands, wives, and children attached to Sleary's circus. In her study of Nelly Ternan, the actress who lived secretly as Dickens's mistress, Claire Tomalin sketches the interconnecting family lives of Nelly's people and the better-known Kembles and Siddonses, Keans and Macreadys. For Nelly Ternan, whose actress mother was known as virtuous, it was possible to choose to seem respectable and even to bring off a plausible semblance of bourgeois morality that successfully concealed a secret life (though people did talk). In France, it would have been much less easy. Not impossible: Samson and his wife were exemplary bourgeois theater folk (their respectability being assisted by the moral cachet which the Théâtre-Français had developed as it had declined in popularity). But the expectation was that an unmarried actress's sexual favors were available, and for sale. She was expected to live as Balzac's Coralie did, or his La Torpille, or the historical Adrienne Lecouvreur, or Mlles George, Anaïs, or Judith, whom Rachel knew—as the mistress of wealthy men who chose wives from their own class.

Although the young Rachel was visibly under the protection of Samson and the state theater, it was well known that her own people were of a world too marginal and murky to mirror respectable society, and too poor to be above suspicion. The Félixes did not, like the Ternans, belong to a sub-society of actors, any more than they were members of the respectable Jewish community which also mimicked the majority. The journalists who dwelt on Thérèse Félix's Bohemian origins meant to suggest that the family were close to Gypsies. Heine thought it hilarious that people talked of Rachel's making a great marriage—and considered the talk to be a symptom of terminal social disorder. Sardonically, he reported that one man made up to Princess Isabella Fernanda of Spain after Rachel's father, "who is descended from a good Jewish family, refused him his daughter's hand." Mocking more than Jacques Félix's arrogance, the German poet proclaimed, "All the ladies-in-waiting of both the Castiles—and those of the whole universe—will hold up their hands in horror. Now, at last, they understand that the old world, the world of traditional respect, has come to an end!"

Heine was overreacting for comic effect. People talked so wildly about Rachel's marrying into the aristocracy partly because she had convinced them of her innate rank, but largely because they did not know what to make of her. On the one hand just a little actress, she seemed to transcend that category. And her aggressive virginity, like any heroine's in a novel or a play, demanded a romantic plot.

It was after her "conquest" of England in 1841 that Dr. Véron, in a mood of expansive mockery, read aloud some compromising letters after one of his famous good dinners; the next day *le tout Paris* tittered over the commonplace truth about *la chaste Rachel*. Devastated by the threat to her career, she claimed to be contemplating suicide; it was also said that she tried to buy the letters to protect her image. Mme Crémieux, the lawyer's wife, wrote urgently to counsel her to marry and save her name at once. (That pillar of the Jewish community had had her children baptized without her husband's knowledge.) But less extreme expedients were to hand.

Sophisticated Paris in the mid-nineteenth century was not really comparable to puritanical America in the mid-twentieth, which felt itself betrayed when Ingrid Bergman, the Nordic nun of *The Bells of St. Mary's*, left her tall doctor husband for the Italian Roberto Rossellini on Stromboli. Disapproval of Rachel could not be so stern, but the objection to being fooled was as real. The star's image was shattered; some fans felt taken. Rachel had little choice but to seize the alternative persona that was awaiting her, as it were, in the wings. She slipped into it easily: youth and impudence, physical grace, a slim figure, a brilliant dressmaker, and an edgy, brittle look equipped her nearly as well as beauty would have for a new, more sexual role. In exchange for glamour, pleasure, and freedom, it was not at all hard to leave her mother at home, along with her white dress, and brave the scorn of the virtuous. People with reason to fear being compromised avoided her—a Mme Crémieux, or a Helen Faucit. On the other hand, a Mme Récamier could rise beyond convention: "Mlle Rachel is a great artist, she is willing to put her talents at my disposal, she has impeccable style," the old woman supposedly declared. "I have nothing more to ask of her." And in England Queen Victoria would continue to be her loyal fan for years, sublimely unperturbed by gossip.

RACHEL'S EVENTFUL LOVE LIFE, like every female star's, lends itself to being read in theatrical terms: as enacting a self fractured by role-playing or softened into insensibility or vice, as a revelation of a "true" concealed self, or perhaps as a response to the repression that was imposed on her by her roles. (In one biographer's view, she made and broke her liaisons, and lived "with utter freedom of mind and body, as though she wished, by dissipations, to divest herself of the chaste and reverent priestly character she assumed on the stage.") As stars of subsequent times would do, Rachel served as an image of the split between the private and the public selves, and also as an exemplary, dramatic instance of their interaction. She was the more fascinating, perhaps, for defying the biographical imperative that a tragic actress must be a *grande amoureuse* in the standard sense, a woman consumed by amorous passion and dedicated to love alone. Onstage, she never found a man to partner her the way Dorval found Lemaître, and Ellen Terry found Irving, and Bernhardt, Mounet-Sully. In private life, she did not follow the model of Adrienne Lecouvreur, who was famed (and admired) for pawning her silver to underwrite her hero-lover's patriotic martial adventure. She was not like Duse, who endured the torments of sadistic Gabriele d'Annunzio, or Marilyn Monroe, who, at the end, let herself be victimized by a series of cynical, powerful men. Rachel had a great many lovers, both men she enthusiastically cared for and more casual ones, but no single passion for a

man that began to equal her commitment to the stage and her parents, her
sisters and brother, and her two children. The story of her love life has lent
itself more easily, therefore, to cynical than sentimental emphasis.

"I am *free,* and mean to remain *free,"* she wrote emphatically to a persistent suitor in 1846. "I will have renters, but not owners," she is supposed
to have quipped during the time she lived openly and lavishly in a house she
shared, as his *maîtresse en titre,* with a man about town. Unlike Bernhardt,
she never risked marriage. The courtesan heroines of the nineteenth century
are victims; their opposite numbers in popular legend are ambitious, heartless
schemers. Rachel fell between the stereotypes, seemed sometimes the one
and sometimes the other, or deliberately both at once. She loved not particularly wisely and not always remarkably well, but energetically—the way she
did everything. "I love to be loved as I love when I love" was one of the
personal "mottoes" the peddler's daughter adopted, aping the aristocracy
with a flashy hint of self-parody. (Another was *Tout ou rien;* was Bernhardt's
Quand même an extension of or a response to it?) The most dramatic and
effective of her corrections of received ideas about women was made by her
professional accomplishment: she made money by acting, not by sleeping
around. But she did like lavish presents, and (therefore) the rich men who
had it in their power to give them to her. And she liked power—the company
of powerful men as well as her own power over them.

The adolescent Rachel seems to have taken her first lover during her
years at the Théâtre Molière. He was an actor who called himself Ancelin,
who lent her parents money. The affair was sordid but the man, committed
to believing in Rachel's genius, was discreet. (No evidence of the connection
was published until Chevalley's 1989 biography.) The somewhat less quiet
connection with Véron occurred during the summer of 1838. Rachel's first
public, indeed publicized, liaison did not take place until 1842, after the affair
of the letters. The man she chose made for a pert rejoinder to those who
bemoaned her "fall": François de Bourbon-Orléans, Prince de Joinville, the
third of Louis-Philippe's five sons and the hero of the expedition to Saint
Helena and Napoleon's Second Funeral. Arsène Houssaye's story of how the
two met is no doubt apocryphal: the prince is supposed to have sent his card
backstage with the scrawled message, "Quand? Où? Combien?" to which
Rachel responded in kind, "Ce soir. Chez moi. Pour rien." While those tel-
egraphic "love letters" were probably the work of another actress more overtly
on the market and another, more sophisticated prince, or even of a single
fabulist, the story has stuck to the legend of Rachel because of the two
significant points it makes: that Rachel had the wit to match even a rude

proposition, and that she didn't want money in exchange for sexual favors. (It was said that in her heyday Rachel "had two bracelets entirely composed of rings given her by her lovers, so heavy that she could wear only one at a time, the other being carried in her pocket.") Joinville was a prince to be enjoyed for the pleasure of it: charming, handsome, and twenty-three, he was a prowler of theatrical corridors who had a private hideaway on the rue Montpensier where he could entertain her. They were a high-spirited couple, even on paper: she writes to her "old dog," he of his "good old Rachel." The solemn tragedienne is nowhere in evidence when, during Joinville's absence, she fondly reminds her lover of her claims on his "tail," demanding that he return to her: "since you're willing to wag your tail in my honor, move your four paws as well and get to Paris." After the young prince made a politically correct marriage she continued to keep his statue on display in her living room. Among her papers she kept the affectionate last letter in which he had taken leave of her: in the margin she wrote dramatically, "Poor Joinville! You take with you my first, my last love. I will live, I will love, *never again.*" For his part, Joinville recalled her fondly in old age (he lived until 1900).

J O I N V I L L E was barely gone on the naval expedition from which he returned with a wife when, in January 1843, Rachel became the mistress of the *amant en titre* of another actress, Mlle Anaïs of the Comédie-Française. Alexandre-Florian-Joseph Colonna, Count Walewski, fell heavily in love with her; and it pleased Rachel to be adored by the son of Napoleon. The product of the Emperor's liaison with the beautiful Polish countess Marie Walewska, he had become a French citizen in adulthood, and lived in Paris dabbling in journalism, playwriting, and Polish and French politics. With some notion of being her Pygmalion, Walewski took Rachel's manners and daily habits in hand: in his biographer's view, it was he who made a lady of her. Walewski was a possessive, protective, suffocating lover who directed her (in writing) to renounce coquetry, tell him everything, and do everything he prescribed, in order to avoid the dangers of her theatrical milieu. That she found him dull and conventional may be guessed from her letters to him: "My conduct is beyond reproach, as you say," she writes him coyly, "but this doesn't prevent me from making a few blunders. Don't go getting worried on my account: they're only *small* blunders." About him, she writes rather dismissively, in a postscript to a long letter to Adèle Samson: "The Walewski begs me to tell you a thousand things (believe they are pleasant things, as he means you to do)."

Count Alexandre
Colonna Walewski,
from an engraving
by Mottez

Seriously domestic, Walewski bought a pretty *hôtel particulier* on the rue
Trudon, where the two of them set up house (Rachel would buy him out in
1850, when their affair was long past). The little street, which was to disappear
in the course of urban renewal later in the century, was a charmingly quiet
retreat within the city, and the luxurious style of living there quickly became
legendary. Guests were received by a servant who bore himself like an English
butler, and were then ushered into a vestibule where rich carpets covered the
marble floor. An elegant curved stairway led to the upper stories: light filtered
down onto it from an Eastern-style cupola made of stained glass. Fresh flowers filled magnificent vases. In the large salon, decorated in white and gold,
a table displayed a variety of bladed weapons with handles wrought of gold
and jewels, and in one case, human bone. Otherwise the room was redolent
of comfort—and glory. The Nine Muses, each one floating over her name in

Greek, looked down from panels on the walls. Thrown on the red damask sofas and chairs were shawls and lengths of lace at least as valuable as the fabrics they protected. The silver and china of the household were marked with a single "R," and other furnishings bore the anti-family crest Rachel had devised for herself, her single initial framed by a buckled belt. The *salonnière* received on regular Thursdays, when everyone who wanted to know everyone in Paris was eager to come to enjoy the food and drink and the gambling that went on in one of the smaller rooms, not to mention the wit of the perfectly charming hostess, and the sense of being enviably in the right place. On a white bearskin in the salon, visitors could watch a pretty child at play—the son of Rachel and Walewski, and the grandson of Napoleon—the real master of the house, some people said. Walewski's friends of course maintained that *he* was the master—at least in the bedroom, a *boudoir de parade* with a bed more magnificent than the one Louis XIV had enjoyed at Versailles. The curious visitor could glimpse its rich hangings, and even the chamber pot of costly Sèvres porcelain decorated with risqué scenes. Off the room was a Spartan closet furnished with a narrow bed and little else: there, they said, the tragedienne devoutly invited her muse, brooding in gloomy solitude.

A widower whose children had died, Napoleon's half-Polish son had none of his mother's beauty or his father's brilliance. But he was steady and uxorious. He was distressed and sympathetic when Rachel miscarried in November 1843, and elated when she bore him a son a year later. She was somewhat less than carried away by maternity: "You ask whether my son is beautiful," she writes to a friend. "Do you want me to answer frankly, and tell you what I think straight out? He is pretty, very pretty, and what is more he promises to take after his father." Walewski recognized his son (who signed himself "Alexandre Colonna W" as a youth, foregrounding the noble Roman part of his name). The surname of Rachel's second son, by the feckless young Arthur Bertrand, was Félix: his mother named him Gabriel-Victor ("Victor-Gabrielle," she ungrammatically wrote, in the note announcing the birth to Mme Samson). Enjoying the nominally huge disparity of class between the boys, legend-mongers like to repeat Rachel's probably apocryphal remark that little Gabriel would be his nobler brother's coachman. But she was equally solicitous about both her children, and encouraged them to be friends. Both boys grew up to be successful in the service of France: Alexandre-Antoine-Colonna Walewski became a diplomat who died at his post in Turin in 1898; Gabriel-Victor Félix, a navy man, died in Brazzaville (Congo), Africa, in 1889, where he was the French consul. From his letters

Emile de Girardin,
photograph by
Pierre Petit

we can know Alexandre as a tender boy and man, who faithfully corresponded, well into middle age, with his mother's servant Rose Halff, whom he called his second grandmother.

DURING HER EARLY YEARS with Walewski, Rachel was proudly monogamous. When she haughtily turned down a proposition from Alexandre Dumas *père*, the novelist retaliated by writing a hearty, elaborately metaphorical letter congratulating Walewski for being the possessor of a city that was impregnable to a siege. But Walewski's territory had a will to wander. Her lover was away on a diplomatic mission when the bored Rachel set about deliberately to seduce Emile de Girardin. The pioneer journalist, brilliant and cold, was a self-made man in a style that probably would have attracted her even if he had not been popularly known as the Napoleon of the press. (He even dressed his hair in Napoleonic style.) He was clever, hardworking, and powerful, famous for having killed a man in a duel and known for the extensive dossiers on everyone important which he kept in alphabetized boxes. He was much older than Rachel—too old for love, he interested her by insisting as their affair began—and committed both to a *mariage blanc* with his literary wife and a longtime liaison with a certain amusing Esther Guimont. Flattered by his attention to her intelligence, Rachel wooed him with arguments that theirs was a singularly advanced and intellectual relationship, and finally he allowed himself to be won. Girardin, who later would be a lover of Sarah Bernhardt's, was an interesting character who had a life that resembled a novel. Understanding as much early on, he wrote it himself. The illegitimate son of a married noblewoman and a man of rank, he had been named after Rousseau's Emile and then abandoned by his parents, who denied him either of their names. At the age of twenty-one he published a well-received autobiographical "fiction," *Emile* (1827), which had the didactic purpose of arguing for the rights of bastards (the title of the first chapter is "The Conquest of the Name"). Literary success and notoriety quickly put him in a position to claim his father's recognition. He went on to further distinguish the family name he had won for himself by virtually inventing the cheap daily newspaper funded by advertising revenues. He founded *La Presse* in 1836, solidified his power by marrying the beautiful, well-connected, and accomplished Delphine Gay, and became a power in political life.

Delphine preferred to avert her eyes from Girardin's sexual life; his mistress of ten years preferred not to. Outraged by Rachel's incursion onto her property, Esther Guimont threatened in a letter by one woman of the world to another that she would inform Mme de Girardin unless Emile was returned to her. Rachel had spent years cultivating the vanity of Delphine, who as a playwright and journalist had a strong hand in her career; she had no choice but to retreat—but not before Walewski returned to Paris, got wind of the affair, and stormed out of the house on the rue Trudon, devastating Rachel by taking his fifteen-month-old son with him. She worked herself up into a state calculated to mollify the moralizing Walewski: "I am a monster indeed!" she wrote him, echoing the accents of Phèdre. Walewski generously returned the child—to be its mother's good angel, he pedantically wrote her—and proceeded to marry a few months later. Rachel was distressed.

She went on to collect a series of new lovers, one of the first of whom was young Arthur Bertrand. He had marched along with Joinville at the Second Funeral; like Walewski, he was the ex-lover of another well-known actress, in his case the mature Virginie Déjazet, who had been chosen by his mother to instruct him in the arts of love. Arthur begged gambling money from Rachel, and pilfered it from her purse when she denied him. For some months Rachel was pleased to play the role of his "little wife," and to enjoy his interest—equal to hers—in things Napoleonic. She writes to Arthur that she regrets missing the celebration of Napoleon's birthday in May 1847 (the Invalides is no place for a woman, she tells him); she describes an encounter on a train with a weathered veteran of the wars whom she felt like kissing. But the *enfant de Ste Hélène* was not closer to Napoleon than several other available men in Europe. In the summer of 1847, pregnant with Arthur's child, Rachel toured England and Scotland, and embarked on parallel affairs with the man who would be the Emperor Louis-Napoleon and his cousin Prince Napoleon, known as Prince Nap or Plon-Plon.

Though parallel, they were unequal—Prince Nap being more interesting and interested—and they intersected from the start. Empress Eugénie repeated the story as her husband had told it: how the three French friends were together in a compartment of an English train when Louis, awakened by a sudden swerve, opened his eyes to see his mistress in the other man's arms. Diplomatically, he shut them again, playing possum ("So like him," was his widow's nostalgic comment). Prince Nap was a different type, a *bon vivant* (a Napoleonic medal dipped in German fat, one wag called him) just a year younger than Rachel. He was famously a republican, and known for his passion for classical art; in respect for Camille and Phèdre, he commissioned a toy Greek temple as a gift for Rachel. He loved her briefly and remained her friend for life, but it was her colleague, Mlle Judith, who was his mistress for years. As for Louis-Napoleon, he also stayed friendly: when he became emperor, Rachel was in and out of the Elysée Palace—the mistress of the house, people said with a knowing wink. And by the way, feminizing the legacy of Talma, who taught Napoleon to carry himself like an emperor, she showed Eugénie how to curtsy while sweeping a crowd with her eyes and seeming to meet the gaze of every single person. (When the palace guards mistook her for the empress one day, Rachel was reportedly insulted.)

Rachel's many more or less anonymous lovers included a country gentleman with whom she dreamed of living a pastoral life. She attracted men individually and also in groups: Michel Lévy and the playwright François Ponsard considered themselves to be members of the *cénacle Rachel;* the so-called "Tuileries Club" of her admirers centered around Dr. Véron. The sentimental Ponsard had loved his "Rachellina" in Italy; back in France, he wrote private poems as well as plays for and about her, including a paean

Prince Napoleon, photograph by Disdéri

of praise describing her as a madonna with her young children at her side in the country. It was a pretty idea of herself that Rachel encouraged and shared—when she was not dining with Achille Fould and Delacroix, deploying canny letters to get what she could from Delphine de Girardin and the Comédie-Française, seducing the likes of Prince Nap, or presenting glimpses of herself on tour in Italy for Véron and his buddies to enjoy. To them, she writes highly rhetorical letters ("Ah! how this Italy has deceived me!!"), reporting on her tours and dramatizing herself: she tells, for instance, how she entered the Pope's garden protected by a phalanx of escorts (the Marquis de Custine and others), and stole two oranges, which she washed in holy water and saved ("Jewess that I am") for luck. Spoken by a representative of France, which had backed the papacy and helped put down the Italian revolution, Rachel-Camille's "Rome" was more ambiguous than ever; she was conscious of her Italian tour as a dramatic occasion.

Unromantically, she enjoyed protracted friendships with her ex-lovers. Not only the Second Emperor remained devoted and useful: Girardin continued always eloquent in her defense; Prince Nap came by yacht to visit her at Le Cannet, and promised to look after Gabriel's career when she was dead. Most shockingly of all, she stayed chummy with Louis Véron, the Balzacian character credited with "corrupting" her in the first place, and "ruining" her in the second. The liaison with Véron that titillated contemporary caricaturists continued to amuse generations of biographers, who savored the spectacle of pure Camille in her toga squired by the fat-necked entrepreneur. Hector Fleischmann's analysis of the association relies on a predictable play of rhetoric and prejudices: "The doubleness of Rachel's character gives itself away clearly here. A woman, that is to say, hot-tempered, passionate, all nerves and anger, she will spurn Véron; a Jewess, that is to say, prudent, calculating, forward-looking and self-interested, she will use him. On the one side, her honor and dignity; on the other, her future and fortune. And would she hesitate? Would she place the one before the other? Do you think she isn't a daughter of Father Félix?" Legend (propagated by the dramatist Ernest Legouvé, in his memoirs) says she once planned to shoot Véron from the stage during a performance, with a gun she took with her for the purpose, but in fact she never even dropped the double-dealing doctor from her acquaintance. The scandalous *affaire Véron*—the reading aloud of the compromising letters—had occurred in 1841; all through the early 1850s, Rachel wrote her old friend boasting letters about the strenuousness and enormous profits of her tours. He was one of the most powerful men in Paris, still; she was an ambitious actress who carefully cultivated public awareness of her international fame. In 1849, before embarking on one tour, she wrote and prettily begged Véron not to forget her during the three months she would be away. She lists proudly, for his benefit, all the cities and the dates on her itinerary, commenting, "What a journey! How exhausting!! But what a take!!!" (Her word is *dot*, which means dowry.) In closing, she professes her love: "I love you with all my heart and am your most devoted friend." The choice of pronouns and gendered nouns is perhaps flirtatious, certainly hard to gloss: Rachel addresses Véron with the formal *vous*, also strangely refers to herself as his *ami*, underlining the masculine noun and its matching article. There may well be a private joke involved. But from here it seems that Rachel, sure that the old ironist would appreciate her self-knowledge, is signaling her amused awareness that she appears unwomanly in a world where energies and appetites and aims such as hers are not the sort of thing a tragedienne, or any woman, can confess to.

AT THIRTY, in a letter to Véron and his friends written from Prague, she reflected on her career and life in general, and therefore on money. Young as she was—and in spite of what the papers were saying, she was still young, she insisted—she had learned a great deal in the course of extensive experience. First of all she had learned that true glory was independence. And what, if not money, makes independence possible? she asks. Noble sentiments are at the root of her strong desire to be rich, she concludes. Rachel was very aware of the limits and the ambiguities of independence. "My dear *older* and *independent* sister," was one of her mock-respectful salutations to the willful Sarah: she knew that independence was not always glorious or noble. "When will I find an independent man who is able to come to visit me during this long exile of a tour?" she writes to Sarah at around the time of the letter to Véron, complaining of fatigue, and of being dirty as a little pig from the dusty roads, and tired of having a lover who was in Paris. "If by chance you take a stroll on a nice day, and run into a man with a nice face and figure, mail him to me *poste restante* to Munich, where I shall be in a fortnight."

3. FATAL WOMAN

Alfred de Musset's account of an evening he spent with the actress in 1839, frequently anthologized as "Un Souper chez Mlle Rachel," is usually read as a telling sketch of her in private, a domestic counterpart to the picture of Rachel the public performer in *Villette.* Like Brontë's chapter, Musset's essay is an exercise in the art of literary portraiture. A portrait, as the aesthete Gabriel Nash explains in Henry James's *The Tragic Muse,* is uniquely "a revelation of two realities, the man whom it was the artist's conscious effort to reveal and the man (the interpreter) expressed in the very quality and temper of that effort." (When the artist and the subject are not both men the process and product are different, perhaps, but Gabriel Nash avoids that issue.) He says that a portrait offers "a double vision, the strongest dose of life that art could give, the strongest dose of art that life could give." When one artist makes a portrait of another, the double dose is even stronger; when the one is a romantic poet and the other a lovely young actress, various more and less artificial flavorings color the "dose."

Musset tells of leaving the theater one evening with the gay young actress and some friends, who invite him to share their supper at the Félix apartment. Once there, Rachel discovers she has left the jewels she wore in the play behind her; she sends the maidservant back to fetch them. There is no other servant, and she is ravenous, so she cooks the dinner herself. The little white hands prove remarkably skillful as they prepare the simple meal of steaks and spinach, and the punch that is set aflame in the dimness. Finished cooking, Rachel snatches up a dish and implements and begins to eat without serving anyone else. But her mother complains that she is also hungry, so pewter plates get laid out for the company. (Showy sister Sarah grumbles about this, but the keys to the silver and china are gone with the maid.) The dinner is delicious; after eating, Rachel reaches for Musset's sword, which she uses to pick her teeth. Relaxed now, she talks freely about her early life, telling how, with the change saved up by careful marketing, she managed to buy herself the works of Molière. Her mother and sister listen, nodding agreement. Then the maid comes back with the forgotten rings and bracelets, which she tips out on the table. The bracelets are magnificent, worth a good four to five thousand francs, and thrown in with them is a really valuable gold diadem: Musset savors the sight of the jewels tumbled together with the salad on the table. After the other guests leave, the mother drowses heavily in a chair like a Rembrandt duenna, while the young actress reads Racine to her poet by candlelight. *Phèdre:* her ambition is to play the great role. Enraptured by the poetry, she is still reading when her brutal father, back from the Opéra where he has just seen Mlle Nathan in *La Juive* (what else?), bursts in to pack Rachel off to bed and dispatch her admirer. Portrait of the artist as Cinderella, of life and art ill-met by candlelight: on the one hand the vulgar family and the vegetables, on the other the brilliant jewels, the great poetry, the adoring poet. Painterly chiaroscuro; also, per- haps, a sly hint of what Roland Barthes would call "Racinian tenebroso," the playwright's characteristic imagery. Musset's Rachel is a white-handed daughter of the Muses misplaced by some ironic fairy in the bosom of the tribe of Félix; also—ardent, earthy, energetic, calculating, ambitious—she is clearly the daughter of precisely those Félixes. She is dead set on playing the greatest tragic role ever written for a woman, and defiantly tells her father she will finish reading *Phèdre* in bed.

The story captures Rachel's energy and frankness, her gift for improvi- sation, above all her steely will. Arsène Houssaye claimed she told him one night at dinner that she had made herself beautiful—straightened out the curves of her nose and forehead—by sheer will. At the height of her stardom, Gérard de Nerval recalled the little actress of the Théâtre du Gymnase who became a great artist not because of fate or talent, but by virtue of her fierce, formidable determination: "the will of Mlle Rachel and the consent of the public have made a tragedienne of her."

Though her public called insistently for that ultimate test and treat, she put off playing Phèdre until January 1843. Gautier considered her reluctance only natural: Phèdre, after all, is the supreme test of whether an actress has real genius or mere talent. Marie Dorval's failure in the role at the Odéon in October, during a rainstorm that drowned out the actors' voices, may have helped Rachel finally to decide to master—or submit to—Phèdre. Gautier admired Dorval, but he had found her natural quality at odds with this role; implicitly, the severe avatar of classicism was urged to show the way it ought to be done. A hasty note Rachel dispatched to Samson on her gold-trimmed stationery embossed with an "R" inside a shield suggests how apprehensively she approached it: "I have studied phedre a lot I will come tomorrow to ask you to judge the result of my profound research."

Racine's Phèdre is based on Phaedra in the *Hippolytus* of Euripides—a mythic figure like that other classical female criminal, Medea, and like her a descendant of the sun. Phaedra's parents are Minos, the judge of hell, and his wife Pasiphaë, mother also of the Minotaur, a half-human monster sired by a bull; her sister is Ariadne, who saved Theseus from the labyrinth; her husband is Theseus himself. That hero's absence from his kingdom provides the situation with which Racine's play begins: the queen alone in a foreign land. In her first words, she confesses she is sick, and the action proceeds to chronicle her illness. Her affliction began on her wedding day, when Phèdre conceived a passion for the young hunter Hippolyte, the son of her bridegroom. In the *Hippolytus* of Euripides, he is a youth whose passionate devotion to the goddess of chastity infuriates the goddess of love; Racine makes him more worldly, and more credible to a courtly French audience, by inventing the new character of Aricie, a young woman Hippolyte loves. Normalized by the introduction of a potentially comic plot, Racine's Hippolyte makes Phèdre seem more grotesque. The character of Aricie, her rival and opposite, points up Phèdre's aberrant nature; and on the level of plot, young Aricie functions to compound the agony of the older woman.

Racine's critics, condemning Phèdre for too quickly believing her husband was dead and she was free, saw her as the archetype of lustful Woman. She defies the divinely given laws of marriage and the family, and the interdiction against incest, as well as the aesthetic rules that structure young love. In the early nineteenth century, Chateaubriand sympathetically interpreted Racine's heroine as a prototypical suffering Christian soul; Rachel's secular audiences probably understood her as a radically self-assertive woman guilty of Camille's scandalous irreverence and Hermione's—that is, of insufficient respect for heroes. The story of Phaedra and Hippolytus, as the classicist Froma Zeitlin writes, explores "the best-kept secret of cultural ideology, that is, the reality of the sexual, even adulterous wife."

In the secular mid-nineteenth century, when the religious resonances of Phèdre's passion—Euripidean-pagan and Racinian-Christian—were muted, the psychological dimension of the action was commensurately intensified. Phèdre is even more self-aware than Camille is. Her unrequitable lust is matched—her agony is increased—by her own intense scrutiny of her symptoms. She can tell her confidante Oenone exactly how she felt when she first saw Hippolyte:

> *Je le vis, je rougis, je pâlis à sa vue;*
> *Un trouble s'éleva dans mon âme éperdue;*
> *Mes yeux ne voyaient plus, je ne pouvais parler;*
> *Je sentis tout mon corps et transir et brûler.*

> I saw, I blushed, I paled at sight of him;
> A strange disquiet seized my stricken soul;
> My eyes could see no more, I could not speak;
> I felt my body burn and freeze in turn. (I, iii)

The lines echo French translations of a famous lyric by Sappho, the poet from the island of Lesbos whose description of love's physical symptoms, from the point of view of the suffering woman, first figured female desire as self-consciousness. Phèdre, distracted, is beside herself, and clear-eyed enough to watch herself in Sappho's way: seeing herself intensifies her passion. She is, as she says, the prey of Venus; she also is obviously in the toils of her own painful self-awareness and self-disgust. The whole play develops this dividedness. When, at the end, a witness reports the horrible death of Hippolyte, whose body is terribly mauled when his horses, frightened by a bull from the sea, drag him behind his chariot across the rocks, it is as if the heroine's psychological struggle has been projected outward into the world. Phèdre's bestial part (also figured by her half-bull half-brother) destroys the youth who rebuffed her. Hippolyte literally, like Phèdre metaphorically, is torn apart by monstrous passion.

The famous representations of Rachel as Phèdre, in which she looks somber, worried, guilty, and queenly, belie the wild stage agonies that terrified her audiences. Annenkov, her most meticulous observer, left a vivid record of what he saw and heard in Russia when Rachel-Phèdre revealed her passion to Hippolyte:

Rachel begins with full voice the tale of her criminal love. Soon the words, the couplets, as if driven by the thought, begin to run as incredible, barely audible speech. A whisper, which betrays her passion with a rapidity almost convulsive, becomes unbearable. Above it, from time to time, are uttered those contralto shrieks, which rend the soul. . . . In mid-monologue, Phèdre, giving herself up totally to a single thought, loses self-consciousness and is almost beside herself. Her lips tremble, her eyes blaze with a maniacal fire, a gesture becomes insanely expressive, that ghastly whisper goes on the whole time, and the words run on, filled with agonizing truth. The paroxysm of passion increases even more, when, after Hippolyte's confusion in striving not to understand his stepmother, she exclaims, "Ah! cruel! tu m'as trop entendue!", these verses must be heard from Rachel's lips in order to realize how much irony can be contained in them! And literally having drawn new strength into it, she bursts out in a thundering confession of her criminal passion in the face of heaven and earth until, filled to the brim with horror and self-revulsion, she seizes Hippolyte's sword and is borne off stage unconscious by her confidante. Only then does the parterre take a breath and rise as one man crying "Rachel!" Such is the scene.

Always best when most thoroughly rehearsed, Rachel was probably more brilliant in 1853 than she had been ten years earlier. But Gautier had been ravished by her very first performance, writing that in spite of a generally inadequate and awkward production, Phèdre seemed actually to live for two hours. "With her first step on stage, her success was assured," he had written of Rachel; "never before was a role more completely expressed in an actor's body and bearing. When she moved forward, pale as her own ghost, her eyes reddened in her marble mask, her arms dangling and lifeless, her body inert beneath its straight-falling robe, we seemed to see not Mlle Rachel, but truly Phèdre herself." Exhausted by her performance, she had chosen not to come onstage to take her bow, tacitly bowing to the greater reality of the tragedy, showing her respect for Racine, suggesting that the actress had merged with, or been overcome by, the character she played.

It was inevitable that Rachel, notoriously amorous, should be identified with the sexual sinner who so brazenly solicits Hippolyte. Her most hostile French critics would goad their readers to hate her by drawing parallels between the stage queen and Phèdre that extended to Marie Antoinette, that also foreign queen who, before she was dethroned and beheaded, had been accused of criminal luxury, including incest with her young son. The loyal Gautier identified Rachel with the role of Phèdre on altogether another level, insisting on the spirit, not the flesh, of the suffering tragic heroines. Like Musset, who called her the vessel in which Racinian gold was purified, he stressed Rachel's truth to a classical ideal. Her Phèdre was no sexual sinner to be condemned from a Christian point of view, Gautier argued, but a being tormented by the gods. "Mlle Rachel understands Phèdre in her own particular way, and it is one that we believe is correct," wrote the critic. "She plays the role not as a passionate woman but as a victim. Her love is like a kind of madness, a malady inflicted by the vengeful rage of Venus, who does not hesitate to sacrifice an innocent woman in order to punish an insensitive man who refuses to worship her." One was invited to extend this interpretation into metaphor, and to see Rachel-Phèdre as an image of the artist-actress victimized by her role and by the theater.

Her triumphant Phèdre made Rachel unquestionably Tragedy's queen— its empress, even. Sainte-Beuve slyly chose a Napoleonic image to applaud Walewski's mistress, writing that Rachel, as Phèdre, had won her Battle of Marengo. The queen devoured by her own lustfulness, burdened by the body Venus feeds on, was taken to be an image of the split between brute sex and exquisite self-consciousness, and furthermore of the actress's self-contradictory, irreconcilable doubleness, in being both Woman and Artist. Sir Theodore Martin was much struck (and stirred) by Rachel as Phèdre, a "woman wasting away by inches in the consuming fires of a passion which she abhorred." In Goncourt's *La Faustin*, the Bernhardtian actress-heroine who painstakingly prepares a Phèdre to rival Rachel's falls victim to an offstage sexual passion that mimics and travesties Phèdre's: seeking her lover at his dueling studio and finding him gone, she is stirred by the male smells, and compelled against her will to invite the crude instructor to make love to her. (At the last minute, she pulls herself together and pushes him away.) Phèdre's criminal sexual desire and her aggressiveness were read as metonymic of the woman artist's ambition, and of Woman's aberrant, monstrous, and fatal aspiration toward greatness. Phèdre's mother mated with a bull; the sister of the Minotaur was herself a monster. Rachel, identified with this role, was no longer just a star but a *monstre sacré*, recognized by her guilty public as its sacrifice to the gods. For the audience came to witness not only Phèdre's suffering and Rachel's great performance, but the spectacle of the star being consumed by her role.

PHÈDRE'S PASSION destroys her stepson's life and her confidante's, and wrecks her husband's, before she kills herself. Her crime is against marriage and motherhood, society and social relations. Because women are conventionally seen as the sum of their social relations—seen as daughters and wives and mothers, first of all—female criminals are particularly shocking and threatening. A contemporary of Rachel's, a writer on prison reform, postulated that "female criminality is more dangerous than men's because it is more contagious."

That an actor is similarly contagious is obvious to the least susceptible member of an audience. Rachel as Phèdre seemed to put her audience in peril along with herself. Is that why people flocked to see her, in the dangerous city of Paris? The actress's growing reputation for greed and sexual excesses bled easily into the images of murderous Roxane and incestuous Phèdre; and as Rachel moved from role to role, it was as if to prove that one crime leads to another. The prejudice that links the stage with sin lent her a sheen of sinister glamour. What might such a woman not do? the virtuous wondered, and the naive filled in the blanks with the sins they recognized. When Rachel performed in Venice in 1851, John and Effie Ruskin did not go to see her, although, as Effie recorded, a couple of their friends had gone on four different nights to *Horace* and *Phèdre*, "and think her very grand." Ruskin's young and still virgin wife had seen Rachel in London and judged her "very pretty," she recalled; but, she commented complacently, "Rachel they say is such a very bad person and although only 32 she looks much older and is killing herself by drinking gin to excess." In *Judith*, the play written by Delphine de Girardin for Rachel and produced three months after her first *Phèdre*, the infatuated, doomed Holopherne says of the heroine, "Her attraction, for me, is the attraction of danger."

It was not until five years after she first appeared in *Phèdre* that Rachel, on tour in the provinces, took time to visit the notorious criminal Mme Lafarge, who was in a prison in Montpellier. The woman had been condemned to death for murdering her husband, after a highly publicized trial in the summer of 1840. Marie Lafarge had then been twenty-four, an orphan of remotely aristocratic parentage, her maternal grandmother having been one of the natural daughters of Philippe Egalité, father of Louis-Philippe, and the celebrated writer Mme de Genlis, his children's governess. Her family had married her off to a much older, loutish ironmaster who had falsely claimed he was rich. (Making the best of things, initially, the romantic youthful bride devised a family crest that included hammers.) Her accusers claimed she had sent her husband a cake laced with arsenic when he was away from home on business, and proceeded to dose him daily with more when he came home to be nursed. Mme Lafarge maintained she was innocent. The celebrity of the case illustrates the vogue for criminal women in the mid-nineteenth century, and suggests some reasons for the enthusiasm for *Phèdre*. During the Lafarge trial, writes the historian Mary Hartman, women had fought "for hours to catch a glimpse of the accused . . . and . . . for tickets for seats in court in the specially constructed ladies' gallery." Engravings of the heroine were sold in the streets, and in the newspapers writers debated whether or not she was beautiful: some observed "that her profile was not really good, that her forehead was too prominent, and her nose and mouth too large. But nearly everyone agreed that her eyes were extraordinary, her smile enchanting, and her soft, deep voice both appealing and seductive." The parallel with Rachel is alarming. The newspapers made Marie Lafarge a national figure, and she followed this up in a memoir she wrote in prison, which portrays her as a proleptic Madame Bovary. Her mind, she wrote, had been molded by books: the plays of Racine and Corneille, and Bernardin de Saint-Pierre's sentimental story, *Paul et Virginie*. She identified herself with George Sand's *Lélia*, "who has suffered all sorrows, doubts, and discouragement; who was riveted to earth by evil passions and raised to the heavens by sublime instincts; who possessed equally the power for good and for evil; who did not want to be a weak woman, and who was unable to become an angel."

It was 1848 when Rachel came to see Marie Lafarge in prison. Her motive was probably rather like that of the actress in Jules Dassin's 1978 film *A Dream of Passion*, who, in the course of rehearsing the role of Medea in Greece, discovers that an American woman has been jailed there for murdering her children. Maia (Melina Mercouri) wants to visit the woman in order to fabricate publicity for herself, and to do some quick research into the mind and heart of a criminal. But a feeling of close kinship with the other develops, which eventually nourishes her play, and makes it better. Rachel, who recorded no such aggrandizement of her art, experienced a more immediate rush of fellow feeling, and a raised feminist consciousness, as a result of her meeting with Mme Lafarge.

She was touring the provinces in her usual repertoire of tragic roles, also rendering those exhortatory recitations of *La Marseillaise* which had led the Republic to sponsor the tour. In the cities outside Paris, the women in the audience were especially enthusiastic: complaints that the tragedienne's visits disrupted family life had already appeared in provincial papers years before. In 1848, the mix of art and politics was particularly heady: at Nîmes the tragedienne was cheered for donating a hundred francs to the unemployed. By visiting an accused murderess in Montpellier she was making another timely gesture toward the unfortunate, as well as satisfying what she called (in a letter to Delphine de Girardin) her "predilection for prisons." The account of the interview she wrote to her sister Sarah suggests that both parties were strongly affected. To the tragedienne's gratification, Mme Lafarge recalled having seen her in *Iphigénie en Aulide*; but when Rachel offered to recite for her she refused to hear her, saying it would make her regret the world too much. Rachel felt intense pity for a person who had been married off without love, and condemned by a petty jury. Such a woman might have done greater things in a different world, where women had more opportunity, she wrote to Sarah in an unaccustomed spirit of revolutionary sisterhood. And she pitied Mme Lafarge for being a victim of tuberculosis: better a tile on the head or a bullet in the breast than such a death, she wrote, in language suggestive of the revolution. (In the event, Mme Lafarge was released from prison in the final stages of her illness, and died of the disease.) Did Rachel see herself in the other young woman who also had extraordinary eyes and a stirring voice, and literary dreams, and violent passions—the other *poitrinaire*? Did destiny, the tragedienne's familiar, grant her a premonitory chill? Had she gone to the prison in the first place seeking sensation, out of curiosity, or looking for a muse? Did she seek deliberately to be affected by another woman as her audiences were by her, as if by contagion? In James's

The Tragic Muse, Miriam Rooth, whose ambition is to be "the English Rachel," stands before Gérôme's portrait of the actress in the Théâtre-Français, preparing for her own career of self-doubling by battening on the other woman's image.

THE MOST SIGNIFICANT other woman in Rachel's life—apart from her mother and her sisters Rébecca and Sarah, and Rose, her faithful maid—was Delphine de Girardin. As the Vicomte de Launay, writing chronicles of Paris life in *La Presse*, she was an early author of Rachel's fame: one of her columns is a witty account of how the actress's visit to the Chamber of Deputies turned the seat of government into a theater, as the nation's leaders craned their necks to get a look at the woman who was sitting in the gallery in order to watch them. The three roles Delphine wrote for Rachel suggest the stages of her career: first, the heroic Jewess of the Bible, Judith; then Cleopatra; and finally Virginie de Blossac, the socialite heroine of *Lady Tartuffe*. Delphine's own life imitated art with the literalness of her husband's: and in her life story, as in Emile de Girardin's and Rachel's, character seemed more than usually implicated in a proper name.

She had been named Delphine after one of Germaine de Staël's heroines. Her mother, Sophie Gay, herself a writer, was one of the so-called "Muses" of the period of Napoleon's Directorate. Sophie was, in the appropriately lush words of a contemporary, one of "those beautiful Grecian idols that, for a moment, made the people of Paris . . . dream of Athens." Young Delphine—her mother's finest work, Arsène Houssaye wrote—was raised to play the role of another de Staël heroine, the rhapsode and poet Corinne. She reveled in it. "Distinguished and crowned by the French Academy in 1822 . . . , Mlle Gay has not ceased to celebrate in verse every important public event," Sainte-Beuve wrote without enthusiasm. "On one day, she could be seen on the top of the dome of the Panthéon, reciting her hymn to Sainte Geneviève in honor of Gros's paintings." She came even closer than that to duplicating Corinne's achievement of being crowned on the steps of the Capitol in Rome. "During a trip to Rome in 1827, she was received at the Capitol as a member of the Tiber Academy. . . . All this created the pretext for people to speak of her (and for her to think of herself) not just as an elegiac muse but as the Muse of the Fatherland." Delphine wrote tributes to her own remarkable "blonde crown"; as Mme de Girardin, she presented her distinguished self to chosen celebrities in her salon. Some gossips whispered about a lesbian relationship between her and Rachel, but on the whole they found female rivalry a more titillating theme and compelling structure.

Anecdotes stress the dramatic differences between the regal well-born blonde and the waif from the gutter: when Rachel first undertook to charm Delphine, people said, she was obliged to subject her complexion to a salon that had been decorated in acid green so as to flatter no one but the hostess. She came out sufficiently in the older woman's good graces to inspire plays and sustain a long relationship. To Delphine Rachel wrote many of her best letters, though not her most unbuttoned ones: the difference in social status, and the fact that Delphine was a journalist, easily account for the palpable constraint. (Before and after her affair with him, Rachel's allusions to "M. de Girardin" are equally distant and respectful.) *Judith*, their first joint effort, was condemned by critics disposed to hoot at the showy collaboration of two women who took themselves—and their subject, the biblical murderess—so seriously. But Delphine's friend, the poet and statesman Alphonse de Lamartine, hailed her on the occasion: "No woman has had such a virile triumph since Vittoria Colonna, whom you resemble in features, in genius, and in heroism." For better and worse, Rachel and Delphine were identified with one another and their heroines: the patriotic murderess; the passionate, dissolute, suicidal queen; and finally the hypocritical Lady Tartuffe, whom, Delphine explained, she had concocted from the characteristics of several society women she knew. Secretly annoyed by Delphine's self-importance, but effusive on paper ("I think of nothing but *Judith,*" she wrote to the author who was drafting it), Rachel honored the connection that literature and legend and their joined talents had made between them. When Delphine died, Rachel sent a wreath with a card that read, "Rachel à Cléopâtre."

IS A WOMAN MONSTROUS for being too much or too little of a woman? Too much like, or unlike, women generally? Self-hatred or dislike of her acting, or both, made Heine, who was a Jew, consistently critical of Rachel. He jeered at her pretensions to rank; backing up distaste with rationalization, he argued romantically that (like that other Jew, Felix Mendelssohn) she lacked the naïveté a great artist needs. The monster-tragedienne is more profane than sacred in a comic story Heine liked to tell about a visit to the actress at home. It ironically underwrites the image of Rachel-Phèdre as a monster, and neatly complements Musset's romantic "Souper":

> When I was to make Rachel's personal acquaintance, some years ago, friends dragged me miles out into the country, where her family had taken summer quarters. I arrive at long last, I am invited to sit

at a table, Papa Rachel appears, then Mama Rachel, la soeur Rachel, le frère Rachel. "Where is Rachel, then?" I asked. "Elle est sortie," they answered; "mais voilà toute sa famille!" At that I began to laugh as though I had gone mad. For I then remembered the anecdote of the man who goes to see a monster which was said to have been produced by crossing a carp with a rabbit. When he arrives and asks, "Where is the monster?" he is told: "We have sent it to the museum; but here are the carp and the rabbit—see for yourself!"—I shall never forget my insane laughter and the way it astonished the civilized Frenchmen around me.

S. S. Prawer points out that often, in Heine's oeuvre, "the analogy . . . for his Jewish artist figure is that of a fairground freak." The contrast drawn by the German-Jewish poet between himself, insanely laughing, and the "civilized Frenchmen" backs up the other one between the real, freakish Rachel (tellingly absent, as tellingly figured by her appalling family) and her too exalted reputation. The poet may have been playing lightly with the image of Rachel as an animal when he dismissed her elsewhere as *bête* (stupid). Was his intense dislike rooted in resentment of a woman who could make a career of flinging her Jewishness in the face of Christian society—while many ambitious Jewish men felt obliged to convert, as he had done, for the sake of their careers? Would a performer like George Eliot's Jewish princess in *Daniel Deronda*, who repudiates her father's religion, have seemed to him more or less of a monster? That the Félix family was a pack of carnival tricksters exhibiting a profitable freak merely capped the comic circumstance of a muse's having any kind of family at all. Of a Jewish muse.

The woman who charmed Chateaubriand at l'Abbaye aux Bois as a girl almost certainly never read *Le Génie du christianisme*, in which he wrote that *Phèdre* is more sublime than its classical model because "this is not a woman in the ancient mode; she is the outcast Christian, the sinner fallen alive into the hands of God: her words are the words of the damned." It was ironic that the Christianized French Phèdre should be played by a Jew—a point not lost on latter-day romantics, whose consciousness of history and their place in it was—Heine said it—ironic. The fashionable secular religion of classical tragedy, with its Jewish high priestess, seemed to many a decadent cult or a vulgar one, or both. In his journal for 1843, Victor Hugo noted a friend's scornful witticism: "M. Nestor Roqueplan said to me the other day, 'Society people go to see tragedies now as women of easy virtue go to Mass.'"

Reverence was compounded with prurient curiosity. When Raphaël Félix played Hippolyte to Rachel's Phèdre, and their younger sister Rébecca played Aricie, the incest theme was exaggerated, Gautier noted; the spectacle of two sisters as rivals for their own brother produced a deliberately bizarre effect. The sexual anxieties of the audience were exacerbated by fear of foreigners. Gérard de Nerval was inspired to sneer inaccurately in *L'Artiste* that "Father Félix, who had previously appeared as an actor at the Frankfurt theater, could have taken on the role of Theseus, and the play could have been kept entirely within the family—but that they were afraid of his Germanic pronunciation, and therefore had to accept a fourth actor, of different blood."

Napoleon too had found significant roles for his relatives to play: people might have accurately observed that this particular repetition of history was just asking to be seen as farce. There were comments about "a Rachelian progeny," and remarks on the conspicuous neglect of actors "not descended from Jacob in general and Father Félix specifically." People asked one another in genuine or mock horror, What polluting deities or demons were being worshiped at the temple of art called the Théâtre-Français?

4. STATUE

From her first performances of classical roles, everyone compared Rachel to a marble statue—because of her pallor, and the sense perhaps of her bony body's hardness; because she was haloed by the aura of the ancient Greeks, whose statues were their most enduring legacy because of the confident quiet majesty with which she stalked onto a stage and stood still for a moment before she spoke; because her eloquent rare gestures were restrained; and of course because the trope was current. By embodying an ideal of classical art, and the hieratic power of a priestess or icon, she increased that trope's currency.

She carried herself with grace and a dignity that was the more striking because she was small. Obedient to the code of gestures developed by the Comédie-Française—the hands never to be lifted above the head, no more than they were in ancient sculptures; the head to be turned only so far to the left, at precisely this juncture—she modified it in its own spirit, by further restraint. If her meager body was merely the foil to her wonderfully rich voice, that body's tension and its stillness were also compelling, conveying the sense that statues give us of space mastered and time stood still—the sense that the most profound meaning is mute. Diderot, who had loved the sculptor's art as well as the actor's, had been critical of the traditional postures of the Comédie-Française. He had much admired David Garrick in an affecting dumbshow he saw the English actor perform for friends: Diderot noticed that he deployed his body so that every pose and movement counted, invested it with meaning as a sculptor invests marble. Rachel, like Garrick and every great actor, could charge a stance or a gesture with emotion or intention, express murderous hatred by the way she pointed her finger. She avoided extravagant theatrical flourishes along with declamation; mostly, she stood still. Because one paid attention to her voice above all, her few, very controlled gestures seemed the more remarkable: it was as if a statue moved.

Gautier insisted tirelessly on the image, even when he described her play—like a film critic *avant la lettre*—as a series of frames. She had, he wrote, "no particular knowledge of the plastic arts or taste for them," but nevertheless "a profound sense of statuary." Not only her poses but her features, he thought, "arranged themselves naturally in a sculptural manner, and broke down into a series of bas-reliefs." The statuesque quality of her Phèdre moved him to ecstasies: "If only you knew how the chaste, pure folds of her white tunic delineate her noble movements, her contained gestures! How dark and deep is her eye in her mask of pale marble! How elegantly the line of her delicate throat leads to her shoulders!" His taste for women of stone can be dismissed as peculiar: in an autobiographical essay, Gautier recalled his shock on first seeing a naked female model in art school, and confessed his continuing preference for statues over fleshly women. In his novel *Mademoiselle de Maupin*, one very refined young man declares, "Sculpture is as real as anything which is utterly counterfeit can be; it is three-dimensional, casts a shadow and can be handled. Your sculptured mistress differs from your real one solely in that she is a little harder to the touch and does not speak—two very trifling defects!" Gautier's enthusiasm for Rachel is not untainted by pride in an aesthete's higher standards, his sense of his own difference from the mob of ordinary, sensual Frenchmen who found her homely. After her death he recalled that "her misunderstood beauty—for she was admirably beautiful—had nothing coquettish, pretty, in a word, French, about it. For a long time she was considered ugly, but meanwhile artists lovingly studied and represented as a paradigm of perfection that black-eyed mask taken from the very face of Melpomene!" To see a woman as a muse was the mark of an artist's ability to savor the spirit as other men relish the flesh. Gautier's love of contradictions and his ideal of art as difficulty overcome informed his admiration of Rachel: in "Art," his most celebrated lyric, he declares, "Yes, the work of art emerges more beautiful from a form that resists working, verse, marble, onyx, enamel. / No false hindrances! but to march straight, put on, O Muse, a narrow buskin."

But he was by no means the only writer to insist that Rachel was like a statue. The image was widely reiterated: it linked her to classical art and to death, to powerful primitive deities and decorative objects, to malleable Galatea and mad Medusa, whose look turns men to stone. Under the intense psychological pressure that was generated by her performances and reflected in her fame, current tropes coalesced into a single phallic object: a woman with snakes for hair who turned men rigid, an evil Other diabolically distorted and disguised. ("She is not a woman—she is a snake," wrote Charlotte Brontë.) Rachel the *pythonisse*, or prophetess, slid into Rachel the terrifying python. (Mrs. Siddons before her, and George Sand in her own time, were also called pythonesses.) The image served to marry—among other apparent opposites—the savage and the sacred; it posed and seemed ready to resolve the paradox of an artifact that could act. The critic Paul de Saint-Victor, her sister Lia's lover, would reflect in marmoreal imagery on Rachel's whole career, after her death: "The entrance of Mlle Rachel, draped in the tunic of a statue, into the theater of her time, with its new plays and poetic license, was a revelation and an enchantment, and had the effect produced by the great Venus de Milo which, scarcely retrieved from the dust, reduced all would-be masterpieces to an inferior rank." Subjecting herself to the rigidities of old plays and selecting new roles to suit her statue image, she rang changes on the theme of a woman hard and soft. In Soumet's *Jeanne d'Arc*, in 1846, she wore a cunning costume of metal and cloth. Gérard de Nerval wrote that she had been "seduced" by the inferior play only because it gave her an opportunity to "realize," in armor, a well-known statue of the Maid of Orléans sculpted by the Princesse Marie, a daughter of Louis-Philippe. Rachel was beautiful, he wrote, "in physiognomy and in attitude. The steel armor, however implausible it was in a prison, suits her to perfection." Implausible and unnatural, she was on her way, as Jeanne d'Arc, to being recognized as the embodied emblem of a glorious, virtuous, martial, monarchical France. When France, within two years, became a republic, and Marianne replaced Jeanne as the nation's symbol, artists competing in a government-sponsored contest for designs of stamps and public monuments were advised to find their model in Rachel. Reiterated and reified, the sculptural trope insisted that she was something between an artist and a work of art, between individual and representative, person and representation— therefore that she was unique and not quite human.

When Mlle Contat had giggled that Talma, in his toga, looked just like

Rachel, statue by Antoine-
Laurent Dantan, 1839

a statue, the point of the simile had been quite different. Talma in his plain republican cloth, in 1789, had been the inspiring image of a citizen; half a century later, Rachel evoked another set of associations. First of all, the severely elegant costume Gautier described her as wearing for *Phèdre* was a far cry from Camille's simple toga. The beauties of her diadem and veil, her peplum sprinkled with gold, her tunic and purple mantle, all in the best possible taste, were admired for their gorgeousness, and cited as proof that she was every inch the queen. Theatrical togas had lost their simplicity after Napoleon's Roman fever converted the classical style into a mode of luxury. Forty years before Rachel first played Phèdre, when the Empress Joséphine had presided over a contest between rival tragedy queens rendering the role, she underwrote the lavish costumes of Mlles Duchesnois and George: a blue cashmere mantle, simply embroidered, for George and a red one with stars for Duchesnois together required more than a dozen yards of fabric, and their tunics called for an additional half-dozen yards of percale. Talma's costume had made a political point about change and republicanism, and promised new heroic action, but in the 1840s the so-called revival of high tragedy looked like an exercise in intransigence and nostalgia—art for artifice's sake, or artificiality's.

Rachel was sometimes compared to a statue in order to make the point that she was implausible and false. Heine declared himself disgusted by the ghosts that stalked the stage of the Théâtre-Français; Baudelaire, in 1846, described the house on the rue de Richelieu as "the most deserted theater in the universe," where audiences were persuaded to believe in people who never existed. He attacked arid classicism in realism's name, asking, "Have you ever seen tragic persons eat or drink?" Writers of tragedy, he wrote, distorted the truth of human nature: they "have . . . created their own temperament, whereas the majority of mankind have to *submit* to theirs." The fleshy Italian actress Adelaide Ristori, whose popularity helped Rachel decide to flee Paris for America in 1855, was of the opinion—she set it down in her memoirs—that her rival clung to the classical repertoire and the toga largely in order to conceal her frightful skinniness. But to those inclined to suspend disbelief, Rachel was a Tragic Muse in her toga—a rarefied idea. Some of the medallions and miniatures and statues artists made of Rachel were realistic, recognizable portraits; but the reiterated statue image linked her to an abstract ideal or idea. The statue that Talma, in his toga, recalled would have been a portrait bust of a Greek or Roman hero or statesman; but the marble figure of a woman would most likely be a goddess or an allegorical representation, or something in between. Anyone could gather as much at the Louvre (where, they said, the young Rachel had been taken by her father to study the statues' poses). Marina Warner writes that "the female form tends . . . to symbolic interpretation; the male resists anonymous universality more robustly, and often manages to retain individuality even while calling higher things to mind." The marble figures sculpted (around Rachel's time) to guard the tomb of Napoleon at the Invalides might be marshaled to illustrate the insight: while the forms of men represent historical individuals, the alternating images of women are allegorical. Tragedy *was* a statue by the mid-nineteenth century: in the portraits of Rachel by Amaury-Duval and Gérôme, the stone statue of a muse or goddess or priestess stands beside the central figure to insist on the point.

To compare a living woman to a statue is to freeze and fix and control her, also to aggrandize her beyond mere womanhood into abstraction or even goddess-head: "Rachel is an antique statue, which is to say, something like ideal beauty," wrote one commentator. The comparison serves to deprive her of individuality; it also makes the connection between Woman and stone. Melpomene blends easily into Galatea, into Medusa. Either Rachel, imagined as stone, was unfeeling and stony, or her baleful look turned those who looked at her to stone, or both. "Her gaze, the eyes enlarged by sorrow, expressed the most violent despair; it was the head of Medusa," one admirer wrote of her. Another image managed to confound the actress and the audience, the victim and the aggressor, by wreathing together the woman and the snake: writing of Rachel as Cleopatra, one critic claimed that he could perceive, "beneath the sculptural folds of her tunic, the moving serpents that sting *our* breast" (my italics). The persistent statue image blurred the distinction between the mover and the thing being moved. In America, a critic characterized Rachel's Camille as "a severe classic figure, a polychrome statue, gliding past the columns"; her Phèdre was admired "for the display of the statuesque grace which is one of Rachel's most marvellous attributes." The critic concluded in some confusion that "Rachel is certainly . . . the first of sculptors," adding that "she seems a goddess chiselled by Phidias in ivory and gold." Repeated, elaborated, literalized and turned on itself, the statue image conjured her strangeness most of all: goddess or priestess of a classical past, marble, not flesh, artist and artifact, she stood for the joined othernesses of Woman and Art, and beyond that for the notion that both were more and less than real. The statue image so often used to class her with the immortals could also condemn her as ephemeral: an 1852 article in the *Revue et gazette des théâtres* described the Comédie-Française as the temple of a "cult of abstractions, of which Rachel is a lively but fleeting expression." A sign of an abstraction, she seemed by virtue of her corporeality to partake of abstraction's immateriality: illogically, incontrovertibly, the comparison with a marble statue insisted on it.

IN THE NINETEENTH CENTURY, genteel ladies entertained themselves and their admirers at parties with *tableaux vivants*. As novelists delight in showing, the game pointed up the emphasis on display and disguise of the female body in social life, and the habit of hypocrisy. Ladies gender-bound to role-playing were obliged to present smooth, objectified public selves, concealing and misrepresenting—and broadly hinting at—their hidden selves. In *Daniel Deronda*, Gwendolen Harleth chooses to play the role of Hermione, the queen who is turned to stone and then to flesh again in Shakespeare's *A Winter's Tale*, in a *tableau vivant* accompanied by music. She is poised at the

Rachel, ivory statue by Jean-Auguste
Barre, exhibited at the Salon of 1849

point where the queen must come magically and dramatically back to life
when a too emphatic chord on the piano—played by her mother—causes a
little door in the wall to fly open; it conceals a painting of a "dead face"
that holds inexpressible terrors for Gwendolen, and she is struck stone-still
in terror in earnest. *Daniel Deronda* explores, among other things, the erotics
of dominance and submission in which coldness, real or assumed, inspires
intense feeling.

The games played in English country houses had their more overtly
salacious counterparts in very different social events like Louis Véron's celebrated suppers, for which naked girls were hired to assume provocative *poses
plastiques.* A social and literary cliché, the statue-woman was susceptible to

different emphases. Germaine de Staël described the heroine of *Corinne* as "a woman renowned only for the gifts of genius," notable for "her tall full figure reminiscent of Greek statuary." Balzac, on the other hand, invidiously compares his hard-eyed and heartless society women to paintings, statues, and—the transition is smooth—to consummate actresses, that is, hypocrites. In Mérimée's story "La Vénus d'Ille," a statue—a primitive goddess dug up by archaeologists—comes sufficiently to life to attack men who don't respect what it stands for, the power of woman and love. In George Sand's *Lélia* (1833), the poet Sténio hotly adores the tormented, haughty, unresponsive heroine because she is cold and pale as death, and unearthly: "Pale as one of those marble statues which guard tombs, you no longer had anything terrestrial about you," he writes to her. Lélia transcends both the earth and death, stands for love and flees it; she is frigid, as the gossips said Sand herself was. (Creature and creator both have duly been read as Phallic Woman.) Lélia's stony appearance indicates her contempt for the flesh, lends her glamour, and suggests her spiritual power: "With her impassive air, her pale, cold brow, and her rich clothing, she resembled one of those alabaster madonnas that Italian women devotedly cover with silken robes and brilliant chiffon. Like the marble Virgin, Lélia was insensitive to her beauty and charm. She was indifferent to the eyes fixed upon her. She despised all the men too much to take pride in their praise." Her lack of responsiveness is a sign of her superiority to the things and the people of this world. At a ball, she is aware that all eyes are on her; refusing to be a mere object of the gaze, she looks back boldly at her admirers—as if she were at a theater, Sand writes, watching the people displaying themselves there. Among them she finds her lost sister, the courtesan Pulchérie, who is at once her antithesis and her second self. When Pulchérie agrees to pretend to be Lélia in bed, so as to fool Lélia's would-be lover—as Rachel would urge Sarah Félix to do, when she wanted to trick Prince Napoleon—she confirms Lélia's own theatricality, her being both herself and not herself, false and true. Known to be the work of the notorious George Sand, the novel invites reading as a spectacle of the (pseudonymous, role-playing) author doubling herself, the woman writer taking on, taking and making over, the meanings of the image of the statue-woman, by merging her own image into it.

RACHEL SEEMED TO BE PLAYING with the image with similar aplomband authority, offstage and on. In one of the letters written for public consumption that she sent back from Florence in 1851, she marvelled that she had been able to "reproduce the folds so beautifully chiseled by the tools of

Michelangelo, Canova, Lorenzetto, Morelli, etc., before having seen them."
She put her self-image through its paces: "But it is my pride to have divined
them; the daughter of the people knew how to drape herself in the antique
fashion, and the Romans have just admired and applauded me with fury, on
many evenings the crowns and bouquets have hidden the floor of the stage."
Houssaye says she told him that as a child traveling through the Alps, she
jumped off the family wagon and rolled herself in the snow "for love of
whiteness," crying that she wanted to turn into a statue. Reiterated, the
figure called attention to Rachel's insistence on her likeness to images, her
making an image of herself. The double role written for her in *Valéria et
Lycisca*, a play about sin in high places in the decadent late Roman Empire,
traded not only on the notion of her moral doubleness—Rachel as queen and
courtesan—but also on the pervasive idea of the statue-woman. One reviewer
attacked her for imitating the sculptor Clésinger (Sand's son-in-law), who had
exhibited twin busts of Rachel as Comedy and Tragedy: the model was accused of aping her own portraits. (For his part, Clésinger was criticized for
giving Tragedy the features of the actress: "he made the mistake of thinking
Tragedy was the same thing as a tragedienne—even though she be Mlle
Rachel," Edmond and Jules de Goncourt remarked.) A grudgingly good
notice of her long-awaited performance of Tisbe in Hugo's *Angelo* includes
an innovative elaboration on the statue image: "It was a rare and moving
spectacle, that first act, when the tragedienne entered the scene, the dead
woman who wanted to live, the marble moving toward the men and women.
It was almost like the Commander's entrance at Don Juan's supper—only in
this case, it was the statue who was afraid." The avenging statue from hell
and the carousing victim struck stone-dead are one: the image suggests the
writer's disturbed sense that Rachel was acting out her own desires and also
someone else's.

The ground floor of the Musée d'Orsay in Paris testifies to the hold
marble had on the nineteenth-century imagination: with a mixture of self-
conscious wit and despair, the sculptors of Rachel's time grasped at eternity,
denying that flesh is not stone, regretting it, defying the fact, always asser-
tively going their predecessors and their contemporaries one better and big-
ger—or two or three. The silent, overstrenuous chorus laments mortality and
history, and links up dreams and reality, sex and death, in the obsessive image
of marble Woman. One recalls the painting (not in this museum) by Ma-
gritte, in which a famous verse by Baudelaire, their contemporary, is spelled
out in crumbling stone letters: "Je suis belle, ô mortels, comme un rêve de
pierre."

•   •   •

THE IMAGE OF A WOMAN who turns from stone to flesh or the other
way round, or who turns men to stone, reflects anxieties about creation,
sexuality, representation, identity. Primary, perhaps, in the nineteenth century, were the particular anxieties of the men who trained their eyes on
female performers, and the men who were trained as artists by copying from
a nude model, usually the only woman, as well as the sole undressed person,
in the room. The group of artist-model-statue, so interesting to writers from
Balzac to James, is related to the group of actress-audience-role: in both,
Woman's mutability is crucial. Nina Auerbach has argued that sexually repressed Victorian men, anxious about the limits of their power, were haunted
by the image of a demonic woman who could enlarge, distort, and transform
herself, turning the natural unnatural, as in a nightmare. As I see it, the
women stars of the nineteenth century fascinated men and women by being
self-contradictory images of womanly power and its containment. Taking on
different roles and selves, they made the female body seem now the image
of a wild idea, then a container of a vulnerable human soul, then again a
commodity. Woman as Image of Nature and Object of Art was complicated
by Woman as Actress, and by romantic ideas of embodied genius, of Art as
Nature's equal and opposite.

In *Crisis in the Life of an Actress* (1848), the Danish philosopher Søren
Kierkegaard meditates on these themes. His essay's avowed scope is modest:
it sets out to be a tribute to one of Rachel's contemporaries, the Danish
actress Johanne Luise Heiberg, having been inspired by her performance, at
the age of thirty-four, of the role of Juliet, which she had first played at not
quite sixteen. Kierkegaard was an acquaintance of the actress, who was known
as Fru Heiberg—no less than the King of Denmark himself having resolved
the national problem of whether she was to be called Madame, *à la française*,
as most actresses were, or Fru, the Danish equivalent of Mrs. Like Mrs.
Siddons's and unlike Rachel's, her stage name marked her married respectability; it furthermore acknowledged the stature of her husband, a writer and
prominent member of the Copenhagen intellectual and artistic community
whose importance augmented hers. Kierkegaard's respectful admiration of
Heiberg's wife strengthens his argument that her mature Juliet is superior to
the one she had created as a girl. He begins by observing that actresses tend
to please by their "playfulness, liveliness, luck, youthfulness"—he does not
quite say sexual attractiveness—which appeal naturally to men. Precisely for
that reason, he goes on, the actress is challenged as an artist only after nature
and time have denied her those assets. He acclaims Fru Heiberg for brilliantly

rising to the challenge, for becoming the antagonist of time itself. Like time, an actress works transformations, metamorphoses; her art is to go against nature. Altering herself, she takes the spectator beyond the simple, natural, vulgar delights a youthful woman offers, thrills him by the sense of a challenge risen to, and met. The thirty-four-year-old Fru Heiberg is a more wonderful Juliet than the younger one, Kierkegaard concludes, because she shows that imagination and art prevail over the flesh.

Such a view evolves logically into *fin de siècle* decadence—Huysmans's preference for art that goes against nature, spelled out in *A Rebours* (1884), and the aestheticism of the Goncourt brothers or Oscar Wilde. Bernhardt's admirers would adore her for flying in nature's face when, playing Jeanne d'Arc at sixty-five, she stoutly responded, when the inquisitors asked her age, "Nineteen." On the other hand, Kierkegaard also sounds like his mid-century contemporaries—Gautier admiring Rachel although she had nothing merely pretty or French about her, or Janin (the former lover of buxom Mlle George!) making a point of his admiration of Rachel's "flat chest." Like these Parisian men of the world, the Danish philosopher is boastful of a taste that marks his superiority to ordinary sensual men. His high regard for the actress is based on an analogous superiority of hers. He honors Fru Heiberg's struggle against time and physical decay, admires the daring and the effective magic of her self-transformation into a young heroine nothing like her real self.

TIME AND TALK together changed Rachel's image: she turned from a pure chaste child into a dangerous mature woman, from Camille to Phèdre, from a princess of the theater to the powerful queen who in 1854 could flatly refuse the Empress Eugénie's special request that she perform *Marie Stuart*, instead of *Cinna*. (The request was brought to her by Fould, the government minister, after ten o'clock in the evening: she claims to have told him that the unfortunate queen of Scots got on her nerves, whereupon "the minister understood me and didn't insist; in return for his tact, I offered him a cup of tea; we then discussed Sebastopol.") But Rachel never had to grapple with the natural changes predicted for her, vindictively, by Mlle George, who had lived to be fat, old, poor, and superfluous. The older actress had complained enviously to Victor Hugo after Rachel refused to assist at her benefit: "Look, I'm all for Rachel," she told him. "She's a clever one. How she brings to heel all these comical Comédie-Française people! She reviews her contracts, makes sure she has warm dressing rooms, time off, and mountains of money; then, once everything has been signed, she says, 'Oh, by the way, I forgot to mention that I'm four and a half months pregnant and I won't be able to perform for five months!' She has it all figured out. If I had her ways, I wouldn't be starving like a dog on the streets." And in her anger George predicted that for all her brilliance on the stage and her equally brilliant backstage maneuverings, the other actress would end quite as wretchedly as she.

Rachel did grow ill, and paler and more shadowy, but she only got to make believe she was old. She was brave enough, at just twenty-six, to undertake the reverse of Fru Heiberg's masquerade: she put gray in her long droopy curls and made lines in her face with makeup for the role of Athalie, startling Paris by the sight of a woman who willingly pretended to be uglier and older than she was. In October of the following year, she played Néron's mother in *Britannicus,* prompting Gautier to wonder whether she proposed to regress instead of going forward, and end up taking the roles of babies at the breast. Appreciative as he was of her flexibility, he counseled nevertheless that she try to stay young as long as she could. If an actress is to make herself a sign of transformative power, she is well advised to transform herself in one direction only: the power to alter the self and change it into a sign is most powerful—most pleasing—when mortality is defied, not invited.

5. SYMBOLIC MOVES

The 1847–48 season was a strenuous one for Rachel. During the summer, in the early months of her second pregnancy, she had left the country retreat she called "Ma Santé" ("My Good Health") to tour England and Scotland. In the fall she retired to the country to read the mixed reviews of *Cléopâtre,* await the birth of her child, and write letters to Buloz, the director of the Comédie-Française, who was trying to force her to play the full nine months in Paris that her contract required, and also to compensate the company for her past absences. Shortly after the court pronounced in favor of Buloz, the government fell.

Rachel's flirtation with the cousins Napoleon in England in 1847 must have seemed to her, in retrospect, shrewdly prescient. During that summer, opposition to Louis-Philippe's government had begun to rally around the cause of electoral reform. Dissidents had held a series of "banquets" designed to circumvent the laws against free assembly, and revolution finally broke out when a banquet planned for Paris was forbidden by the apprehensive authorities. Workers rioted; barricades were thrown up; people were killed; bodies were paraded in the streets. At the end of the month the king abdicated in

Rachel as Athalie, 1847, photo illustration from Jules Janin's *Rachel et la tragédie*

favor of his grandson, and fled, disguised, to England, with the queen. "Your Majesty, it's time to leave," Rachel's old friend Adolphe Crémieux had told him on 23 February, escorting the king to his carriage. Caricatures of Louis-Philippe bustling off with his umbrella delighted the large but fatally divided camp of his enemies.

The Comédie-Française, renamed Théâtre de la République, had closed its doors during the most severe days of street fighting, but opened them soon again; people were not in the mood for stage entertainment, but the management, hurting financially, was eager to feature its star—and make a show of her obedience. Rachel begged to be excused from scheduled performances, saying the doctors had ordered her to rest for six weeks after childbirth. She was suspected of lying, and of maneuvering to arrange the replacement of Buloz with her candidate, Lockroy, who promised to be more indulgent of her demands for long vacations and short seasons. Lockroy was indeed installed by the new republican government on 3 March. Three days later, probably at his suggestion, Rachel made a dramatic appearance onstage after Act IV of *Horace*, celebrating the people's victory over the king by reciting the hymn of revolution, *La Marseillaise*.

It was electrifying. Gautier enumerated her perfections: the menace and power of the pale mask, the black eyes agleam with suffering and revolt, the brows twisted like serpents, the nostrils flaring as if to inhale the air of freedom upon emerging from a fetid prison. When she lifted her arm with a gesture of "tranquil violence," he wrote, letting the sleeve of her tunic fall back, it seemed to all the world as if Nemesis, sculpted by an invisible artist, were emerging from a block of Grecian marble. She neither sang nor recited, but spoke in a musical antique manner that could be described only with a Grecian term, as a *mélopée*. It was the word that had been used of the traditional tragic style of declamation that Rachel—and Talma and Adrienne Lecouvreur before her—had rejected for more "natural" acting. But these measured, dignified cadences transcended both declamation and natural speech. It was indeed the tocsin of revolution that made her voice vibrate, the fever of vengeance that made her frail body tremble, Gautier wrote. At the end of the hymn she collapsed on her knees, as if overcome by the sacred idea of the nation; she buried herself in the folds of the tricolor. The bravos and the stampeding shook the theater; the applause was like thunder.

IT WAS THE APOGEE of her career as a symbol. The British impresario Lumley believed that a symbol was her model: for the *Marseillaise*, he wrote, "she took her attitude from the figure of liberty among the victories on the

Cover of sheet music portraying Rachel as *La Marseillaise*

Arc de Triomphe." He had in mind the famous muscular fury known as *La Marseillaise* in the high-relief carving by François Rude. Celebrating the partisans of 1792, it had been installed on the Arc after the revolution of 1830, which had installed the regime that the revolution of 1848 overthrew. Embodying Revolution for her generation, Rachel staked the claim—as Rude's statue did—that its spirit was high, irrepressible, and immortal. The slender actress hardly resembled the muscular allegorical female figure on the Arc; but if we set Annekov's description of Rachel's black-mouthed Camille beside the face of Rude's marble fury we can get some idea of the sense she conveyed of the creature possessed by violent passion, intent on inspiring it in others. Her blazing eyes and extravagantly distorted mouth recalled the Gorgon. At the same time, as she chanted the patriotic hymn, she gave republicanism the sanction of high art. She also presented herself more directly than ever before as France, embodied: not its mock queen now, but a child of the people who had suffered and earned the right to represent the spirit of the whole nation. She did thirty-seven performances of the hymn in the Théâtre de la République, and more in the suburbs for benefits organized by George Sand. A trace of her popular appeal is retained in a small, crude terra-cotta figure (found near Metz, and now in a private collection) of a strong-faced stalwart woman—a mature and very Jewish-looking Rachel—on her knees, holding up the flag. In April 1848, the editor of *La Fraternité*, the organ of the communist party, requested tickets for her performance for his wife and daughter. He himself had been overcome when he heard the patriotic hymn of "our great tragedienne," he wrote; "if her heart and soul are like her play," he added a little warily, "I acknowledge her as the first Republican of the French Republic."

Foreigners had no trouble identifying Rachel with republican France, reborn. In Germany, young radicals like Carl Schurz were cheered by reports of her "throwing her audiences into paroxysms of patriotic frenzy," celebrating the fall of a king. For visitors who came to Paris to see the revolution, Rachel chanting *La Marseillaise* was high on the list of spectacles. Arthur Penrhyn Stanley, the future Dean of Westminster, was wildly enthusiastic. He was impressed by "her great simplicity, and the total absence of rant" in Ponsard's *Lucrèce;* when she followed up the play with *La Marseillaise* he was stunned by the transformation:

> she came forward for the "Marseillaise," in white, as before. It is difficult to describe it. She had seemed to be a woman—she became a *"being"*—sublime irony, prophetic enthusiasm, demoniacal fierce-

ness, succeeded each other like flashes of lightning. And then, with
a solemn march, she advanced at the last stanza to the tricolour
standard and knelt, folding it in her embrace, as if with a determination that nothing should ever part her from it—a love, an adora-
tion as if it were an animated creature. It was very grand—Morier
declared that it was itself enough to annihilate a monarchy. Madame
de M. thought it the "most shocking sight she had ever seen."
Certainly it did seem as if the expression of such feelings was beyond
what the occasion called for. Had Nero fallen instead of Louis Philippe, the impression conveyed could not have been more ferocious.
They say Rachel enters into it herself heart and soul, and is so
wrought up by it that she faints away when it is over.

Samson (after Diderot) might deplore this kind of passionate acting that leads
to a collapse, but the general public was thrilled. As she knelt to adore the
French flag "as if it were an animated creature," the exhausted actress seemed
to strip herself of her own creatureliness, to be somehow elemental, a "being." To the English especially—Arnold and Brontë as well as Stanley—
Rachel seemed remarkable first of all for her strangeness, for being at once
human and not human, physical as well as spiritual, a woman but somehow
male. Gautier had written that she made Rouget de Lisle's "very male hymn
of such great musical thrust" more virile than ever, "more energetic, stronger,
more fierce, and more impressive, by the incisive sharpness, the rancorous
thunderings, the metallic flashes of her diction."

Gautier became sardonic when she added a tricolor belt to her costume,
altering her persona, as he saw it, from Nemesis into a provincial mayor, or
a police commissioner on parade. And the American Ralph Waldo Emerson,
impressed by Rachel's *Marseillaise*, observed it did not bear hearing more
than once. But by its very lack of subtlety the spectacle claimed world-
historical importance. Among the foreigners who thrilled to it was the
German-Jewish writer Fanny Lewald, best remembered now as a friend of
Heine and recorder of his conversational sallies. Lewald took Rachel most
seriously. As Charlotte Brontë would do three years later, she responded with
special intensity to a fellow woman artist, and for her as for Brontë it was
crucial that Rachel became something other than human on the stage, as if
to reflect the otherness that the woman in the audience saw in her and sensed
in herself: "Rachel is the personified Marseillaise become human, the concept
of the struggle for freedom incarnate," Lewald wrote. "On and on 'and the
word became flesh!' resounded in my soul! Yes! The word should do that! It

Rachel as *La Marseillaise,* terra-cotta statuette, ca. 1848

should, it must become flesh in order to be! And there is also good in that this Marseillaise become flesh is a Jewess, the daughter of the oppressed." The evening Lewald saw her and was moved to quote the New Testament, Rachel played Pauline, the convert to Christianity in *Polyeucte,* before she declaimed *La Marseillaise.* The performance seemed to dramatize the difficult coexistences of the daughter of the oppressed and the *reine de théâtre,* the Jewess and the new Christian, and in doing so to confirm miraculous transformations of the literal into the metaphorical and back again: of the word becoming the flesh, and the flesh becoming the word—of the actress become an idea incarnate, her speech-act not merely affirming but making historical reality, and identifying her with the nation.

A generation earlier, another woman, German-Jewish like Fanny Lewald and bearing the same Hebrew name as Rachel, had speculated excitedly in her journal that it was possible for a Jewish woman undistinguished by beauty to represent, therefore to be, anything. Rahel Levin Varnhagen, the friend of Goethe, had argued that unlike a princeling, who represents his hereditary lands and people, or a Goethe who can speak for all of Germany, a woman like herself, in and as herself, stands for nothing at all; therefore she can make what she wants of herself. Rahel's Jewish family was very different from Rachel's, being German, wealthy, urban, and well-placed; and unlike Rachel, Rahel lacked a remarkable gift. Nevertheless, it is not only the nominal similarity between the two women that makes Rahel's private reflections (as re-presented by Hannah Arendt) seem relevant to Rachel's condition as a representation. Rahel, who was celebrated as a *salonnière*, struggled to erase her Jewishness and to make herself up as a member of the new aristocracy of the cultured that emerged in Europe in the years after Napoleon, after the old hierarchies had collapsed. This "class" was peculiarly inviting to Jews. It was cosmopolitan and international; its characteristics were acquired, not inherited; and its members might quite naturally, as it were, include a people that identified itself as "of the book."

The two Rachels were in many ways opposites—the important difference between them being that Rachel the tragedienne had what Rahel thought she lacked, a great gift (and great confidence in it). Where Rahel aimed credulously at assimilation, Rachel flaunted her Jewishness as something that looked good on her, therefore was quite good enough for anyone. She disdained to marry a gentile aristocrat; she made no claim to be a member of a cultural aristocracy, only to embody the best that had been written and felt. As a star who took care to keep her persona present in the minds of her audiences, she stood (metonymically) for the Jews, all the while standing (metaphorically) for Camille or Hermione or Phèdre, Corneille and Racine and Tragedy, the Classics, and Art. So doing, legitimizing herself as no actress, gentile or Jew, had done before, she raised questions about what it means for a person to stand for something. They were the quintessential questions that nourished the romantic distaste for the bourgeoisie, and encouraged the romantic interest in actors.

The hero of Goethe's *Wilhelm Meister's Apprenticeship* becomes infatuated with an actress and runs off with a theatrical troupe because he desires to develop himself "harmoniously," in the manner of a nobleman. He explains:

> A nobleman can and must be someone who represents by his appearance, whereas the burgher simply is, and when he tries to put on an appearance, the effect is ludicrous and in bad taste. The nobleman should act and achieve, the burgher must labor and create, developing some of his capabilities in order to be useful. . . . I have an irresistible desire to attain the harmonious development of my personality such as was denied me by my birth.

Therefore he resolves to be an actor.

R ACHEL BEGAN the summer of 1848 with a tour of the Low Countries and Switzerland, where she performed *La Marseillaise* along with her standard repertoire. At the end of June, an insurrection of workers, provoked by a government decree, was suppressed by the troops of General Cavaignac; three thousand people were killed, and fifteen thousand transported without trial. The Second Republic ceased being the party of the working people, and as the Catholic, legitimist Party of Order struggled with the conservative bourgeoisie for control, the way for Louis-Napoleon was prepared: he would be elected president of the republic in December. The nervous government underwrote the tour of "Citizen Rachel" to the French provinces in an effort to retain or regain confidence. For her part, she was hopeful that chanting *La Marseillaise* would prove more profitable than touring Holland had been. But France, when her traveling troupe reached it in June, was distressingly unstable: "the provinces are stricken, as Paris is," she wrote Sarah from Liège, a week before the bloody June Days. In the south, *La Marseillaise* was generally well received: pure-blooded reactionaries were heard to hum the anthem as they exited the theater. But there were a few violent protests in the streets: two years later, when she refused to play Charlotte Corday, the murderess of Marat, in a new drama written for her by Ponsard, Rachel would deplore having acted as an agent of the revolutionary government and therefore as an "angel of death." (The actor Edmond Got suspected she had other reasons for refusing the role, which Mlle Judith accepted: he observed waspishly in his journal that *La Grande* was "ever attentive to the capricious winds of success," but had "small interest in republican issues.")

She was convincing in the role of Muse of the Republic, and her legend was embellished with new stories. People liked to tell how she had graciously chanted *La Marseillaise* in a forest, at the request of some soldiers who had helped her out after a carriage accident on a country road. There was praise of her charities in the provincial papers—also some complacent right-wing reflection that, at least in the theater, royalty still lived. Rachel herself would claim, after the revolution, that her prime allegiance had always been to her profession and to the Théâtre-Français. Preparing one of her many professions of loyalty to the company, she charged Lockroy to recall "that I sang *La Marseillaise* only out of devotion, at a more than critical moment, since without it, after all, the Théâtre-Français would have perished like so many others in that shipwreck of revolution." If her timely fervor of patriotism was self-serving and pragmatic, it was also appropriate to the shifting state she served.

In 1846–47, she had been applauded at home and abroad as Jeanne d'Arc, symbol of Catholic, monarchical France. In 1848–49, chanting *La Marseillaise*, she persuasively embodied the counter-image of Marianne. In 1852, she would appear at the Théâtre-Français as the Muse of History, welcoming Louis-Napoleon's Second Empire. Too bad she didn't live to see—to be—the Third Republic! Rachel's politics of expediency and theatricality reflected the dominant mode. The darling of the right had always been a dubious version of the Catholic Maid of Orléans; the "child of the people" was expected to whine that "the republic is costing me dearly." One did not have to be against the people, of course, to deplore the violence and bloodshed of the June Days and the torching of the Rothschild château, as Rachel did, or to pray as she said she did that God would preserve France, since men knew only how to destroy. And it is only reasonable for a *grande tragédienne*, reduced from Racine to Rouget de Lisle, to write, as she did in a letter, that she hoped for a king to release her from endless recitations of *La Marseillaise*. And only reasonable for an actress to love a good show. On the first of October 1852, Rachel wrote with evident excitement to her young son Alexandre, "Tomorrow the republic exits France, our climate does not favor it. Tomorrow will be the Empire, tomorrow Paris will be bright with lights, I am sorry, my sweet little angel, that you will not be able to help me hang up my lanterns. I am a bit ill, I will unfortunately not be able to go to the Champs-Elysées to see the Emperor's entry into Paris."

She had always admired an emperor, and enthusiastically she helped arrange the November gala to celebrate the new regime. Houssaye had written a poem for the occasion, based on a slogan taken from a speech by the new leader; the plan was for Rachel to recite it after a performance of Molière's *Le Malade imaginaire.* But she wrote to urge Houssaye to change the program, and substitute Corneille's political play, *Cinna, ou la clémence d'Auguste*—with her in one of her best-known roles, as Emilie. Comparing a recent act of the French head of state to Augustus's clemency, she praised "our Emperor Louis." Furthermore, she added, even though His Imperial Highness would not be in his box until the middle of the tragedy, playing Emilie would give her the energy for interpreting Houssaye's verses, and making sure they were heard. The mix of flattery and subtle put-down is professional; the desire to shine in the imperial eyes is clear. More interesting than either is the actress's apparent conviction that playing the one role would give her the verve for the other.

She did her reliable, rousing Emilie. Then, in her all-purpose toga, standing beside the flag she had held while chanting *La Marseillaise*—the flagpole that was surmounted, now, by an imperial eagle—she reappeared as the Muse of History. Respectfully, she intoned the tinny stanzas that hymned the new imperialism, Houssaye's confused, toadying verses ringing variations on Louis-Napoleon's self-serving phrase, *L'empire, c'est la paix.* (The poem describes Phidias as another Prometheus, sculptor of a goddess whose feet are on the ground.) If Rachel had trouble emoting lines that did not even aspire to Corneillian eloquence, she had none at all accepting the diamond bracelet that Louis-Napoleon sent her with his note of thanks and congratulations.

MORE RELEVANT than Rachel's own politics are the changes in her career that accompanied the political changes in France. *La Marseillaise,* Gautier noted, was her first modern role. She went on from it to plays by Dumas and Hugo, and virtually a second career as a romantic actress. In her brief maturity, she increasingly took control of her performances and her image, using men like Lockroy and Houssaye and her brother Raphaël to front for her. She created an ever more authoritative persona.

In December 1848, Louis-Napoleon was elected president of the republic. As if to reflect the apparent abatement of national tensions, Rachel appeared in her trademark toga the following March as a clever and seductive Roman courtesan, in an insubstantial, amusing playlet by Armand Barthet, *Le Moineau de Lesbie.* Playing the mistress of the poet Catullus, she traded wryly on her classical aura: Lesbie was a far cry from what Rachel referred to as the "solemnities" of *Phèdre.* On 14 April 1849, she made her decisive shift into contemporary drama, in the consummately self-reflexive role of an actress that the popular playwrights Eugène Scribe and Ernest Legouvé had written for her. *Adrienne Lecouvreur* was a huge success: at every one of the nineteen performances before Rachel left in May for her long vacation, the box office took in five thousand francs. 1849 was the year Rachel was described in the *Revue des deux mondes* as "ce que les Anglais appellent *une étoile (a star)."*

Playing a classical tragedienne in a modern melodrama was something like a rehearsal for the romantic repertoire, in which women victimized by passionate love rise, like Adrienne, to heroic, pathetic self-sacrifice. In January 1850, Rachel made her debut in *Mlle de Belle-Isle* by Alexandre Dumas. The role had been created by Mlle Mars in 1839, and audiences still had fond memories of the older actress, who had died only three years before. There were unpleasant comparisons to her predecessor's charm and beauty, but Rachel successfully made the role her own. Loyal Gautier called her superior to Mars. (And Dumas never forgave her for doing only seventeen performances.) The triumph was followed up in May when Rachel played a Venetian courtesan, Tisbe, in Hugo's *Angelo*—once again, quite in her own *grande tragédienne*'s mode, a brilliant re-creation. Marvelling at her brilliance, Gautier modified his favorite trope, praising the way she had changed from a classical statue into a Renaissance painting, with all the warm tones of the Venetian school. Her sister Rébecca played against her; it was to celebrate their joint triumph that Rachel surprised her with the extravagant gift of a fully furnished house.

There was almost universal applause for Rachel's breadth and versatility as an actress, and her condescension in performing the works of her contemporaries, as only she among actors had so long refused to do. But romantic drama had already gone into decline: rather than changing, herself, in performing Hugo and Dumas, she could fairly be seen as conferring on their plays canonical status and literary-classical cachet. Her success with *La Marseillaise* had perhaps emboldened her to make any text over in her own image. Did it make her want to be a symbol of all of France, the romantic party as well as the classical? Or did she "stoop" so as to conquer in nonclassical plays in order to save the Comédie-Française from its abiding financial problems? Did she act under the gun of a legal judgment the management was once more seeking against her, for the long vacations when she made money only for herself? Or was she responding to an inviting artistic challenge? Was she finally taking charge of her own career? Or merely acquiescing in the role of Louis-Napoleon's cat's-paw, and helping him rehearse, within the Théâtre-Français, the larger coup he was planning to make of the nation?

Some critics and most actors took that view of the Prince-President's appointment, in November 1849, of Arsène Houssaye as director of the

Comédie-Francaise. Houssaye himself disingenuously described it as simply the replacement of a parliamentary with an authoritarian republic. Napoleon's nephew, protesting that he had no desire to tamper with the administrative structure his uncle had put in place by the Decree of Moscow, claimed in his modern way that his only aim was to make the state theater a better business. (A few months later, having put the big one in his pocket, he imposed censorship on all the other theaters.) Neither the politics of the coup—Louis Bonaparte's, Houssaye's, Rachel's—nor the mechanics of it were probably as dramatic or operatic as they are in Houssaye's version, which is, on the other hand, too good a story to be altogether without truth.

He was sitting quietly at home one evening, Houssaye recalled, when two men dressed in black suddenly appeared and instructed him to accompany them to the Elysée Palace. Sure that he was being arrested, as so many others had been, he reminded himself, as he kissed his weeping wife and child good-bye, that the palace had been named, not the police station. Arrived there, he was graciously greeted by *la grande Rachel*, who seemed quite the mistress of the house. Houssaye had met her only a few times before. They chatted; she asked him to write her a play about Sappho (but whom did she not ask to write her plays? modest Houssaye later reflected). Soon the Prince-President himself appeared, and made Houssaye the startling offer of the directorship. He had Rachel to thank for it, Louis Bonaparte said: she had chosen him from a list of six men of letters—chosen him because she knew him least well, Rachel pertly added. (Like almost all women, she loved the unknown, sanguine Houssaye comments.) He heard the Prince-President urge his star to undertake Hugo, Vigny, Dumas, and Musset, and heard Rachel agree to set about to study the modern repertoire. And he agreed to take the job.

Popular objection to Louis Bonaparte's conquest of the Théâtre-Français was based in part on resentment of Rachel; her enemies argued that the theater was in its weak position, and susceptible to such a takeover, only because she had been spending so much of her time abroad. The other actors blamed her for their losses; Parisians blamed the company's inability to control its star. Houssaye's appointment was delayed. But here as elsewhere, as business interests increasingly dominated and France moved farther to the right, the Prince-President's project of administrative streamlining eventually was seen as an attractive solution. Like all the efforts of the Nephew, as Marx memorably denominates him, this venture into the affairs of the Théâtre-Français is easily read as a debasement and a parody of the Uncle's. Napoleon I had structured the Théâtre-Français as a democratic meritocracy, in which voting privileges and profits were shared in exchange for clear obligations; the man who would be Napoleon III brought in an amiable, politic outsider to rule the company, and kept only the appearance of democracy. In their personal relations with the star actors, the two were also dramatically different. Where Napoleon I had had the grace and acumen to recognize Talma as his counterpart, people said, the Prince-President who honored Rachel's wishes was merely giving the run of the palace to his mistress, letting a woman manage him.

If her connection with Louis-Napoleon was not the finest chapter in Rachel's story, it did allow her complete administrative and artistic victory. With his help, she chose a director she could manage for the Comédie-Française: on her own, meanwhile, she won the legal case the company had brought against her, and prevailed on the management to allow her to sign a contract that changed her status from *sociétaire* to *pensionnaire*, or mere employee, of the theater, who had a full share of neither its profits nor its obligations. It was a demotion—a move quite as unprecedented and scandalous as her youthful elevation to a status that Lemaître and Dorval never attained. But it was what she wanted. The change granted her six months of vacation a year, during which she could tour at will; during the other six months, she was obliged to play in Paris forty-eight times, for thirty thousand francs. The potential profits the change allowed for were enormous: in 1850, she signed a contract that would bring her one hundred twenty thousand francs—ten times more than Mrs. Siddons ever got!—for a single month in England and Scotland. She went on from there to a four-month tour of Germany, where she looked up an old and poor aunt, and lavished gifts on her. On her return to Paris she was pleased to learn that her friends had successfully undertaken a commission she had given them, and managed to reacquire the statue of herself by Barre that she had given to Prince Napoleon. (He had passed it on to his mistress, Judith, who got a portrait of Nap in exchange.) Rachel was in control of her image.

Her letters to Houssaye in the early 1850s are those of an accomplished charmer, a star weighing the demands of her management and her public, consciously husbanding her physical and emotional resources. She cannily hoarded and deployed her *moyens tragiques*, as she called them, by alternating the classic and the romantic repertoires. It was she who chose her roles and the days she would appear at the Théâtre-Français, the management reserving the right to require a certain number of performances. Somehow, she managed to return to the status of *sociétaire* in 1851, and retain her right to long vacations. Sending Raphaël before her to make arrangements, she embarked on an extensive, strenuous, and successful tour of Italy. The splendid Gran Teatro La Fenice in Venice was opened for her; in Rome, she reported, the thirty thousand French residents of the "country of Camille" loaded her with flowers. Looking around, she deplored the wars that had impoverished the most beautiful of countries; and she decided on the role of the New Christian Pauline in *Polyeucte* for her *rôle de rentrée* in the fall, as she had the costume all ready. The next summer, when she performed for a collection of foreign royalty in Potsdam, the Czar of Russia, one of the guests, invited her to his country.

6. STAGE EMPRESS

"Travel makes one's youth and breaks one's hatboxes" was an epigram attributed to Rachel. The exhilaration she felt on the road was perhaps a function of her faux-Napoleonism. "Another nation conquered!" she exults in a letter from Brussels to Samson's daughter Adèle. She had a general passion for accumulation—of lovers, bracelets, francs, furniture, applause, roles, mileage, countries. "I have traveled across Belgium, Prussia, and Saxony, here I am in Bohemia, the day after tomorrow in Vienna, all in one month," she writes from Prague in 1851. More than eight hundred leagues covered, by rail; twenty-five performances in a single month. The spectacle of her own heroic exertions gave her energy, even, for other people: abroad, she thought about her little sister Dinah's problems, and planned to solve them by taking her along on the next tour. Although Rachel's critics insisted on the fact that she cared little about her supporting casts, and hired inept provincial actors in order to save money, one *comédien* who toured with her, Jean Chéry, gratefully remembered her showing him how to enter the stage in the role of Old Horace, while they strolled together in a field near a train station in Germany. But her own letters usually focus on herself: she makes only sketchy observations of what she saw (the houses of the poor were white in the manufacturing towns of Belgium, where the coal was produced more noiselessly and cleanly than she had been led to believe). One August evening in Brussels she played Phèdre in a theater that was so hot she felt "like a bit of ice in a pot of hot water," she reports (her metaphor suggesting that as the critics said she was cold, *au fond*); but the audience response miraculously restored her, she gained substance with every bravo and sympathetic murmur. (Describing another performance to a lover she had left behind, she writes

"The Grand Tragédienne
Has Made Her Ninety-
Ninth Return,"
caricature by Marcellin,
Le Journal pour rire,
20 November 1852

that the whole house rose like one man to applaud her, adding, "Was it I who aroused the public or the public who aroused me? I don't know: all I know is that we were both hot.") She enjoys totting up her triumphs, reveling in her exhausting schedule: tomorrow *Phèdre* at Namur, the next day Hugo's *Angelo* and Ponsard's *Horace et Lydie* back at Brussels, the day after that at Anvers, etc., etc.; and the receipts are better than ever. She is exultant: one needs a body of iron to go on this way without letup, no? And a head of Rachel? Preening in the sun of her success, proudest as always of her intellect, she glances back at her critics in Paris: this tour of mine might not suit the public, but it's good for my health, she boasts—and people who complain aren't worthy of living. Watch me light a candle instead of cursing the darkness, is the rather plaintive message to Véron and his friends of the Tuileries Club. Legible beneath the bravado are a need for love and a sense of doom—and a romantic, resentful sense that love and doom are causally connected: "Life, finally, is sad without friends, and nothing seems sadder to me than not satisfying, at all points, the people who lead us gaily toward the eternal end, *Death.*" Look at me, she was telling her correspondents, just like you I'm watching myself play out the play.

Like a Chorus in a Greek tragedy, Paris journalists lamented Rachel's greed and disloyalty, and hurt her more by observing that she was growing old; her travels were diagnosed as symptoms of insatiable desire, or of the peddler's daughter's compulsion to repeat her infantile wanderings. As early as 1843, a year after she was first named a *sociétaire*, she was criticized for giving fewer performances in Paris than her contract mandated. In the beginning Pa Félix had been excoriated for exhausting her abroad, for his profit, during her "vacations"; later Rachel herself was attacked for thinking that her genius (and ill-timed pregnancies) excused her from her legal obligations. In 1846, when the star wrote her first letter resigning from the state company, and again in 1847–48, her quarrels with the Comédie-Française had focused on her foreign tours.

She accepted the Czar's invitation to visit Russia at an especially delicate moment, in the fall of 1853, on the eve of the Crimean War; France and England broke diplomatic relations with Russia the day before she opened in Moscow. Paris reacted, understandably, with vituperation. Although the Russian government was merely opening the theaters to her, and all her profits were to derive from box office receipts, she was perceived in France as an employee of the national enemy. (The tour brought her three hundred thousand francs.) She claimed her goal was to make peace between the French and Russian peoples; Véron's *Le Constitutionnel* rated her for greediness, but in *La Presse* her friend Emile de Girardin argued fluently in another vein— or two or three—that the tour was part of her star's inevitable triumphal progress, that it would extend French civilization, and furthermore that as a great artist she belonged to the whole world. This was not very convincing; Mlle Plessy—another Samson student—had gone to Russia earlier to gather the gold and jewels of what was already known as the Eldorado of French actors.

In Russia Rachel was received with excitement and respect, and Latin verses that praised her as Melpomene; princes plied her with jewels and furs; busts and portraits of Rachel, and powders and pomades called by her name went on sale in the shops. Jean Chéry described young ladies from the very best families crowding around to touch her bouquet, and scrambling to pick up the flowers from the floor, when it broke. From the land of the brutally

Souvenir d'un voyage sentimental à Saint-
Pétersbourg.

"Souvenir of a
sentimental voyage
to St. Petersburg,"
contemporary
caricature

anti-Semitic Czar Nicholas she punned delightedly that she was treated "like
a sovereign, not a make-believe sovereign of tragedy, with a crown of gold-
colored cardboard, but a real sovereign made by the Mint." She enjoyed the
Napoleonic echoes: "Moscow will soon be taken; the Muscovites are paying
back with interest all that they took from us in 1812," she wrote. Moscow
was burning with ardor for her, she reported later, and, at the end, that she
had left it in flames. Better read than their English counterparts in the classics
of French literature, the aristocrats of Russia were delighted by the star of
the Comédie-Française. But her art and style were ultimately rejected in
Russia, where critics and actors preferred the indigenous tradition. Like Sir
Theodore Martin, who wrote in the 1880s that England had wrongly praised
an actress whose talents were not up to the subtleties Shakespeare required,
Rachel's Russian admirers ultimately decided that her very French art was
not for them. Her foreign conquests were brilliant but fleeting; her tours,
like many ventures of cultural imperialism, ultimately stirred nationalist
reactions.

Rachel was dazzled by the wealth and amused by the crudeness of Russia:

when she performed before the court, after a banquet in her honor, she watched incredulously as men climbed onto the tables, heedless of the gold plates. It tickled her to see "a whole tralala of princes" devouring the least words and sighs of "the daughter of Ma and Pa Félix." With an eye on her critics in France, she insisted on her patriotism: when some Russian soldiers boasted that they would be drinking champagne in France soon enough, she retorted that the French didn't treat their prisoners *quite* that well. The witticism was repeated with pleasure in Paris, where Rachel's Russian tour was quickly written into her legend. The last role she would create exploited that tour: she wore the ermine-trimmed robes of Catherine the Great in *La Czarine* (1855).

RACHEL'S TRIUMPHANT RETURN to Paris was interrupted by personal tragedy: in June 1854, Rébecca Félix died of tuberculosis at twenty-five. It was the first death in the Félix family, and it seems to have brought them even closer. Rachel recovered with difficulty from the loss, in a year when war in the Crimea increased the general gloom. The press remained resentful of her Russian adventure, and the theatergoing public was encouraged to embrace a rival star when the Italian actress Adelaide Ristori arrived in Paris. Ristori was simultaneously new and familiar, as a star must be—and flamboyantly a romantic. Demonstrative and emotional, she performed Corneille's and Racine's tragedies with none of Rachel's sense of their constraints, and—the more operatically—in her native language. Rachel, one critic explained, had played only one side of Phèdre—"the fatal side, the majestic breadth, the calculated effects, the statuesque posture undercut by frenetic fits, the funereal threnody deployed in five dramatic monologues worthy of her gifts: the diction." Mme Ristori showed the other side, "the one most in accord with her instincts; tender, burning love, jealous fever and secret terrors, expressive pantomime: in a word, passion. She makes her a woman." Genius was pitted against instincts, artist—once again—against woman.

G. H. Lewes took Rachel's side: the difference between the two actresses, he wrote, was "the difference between talent and genius, between a woman admirable in her art and a woman creative in her art." Ristori was merely an imitator, he wrote, who lacked the transformative power Rachel had shown she possessed by rising as she had above herself ("Rachel made a common Jewish physiognomy lovely by mere force of expression," Lewes had written with offhanded anti-Semitism). What Ristori lacked was soul: "Ristori has complete mastery of the mechanism of the stage, but is without the inspiration necessary for great acting." Fanny Kemble was of the same opinion, and so, engagingly, was the generous Ristori herself, who wrote that after seeing Rachel she agreed with the people who thought there was no comparison between them. For her part, Rachel expressed admiration for her *camarade;* she went to the theater, heavily veiled, to see Ristori perform, and sent her rival tickets to a performance of her own. But the papers polarized the women: the war of divas is a compelling concept, especially provocative when coupled with a rivalry of nations. Rachel represented artful, intellectual France, Ristori passionate and natural Italy: decades later, the equation would subtly alter when some of flamboyant Bernhardt's followers betrayed her for the more soulful and spiritual Eleonora Duse.

Rival actresses had been set up as the superiors of *La Grande* before: Edmond Got was of the opinion that her own sister Rébecca had run rings around her in *Angelo.* But since Rébecca had died in her arms—pathetically protesting it was impossible that death should come to one so young, and the sister of the great Rachel—mortality had oppressed her. At thirty-three, she was thinking of herself as no longer young, and worrying more than ever about the future of her children and her parents. Looking back over her life, she reflected that she had never been beautiful, and therefore had aspired to be a great artist. Wounded, she was seeking to retreat—away from Paris, toward her family. Her enterprising brother Raphaël, who had managed her successful tours of Italy and Russia, seized the moment, and called on the Félix family to close ranks around their star, and go off to make a spectacular fortune. He proposed to take all but the mother and Rachel's two children to America.

In letters she wrote before she left to two of the more persistent men in her life, Rachel betrays her nervousness by invoking her sense of distance— now morbid, then mocking—from herself. To Prince Nap, the fancier of classical subjects and women, she writes *en grande tragédienne,* calling the voyage pure madness, describing herself as driven, like Phèdre, by a tragic fatality toward the abyss. To Michel Lévy she sends a note together with a tapestry seat cushion embroidered with her own hands, she explains, for "M. ton derrière." She takes a tone of cozy vulgarity with an intimate who felt like family, but less demanding: "My good old friend Michel, I make you the judge of my devoted attachment to your very dear person; for don't forget that I am a tragedienne, that my loves are out of the pages of Corneille, whose male and virile tastes are also mine."

IN SECOND EMPIRE PARIS, it was hard to believe that Americans could possibly appreciate a tragedy queen. What would the republic make of

Rachel as Phèdre, photograph by Mayer and Pierson

Mlle Rachel,
caricature by Carjat

her aristocratic art? Louis-Napoleon's subjects wondered condescendingly, and
concluded that the rabble could only admire her as a rabble-rouser. Janin
imagined that a voice in the American audience would demand *La Marseillaise* at the moment when Rachel, as Emilie in *Cinna,* urged her lover to join
the conspiracy against Augustus. She would debase her gifts before crowds
used only to the crudest spectacle, uncomprehending of her language, deaf
to the subtleties of art. Janin summed up the case against the American tour
in the *Journal des débats* of 13 October 1855, when Rachel was already in New
York: "Indeed, by virtue of the art she practices and the masterpieces she
performs, she belongs to all that a Republic or a Monarchy can have of
elegance and courtesy, of the elevated, the aristocratic, the refined. Athens is
a court; the Rome of Augustus is a court; Louis XIV is a sun which gives
its light to the stars; the great poets Euripides, Sophocles, Corneille, and

Racine address chosen spirits, elite souls, elegant feelings, speak to grandeur, omnipotence, and majesty. Their dramas take place in a complex and exigent world apart; they speak to the souls of discriminating audiences, not the passions of masses." Janin's argument against American audiences might have been strengthened by a reference to the bloody and destructive Astor Place Riots of 1849, in New York, in which drunken patriotic supporters of Edwin Forrest had protested the visit of the English actor William Macready (both were early admirers of Rachel). New York was tough territory in the mid-nineteenth century. The actor Léon Beauvallet, a member of the Félix troupe, would write incredulously of the frequent fires in the city, and the people who enjoyed nothing so much as running after fire trucks; Rachel would report that when she went out alone one evening in a taxi, and the driver got lost, she feared for her diamonds and her life. Many respectable women would not be seen in New York theaters—not that Parisians credited American women (les blooméristes, as they called them) with an elevating influence. The elite of the Second Empire shuddered delicately at the idea of the pearls of French literature cast before swinish American crowds. Beauvallet would duly report back to them that American audiences could only respond to large movements and a raised voice, being deaf not only to niceties of diction but to the subtle play of features and gestures that French connoisseurs admired. By 1855 some discriminating Parisians had ceased to admire Rachel; and, of course, there were some who had never begun. Auguste Vacquerie wrote dismissively of Rachel in America: "May she stay there and succeed there, and be crushed by all the dollars, and take her pleasure, and make love to Racine there and marry him, and may they have many little tragedies!"

Raphaël Félix aimed to emulate and equal P. T. Barnum, who had arranged the enormously profitable American tour of Jenny Lind in 1850. The Swedish Nightingale was adored by the American public that had paid to see Mr. and Mrs. Tom Thumb, and an aged black woman who was billed as the former nurse of George Washington: why should it not queue up for a bona fide French tragedienne? Barnum's retirement in 1855 gave Raphaël what looked like an opening, and Rachel's depression inclined her to yield to her brother's superior energy. During a stopover the company made in England, on the way to America, the manager-brother made a public point of his authority over his star, fining Rachel for some small infraction, and posting the fact and the sum in the theater lobby. (Although she had for years done without her surname, in a show of either closeness or estrangement she had signed her contract with him "Rachel Félix.") In a letter written as the steamer approached the United States, the tyrannical brother's employee—responsive as ever to her context—compared herself, in a letter to her mother, to a Negro slave.

"THE EMPIRE OF FRANCE," according to *Mitchell's School Geography*, published in 1854, "is a great and powerful state. The French are a brave, active, and polite people . . . fond of show and amusement. The French language is the most refined, and the best adapted to conversation, of any in Europe, and is much used in polite society. The upper class in France excel in dancing, fencing, and other graceful accomplishments; and the women take an active share in all the affairs of life." New York was pleased to welcome the elegant empire's representative, selling restaurant desserts and painted fans à la Rachel, as the Russians had done, and newspaper articles that described the contents of her trunks and hinted at sexual scandal. In an effort to educate the public and control his star's image, Raphaël had an instructive pamphlet drawn up, "The Biography of Mdlle Rachel with Contemporary Criticisms by the most Eminent Writers, and Analytic Notices of the Characters in her Repertoire Written and Compiled from European Authorities." Rachel appealed to the republican imagination as a celebrity, as an import fresh from Paris, and as a queen risen from the ranks of the people. She was an actively reigning queen; given the choice, what woman would not prefer to be her rather than a figurehead like Queen Victoria or the Empress Eugénie? one American journalist asked rhetorically.

Her personal power and its political dimension would make a lasting impression in America. Harriet Beecher Stowe's essay, "Sojourner Truth, the Libyan Sybil" (1863), compares the famous black preacher and abolitionist to Rachel. "Perfectly self-possessed," endowed with "that silent and subtle power which we call personal presence," the other dark and dignified performing woman resembles the actress, Stowe writes. "It is said that Rachel was wont to chant the Marseillaise in a manner that made her seem, for the time, the very spirit and impersonation of the gaunt, wild, hungry, avenging mob which rose against aristocratic oppression; and in like manner Sojourner, singing this hymn, seemed to impersonate the fervor of Ethiopia, savage, hunted of all nations, but burning after God in her tropic heart, and stretching her scarred hands toward the glory to be revealed." (The former slave's performance of a religious hymn in the Stowe living room is evoked in the terms of romantic theater critics: she sings "with such an overwhelming energy of personal appropriation that the hymn seemed to be fused in the furnace of her feelings and came out recrystallized as a product of her own.")

The "Jewish sorceress" was not invited into good company in New York, which had its doubts about actresses from Paris, but her legend caught the imagination of a country already intensely interested in any kind of royalty. Everyone who was anyone went to hear Rachel perform, first in New York and then in Boston: Longfellow and William Cullen Bryant went, and Horace Greeley, who reportedly fell asleep and was awakened only by the pistol-shot in *Lady Tartuffe*. Ralph Waldo Emerson, who had seen her in Paris in 1848, had been impressed by her "goodness," and by her speaking so clearly that he could understand her, but only one out of twenty people in the audience in New York and Boston and Philadelphia were expected, by her manager, to follow her lines. Accordingly, Raphaël Félix had arranged with the New York firm of Darcie and Corbyn to publish and sell at the gate copies of "her" plays in pamphlet form, the French texts accompanied by what was described as "a literal English translation." They were decorated with a "Certificate of Authority" signed by both Rachel and her brother, to imply their superiority to any versions of the plays people might already own. The side venture was profitable: it was said that the tragedienne was obliged to pause, mid-*tirade*, by the rustle of folio-sized pages turning. Advertisers augmented Raphaël's profits: space at the back of the books was bought by the manufacturers of Mexican Mustang Liniment, of D. J. Allen's Improved Artificial Teeth, of the manufacturers of elegant pianofortes and melodeons. We can get some idea of what Rachel's New York audiences were like by the kinds of merchandise that tempted them: "The Balm of Thousand Flowers," which "removes all tan, pimples and freckles from the face, removes grease spots from clothes or carpeting, beautifies the skin, cleanses the teeth, or curls the hair," was promoted with encomia from the *London Mail* praising its inventor, "Dr. A. De Fontaine, of Paris"; Molyneux Bell, of 58 Canal St., Importer and Manufacturer of Cloaks and Mantillas, reported he was "receiving from his Parisian modiste New Styles by the Steamers as they are issued in Paris."

Rachel's greatest fans in New York were the members of the small French colony, who invited her to meet their wives and daughters at dinner. For them, she cast her voyage to America as a selfless and heroic act, rather like a journey to a war zone; she included in her repertoire a rousing poem by Régis de Trobriand, editor of the *Courrier des Etats-Unis*, the newspaper of the French community. The translation in the *Boston Daily Advertiser* of 20 November 1855 begins: " 'O go not,' they cried, 'to that far distant land, / Oh venture not life on America's strand; / 'Tis a nation of labor, they ask but strong arms / For genius they seek not, they know not its charms,

/ The sweet speech of Corneille to them is unknown— / Oh go not,' they tell me, and I—I have come."

Rachel's exalting sense of her own heroism intensified as she began to suffer the first stages of her final acute illness: she had carried her name as far as she could, she wrote home in Camille's tones. On the long ride from New York to Boston in an unheated train, she caught a severe cold that was the beginning of the end. Periods of weakness alternated with energetic and even elated days, as residents of the New Athens, as Bostonians proudly called their city, sought to prove its high cultural tone by applauding Rachel, and she, as ever, responded with enthusiasm to applause. Harvard students— the scions of America's best families, Beauvallet reported—volunteered for walk-on parts in *Virginie*; they barely had time to throw off their costumes before crowding the wings to applaud *La Marseillaise*. The actor was amused by this American lack of dignity. "Some had put on their trousers and shoes but were still in their tunics; others were wearing their coats over flesh-coloured tights, etc., etc. It was a strange sight to see the wings packed with men in this odd sort of fancy dress." Bostonians joked uneasily about the pharmacist whose sign advertising "European leeches" brought people to his shop to purchase pricey theater tickets. William Wetmore Story, the sculptor, wrote to James Russell Lowell: "Rachel made a great sensation here . . . nobody understood what she said; but everyone thought her wonderful. . . . Nobody cared for her character. She was wretchedly supported by a set of dirty Jews, and they too were taken into the general admiration. She was jewier than ever and tried to skin a flint in Boston, which created a little reaction. But you know we go by fashion, and it was the fashion to consider her unequalled." (Story had seen Ristori in Paris and decided that "Rachel seemed a sham after her. The Italians have the real *clou* of passion.")

Rachel explained with forced gaiety, in a letter from Boston, that "because I imprudently failed to dress warmly enough, I cough like a tubercular woman, which I assure you I am not, believe me, for all my pale complexion and apparent thinness." Her doctors were agreeing with her, conspiring with fate to send her to an early grave. She reported exhaustion so extreme that she actually yawned onstage as Adrienne, in the face of her fat Maurice de Saxe, a certain M. Randoux who always had the effect on her of a large piece of ice thrown into a glass of warm water. Catching herself using a favorite metaphor, she wondered how the rest of the cast would like that analogy. She wrote poignantly to her friend Louise de Saigneville of her regret that "our beautiful French language" was little known, even in New York, where applause came at all the wrong moments. As an artist, she wanted first of all to be understood, she explained. The discomfort was not only professional: she felt thoroughly *dépaysée* in Boston, where she was unable to make herself understood in her hotel, and had to move to Sarah's, her sister having had the foresight to bring along an English maid. Rachel insisted she was not sorry she came to America: the twenty-four performances during the first run in New York had brought her more than she had made in Russia. "I am making myself commercial, I take and I pile up the dollars," she wrote to Louise.

In another letter, in another mood, Rachel—feverish, coughing, exhausted—acknowledges failure in her killing tragic-heroic tones: "My body and mind have dwindled to nothing. I bring back my routed troops to the banks of the Seine, and perhaps, like another Napoleon, I will go to die at the Invalides and request a stone to lay my head upon." The Napoleonic self-image had always required a fall. She had looked forward to playing in Philadelphia and then in Charleston, South Carolina, where there was a substantial French community, and perhaps the sun. But there, as Adrienne Lecouvreur, she collapsed onstage. The reviewer of the *Charleston Mercury* proved correct when he wrote that in Adrienne's farewell to the theater—in which she mourns the ephemeral lives of actresses, and charges her friends and her audience to remember her—he heard Rachel's own.

Adrienne dies of smelling poisoned flowers; tuberculosis destroys the lungs less melodramatically. Rachel dragged herself to Cuba, where the doctors gave her hope that she would recover; shivering with fever, she was astonished by the Creoles in their light muslins. She sailed back to New York in January and from there to France in early February, arriving in Le Havre on the twenty-fifth of that month. "Notwithstanding the losses which she is said to have sustained by her visit to America, she continues the embellishments of her hôtel in the rue Trudon on the most expensive scale," the English papers noted disapprovingly in March. Rachel was spending much of her time recovering in the country, receiving visits from her admirers, and planning her return to the theater. But in May her doctors advised her to go to Ems, to take the waters, and her leave of absence from the Comédie-Française was extended for another year. Diligently, at the spa, she worked at her health—ass's milk, rest—and at avoiding the curious; she played cribbage, a card game she thought was called "garbage," and squabbled with her maid Rose. In September she left Paris for Alexandria, which was more like Europe than she had expected; she wrote that she felt more comfortable there than she had in the New World. She set off from that city to be rocked on a barge on the Nile in the sun. Accompanied by Sarah and Rose, she

Rachel, photograph by Julien Vallou de Villeneuve, 1853

rested, receiving some visitors, doing some sewing, reading, and writing letters. But her fevers and cough continued, and, as always when she wasn't
acting, she suffered cruelly from boredom. She wrote her father hopeful
descriptions of her abating symptoms; she sent orders to her agent, Bellevaut,
about selling her furniture—except the armchair, recently reupholstered, that
had come to her from M. Walewski, and the round table with gold feet and
marble mosaic from Florence, a gift from Prince Napoleon. Did she hope to
live yet among her keepsakes, or think her children would be able to sell
such historic items at a greater profit later on? Or was she holding onto the
solid evidence of her history and identity? To Arsène Houssaye she wrote,
"I have no more hopes, no more expectations. And frankly, rather than lead
the beastly life through which I have dragged myself since the onset of this
long, painful, and sad illness, it would be a hundred times better to be
enclosed within four tightly sealed boards and to wait there to be disposed
of as we now dispose of Egyptian mummies. Perhaps I will not die of consumption after all, but of boredom. What a sad loneliness has settled in
around me! Imagine me alone with a Polish doctor who is nothing more
than that, a cook, and my maid Rose. Still, I always have before me a clear
sky, a mild climate, and this hospitable river that carries its patient's boat as
gently and maternally as a mother her newborn child. But the majestic memories of ancient Egypt, the partial ruins of marvellous temples, the enormous
giants carved in the flanks of granite mountains, so many works and masterpieces ravaged by the force of the centuries, toppled from their pedestals by
earthquakes—when all of this spectacle is seen up close, even discounting
the ways the imagination makes it even more frightening, it is far too much
for weak creatures and worn spirits to bear." It pained her to be unable to
rise, as she had been able to do in the past, to the level of spectacular circumstances.

While the vestiges of past glory in Egypt oppressed her spirit and increased her sense of her own impending doom, she carefully monitored her
body and her emotions: Phèdre dies of self-awareness, and like every patient
Rachel clung to physical facts as if it would preserve her life to know them.
Having been taken by litter to the foot of the Pyramids, she checked her
pulse: she reported eighty-six beats. She pitied her children and herself, and
managed as always to transcend herself through irony that was perhaps innate, but surely also informed by the grandiloquence of Corneille's and Racine's heroines, which she had absorbed and made her own. Napoleon,
exhorting his troops to glory in Egypt, had told them that the centuries were
looking down on them from the peaks of the Pyramids; Rachel wrote in this

vein, "At the foot of the Pyramids, I contemplate twenty centuries lost in the sands. O my friend, how I see here the nothingness of tragediennes. I thought I was pyramidal, but realize now that I am a mere passing shadow. I came here to find the life that is fleeing me, and all around me I see only death." Recalling the imagery of marble that had been invoked so often to describe her, she reflected that it had foretold the graveyard.

Virginia Woolf speculated of Rachel that her most real life was lived in the course of acting out the passions of the women she imagined—in other words, that the reality of her own life pales beside that. I have argued to somewhat different effect that her life was embroiled with fictions—and that her star-struck public correctly understood her, and her romantic biographers have portrayed her with inadvertent accuracy as a woman part real and part ideal. The theme was underwritten by insistence on her doubleness: Rachel the child of the streets and stage queen; chaste courtesan; classical tragedienne and romantic actress; monstrous egotist and loving daughter, mother, and sister. Her self-consciousness was a function of her métier and the mechanisms that made her a star. Different plays, surely, would have formed her otherwise—the new tragedies that Alfred de Musset called on his contemporaries to write for her, the one he himself began to write and failed to finish. They do not figure in her story; but one play she never appeared in does.

Like so many of the stories about Rachel, the one about the role she turned down with great éclat, at great expense, features a man who imagined that he had made her and was therefore entitled to break her. Ernest Legouvé was a feminist and a prodigiously prolific playwright, the author, with the equally prolific Eugène Scribe, of *Adrienne Lecouvreur*. In the memoir he wrote in old age, he tells the story of how Rachel had refused that role at first, and then in a lucky intuitive flash decided she had to have it: he goes so far as to reprint the prettily penitent letter she wrote saying so. It was he who told, with the same complacency, the spooky story of how he came upon her rehearsing Adrienne's death scene alone in a darkened theater, tears rolling down her cheeks, and she told him that she was mourning her own death in Adrienne's. The impulse to mythmaking is inspired by success—which perhaps in turn encourages myth-unmaking.

The historical Adrienne Lecouvreur, as Scribe and Legouvé depict her, is adorable and witty, and a mistress of artifice; no spontaneous romantic Dorval, she depends (as Rachel was known to do) on the teacher who instructs her in the traditions of the Comédie-Française. In parallel scenes set in a princess's boudoir and a greenroom, Scribe and Legouvé elaborate the

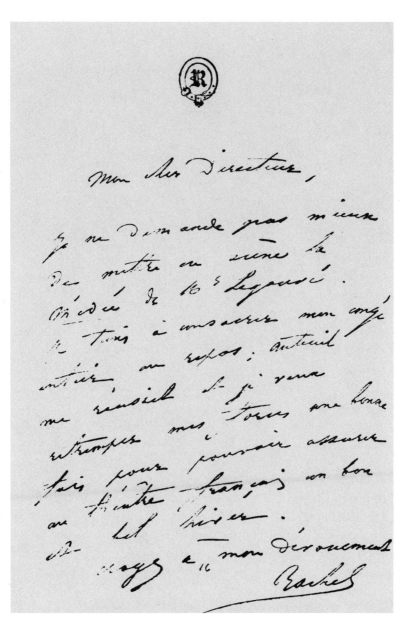

Letter from Rachel to Arsène Houssaye

Balzacian point that the artifice involved in a society lady's life is the same
as an actress's. The connections between low life and high; the difference
between the true love of Adrienne for Maurice de Saxe (George Sand's grandfather) and the schemes of the aristocratic adulteress who also wants the hero;
above all the rivalry between the actress and the Princesse de Bouillon, which
titillatingly joins and evades the themes of class warfare and the differences
between "good" women and "bad" ones—all these gave authenticating "historical" narrative form to themes inherent in the image of Rachel. As the
play depended on the celebrity of its star, the plot depends on playing real
life against the stage: Adrienne, who is first seen rehearsing the role of Roxane
in *Bajazet*, later humiliates the Princesse de Bouillon by pointedly alluding to Phèdre's comparison of herself to "those brazen women who . . . Dare
flaunt a face where not a blush is seen" (III, 3). The infuriated princess
retaliates by sending Adrienne a bouquet of poisoned flowers. Adrienne in-
hales their perfume and dies, exhorting her audience to remember her:
"Nothing survives us . . . nothing but memories. Your memories, is that not
so?" Delighted by her great success in the role, the star insisted on the
connection with the earlier actress. Apprehensive that she would die young
as Adrienne had before her, Rachel had nevertheless insisted on identifying
herself with her role. She hung a picture of Adrienne in her home; she made
up a quarrel with Samson onstage during a rehearsal of the play, when, at
the moment Adrienne thanks her teacher Michonnet for all he has done
for her, Rachel turned to him despite the fact that he was not playing that
role. The rest of the cast applauded them both: Adrienne-Rachel was a collaborative creation.

To conjecture that Legouvé subsequently wrote *Médée* in order to kill
the thing he imagined himself to have made is not quite fair: simple personal
ambition was surely involved. Also, it is a logical step from Phaedra to
Medea; people (Lamartine, for instance) urged it on Rachel when they got
wind of Legouvé's project. Initially she seems to have been interested in the
role of the mother who kills her children, but she was always a little dubious;
Legouvé, however, imagined on the basis of her past behavior that he could
overcome her reluctance. But after she agreed to take the role, she set about
avoiding both the author and the play. She claimed to be incapacitated, first
by anxiety about her sister Rébecca's illness and then by despair soon after
Rébecca's death; then she said she was obliged to leave town for her health;
then she began rehearsals, broke them off, and decided she was in no position
to refuse a very profitable offer from the King of Prussia. (She had used the
business of a *grande tragédienne* to get rid of unwanted suitors all her life.)

Legouvé, who fancied himself her more than intimate, was enraged. He pursued her into the courts, and she called upon the lawyer Adolphe Crémieux—from whom she had been alienated since the Véron affair—to save her. He tried, but this time he failed. A final court order required Rachel to pay the disappointed playwright five thousand francs for breach of contract.

She was predictably accused of skittishness, vanity, and cowardice, also of maternal sentimentality: she had said that as the mother of two young boys she was reluctant to play the infanticide. A look at the play suggests why Houssaye supported her decision to refuse the role, and why Rachel, who cared so much about money, was willing to risk paying, indeed to pay, to avoid it. If a writer had aimed to travesty her image, he would have been hard put to devise a better vehicle than Legouvé's *Médée*. It is a debasement of Greek tragedy so thoroughgoing as to seem deliberate. Where the Medea of Euripides is a heroic figure larger than life, a sorceress who helped Jason to the Golden Fleece, this one is a cast-off wife, a woman scorned and driven mad by a man who is bored by her. Jason, here, is an enterprising rake, compared in the author's preface to slick Parisian seducers of poor girls from the country; and his proposals to Médée, about divorce and child custody, are hardly evocative of more spacious antique times. Médée's feelings for her children are narrowly possessive: as Legouvé saw the character, "Medea is to maternal love what Othello is to romantic love, the image of the passion that kills." The play emphasizes the lust of the young barbarian who is driven to commit terrible crimes for Jason's sake. She is a foreigner used to strange gods, including a Venus thirsty for human blood. Cast off in Corinth, Médée is bewildered and pathetic, and the pathos of her situation is intensified by her more pathetic children, to whom Legouvé gives names and speaking parts. (In the play by Euripides the unnamed children have a scant two lines.) The two boys—like Rachel's own Alexandre and Gabriel—whine realistically about how tired and hungry they are; Jason's new love, Créüse, exclaims over them and covers them with kisses, and declares she longs to adopt them; and they are heart-wrenchingly afraid of their terrible mother, who repels them at one point with the declaration that "Jason's children are not my children." In the tragedy by Euripides, Medea agonizes, arguing with herself, over whether to kill the children; here, the decision seems impulsive.

It is, in other words, a vulgar play that might have vulgarized its star. In an essay on Mme Ristori written in 1875, Henry James indicates he knew as much, although he puts the blame on the actress rather than the role: "The objections to Madame Ristori's Medea are obvious; the lady is too much of a termagant—no wonder poor Jason would not go back to her." Even if the play itself is "a dense tissue of superb action," as James would call it, Rachel was right in believing it was not suited to her gifts. She pointed out one problem in a letter to Legouvé: her forte was conveying emotions through a pose or an attitude or a restrained and measured gesture, she wrote, but "at the place where large, energetic pantomime begins, my talents cease." (Act II, Scene 5, of Legouvé's play opens with "Medea, distraught, taking great strides.") The playwright seemed to avoid exploiting or even acknowledging her strengths, not only the graceful gesture that was the more emphatic for being so rare, but the long, brilliantly modulated sustained monologue. Legouvé's Médée has mostly broken half-lines and staccato exclamations; dignity, along with language, is beyond her, for she suffers from high romantic madness, the delectable "rich anger" of the mistress whose soft hand Keats counsels the man who would be melancholy to imprison—the craziness generally attributed to women who kill. Rachel had made her name and fortune by acting self-possessed and single-minded, as scrupulous Camille, as scornful Hermione and imperious Roxane, even as Phèdre observing her own passion and disintegration. Legouvé's distracted Médée can pull herself together only with her last breath, in the final, hollow claim that it was really Jason who killed the children.

Recent critics have argued that the classical Medea was, for the ancients, a figure of the archaic heroic that was meant to horrify. Legouvé's version of Euripides does not interrogate concepts of heroism, as the Greek play does; instead, it makes Médée a sentimental, banal heroine. Had Rachel consented to play the role at the end of her career, she would have seemed to be revealing some secret cracked self she had hidden behind her smooth marble facade, and to be acknowledging—finally—that she was really a welter of disordered, horrific female passion, a mad mother pathetically without a man, needy and violent and guilty even of the least forgivable of crimes. Fidelity to her image and herself demanded that she turn the role down; and Adelaide Ristori arrived in Paris just in time to take it up. Legouvé's journalist friends encouraged audiences to love Ristori as Médée—love her, quite pointedly, more than they loved Rachel. The hero of the day was the playwright, who had been thwarted by a temperamental woman's promise; the heroine was the lusty, new foreign actress, who performed operatically in Italian. Ristori was commended as the true romantic woman, passionate rather than artful, a successor to the timid, tradition-bound Rachel; also a mother, she was hailed as more thoroughly the artist for being willing to act the role of the woman who kills her own children.

Unlike Rachel, Ristori was also safely a wife, as well as a genuine foreigner from another country, and an actress unencumbered by a legend. Rachel's children had hardly figured in her myth—had been hard to assimilate into it. Although François Ponsard, who adored her, had described her as a tender mother, his version of Rachel did not catch on; most biographers have preferred the stereotype of the egotistical actress, who left Napoleon's grandson in the care of that slatternly wife of a vendor of eyeglasses, her mother, who taught him to repeat vile things about his father and other actresses. An unmarried star is supposed to be a bad mother: it is part of the fantasy of her monstrous unwomanliness. In the early 1840s, childless Delphine de Girardin, writing as Vicomte de Launay, had mocked the idealization of secular maternity; it only increased as the century wore on. Legouvé's *Médée*, about a woman driven so mad by love for a man that she sacrifices her two children, did a standard lurid turn on the reigning stereotype. It would have been that much more lurid had it starred Rachel. The story of Rachel's refusal of *Médée* did cast her finally, ironically, in the maternal role, however—as it was explained that her nervous, out-of-control superstitiousness about miming the murder of her sons had made her break her contract with Legouvé. In the event, as a capping irony, she was indelibly fixed as Médée after all: the expression of Medea about to kill her children, in a painting by Delacroix, recalls—or did to Gautier, in 1855—not Ristori's face but Rachel's.

On her deathbed, Rachel refused Legouvé's request to visit her. (This did not stop him from describing the statuesque poses she struck there.) In the gracious little note turning him down, the tragedienne wrote that if she were to return to the stage, she would have him write her *rôle de rentrée*, but begged him not to take her to court if she proved unable to fulfill the obligation.

CHAPTER FIVE

～

Afterlives

During the first stage of Romanticism, up till about the middle of the nineteenth century, we meet with several Fatal Women in literature, but there is no established type of Fatal Woman in the way that there is an established type of Byronic Hero. For a type—which is, in actual fact, a *cliché*—to be created, it is essential that some particular figure should have made a profound impression on the popular mind.

MARIO PRAZ, *The Romantic Agony*

Fame is made up of four elements: a person and an accomplishment, their immediate publicity, and what posterity has thought about them ever since.

LEO BRAUDY, *The Frenzy of Renown*

A subjective account by an impressionable spectator of one of the most mercurial of human activities, an actor's performance, is open to the widest misinterpretation, and the Victorian era, with its plethora of newspapers and periodicals, further confuses the picture by sheer abundance of detail.

GEORGE ROWELL, *The Victorian Theatre*

What do you think of Rachel—greater in what she is than in her
creativity, eh?

MATTHEW ARNOLD, letter to Arthur Hugh Clough

REAL PEOPLE are special effects in fictions. When Edward Waverley is
received by Prince Charles James Stuart in person in Walter Scott's novel,
or Napoleon himself appears in *War and Peace,* or when Steve Rojack, in
Norman Mailer's *An American Dream,* recalls the time he first met "Jack
Kennedy," the reader thrills to the superior glamour of historical fact. In
imaginary worlds, real persons thicken the illusion of verisimilitude, also
remind us of the private and fabricated nature of the novel and the self. The
fact that Bonnie Prince Charlie once lived would argue that Waverley did
too; on the other hand, at the prince's side Scott's hero is shown up as a
fiction, so that one nearly begins to wonder how real the fabled Stuart was.
Roland Barthes remarks that when historical persons play disproportionately
small roles in fictions, being "merely mixed in with their fictional neighbors,
mentioned as having simply been present at some social gathering, their
modesty, like a lock between two levels of water, equalizes novel and history." He sees them as serving as "superlative effects of the real." By con-
spicuously standing out as "effects," he suggests, they call attention to the
line between novel and history that they seem to challenge or erase. Men
like the prince, or the emperor, or the president, importantly world-historical
but half-legendary as well, also draw our attention to the difference between
public and private persons, the fact that (in fiction, at least) only members of
the second group can be satisfactorily known.

The name of the famous actress Berma in Proust's *A la recherche du
temps perdu* does not have the same resonance as "M. Grévy" or "Maréchal
MacMahon" in that novel. First of all, it is not in fact a name from real life,
being only evocative of Sarah Bernhardt's surname; and secondly, it names
an actress, a public woman, not at all the same thing as a public man. While
the name reminds us of Sarah Bernhardt and inspires us to savor her historicity as we savor Bonnie Prince Charlie's, it also suggests that she was not
quite, not altogether, and not only a person in history. It begins to raise the
questions, explored by the text, about the extent to which she is a living
image of something in the narrator's mind. In other words, her very name
suggests the equivocal nature of her identity, as does "Vashti," the name of
the actress in *Villette.* Single and singular, these names mark the actress's

difference from ordinary persons, real and fictitious, and suggest something about the spectator-narrator who names her. Proust's narrator sees his actress and Lucy Snowe sees hers as not altogether separate beings. Berma and Vashti stimulate and extend the narrators' selves. They are symbols as well as persons, arbitrary signs of persons, creatures in the phenomenal world and also openings into a place at which the self bleeds into that world, into another self. Signs of the self, they are also signs of its instability.

WRITING UP Rachel's New York tour of 1855, *Putnam's* and *Harper's* magazines reminded American readers that she was the original of Brontë's Vashti. Having been mentioned in a novel lent her a certain importance and a glamorous increment of fictitiousness. The novel readers of her time might have been primed for Rachel's appearance in Brontë's novel by earlier works—Balzac's *La Cousine Bette* (1846) and Disraeli's *Tancred* (1847); they might even have noted the difference between the Frenchman's Josépha and Josephine, the child actress imagined by the English writer. Josépha evokes Rachel less directly and specifically than Josephine does. She is not a trage-dienne but a diva—born in 1814, the pseudo-historian painstakingly tells us, and a star at the Opéra, in Rossini's *Guillaume Tell*, in 1843. A Jew (the natural daughter of a rich German banker), she is compared to a portrait of Judith in the Pitti Palace, which may be an allusion to Rachel's role in Mme de Girardin's play; but Balzac means his character to remind us of prominent Jewish divas, such as Pasta and Grisi, as well. She recalls one legendary aspect of *La Grande* largely by her manner of being confidently and effectively superb. The scene between her and poor Mme Hulot, who comes to her in an effort to find her straying husband, sets up the large-souled, free and generous public woman against the pinched and virtuous little wife. Triumphantly aware of their relative positions, the courtesan makes a deliberately theatrical appearance in greeting the other woman, and follows it up with a grandly generous offer to help her.

The difference between French and English literary versions of Rachel continued to prevail in her afterlife. In her own country, especially after her image was conflated with Sarah Bernhardt's, Rachel was sunk into the ste-reotype of the glamorous demimondaine; in England she remained a (prob-lematic) sign of high seriousness and of art. Disraeli, George Henry Lewes, and Matthew Arnold helped define the English Rachel, Lewes insisting influ-entially on "her *distinction,* her simple dignity." But Charlotte Brontë's vision of Rachel has most effectively preserved her memory. Brontë brought her figure into the moral tradition of British fiction—the tradition of Richardson, in which Woman represents the inner life. Figuring a sort of conduit between inner and outer, real and fantastic, private and public worlds, revisionary versions of Brontë's Rachel haunt later novels by George Eliot and Henry James. These writers in the English tradition insist, as the French do not, on the actress's uniqueness and her genius, and on the charged play of oppositions she embodied; they invoke her as a compelling link between psychosocial reality and aesthetic ideals, the provocative sign of a set of unstable opposites that especially interest them: between novelistic density and theatrical illusion; fiction and history; singularity and representativity. Above all, in the most psychologically minded of literary forms, she figures the attractive idea and unstable substance of character.

I. A Woman and an Artist: Vashti

When Charlotte Brontë went to London in the early summer of 1851 she was an accomplished and well-known novelist, and a painfully lonely person. Her brother and two sisters had very recently been consigned in swift succession to the graveyard beside Haworth Parsonage, leaving her with a father whose irascibility had been intensified by tragedy, illness, and age. Even the countryside she had lived in and deeply loved since childhood seemed alien: "I am free to walk on the moors," she wrote from Yorkshire, "but when I go out there alone everything reminds me of the times when others were with me, and then the moors seem a wilderness, featureless, solitary, saddening." Her friends hoped a visit to London would cheer her with the balm of fellowship: there were people she knew there, and a wider literary society eager to honor the author of *Jane Eyre*, as well as a range of convivial distractions. It was the year of the Great Exhibition, and Brontë went five times to the Crystal Palace, though "under coercion rather than my own free will," to see scientific wonders she confessed she did not know enough to appreciate. She—who had shrunk almost ostentatiously from being known—began to flirt, finally, with celebrity. She heard Thackeray lecture, and finally met him; she breakfasted and dined with various other prominent persons. And she went twice to the St. James Theatre, to see Rachel in *Horace* and in *Adrienne Lecouvreur*.

To Brontë in 1851, the metropolis was an alien place; "this great London" and "this great Babylon" are interchangeable phrases in her letters. The cranky parson's spiky daughter was not disposed to be enthusiastic about people or

Rachel as Phèdre, drawing by Eugène Delacroix, 1843

crowds. In the St. James Theatre in 1851, she would have felt further isolated by feelings of superiority: unlike the others who came to gape at a star, she was proficient in Rachel's language. (She would have shared the scorn of G. H. Lewes, who was embarrassed by the provinciality and ignorance of Rachel's English audiences. "We once saw a lady in a private box not content with her book, but absolutely hunting out the words in her dictionary!" Lewes reported, in a review of 1850.) She, after all, had lived abroad, had even written love letters in French. Her memory of the passionate feelings she had expressed on paper for Constantin Héger, the teacher she fell in love with in Brussels, would have complicated the emotions that going to the French Theatre stirred. Her companions for the evening were her publisher and sometime suitor George Smith, a tall fair man, and his mother. John Graham Bretton, the bland, blond, handsome English doctor who takes Lucy Snowe to see Vashti in *Villette*, is based on Smith: in the novel Lucy gets to go because his mother has decided to give up her ticket. Lucy's story develops a contrast between the tall Englishman, her first love, and her second, a passionate, peppery, French-speaking little professor rather like the one Brontë had known when she was a student.

Brontë prepared for going to the theater in a mood of wary ambivalence. "To-night—(if all be well)," she wrote to a friend, "I expect to see Rachel—at the French Theatre. I wonder whether she will fulfil reasonable expectation—as yet it has not been my lot to set eyes on any serious acting for which I cared a fig." Brontë was not one of those English ladies bred up to play genteelly at charades. But the country childhood that had taught her to scorn worldliness and display had also prepared her to take playacting very seriously. In her biography of the novelist, Elizabeth Gaskell relays Patrick Brontë's account of an event he staged in the early years at Haworth Parsonage: "When my children were very young, when, as far as I can remember, the oldest was about ten years of age, and the youngest about four, thinking that they knew more than I had yet discovered, in order to make them speak with less timidity, I deemed that if they were put under a sort of cover I might gain my end; and happening to have a mask in the house, I told them all to stand and speak boldly from under the cover of the mask." He asked each of the children what they most wanted: "I asked Branwell what was the best way of knowing the difference between the intellects of men and women; he answered, 'By considering the difference between them as to their bodies.' I then asked Charlotte what was the best book in the world; she answered, 'The Bible. . . .' " Oscar Wilde intended to shock the middle classes when he declared, "Man is least himself when he talks in his own person.

Give him a mask, and he will tell you the truth." Did the Yorkshire parson share his view? Or did he shrink from his children's clear gaze? As for his dutiful oldest daughter, was she telling him the truth or maintaining a mask that she always wore when she gave him precisely the answer he wanted? Whatever else, the anecdote certainly suggests that Charlotte Brontë, long before she wrote her novels as Currer Bell (and as the first-person narrators William Crimsworth, Jane Eyre, and Lucy Snowe), was well acquainted with the attractions of theatricality, and the connections between self-revealing and self-concealing.

Coming to examine, ready to dismiss Rachel, Brontë stayed to admire her; four days later she reported to her friend Amelia Ringrose Taylor, "I have seen Rachel—her acting was something apart from any other acting it has come in my way to witness—her soul was in it—and a strange soul she has—I shall not discuss it—it is my hope to see her again." Discussion of Rachel's soul having been thus deferred, she added only that the actress and Thackeray, whose lectures she had been attending, "are the two living things that have a spell for me in this great London—and one of these is sold to the Great Ladies—and the other—I fear—to Beelzebub." After she went a second time to see Rachel perform, Brontë gave a milder account of Thackeray to Elizabeth Gaskell. As one novelist writing to another of a third, she sought to be tactful; and the great man had charmed her by introducing her to his mother; but she also was beginning to work at sharpening the contrast between the novelist's and the actress's performances. (She never met Rachel.) "Thackeray's lectures and Rachel's acting are the two things in this great Babylon which have stirred and interested me most," she wrote to Gaskell; and to Sydney Dobell, "Thackeray and Rachel have been the two points of attraction for me in town: the one, being a human creature, great, interesting, and *sometimes* good and kind; the other, I know not what, I think a demon." She had told Gaskell that in London she had found in Thackeray and Rachel "most of what was genuine, whether for good or ill"; amid the false Great Ladies, in the Vanity Fair of the city, she thrilled to anything that seemed real and authentic, even real evil. "I shall *never* forget her—" she reiterated to Dobell from Manchester, where she was reflecting on Rachel after talking about her with Gaskell. "She will come to me in sleepless nights again and yet again. Fiends can hate, scorn, rave, wreathe, and *agonize* as she does, not mere men and women." With "wreathe" she conjures the image of a snake.

Her last Rachel letter is her most revealing—as a social transaction if not as a text. Deliberate and highly wrought, it was written in November 1851, six months after her visit to the French Theatre, and directed to James Taylor in Bombay. Taylor, an editor at Smith, Elder, had recently been stationed in India—perhaps, one Brontë biographer suggests, because he was George Smith's rival for the novelist's affections. Before going abroad, he had visited Haworth to press his suit, and had been firmly turned down. To her close friend Ellen Nussey, Brontë had reported then that "each moment he came near me—and that I could see his eyes fastened on me—my veins ran ice. Now that he is away I feel far more gently towards him—it is only close by that I grow rigid—stiffening with a strange mixture of apprehension and anger—which nothing softens but his retreat and a perfect subduing of his manner." The woman who stiffened when the man came near was relieved when the taxing Taylor went off to India. She wrote to him about Rachel partly by way of keeping him abreast of the cultural news of home, partly because she was drafting or thinking about a crucial section of her novel, but also because Rachel seems to have reminded her of him:

> Rachel's acting transfixed me with wonder, enchained me with in-
> terest, and thrilled me with horror. The tremendous force with which
> she expresses the very worst passions in their strongest essence forms
> an exhibition as exciting as the bull-fights of Spain and the gladia-
> torial combats of old Rome, and (it seemed to me) not one whit
> more moral than those poisoned stimulants to popular ferocity. It is
> scarcely human nature that she shows you; it is something wilder
> and worse; the feelings and fury of a fiend.

Less distanced than the letters to Gaskell and the others, less urgent than the letter to Ellen, this like the violent language of Lucy Snowe describing the transformative impression made on her by the actress she calls Vashti.

LUCY'S ACCOUNT of her evening at the theater is in the hot center of *Villette*, the twenty-third of forty-two chapters. She interrupts her relation of her own story to focus on the actress who seems to reflect her. We have come to know Lucy, who calls herself "a looker-on at life," as a woman who is fascinated and repelled by other women, both the enviably self-contained ones and those who flaunt their feelings. (The way she categorizes people is a clue to her character.) She prides herself on concealing who she is, carefully dressing so as to appear invisible—but she can be "read" by an expert in phrenology, the penetrating Frenchman Paul Emanuel, with whom she will fall in love because he recognizes the self she conceals. (But her self is not simply buried; her reflection can also be "read" when it is set beside another woman's in a mirror.) Her narrative insists there are two Lucys, inner and outer, also that there is a single contradictory one, which the actress thrills, transfixes, enthralls, enchains, and animates. As Lucy watches Vashti perform, she tells us,

> The strong magnetism of genius drew my heart out of its wonted orbit; the sunflower turned from the south to a fierce light, not solar—a rushing, red, cometary light—hot on vision and to sensation. I had seen acting before, but never anything like this; never anything which astonished Hope and hushed Desire; which outstripped Impulse and paled Conception; which, instead of merely irritating imagination with the thought of what *might* be done, at the same time fevering the nerves because it was *not* done, disclosed power like a deep, swollen, winter river, thundering in cataract, and bearing the soul, like a leaf, on the steep and steely sweep of its descent.

Watching Marie Dorval, George Sand imagined she could see her own soul on the stage; Hans Christian Andersen, after seeing Rachel in *Phèdre*, wrote, "You get ice-cold shivers down your back, as if you were watching a sleepwalker who expressed your hidden, deepest feelings." Lucy's fusion with Vashti is more difficult: she mirrors the haughty actress who "stood before her audience, neither yielding to, nor enduring, nor in finite measure, resenting it . . . locked in struggle, rigid in resistance." Lucy, the looker-on who avoids being looked at, identifies with Vashti's suffering and her disdain of the crowd. She is possessed by Vashti as Vashti is possessed by her role. Vashti is her alter ego—what Lucy, had she read Baudelaire, might have called her *semblable* and *soeur*.

LUCY'S NARRATIVE of her life story is generally adversarial in tone. It alienates the reader by obfuscating vital details, and by using a lot of French words for which the foreign setting provides but a slender pretext. This first-person narrative refuses to take the tone of an intimate confidence. The flirtation with identifying the actress, like the title page that names the author as Currer Bell, author also of *Jane Eyre, An Autobiography*, is part of an authorial performance that might fairly be termed theatrical. Lucy describes herself as a "rising character," and tells the story of her emergence from humble obscurity, as a lady's companion and a children's governess, to the elevation at the head of a classroom, the stage-like "estrade" on which a teacher rules over her frivolous and sottish girl students. But her position isolates her: outside the classroom, the girls are enviably more powerful—richer, more beautiful, luckier—than their teacher is.

Lucy has a single try at playacting which convinces her that literally as well as figuratively she belongs in the audience. She is half-forced, half-cajoled by Paul Emanuel, her colleague, to take a role in a silly school play—to misrepresent herself, as she sees it, by assuming the part of a foppish man. She cons her part in a hot attic that is infested by rats and black beetles which threaten to climb her skirts; M. Paul feeds her with sweet cakes by way of reward. After a pseudo-erotic struggle over her costume, she succeeds in retaining her woman's clothes, adding a symbolic cravat to indicate she plays a man. The phallic addition nearly makes Juliet Dusinberre's point about actresses *en travesti*: "Disguise makes a woman not a man but a more developed woman." Lucy becomes involved in the play after she observes—from the stage—how it reflects the sticky social situation into which it is inserted: the story about a beautiful young woman desired by two men resembles the plight of the flirt Ginevra Fanshawe and her two suitors, one of whom is Lucy's Dr. John. When Lucy, onstage, begins to understand that she is playing the part of Dr. John's rival for Ginevra, she "recklessly alter[s] the spirit of the role" while "retaining the letter," and throws herself into the experience. Acting, she is transformed: "Cold, reluctant, apprehensive, I had accepted a part to please another; ere long, warming, becoming interested, taking courage, I acted to please myself." In the role of the fop, she manages to express herself, to act on her secret ambition "to win and conquer." Later, she compares the exhilarating experience to an ascent in a balloon. Having learned how much she likes acting, she renounces it, in a characteristically self-punishing, self-abnegating move. It is some months later that she is taken to the theater by Bretton, and sees Vashti.

Villette on the one hand invites us to regard the famous actress as an image of Woman that Lucy compares herself to, a "flat" character who has less substance than the heroine, and meanwhile it takes the invitation back by insisting on Vashti's extraordinary power. Even John Graham Bretton, that "cool young Briton," bites his underlip as "the deepening tragedy blackened to the death scene." And then, as his and Lucy's and everyone else's attention is riveted to Vashti in her final struggle, there is the cry of "Fire!" and panic in the theater. Unanswerable questions hang in the air: has Vashti's passion provoked the flames? has her effect on the audience caused the explosion of popular ferocity, in which people trample one another in panic? does the imagination of danger and death produce the reality? Lucy avoids those issues by shifting her attention to the audience, where long-lost threads of plot are picked up. The polymorphous Vashti is dismissed; the fiery actress who was described as a fallen angel still haloed with Heaven's light, a shooting star "half lava, half glow," a creature "wasted like wax in a flame," vanishes utterly.

> On our way back we repassed the theatre. All was silence and darkness: the roaring, rushing crowd all vanished and gone—the lamps, as well as the incipient fire, extinct and forgotten. Next morning's papers explained that it was but some loose drapery on which a spark had fallen, and which had blazed up and been quenched in a moment.

In other words, all the fuss was over nothing: Vashti's fuss on the stage, Lucy's fuss over Vashti, as well as the rumor of fire. Lucy's resumption of her narrative suggests that Bretton's calm reality is the stuff of the real world, the world of ordinary phenomenal bourgeois reality, of realistic novels. What had flamed up so wildly had been only bits of rag; what had moved Lucy to poetry is written off by that reliable record of facts, the daily paper.

Like the paper, the novel tells us nothing about the play. We know only that it is a tragedy. The absence of plot summary or description—which the ordinary visitor to the theater would report on—allows us to separate character from plot, to attend to Lucy's fusion with the actress who is fusing with her role. At first Lucy looks askance at Vashti, as if at any woman publicly displaying herself. But then Vashti's spirit visibly takes her body over, consumes it; her flesh is transfigured into light (suggesting Lucy's first name?); therefore she can only be described in images, of stars, candles, daylight. Transcending her womanly body, she transcends the physical condition of woman, indeed of humanity:

> For awhile—a long while—I thought it was only a woman, though an unique woman, who moved in might and grace before this multitude. By-and-by I recognized my mistake. Behold! I found upon her something neither of woman nor of man: in each of her eyes sat a devil. These evil forces bore her through the tragedy, kept up her feeble strength—for she was but a frail creature; and as the action rose and the stir deepened, how wildly they shook her with their passions of the pit!

"The pit" is the haunt of devils such as sit in Vashti's eyes, but also the place where the audience sits. Lucy's pun suggests Brontë's awareness that the evil forces twisting the queenly face have sources on both sides of the tragic mask: that in the pleasure-pain of tragic acting and tragedy-viewing, audience and actress melt together in an acutely felt agon. The respectable audience helps transform the performer into a fiend. She openly experiences the violent passions that middle-class people do not acknowledge, the ones they repress and deny; she reflects them, caters to them, produces them. Brontë picks up the bloody imagery of gladiatorial combat she used in her letter to Taylor:

> Swordsmen thrust through, and dying in their blood on the arena sand; bulls goring horses disembowelled, make a meeker vision for the public—a milder condiment for a people's palate—than Vashti torn by seven devils: devils which cried sore and rent the tenement they haunted, but still refused to be exorcized.

The actress, their agent and scapegoat, is suffering for the audience's blood lust; her acting *is* suffering. Watching the other woman, Lucy is divided by what she sees, and by the difference between what she sees and the words to describe it—other people's words and also her own: "Vashti was not good, I was told; and I have said she did not look good." Vashti, standing "draped in pale antique folds, long and regular like sculpture," against a background "of deepest crimson," is "white like alabaster—like silver: rather be it said, like Death." She dies excruciatingly at each night's performance (her terrible struggle surely recalling, to Emily Brontë's surviving sister, that other thin woman's last agony); her acting is awesomely transformative and regenerative, but on the other hand it seems to be killing her. Lucy must ward her off: the baseless rumor of fire is a bitter, dismissive last image of the passionate woman, a reiteration of Lucy's first observation about the meteoric performance and career of the dead star she saw in her youth. To insist that her effect was but fleeting is, like Brontë's claim that Vashti is dead, a way of arguing against its force.

MATTHEW ARNOLD, the stern critic of the "hunger, rebellion, and rage" that marred Charlotte Brontë's fiction, could not possibly have read the private letter in which the novelist wrote that if she "could bear the high mental stimulus," she would go every night to see Rachel. But in an essay recalling the days of his youth, he precisely echoes the sentiment. Arnold was free to go every night to the theater, if he chose, and he did. "After a first sight of the divine Rachel at the Edinburgh Theatre, in the part of

Hermione," he remembers, "I followed her to Paris, and for two months never missed one of her representations."

A comparison of his Rachel and Brontë's is unfair. The vivid chapter that stops *Villette* in its tracks not only introduced Rachel to her audiences in America before she went there, but remains most of what most English-speaking readers know of her; in sharp contrast, Arnold's three didactic sonnets are forgotten, except in the playful allusion, in Randall Jarrell's novel *Pictures from an Institution* (1954), to the "accents of Matthew Arnold appreciating Rachel." I make the contrast in order to suggest why Brontë's vision begins to be true to Rachel: because Brontë takes her more personally than Arnold does; because instead of universalizing her as a symbol, she implicates her in a tissue of fictions; and because she refuses to resolve the lambent contradictions Rachel presented.

Arnold's accents, in his sonnets, are different not only from Brontë's but from those we might reasonably expect of the young Matt who, his friend Clough reported in a letter in 1847, was "full of Parisianisms; Theatres in general, & Rachel in special: he enters the room with a chanson of Béranger's on his lips—for the sake of French words almost conscious of tune: his carriage shows him in fancy parading the Rue de Rivoli; & his hair is guiltless of English scissors: he breakfasts at 12, and never dines in Hall, and in the week or 8 days rather (for 2 Sundays must be included) he has been to chapel Once." It was a much more sober Arnold who wrote the sonnets—one more like the man who, on the occasion of Sarah Bernhardt's visit to London in 1879, would praise Rachel as Bernhardt's superior in "intellectual power." In the cloud of Bernhardt's steam—Shaw later disparaged the "mere head of steam needed to produce Bernhardtian explosions with requisite regularity"—the memory of Rachel's star shone in England with a cool, cerebral light. In his essay on French drama, Arnold duly praises Rachel for putting Shakespearean fire in Racine: she and Talma before her, he writes, had "filled out with their own life and warmth the parts into which they threw themselves, [given] body to what was meagre, fire to what was cold." But life and warmth are not what he praises her for, in the end.

Nor did he praise those qualities in the sonnets he wrote in 1863 and published in his *New Poems* of 1867. They were inspired by the biography by Mme de B., and Arnold's gloom about Rachel's early death pervades them. The heroine of the sonnets is not the fiery stimulating actress who had once been followed to Paris by a passionate youth, but Tragedy decked out with pathos. It is as if, in response to the caviling of Mme de B., Arnold set about to make a higher-minded monument of his own to the tragedienne of his past. Imagined by him, Rachel's dying becomes a drama in three acts, a tragic ritual that transforms its central figure into multiple abstractions. Although Arnold does not, like John Graham Bretton, "judge" the actress "as a woman" and damn her as unwomanly, the point of view from which he sees her is nevertheless peculiarly male.

Echoing two different traditional forms—the elegy for one great artist by another, and the sonnet sequence that numbers a woman's virtues—Arnold begins with a description of the classical actress, mortally ill, revisiting the Théâtre-Français for a last farewell as she deliberately prepares to go south to die. Mme de B. and others had etched the affecting scene in the popular memory: it was indeed as if audiences had witnessed it. Arnold evokes the tragic heroine approaching her end with noble dignity:

> *In Paris all looked hot and like to fade.*
> *Sere, in the garden of the Tuileries,*
> *Sere with September, drooped the chestnut-trees.*
> *'Twas dawn; a brougham rolled through the streets and made*
>
> *Halt at the white and silent colonnade*
> *Of the French Theatre. Worn with disease,*
> *Rachel, with eyes no gazing can appease,*
> *Sate in the brougham and those blank walls surveyed.*
>
> *She follows the gay world, whose swarms have fled*
> *To Switzerland, to Baden, to the Rhine;*
> *Why stops she by this empty play-house drear?*
>
> *Ah, where the spirit its highest life hath led,*
> *All spots, matched with that spot, are less divine;*
> *And Rachel's Switzerland, her Rhine, is here!*

The flesh is pitted against the spirit, the worldly against the "divine," and Rachel represents the latter forces. "She represented for him that profound emotional force and inward concentration he desired," writes a biographer of Arnold. The tableau of the dying Rachel's return to the place where she had lived most intensely—the theater where she had had her "highest life"—allows an imaginative return of the poet's own: a French scholar was the first to observe that Arnold identifies Rachel with himself when twice he repeats, "Switzerland and the Rhine," the names of places where he remembers that *his* spirit had had its own best and most intense moments. But the actress is hardly acknowledged in this sonnet as a second self. She is distanced, a figure in a foreign city acting out a strange tableau, a ghost in a chilling charade.

In the next poem Rachel is no longer feverish and fading, and no longer in apparent harmony with what passes for nature in the parks of Paris. Instead, she mimes art. The contrast is neat: being moved from the cool pine forest to a bed shadowed by a marble bust, she acts no longer, but line by line grows colder:

> *Unto a lonely villa, in a dell*
> *Above the fragrant warm Provençal shore,*
> *The dying Rachel in a chair they bore*
> *Up the steep pine-plumed paths of the Estrelle,*
>
> *And laid her in a stately room, where fell*
> *The shadow of a marble Muse of yore,*
> *The rose-crowned queen of legendary lore,*
> *Polymnia, full on her death-bed.— 'Twas well!*
>
> *The fret and misery of our northern towns,*
> *In this her life's last day, our poor, our pain,*
> *Our jangle of false wits, our climate's frowns,*
>
> *Do for this radiant Greek-souled artist cease;*
> *Sole object of her dying eyes remain*
> *The beauty and the glorious art of Greece.*

It is the inevitable final stage of the Pygmalion motif: the dying actress—the poet's muse—turns finally to stone, grows cold under the gaze of a "marble Muse," calm and maternal, Polymnia, not Medusa. The woman dies; what looks on and is left is an antique statue that embodies her soul. Mme de B. emphasized Rachel's last, alabaster bed, told the story that the dying actress passed her final days running her fingers through the coffers of cold jewels she had vainly collected from kings and princes. Arnold imagines Rachel leaving "our northern towns" (more London than hot Paris?) and chill human misery to attain a final Keatsian union with Provence and the Greek Art which nineteenth-century English writers so often opposed to mortality, bad weather, and urban confusion. The spirit of this art attends her spirit's departure as her dying eyes rest on the bust of the muse. With this "sole object" in view, the "Greek-souled" artist dies alone; it is as if her sister muse—the muse of mimic art—turns Rachel "naturally," as it were, into stone.

Reaching the apogee of his hymn to contradictions, Arnold contradicts himself. In his final sonnet he denies that Rachel was simply "Greek-souled," insisting instead that many nations—"contending powers"—were the source of her spirit and strength. As a mixture of faiths and nations she is, furthermore, not unique and isolated, but "like us" after all; and there are other people at her bedside, it turns out:

> *Sprung from the blood of Israel's scattered race,*
> *At a mean inn in German Aarau born,*
> *To forms from antique Greece and Rome uptorn,*
> *Tricked out with a Parisian speech and face,*
>
> *Imparting life renewed, old classic grace;*
> *Then, soothing with thy Christian strain forlorn,*
> *A-Kempis! her departing soul outworn,*
> *While by her bedside Hebrew rites have place—*
>
> *Ah, not the radiant spirit of Greece alone*
> *She had—one power, which made her breast its home!*
> *In her, like us, there clashed, contending powers,*
>
> *Germany, France, Christ, Moses, Athens, Rome.*
> *The strife, the mixture in her soul, are ours;*
> *Her genius and her glory are her own.*

It is not a triumphant conclusion. Arnold begins with Rachel's Jewishness—the "scattered race," in a phrase that adds to his emphasis on fragmentation; he complicates it with the story of her reading Thomas à Kempis, which Mme de B. told; then in the end he returns to the hard fact of her origin. He mixes up Moses with Christ, nervously adds Germany to the brew of France and Athens and Rome. Making his monument to her uniqueness, the poet shores up fragments against ruin. Lionel Trilling remarked on the gloom that led Arnold to see Rachel, dying, as a symbol of modern Europe; more striking is the ragtag amassing of observations and names that suggests a clash of ignorant armies. Arnold's intention is to affirm the truth of Rachel's heroic uniqueness, an individuality that transcends multiplicity, but his litany of names, people's mixed with those of places, makes a recalcitrant line: "Germany, France, Christ, Moses, Athens, Rome." The dying actress is forced to encompass too many contraries: the Hebraism and Hellenism that Heine had been the first to formulate, and classicism and romanticism, and multiple political, religious, and aesthetic contrasts, and comparisons of the present with the past. (There is even perhaps an echo of Arnold's personal past, as the lost accents of the gay young Matt who sang Béranger's songs are audible in the slangy "tricked out" of line 4.) The actress is imaged as a creature of warring forces, therefore proposed as an aesthetic ideal based on the tensions of opposites; the human ideal she is supposed to represent is of individuality, separateness, and uniqueness, a coherent identity. "Her genius and her glory are her own": the eulogy ends in the present tense to suggest that in death— in Arnold's monument? where else?—the actress continues to live and enjoy her selfhood. It is unconvincing.

Arnold ends by affirming Rachel, Brontë by dismissing her; the latter has, ironically, been a more effective preservative of her memory. Rachel, the tragic actress whose role it was to die, represents death aestheticized, subtly eroticized, as the story of her dying is recounted. Meditating on the pains of existence in the heart of modern muddle, longing for a lost aesthetic absolute, hoping for a solution through synthesis, Arnold fixes on Rachel as symbolic of all three. But in the end—in the last sonnet, specifically—things fall apart. In his poems to her memory, what he shows is the close connection between the hopeless sense of chaos and confusion, on the one hand, and the dream of ideal art and dead women and lost heroics on the other. Rachel is called heroic, but her heroism finally seems to be a graceful submission to death, set up for us to contemplate with pleasure. The connections between the ideals of woman as art object, heroic individuality, and a lost better world— the connection between those ideals and death—are clearly legible.

2. SEPARATENESS AND CONNECTIONS

Vashti appears in *Villette* only onstage: her private and personal history is only (darkly) hinted at, and John Graham Bretton is shown up as worse than stuffy for drowning the artist in the woman, privileging "real" life over the livelier stage. Only an object of the gaze, never seen out of character, the actress lacks what people usually have in life and in novels, a social context and a history. On the one hand she resembles Lucy Snowe, an alienated English Protestant in a Catholic, French-speaking city, who is also cut off from parents and past; on the other hand she is nothing like anyone, less a character in a novel than an image.

Vashti's private life and her exotic religion or race are only hinted at,

Rachel in costume, photograph by Julien Vallou de Villeneuve

ambiguously and perversely, by her biblical name: the Vashti of the Book of Esther is not a Jew. The actress's Jewishness is only lightly and fleetingly alluded to by Brontë in a wild and violent passage in which Lucy compares this living, dying, dominating creature to a painting of a passive, sexy Cleopatra, which she has scornfully described in an earlier chapter: "Place now the Cleopatra, or any other slug, before her as an obstacle, and see her cut through the pulpy mass as the scimitar of Saladin clove the down cushion. Let Paul Peter Rubens wake from the dead, let him rise out of his cerements, and bring into this presence all the army of his fat women; the magian power or prophet-virtue gifting that slight rod of Moses could, at one waft, release and re-mingle a sea spell-parted, whelming the heavy host with the downrush of overthrown sea-ramparts." Picturing the "heavy host"—fat sensual women and the male army of their admirers—as overcome by spiritual power, small, large-souled Lucy imagines her own victory over her enemies: Vashti, the vital, creative, powerful antithesis to woman-as-art-object and woman-as-flesh, is her righteous surrogate. The "slight rod of Moses," Vashti is an agent of the avenging Old Testament God, more an antique Hebrew than a Jew.

G. H. Lewes borrowed the phrase from Brontë for one of his reviews. Lewes was astonished, each time he saw Rachel, by her power and her persuasive demand to be taken seriously. His response was intense: "Scorn, triumph, rage, lust and merciless malignity she could represent in symbols of irresistible power; but she had little tenderness, no womanly caressing softness, no gaiety, no heartiness. She was so graceful and so powerful that her air of dignity was incomparable; but somehow you always felt in her presence an indefinable suggestion of latent wickedness . . . a beautiful devil." Lewes strung those phrases together in an essay for his book *On Actors and the Art of Acting* (1875), compiling them from reviews he had been writing since the 1840s. A serious student of dramatic art, he shrewdly located the actress's seriousness in her play: "Speaking or listening she is wholly absorbed in her character. The effect of this is incalculable. You never take your eyes off from her; because she is so much in earnest, you are so interested."

But like nearly everyone else Lewes was bothered by her being a Jew. His early reviews, as John Stokes observes, are marked by "a crude and casual anti-semitism." In one, for example, he declares, "It will ever remain a curious problem how this little Jewess, this *enfant du peuple*, should, from the first moments of her appearance on the stage, have adopted—or let us rather say *exhibited*—the imperial grace and majesty which no one but herself can reach. . . . If you wish to form an idea of what Rachel would be without

her exquisite intelligence, look at her brother Raphaël Félix, who so closely
resembles her. Is he not a vulgar Jew Boy? Can anything wipe out the original
stain of his birth? Yet Rachel herself physically is no better; and were it not
for the 'o'er-informing spirit,' she would be as vulgar." Queen Victoria's
subject agonized over the mystery of the *reine de théâtre's* majesty—and the
experience of being subjected to the stage passions of a lower-class woman,
actress, Jewess. "Where has she learnt her dignity?" he asked in one of many
columns he wrote about her as "Adrian" of *The Leader*. He answered himself
promptly, "It was given her by God! This little Jewess picked up from the
streets, whose face would be common and insignificant were it not lighted
up with an expression which makes it ever-memorable, she carries herself
with *more* queenly grace of deportment than any throned monarchy." In
Lewes's novel *Three Sisters and Three Fortunes, or Rose, Blanche, and Violet*
(1848), a group of fashionable Londoners talk about Rachel in language just
like this, and one character coins a phrase Charlotte Brontë would borrow,
describing the actress as "a little Jewess they call Rachel, quite a girl, picked
up from the streets, but an empress on the stage."

Lewes and Brontë read one another's work with nearly the same ardent
attention they gave Rachel, and Brontë may perhaps rightly be read as deliberately rejecting Lewes's emphasis in her portrait of a not-particularly-Jewish,
purely artistic Rachel. He is more pointedly, painstakingly, and passionately
corrected by a woman novelist who was much closer to him. George Eliot
wrote her last novel, *Daniel Deronda*, while Lewes assembled his essays on
acting—minus the anti-Semitic slurs—in another room in the house they
shared. For her, Rachel's being a Jew mattered more than it had to Brontë—
and Rachel's woman's body meant something different from what it meant
to Lewes.

IN THE MIDDLE of the nineteenth century, when Rachel was at the
summit of her glory, women writers were beginning to redefine the actress
as a sign of female power. They did so in a gingerly fashion, with a perceptible anxiety focused on the body: the unspeakable issue between their lines
is the connection of women's moral strength and worldly ambition with female sexual desire. Rachel was the appropriate muse for these writers. On
the one hand, haloed by Racine and Euripides, her spectral body chastely
draped in Attic folds, she presented the actress as a legitimate subject for
moral people's attention; but then there was the other hand, not only the
gossip about her "real life" but the terrifying hyper-reality of the stage passions that so shake Lucy Snowe. Margaret Fuller invokes her as an example

of the woman of genius, "enslaved by an impassioned sensibility," who is detested by imperious men; in *Woman in the Nineteenth Century* (1845), she pleads that given "room enough," the "electric fluid" in women like Rachel will "invigorate and embellish, not destroy life." The power of such a woman is "direct from the spirit," Fuller argues: a force like magnetism or mesmerism is manifest in her "depth of eye and powerful motion." Manifest in the body, this powerful natural spiritual force threatens to destroy it, as if to prove soul and body are at odds. "Sickness is the frequent result of this overcharged existence," according to Fuller, whom James called "the American Corinne." She sees the actress as a type of woman whose art is an expression of her character, a vocation rather than a profession.

The more conventional Dinah Craik is more radical. In *A Woman's Thoughts about Women* (1860), Craik argues piously—as Elizabeth Gaskell did about Charlotte Brontë—that talents given by God should not be denied. She protests that "a Sarah Siddons, a Rachel, or a Jenny Lind, being created, was certainly not created for nothing"—that gifts like theirs should not "be hid under a bushel." But the female performer's display of herself disturbs Craik, who laments the "sad selfishness" of the *artiste*, the fact that "she needs to be constantly before the public, not only mentally, but physically: the general eye becomes familiar, not merely with her genius, but her corporeality; and every comment of admiration or blame awarded to her, is necessarily an immediate personal criticism." Craik's main concern nevertheless is to exonerate the acting profession as one of several legitimately open to women. In defense of acting, she elevates it into a calling: she writes that it is no "small thing for any woman—be she governess, painter, author, or *artiste*—to feel that, higher or lower, according to her degree, she ranks among that crowned band who, whether or not they are the happy ones, are elected to the heaven-given honour of being the Workers of the world." Redefined as workers, women who are governesses, painters, authors, and even actors may be defended against the sexual innuendo that was often directed against them all in Victorian England. As Helena Michie points out, the ideal of useful work, central to the bourgeois ideology of domesticity, is invoked here to validate the use outside the home of the female body— including even its pleasure-giving and pleasurable display.

Craik's actress ranks, at best, where "good" men and women would place her, among the lower and less happy respectable women. Florence Nightingale, more radically, refuses to concede that point. In *Cassandra* (1852), she raises the actress into middle-class society by refusing to look as usual at her body. The emphasis is deliberately eccentric. "Women, when they are young, sometimes think that an actress's life is a happy one—not for the sake of the admiration, not for the sake of the fame," Nightingale writes, "but because in the morning she studies, in the evening she embodies those studies." Embodying what she takes in is redefined as a stage in that most unimpeachable nineteenth-century process, self-improvement; by studying in the morning and testing herself in evening performances, Nightingale observes, the actress may make progress "even after middle age." The actress figure is purified; in her, of all people, mind and body are reconciled. A related feminist paradox would be presented in different terms by Simone de Beauvoir nearly a hundred years later. Having made the polemical point that in a man's world a woman is confined to immanence and narcissism, *Le Deuxiéme sexe* (1949) concludes that only the extraordinary rare actress can achieve transcendence. While the usual run of third-rate actresses virtually caricature women's plight, de Beauvoir writes, the great women performers renowned for intellectual and spiritual power—"the Rachels, the Duses"— manage marvellously to "make their persons the instruments of their art instead of seeing in art a servant of their egos." They are, she insists, the rare exceptions; but her peculiar plurals are promising.

WE CAN CATCH George Eliot in the act of conceding that the body of an actress is a problem when we look for the Rachel figure in *Daniel Deronda*. She is dissolved there, not framed and set apart as in *Villette*; there is more than one rare, unique actress in the novel. Not only does the text name her outright—along with Ristori and Jenny Lind—but it conjures her by almost all its themes: Jews; performing and criminal women; above all, the separateness and connectedness of individuals and peoples. She is recalled by three separate characters: the diva who turns up toward the end to inform her son, the eponymous hero, that he really is, by blood, the Jew he wishes to be; the English society girl Gwendolen Harleth, who frivolously imagines she can be a tragic actress like Rachel; and poor, gentle Mirah Lapidoth, whose mountebank father stole her away from her mother and put her onstage for his profit. Arguably, the Jewish tragedienne provided the germ out of which George Eliot's extraordinary, ambitious last novel grew. *Daniel Deronda* quite explicitly casts the Jews as the heroes of history's longest-running tragedy, currently being revised by Zionists into something between tragedy and history, therefore fit subject for a novel about the confluence of will and destiny. Coming to the novel from the history and legend of Rachel, one is ready to suspect that the actress's notorious passion for jewelry helped to motivate the twinning of Jews and jewels that unites the Gwendolen and the Deronda plots. *Daniel Deronda* turns on the paradox that Jews like jewels are at once valuable in themselves and symbols of other, more abstract values, representations of tradition and affiliation which can be loaded with meanings that contradict those they already have. As signs of (economic) change and changing signs, Jews and jewels together illustrate one of the novel's major themes: the arbitrary nature of signs, and how their names inform the way we look at things and people.

The connection (made by pawning, not punning) is insistent, and by tracing it one may summarize much of the story. Gwendolen Harleth loses at roulette in the first chapter, which is set in a gambling casino on the Continent; she pawns her turquoise necklace to a Mr. Wiener in order to pay her gambling debts. Daniel Deronda, who watched her play and felt mysteriously drawn to her, helpfully redeems it and returns it to her anonymously, forging a bond between them, making her look to him for redemption later, and oddly prefiguring his ultimate redemption of his people. The turquoises were the legacy of Gwendolen's dead father, who was replaced, in her childhood, by a stepfather who was perhaps worse than inadequate. Later, after she has married sinister, sadistic Henleigh Grandcourt, Gwendolen sees Deronda again at a country house party in England; she winds the turquoises around her wrist to signal to him that she is again in trouble. By then she has been further burdened by other jewels which are more valuable, also more negative in their symbolic valence: the diamonds sent her by Lydia Glasher, her husband's cast-off mistress, on her wedding day (they were originally his mother's). By marrying Grandcourt, Gwendolen betrayed a promise she made to Lydia, and in effect denied her connection with victimized womankind; the poisoned diamonds are a sign of her instability, her vanity, her greed.

While Gwendolen has been marrying and betraying, Daniel has saved Mirah, another pretty and desperate young woman, from drowning herself in the Thames. That action takes him to another pawnshop, where he hopes to find her lost mother. In order to have an excuse to come back to the shop (run by Jews, of course), he pawns a jewel of his, a diamond ring. That will turn out to be *his* father's legacy: *his* mother, when she commands him to visit her in Genoa, will ask him to wear the ring. In the end Mirah's father will steal the ring, freeing the orphaned young couple to marry and go eastward out of the fallen world of Europe into Zion, cleansed of material things like jewels, ready to effect a visionary action in a place where physical signs of spiritual relationships (like objects and parents) don't figure. Gwendolen, also purged by the tragedy of her marriage and Grandcourt's drowning, will stay at home, also freed of unnecessary baggage: Grandcourt's estate goes to Lydia's son.

THE IDEA OF RACHEL impressed George Eliot to the extent that the actress did not. She was sufficiently curious to go to see her more than once, but never enthusiastic. "We went to see Rachel again, and sat on the stage between the scenes," Mary Ann Evans wrote from London to her friends Cara Bray and Sara Hennell, in June 1853. "When the drop-scene fell, we walked about and saw the green room and all the dingy, dusty paraphernalia that make up theatrical splendour. I have not yet seen the 'Vashti' of Currer Bell in Rachel, though there was some approach to it in Adrienne Lecouvreur."

"We," of course, were Evans and George Henry Lewes, who along with Charlotte Brontë had raised her expectations of Rachel—too high, she judged. ("Her acting is not acting," one character says of Rachel in Lewes's novel *Three Sisters and Three Fortunes, or Rose, Blanche, and Violet;* "No, . . . it is *suffering,*" replies another.) Evans was falling in love with Lewes; just a year later, in July 1854, she would make the bold decision to live with him although he was married to another woman. When Lewes and Evans first went off together they visited Germany, where Lewes introduced his companion to Count Varnhagen von Ense. The widower of Rahel Levin Varnhagen might well have talked to this literary, learned woman interested in the historical roots of the Bible, and therefore in the Jews, about his dead wife, the friend of Goethe. Rahel had espoused assimilation and believed it possible; she had also believed that because she represented nothing intrinsically, she was free to stand for anything. George Eliot, concerned with what she herself represented in a world that would scrutinize her closely, would have been interested in Rahel's notion, and struck by the similarity of Rahel's name and that of the great tragedienne. Some years later, while she was writing *Daniel Deronda* (which contains some scenes set in Germany), the Jewish subject matter she had researched—the questions of assimilation and Zionism, the theme of "separateness with communication"—might have reminded her of Rahel and the Jewish actress.

The source of identity is one stated subject of *Daniel Deronda:* "Men can do nothing without the make-believe of a beginning," the epigraph to Chapter 1 memorably reads. The parallel, intersecting stories of Gwendolen Harleth and Daniel Deronda present alternative visions of how biological beginnings are related to character and the plots of lives. The Gwendolen story takes the conventional chronological view of personal development, for all that its heroine is seen first, in the gambling "hell," *in medias res*. As most nineteenth-century novelists and twentieth-century psychologists would do, George Eliot explains the heroine's (spoiled) character by an account of her early life. She is the child of a weak mother fallen on hard times, who encouraged her to imagine herself a princess in exile. Gwendolen's feelings of superiority to her half-sisters, her beauty and wit and social success, make her imagine she deserves applause and distinction, therefore that she can go on the stage professionally. After she is discouraged by the pianist Klesmer (a genius, "half-gypsy, half Jew," who advises that art requires hard work), she makes a show of a marriage that leads to tragedy. (The ironies are multiple: the history of the Jews is insistently called a tragedy, and Gwendolen's opposite realm seems to be romance; but she does become a tragic figure in the end.)

In contrast to Gwendolen, Daniel Deronda is introduced as parentless, and virtually without a character-determining childhood. He has been brought up by a tutor and a pleasant but remote guardian, Sir Hugo Mallinger, and suffered no equivalent of the turbulent formative experiences Gwendolen has had. (The modern reader will remark that this void has left him affectless.) Where Gwendolen's life is shaped by her desire to help and her need to separate from her mother, motherless Daniel's story moves him, all unknowing, *toward* his mother. It is as if his desire (to be a Jew) conjures her up: on the one hand she is proof of his real identity, but on the other hand she is the mother he dreamed. It is not altogether a good dream: the Princess Halm-Eberstein is spectral, dying, and she explains she has only asked to see him because she is compelled by her own father's avenging ghost. Here, as in Gwendolen's case, the mother is the significant parent, the clear point of origin, but here, as there, a shadowy man lurks in the background behind her. Raising the question of how destiny is determined for man and woman, gentile and Jew, the parallel plots interrogate one another. Doing so, they in effect deconstruct two of the most resonant pronouncements of the nineteenth century, Freud's assertion that anatomy is destiny and the cliché pronounced by Disraeli's Sidonia, among others, that race is the only truth.

Gwendolen, born a woman and beautiful, generally admired for being that, is embedded in artifice. She playacts very successfully in society, therefore imagines she can be an actress; she finds it hard to accept Klesmer's advice that acting is work, not play. Her incredulousness is conveyed by a startlingly violent image: "The belief that to present herself in public on the stage must produce an effect such as she had been used to feel certain of in private life, was like a bit of her flesh—it was not to be peeled off readily, but must come with blood and pain." Later, reflecting on what Klesmer told her, it seems to her that "his words had really bitten into her self-confidence and turned it into the pain of a bleeding wound." The Freudian critic is invited to discuss castration, but there are other options as well. In the world of this novel, private images—products of fear, guilt, hope, and desire—have the potential to become material.

The most important of the dreams that the plot realizes is Daniel Deronda's desire to be a Jew. His mother makes it true by telling him her life story: her word legitimizes his flesh, and significantly qualifies it. In its overarching plot as in its details, the novel asks whether the "natural" qualities seemingly lodged in the flesh—the race, the sex—are not rather formed and informed, created, as it were, by desire and dreams and language, the uncontrollable imagination and the conscious will, awkwardly collaborating. The figure of an actress presents itself to embody, if not answer, these questions.

THE PRINCESS Halm-Eberstein appears in only two scenes, dramatically, as if in a play of her own devising, before an audience of one. She receives her son in "the manner of a queen rather than of a mother," and is so remote that she seems to him a mythological enchantress, "a Melusina, not a human mother." (Melusina, a fairy of French legend, changes into a serpent from the waist down on one day of each week.) This cold and powerfully self-controlled mother is also a tragic victim—of her own dead father, whom she thinks she wronged, and of the desire that drove her to rebel against his repressive patriarchal will. Dying, consumed by guilt and disease, she is punished like the Ancient Mariner by having to tell her story. "I obey something tyrannic. . . . I have been forced to obey my dead father," she explains. And the truth that will complete and satisfy Deronda visibly depletes her as it is wrenched out of her in a speech described as a piece of "sincere acting."

As a girl, she explains to her son, she defied her father's commitment to the past and future of the Jewish people, and only for that reason to his daughter. "He wished I had been a son; he cared for me as a makeshift link," she says. She was eager to develop "the born singer and actress within me," the talent she derives from the female line. She tells her son that he can "never imagine what it is to have a man's force of genius in you, and yet to suffer the slavery of being a girl." But she tries to convey it to him, in vivid and markedly "feminine" imagery: "To have a pattern cut out—'this is the Jewish woman; this is what you must be; this is what you are wanted for; a woman's heart must be of such a size and no larger, else it must be pressed small, like Chinese feet; her happiness is to be made as cakes are, by a fixed

receipt.' That was what my father wanted." The princess tells her son she
never felt the mother-love that is said to be natural in women: "People talk
of their motives in a cut and dried way. Every woman is supposed to have
the same set of motives, or else to be a monster. I am not a monster, but I
have not felt exactly what other women feel—or say they feel, for fear of
being thought unlike others. When you reproach me in your heart for sending you away from me, you mean that I ought to say I felt about you as
other women say they feel about their children. I did *not* feel that. I was
glad to be freed from you." Cold as a daughter and a mother and a wife,
eager for freedom and ambitious for herself, she knows she seems a monster
in a world where women are defined by their (warm) relationships to men.
But she is bound to realize her own nature, to rise to the challenge of
opposing her adversary. She struggled with her father, and not for the conventional aim of choosing the husband that she wanted. Indeed, in order to
live for her genius and herself, she went so far as to marry the man he chose
for her, her cousin. When she thought her voice was going and wanted to
leave the stage gracefully she married again, as pragmatically: her art is her
most deeply felt life. As she prepares to leave her son for the last time, she
tells him, " 'I am not a loving woman. That is the truth. It is a talent to
love—I lacked it. Others have loved me—and I have acted their love. I know
very well what love makes of men and women—it is subjection. It takes
another for a larger self, enclosing this one,'—she pointed to her own bosom.
'I was never willingly subject to any man. Men have been subject to me.' "
Wise young Deronda, "with a grave, sad sense of his mother's privations,"
suggests the men were perhaps happier. He is committed to connectedness. But
separating is necessary as well. Leaving his mother, he reflects that he had "gone
through a tragic experience, which must for ever solemnise his life, and deepen
the significance of the acts by which he bound himself to others."

During their interview, Deronda assures his mother that he will understand her: "What I have been most trying to do for fifteen years is to have
some understanding of those who differ from myself," he explains, and ventures to say he can "enter into the painfulness" of her early struggle. She
rebuffs him: " 'No,' said the Princess, shaking her head, and folding her arms
with an air of decision. 'You are not a woman.' " Her position on the
insuperable gulf between men and women recalls the plight of Gwendolen,
who is also a performer, and also cold. In the context of a novel that preaches
understanding among different peoples, it is ominous.

Lewes had the idea that George Eliot should write *Daniel Deronda* as a play. But of course it had to be a novel, to allow her to expatiate largely on the difference between acting and suffering, and to elaborate the connections between separateness and connectedness, and history and tragedy. Although she did write that the actress Helen Faucit might serve as a moral model for girls, George Eliot was committed to a belief in the supreme moral power of fiction, which exercises and strengthens the sympathies, she thought, and trains people to love one another better. With *Daniel Deronda*, she hoped specifically to equal the achievement of Harriet Beecher Stowe, whose *Uncle Tom's Cabin* had changed American readers' views of slavery, and helped to alter the social and political world. She wanted, she said, to correct the error of anti-Semitism in England; she proposed to show in her novel that Jews were more like Christians than not. But the Jews themselves, she recognized, insisted on their difference, stressing the "separateness with communication" that had helped keep them a distinct people throughout diasporic history.

George Eliot could not resolve the paradox any better than anyone else has been able to, and suggests her impatience by a flaw in her novel. On the one hand, Daniel Deronda and his party, representations of the idea of Jewry, are too moral, idea-driven, and impalpable to be believable, or even redeemable by the several rueful or ironic acknowledgments of this; on the other hand, the "realistic" other Jews conform too well to stereotype. "Everything *specifically* Jewish is of a low grade," she had written in 1848 about Disraeli's novel. Later, she denounced anti-Semitism explicitly and emphatically. Nevertheless, when the poetic Daniel and Mirah go off to realize their ideal nation in the promised land, the Jews left behind in London for the gentile reader to love as neighbors are repugnant and reminiscent of hostile stereotypes: the too shiny, ingratiating pawnbroker Ezra Cohen, his dressy wife and daughter, and his "whinnying" son. These real Jews in their repellent physicality are the ones who abide in England; what the reader is meant to learn from is their kinship with the ideal ones, people Sir Hugo and Lady Mallinger would be happy to dine with, who go off the map to never-never land, where they belong. A deliberate irony or a telling slip? It is difficult to say.

And Gwendolen? Can she try to be, learn to be, get to be better, as she promises her mother, or must she perforce be what she physically is, even after (in a startling image, at the end) she shucks her old skin, the way a Lamia (something like a Melusina) or a snake does? Via Rachel, it is easy to slide from the Jewish Question to the Woman Question; and indeed the comparative success of the Gwendolen plot suggests that the earnestly pursued first Question may be something like a cover for the second. The actress,

Jew and woman, haunts a novel concerned to ask in multiple ways whether or not one must keep to old patterns, whether one can remake oneself to accord with an idea, whether ideas do not impress themselves upon and virtually create physical facts. Rachel interested Mary Ann Evans, who re-created herself as George Eliot to become an original and effective image in the world—even, in the end, as she received her reverent visitors at the Priory, a quite theatrical personage. The actress represented both Woman and Jew; the way she handled her particular physically determined differences seemed to the novelist to represent, more generally, the fact that everybody can stand for something beyond her self, and the possibility that by will and imagina-tion one might conceivably elude the body's imperatives and history's, and transform one's self into an image of the imagination and the will.

3. TRAGICOMIC MUSE

The *femme artiste* is doubly, therefore monstrously, a woman: the truism, solemnly and salaciously propounded by Parisian boulevardiers, was explored throughout the nineteenth century by serious novelists, female and male. The first *femme artiste* of fiction, the heroine of *Corinne, or Italy*, is a figure for her mother country (which is not her father's). Like Italy, Corinne inspires and contains and stands for art. In her, as in all romantic artists, genius is pure instinct; it drives her into the fever of creation and the glare of publicity; but the same pure instinct also impels her to a love which cannot be recon-ciled with her outward, self-expressive artist's life. Womanhood binds her to the heterosexual plot; because that plot demands she be something other than an artist, it must have a tragic resolution. (Byron told Germaine de Staël that the moral of her story was more harmful to girls than anything *he* had ever written.)

The *femme artiste*, doubly a woman, is doomed. In the course of the century, as novels and plays about performing heroines intersected with the careers of stage performers and excited gossip about them, the theme was reworked with more and less erotic and tragic variations. English women writers—Brontë and Eliot, Geraldine Jewsbury and Elizabeth Barrett Brown-ing—brooded over the irreconcilable obligations imposed by genius, which seeks to show itself, and womanly love, which is private. The different em-phasis of men's writing is suggested by two very different minor novels that were published, in Paris and in London, the same year as *Villette*: Gérard de

Rachel, miniature
by Adelaïde Isabelle
Antonine Chéreau,
dame Lapoter,
exhibited at the
Salon of 1850

Nerval's wispy, poetic *Sylvie* and Charles Reade's comic *Peg Woffington* have nothing in common but the theme of the actress who is false and flawed and dangerous to men.

Rachel, who seemed to make the inner life of the woman artist manifest, is a haunting dark figure of the *femme artiste* in Brontë and Eliot, an image of the contradictions between the outward and the buried life of women. Virginia Woolf may be pointing to that image of the actress by giving the name Rachel to the heroine of her first novel, *The Voyage Out*, which was written in 1911, the year she reviewed the Gribble biography of Rachel. Like Lucy Snowe and Gwendolen Harleth, Woolf's Rachel Vinrace cannot reconcile the person she feels herself to be and the outer life she lives; she dies young. But in an American novel published a few years later, thoroughly revisionary feminist version of the performing heroine alters the trope: Thea Kronborg, who at the end of Willa Cather's *The Song of the Lark* (1915) chooses her career as an opera singer over love—and is happy, and warmly supported by the men in her life, for doing so. Of equal but subtler feminist import is a novel published twenty-five years before Willa Cather's, Henry James's *The*

Tragic Muse (1890). James reverses the emphasis of nearly a century of moral and not-so-moral fiction by imagining an actress for whom the stage life is the most real life. The story of Miriam Rooth, who wants to be "the English Rachel" and gazes with desire at Gérôme's "cold portrait" of the French actress, is about the play between the inner and the out ward life, the psyche and the stage, the literal, the metaphorical, and the metonymic.

As if to signal his departure from the earnestness that governs even Goncourtian portraits of *femmes artistes* in novels, James does not fictionalize a historical actress but imagines, instead, the predicament of a young person who aspires to be a star like one she admires—aspires, that is, to the condition of representation. Miriam aims to make herself an actress and an image of her art. Rachel is her model just as she was Gérôme's, and just as Miriam herself becomes the model for young Nick Dormer's painting of The Tragic Muse. In Rachel's lifetime, Théophile Gautier had identified Rachel's brittle, nervous, mocking quality as modern; when James's Miriam, following Rachel, makes herself into an excellent actress and ultimately a great star, she is described as "the great modern personage" by someone who recognizes her as an effect and an image of theatricality—of what we now call the postmodern.

Set in Paris and England, *The Tragic Muse* concerns six young people—four of them members of the same family—who either face, or fancy they face, the choice between living a safe, conventional life and devoting themselves to art. Nick Dormer and his sister Biddy are the children of an upper-class but impoverished British family. Nick's mother wants him to stand for Parliament; a friend of his father has promised him a fortune if he does so; but his desire is to be a portrait painter—to represent people on canvas. Biddy sculpts. Their cousin, the rich, beautiful, domineering Julia Dallow, is in love with Nick, but will marry him only if he gives up art: she is the widow of a collector, and prefers politics to her surfeit of beautiful things. Biddy is in love with Julia's brother, Peter Sherringham, a diplomat and an impassioned amateur of the theater, but Peter is no more interested in his cousin than Nick is in his. "I'm fond of representation—the representation of life: I like it better, I think, than the real thing," Peter says. Drama and possibility enter these not-quite-incestuous young people's lives in the persons of two less than respectable individuals: the drawling, decorative aesthete Gabriel Nash, Nick Dormer's college friend, and the intense aspiring actress Miriam Rooth, an acquaintance of Gabriel's. "Ah, you're a queer family!" says Miriam. From the point of view of the traditional novelist of manners, she, of course, is the queer one—the sort of woman who is usually a minor character in fiction, the daughter of a man originally named Roth, now dead, and an ambiguous, lower-case-bohemian mother. As if to keep Rachel in the knowing reader's mind, James rings semiprivate, nearly inaudible changes on her legend: Mrs. Rooth reads novels by Sophie Gay (the mother of Delphine de Girardin), and constantly readjusts a paisley shawl reminiscent of the one an English duchess gave *la grande Rachel*, who passed it on to her mother. James describes the girl's dead Jewish father wryly as a variant on the peddler, a collector whose "love of old pots and Christian altar-cloths, had supplied, in the girl's composition, the aesthetic element, the sense of form."

This man's daughter has tendencies toward being an object of art; she also wants to be an artist. James shows that the two are connected in parallel theatrical scenes. In the first, which is set in the greenroom of the Théâtre-Français, Peter Sherringham watches as Miriam gazes passionately at "Gérôme's fine portrait of the pale Rachel, invested with the antique attributes of tragedy." Looking from the real woman to the painted one, and back, Peter reflects that she "suffered little by the juxtaposition": Miriam is as pale with her ambitious passion, as clearly marked by the muse, as a muse is. The second scene, set in an artist's studio, not a theater, echoes the first and underscores it. Julia Dallow, on a surprise visit to Nick, catches Miriam in the act of modeling for his painting of The Tragic Muse. To Julia their intimate joint enterprise seems a nearly sexual transgression, and she grows "so pale that Nick, observing it, instinctively looked back to see what Miriam had done to produce such an effect." (Pallor like Julia's, and Miriam's when she looks at the picture of pale Rachel, has signified desire since Sappho.) Nick finds that his model has merely kept her pose, stayed as still as a painting: "She had done nothing at all, which was precisely what was embarrassing; only staring at the intruder, motionless and superb." Miriam looks back to more effect than Nick; her "largely gazing eyes" challenge the distinction between those who look and those who are looked at—between actual and painted women, respectable ones like Julia and spectacular ones like herself.

The circumstances of the novel's production are echoed in the twinned artist-and-actress-model scenes. James was living in London and planning to write for the London stage—although, as the critic Peter Brooks observes in passing, he would have preferred to write for the Comédie-Française. The real-life muse for the novel was his friend, the aged Fanny Kemble. She served him as the model for old Mme Carré, late of the Comédie-Française, the teacher whom Peter Sherringham hires to train Miriam. More importantly, she was the inspiring historical link to Mrs. Siddons—Reynolds's Tragic Muse was her aunt—and to Rachel. In 1851, Kemble had given readings from Shakespeare, in the afternoons, on the same London stage where Rachel performed in the evenings; in the 1880s, she was doing imitations of the great tragedienne for friends. Still wonderfully talkative, she liked to recall Rachel's superiority to Ristori, and would not tolerate comparisons of Sarah Bernhardt to Rachel. James was enchanted by the friendship of a woman who "reconciled being alive today with having been alive so long ago," as he puts it of Mme Carré; he loved being linked, through her, not only to the English theater but to the high traditions and high polish, the "ideal and exemplary world," of French theatrical productions, a world where, he had admiringly written, although the women were not all beautiful nor the men handsome, there was never "an awkwardness, a roughness, an accident, a crude spot, a rough note." He was very proud of his knowledge of the French theater ("I may say that I know the Comédie-Française," he confided to his notebook). Chatting with Fanny Kemble, plotting *The Tragic Muse*, he was thinking about Rachel, whom he wished he had heard: "Her artistic being, so vivid, yet so purely instinctive," he jotted in his notebook, apropos of Miriam. "Ignorant, illiterate. Rachel."

Closeness to Kemble also encouraged James to be proud of a real or imagined working knowledge of the theater that put him in a position to recognize, criticize, and correct the *embourgeoisement* to which novelists subject actresses. He mocked, for instance, the diva of *Daniel Deronda*: her excessive earnestness seemed to him incredible. In a critical essay written as a playlet, or "conversation," he set two characters to debating her plausibility:

> PULCHERIA. I don't see the princess, in spite of her flame-colored robe. Why should an actress and prima-donna care so much about religious matters?
> THEODORA. It was not only that; it was the Jewish race she hated, Jewish manners and looks. You, my dear, ought to understand that.
> PULCHERIA. I do, but I am not a Jewish actress of genius; I am not what Rachel was. If I were, I should have other things to think about.

His Miriam, with her "pale face, a low forehead, and thick, dark hair . . . [and] largely gazing eyes," her look from under dark brows that makes her appear "unconciliatory, almost dangerous," physically resembles Rachel. She is "more than half a Jewess," but thinks not at all about religious matters—

or indeed about very much except herself and her career. In her lack of susceptibility to others (inherited or borrowed from her father's insensate old pots and the cold portrait she contemplates), Miriam radically contrasts with the performing heroines of two novels of the 1880s: James's own *The Bostonians* (1886) and Mary Augusta Ward's *Miss Bretherton* (1884).

Verena Tarrant, in the Boston novel, is not an actress but a rhapsode—"an American Corinne," to adopt the phrase James used to describe Margaret Fuller. Her father, a religious mountebank, exploits her; her other rival would-be possessors are a feminist activist with fantasies of a "Boston marriage" to the beauty, and the reactionary southerner Basil Ransom, who means to take her out of circulation and make her his wife. (In what I take to be an inter-oeuvre joke, his name is recalled by Basil Dashwood, the compliant cipher Miriam Rooth finally marries.) The forces that vie to possess Verena are still in conflict in the novel's last scene, where Verena weeps as Basil sweeps her off after her final performance. The reader is invited to wonder: what if she had given herself neither to father nor lover, woman or man, and stood up for whatever it was that might be, or pass for, her own self?

When he first read Ward's *Miss Bretherton* James had considered such questions. In a graceful letter of congratulation to the author, he confessed his own interest in what seemed to him her subject, "the private history of the public woman, the drama of her feelings, heart, soul, personal relations, and the shock, conflict, complications between these things and her publicity, her career, ambition, artistic life." James was generously overreading: a better account of Ward's meaning was given by the *Fortnightly Review*, on the occasion of the author's death in 1920, which interpreted *Miss Bretherton* as "the story of an actress vindicating the honour of her profession." Ward's heroine is a moralizing correction of French versions of the *femme artiste*. Miss Bretherton, who is English, is spontaneous and virtuous; she lacks the sinister craft, polish, and (associated, implicit) sexual promiscuity of the Frenchwoman Mme Desforêts, brilliant in the role of Adrienne Lecouvreur, who is a version of Sarah Bernhardt. Ward's hero, an Oxbridge don, is a literary scholar (his subjects are Musset and Stendhal) and a connoisseur of the theater. He is enchanted by Miss Bretherton's beauty but distressed by her lack of art, so he sends her to his sister, Mme de Châteauvieux, for polishing. That lady is married to a Frenchman, and has "that *mélange du meilleur ton*" which, Ward quotes an authority as saying, "is found in its perfection only in the best society of France." Being French, she is equipped to instruct Miss Bretherton in artifice; being English, she can ensure that the young woman will remain virtuous. In three weeks, the actress is transformed into an artist. She vindicates her profession, but she must abandon it.

"It will break her down," Mme de Châteauvieux tells her brother on her deathbed. "You can save her and cherish her—you will. It seems as if I saw you—together!" Of course they marry. Plausibility requires that the actress be less than perfectly genteel, but Miss Bretherton is luckily nearly good enough for Kendal, being the daughter of the Scottish overseer of a sugar plantation in Jamaica, who "married an Italian, one of your fair Venetian types—a strange race-combination." Emphatically, she is not "one of your thin, French, snake-like creatures who have nothing but their *art*, as you call it; nothing but what they have laboriously learnt with time and trouble." She reconciles spontaneity and goodness, art and nature, France and England, as Kendal and Mme de Châteauvieux manage to do; but to marry the public and the private woman remains beyond her. Having been perfected by the stage, to suit Kendal's exquisite taste, she must give up the theater, and give herself up to love or connoisseurship.

KENDAL FIRST SEES Miss Bretherton at an art exhibition at the Royal Academy, where a friend points her out as the most beautiful object on display. James copied Ward's opening strategy exactly in the first chapter of *The Tragic Muse*, where Miriam Rooth presents herself to public view in the garden of the Palais de l'Industrie, at the annual exhibition of the Salon, among sculptures that raise bourgeois eyebrows. Like Vashti, like the Princess Halm-Eberstein (and Gwendolen Harleth at the gambling casino where we first see her), like Miss Bretherton at the Royal Academy, Miriam Rooth is there to be seen, filtered by the regard of those who consider her and perhaps altered by her admirers into someone more complex and serious and substantive than she might really be. She is partly other people's projection. Disingenuously, James evades the mystery of her inner life, which "would be cleared up only if it were open to us to regard this young lady through some other medium than the mind of her friends." The theatrical approach to an actress is chosen as the most appropriate and most telling: "We have chosen, as it happens, for some of the advantages it carries with it, the indirect vision."

Miriam is interesting rather than beautiful; she is messy and vulgar, with a troubling appeal that is not altogether erotic. The matter of her sexual availability is elaborately and euphemistically danced around, conflated as always with matters of class and even of species: "Miriam Rooth was neither fish nor flesh: one had with her neither the guarantees of one's own class nor the immunities of hers." What is different and distinguished about her is her "instinct" for art, which is genuine and innate. Unlike de Staël's rhapsode, Corinne, she is by nature a deliberate and self-conscious artist—not that she is able to discuss Diderot's or Talma's aesthetic creed, or Coquelin's or James's own. "She had no knowledge that it was publicly discussed; she was just practically on the side of those who hold that at the moment of production the artist cannot have his wits too much about him. When Peter told her there were people who maintained that in such a crisis he must lose himself in the flurry she stared with surprise and then broke out: 'Ah, the idiots!' " Ignorant about everything else, she is no idiot where art is concerned. It is her life: to make herself an artist, she becomes "a drudge," for art's sake. She does not succeed by being polished into a lady, like Miss Bretherton; instead, she earnestly studies Shakespeare and the techniques of her craft.

Peter Sherringham is shamelessly in love with the theater, and when he begs Miriam to marry him he offers her the comfortable role of ambassadress, telling her she can play it all her life. Nevertheless he is wary of the actress, and has doubts about Miriam's character. What bothers him is not exactly her class or her morals, but something that embraces and evades both: the accessibility and outwardness of the public woman seems to him to threaten something beyond her womanhood—her very humanness. Peter wonders about the substance of "a woman whose only being was to make believe, to make believe that she had any and every being that you liked, that would serve a purpose, produce a certain effect, and whose identity resided in the continuity of her personations, so that she had no moral privacy, as he phrased it to himself, but lived in a high wind of exhibition, of figuration—such a woman was a kind of monster, in whom of necessity there would be nothing to like, because there would be nothing to take hold of." Monstrousness here is not, as in Brontë and George Eliot, contingent on the refusal of normative female "goodness." The indictment of the actress here is less obviously gender-based, and more devastating. Miriam is more frankly vulgar and available than Vashti, or the princess, but less sexual: she has less of a secret dimension. Peter's male emphasis on taking hold is almost ironic. What the actress refuses or simply lacks—it is unclear which—is character. She wants the complexity and privacy and personal richness that heroines of fiction conventionally represent, the psychological denseness which the tradition of Richardson and Brontë and Eliot and James never tires of identifying as the highest human value. Constantly acting, impersonating, living only to display herself,

Miriam is a character of whom it might be said—Peter says it—that "the representation was the substance." She embodies her art; it is her most real being.

Peter is saved from solving the problem Miriam sets a man like him—a man, that is, who prefers representation to the real thing. Single-minded in her commitment to herself, her art, and her image, Miriam easily decides to turn him down, and choose a husband whose only asset is a willingness to serve her and her success. Like Rachel, she cannot imagine putting love and marriage before glory, and like Rachel she is determined to remain independent. Basil Dashwood is no Svengali; he will manage only the business end of her career. She therefore rejects Peter, who was temporarily useful to her in finding Mme Carré, who formed her for the stage; earlier, she found Nick Dormer useful to the extent that he could make her image real. Otherwise, her shady, shadowy mother and co-conspirator, and her shallow young actor-husband, are all the people she needs, all she wants. Dismissed, Peter Sherringham will learn to make do with reality at the side of the charming, compliant Biddy; he will in other words stay in the family, within the cozy upper-middle-class sphere he was born to, while Miriam goes off into a wider, wilder, riskier world. Gabriel Nash, the other outsider, lazy aesthetic man to Miriam's hardworking artist-woman, also drifts off—less purposefully—somewhere indeterminate. Before he does so, he speculates brilliantly about what will become of the monstrous brilliant girl. In this novel about painting and surfaces, Miriam's future is suggestively "brushed in" as Gabriel paints, in words,

> a large bright picture of her progress through the time and round the world, round it and round it again, from continent to continent and clime to clime; with populations and deputations, reporters and photographers, placards and interviews and banquets, steamers, railways, dollars, diamonds, speeches and artistic ruin all jumbled into her train. Regardless of expense the spectacle would be thrilling, though somewhat monotonous, the drama—a drama more bustling than any she would put on the stage and a spectacle that would beat everything for scenery. In the end her divine voice would crack, screaming to foreign ears and antipodal barbarians, and her clever manner would lose all quality, simplified to a few unmistakable knock-down dodges. . . . It would be curious and magnificent and grotesque.

Gabriel's canvas is broad, his strokes impressionistic. In contrast to Gérôme's academic "cold portrait" of Rachel, this picture places the modern actress in the chaos of the modern world. Behind James's mordant vision of what a career like Miriam's would come to in the twentieth century hovers the legend of Rachel's last journey to America, the story that she was Barnumized there, and destroyed. Enlarged into a spectacle, Miriam is flattened and reduced; hawking herself, hustling others, she is finally transformed into "the pure commodity: as fetish," in Walter Benjamin's phrase, "saleswoman and wares in one." Spectacular only, the star is finally "the great modern personage," a dismaying sign of the modern marriage of commerce and art.

But James nevertheless insists on Miriam's brief extraordinariness, the wonder of her creation of herself as "a beautiful, actual, fictive, impossible young woman, of a past age and undiscoverable country, who spoke in blank verse and overflowed with metaphor, who was exalted and heroic beyond all human convenience, and who yet was irresistibly real and related to one's own affairs." He insists as well that Miriam, on her progress toward inevitable vulgarization and destruction, energetically collaborates in the star-making process—that she herself desires and controls it. ("I am making myself commercial," Rachel had written from America.) Miriam is not swallowed up by publicity and spectacle and the legend of her life, not managed or owned or victimized by even her admirers. As Rachel did, and Bernhardt did after her, she tells the papers what to say about her.

> She made almost an income out of the photographers (their appreciation of her as a subject knew no bounds), and she supplied the newspapers with columns of irreducible copy. To the gentlemen who sought speech of her on behalf of these organs she poured forth, vindictively, floods of unscrupulous romance; she told them all different tales, and as her mother told them others yet more marvellous publicity was cleverly caught by rival versions, surpassing each other in authenticity. The whole case was remarkable, was unique; for if the girl was advertised by the bewilderment of her readers, she seemed to every sceptic, when he went to see her, as fine as if he had discovered her for himself.

James wrote elsewhere of Sarah Bernhardt, "She has in a supreme degree what the French call the *génie de la réclame*—the advertising genius; she may, indeed, be called the muse of the newspaper." An echo of *Villette*'s condescension is audible at the end of *The Tragic Muse:* the papers had the last word about Vashti, too.

On the other hand, we are told that even the skeptics who see her enjoy a thrill of discovery, think Miriam "fine"; we are asked to think her case unique. She is a marvel precisely because she is altogether and only committed to aesthetic values. Like Rachel, she is low and also high; as Rachel said of herself, she has nothing at all about her that is bourgeois. She is contemptuous of pieties, and frankly avows the materialism and the selfishness that smug, safe, genteel families pretend not to have. "Curious and magnificent and grotesque," Gabriel calls her, and the last word is perhaps worth pausing over.

The feminist theorist Mary Russo has proposed "the female grotesque" as a mode of subversion. Women, Russo argues, are conventionally cautioned to avoid "making a spectacle" of themselves; she suggests that deliberately doing so, flaunting the fact that what's called "natural" is constructed, can be a way of attacking and undercutting cant and false values. I am not suggesting that James proposes Miriam as a model for a feminist, nor am I proposing her myself: she probably is, just as Peter suspects, shallow. On the other hand, by being so consciously, brilliantly, generously, and grotesquely theatrical, she challenges conventional ideas of what Woman is and must be; she represents something newer and more vivid and vital than a Tragic Muse. Is she its comic opposite? "Never, never . . . ," says Peter Sherringham, when the suggestion is made. "I'd rather see you as Medusa crowned with serpents." But James leaves it open for us to see her that way, by leaving her free and still thrilling, at least for a while. Her marriage does not impose the closure on her story, the limit on her freedom, that constrains standard heroines of fiction. Gabriel predicts that Miriam will be destroyed by her stardom, but *The Tragic Muse* stops short of tracing her path to tragedy—if that's where she is going. She has yet to peak. The narrator is "warned," he says, "by a sharp sense of modernness" that "renders it difficult . . . in taking leave of our wonderful Miriam, to do much more than allude to the general impression that her remarkable career is even yet only in its early prime." The final emphasis is on possibility, and indeterminacy. In Gabriel's vision of Miriam flattened into a commodity and a celebrity, an indeterminate shimmer of facts and fictions and reflections, she is vulgar and hard to define, but more vital than any of the others.

CARL SCHURZ, the American politician and journalist, was somewhat older than James; he saw Rachel when he was a young German revolutionary in Berlin, in 1850. In his later life, he recalled the "spell of intense astonishment" when she first stepped upon the scene; the eyes that glowed like two black suns; the voice that seemed to rise from the bowels of the earth and carried the soul of the listener through all the sensations of joy, sadness, pain, love, hatred, despair, jealousy, contempt, wrath, and rage, even if he did not understand the language; and finally the force of the climaxes in which the beholder would feel his blood run cold and gasp for breath, and moan, "God help us all." Schurz insists that "there was in my admiration of Rachel nothing of the infatuation of an ingenuous youth for an actress which we sometimes hear or read of. If anybody would have offered to introduce me personally to Rachel, nothing would have made me accept the invitation. Rachel was to me a demon, a supernatural entity, a mysterious force of nature, anything rather than a woman with whom one might dine, or speak about every-day things, or take a drive in a park. My enchantment was of an entirely spiritual kind." He even cites the concurrence of other "persons of ripe years" and "cultivated artistic judgment" to prove that his view of this actress was more than "an extravagant picture produced by the overheated imagination of a young man charmed by a stage-goddess." This most sublime of actresses whose appeal was higher than sexual did not hold the mirror up to nature, he concludes; rather, she embodied extreme emotions "in an ideal grandeur, in their highest poetic potency, in gigantic reality." He apologizes for his inadequate language.

Clearly Schurz—like Matthew Arnold—protests too much; the stress on Rachel's spirituality and intellectuality suggests a reluctance to acknowledge her vexing corporeal attractiveness, the implication of an unbeautiful, "low" woman's body in "high" art, great ideas. ("Was that the voice of a woman?" Schurz asks, and goes on to describe the enchanting grace of her palms outstretched beseechingly, and "the disdainful wave of her arm, which seemed to sweep the wretch before her into utter nothingness.") Keeping high and low separate is basic to a man's respectability and a culture's; denial, we have learned, is a common habit. Well before Freud wrote, Germaine de Staël and George Sand suggested that passionate female performers are ambivalently admired by masochistic Northern men, who are threatened by a female sexuality they ultimately condemn as perverse. It is tempting to overread the sexlessness of *The Tragic Muse* as a function of denial, and to interpret the aesthetic passion the novel analyzes as a mystification of the bodily feelings that are virtually unacknowledged in this text. When Peter Sherringham reflects that there is "nothing to take hold of" in Miriam, the skeptical eyebrow, after Freud, tends to lift; the modern instinct to psychologize stirs.

Is the novel "really" about the lure of a forbidden object of desire? Or, perhaps, does Peter's wish to marry Miriam, along with Nick's sentimental link with Gabriel, encode a love that dares not speak its name? The problem with such a reading is that Peter's desire is less interesting than Miriam's—for all that James shows the latter only from the outside. Her passion is for her art and herself as an artist; and the comical, ironical truth James insists on is that, helped along by much hard work, it gets realized. Readers have long discussed what the theater meant, here and elsewhere, to Henry James, and how he ranks it in relation to that art of the novel which he took so seriously. What Miriam represents in *The Tragic Muse*—the theater and theatricality—is apparently the shallow opposite of "high" and moral inward-looking art, but also, paradoxically, it is art at its most vital and single-minded. The actress's evocative figure seems to suggest it would be a mistake to put sexuality on one or another side of a moralized false opposition.

THE TRAGIC MUSE plays out most of the themes implicit in the legend of Rachel, neatly pulling my themes together. For many reasons, it seems appropriate to end this book about Rachel with a reading of that novel. But even the ambivalent biographer must yearn for more theatrical closure than a reading of James's portrait of the actress—cold like Gérôme's—provides. And while it is only an appropriate act of homage to bathe the image of Rachel in the flattering afterglow of high culture, that image also demands wider notice and applause. Finally, for all the fascinating rewritings that followed it, Brontë's remains the most vivid vision of Rachel. And therefore two novels by women that in different ways recall Brontë's present themselves here to give Rachel something like a curtain call.

Sylvia Townsend Warner's *Summer Will Show* was published in London and New York in 1936, a hundred years after Rachel's Paris debut in the legitimist-Bonapartist-Orléanist melodrama *La Vendéenne*. The author of the novel, a communist, went off to Spain to support the anti-fascists soon after finishing it. The Rachel she evokes (without ever naming her) in her novel about the 1848 revolution is a far cry from a heroine of a Napoleon play. She is the spirit of popular revolution, of *La Marseillaise*—not the tool of government who calmed the mob, as cynical versions of Rachel's legend have it, but the child of the people who voiced its righteous fury. Recognizably a rewriting of very different French and English nineteenth-century novels—of Flaubert's novel about 1848, *L'Education sentimentale*, and of a tradition of English novels about passionate, genteel heroines—it celebrates, as Charlotte Brontë's Vashti chapter began to do, the twinning of a repressed Englishwoman and her opposite, counterpart, and reflection. Here the usually marginal figure of the dangerous, foreign, fallen woman, the *femme artiste* who unsettlingly combines Nature and Art, is drawn, with clearly subversive intent, into the center of the narrative.

Warner's novel tells of the erotic and political liberation of Sophia Willoughby, a Victorian lady with a talent for commanding. We first see her reigning severely over her estate, her horses, her servants, and her two young children. Her estranged husband, hardly the man she herself might have been, is living, she reflects contemptuously, in Paris with his mistress—a "byword, half actress, half strumpet; a Jewess; a nonsensical creature bedizened with airs of prophecy, who trailed across Europe with a tag-rag of poets, revolutionaries, musicians, and circus-riders snuffling at her heels, like an escaped bitch with a procession of mongrels after her; and ugly. . . ." When Sophia's two children die of smallpox, she abruptly decides to go after Frederick in Paris—in order to get him to impregnate her, she thinks, but really because she is drawn by Minna Lemuel's compelling voice, which Frederick echoed at the bed of his dying little daughter, repeating the French phrase, *Ma fleur.*

Arrived in Paris, Sophia soon finds herself at a bohemian evening party on the Left Bank, at the home of this mistress, where Minna is at the center of an international crowd of worshipers. Pressed to recite a fairy tale—reciting is her métier—she tells instead, by flickering candlelight, the true story of her own girlhood in Lithuania. The child of religious, persecuted, poor Jews, she was spiritually nourished, she says, on "the stories of good Jewesses, faithful women: Jael, who slew Sisera, and Judith, who slew Holofernes; Deborah, who led an army, and Esther, who saved a people." As Minna's beautiful contralto continues, Sophia thinks, "You are exactly like a Jewish shopkeeper, the Jew who kept the antique shop at Mayence, staring, gloating round his shelves, with a joy in possession so absorbing that it was almost a kind of innocence. In a moment you should rub your hands, the shopkeeper's gesture." And as if in response to her auditor's derisive thought, Minna does. For Minna, as she will tell her later, is addressing and responding to only Sophia. The common fantasy of members of audiences, the delusion that the performer on the stage speaks directly and specifically to oneself alone, miraculously comes true.

The two women's rapturous love affair takes place against a background of radical upheaval. Caught up by her passion for Minna, caught by history, Sophia becomes a traitor to her class, increasingly radical. She gives what money she has to the revolution; she collects metal to be made into bullets

by the insurgents; she ends up, together with Minna, on the barricades in
June. Minna is a sloven and the opposite of a lady, but like Vashti, like
Rachel, she carries herself with queenly dignity, as if she were ennobled, not
so much by her art as by her honesty in presenting her self. She is a defiant
rewriting of the cliché that the public woman is the lady's traditional opposite, "fallen" and inferior. Here as in Brontë's novel, the Rachel-figure reit-
erates the traditional identification of Woman with art and emotion,
redefining art in romantic terms to mean rapture and freedom, not artifice
and pattern and enclosure and control. Minna the rhapsode began her career
by memorizing and declaiming French classical tragedy, but she transcended
alexandrines to become the more original and more personal artist—a Jewish
Corinne. Loving Minna, glorying in the power of her own body and her
own life, the lady of the English manor becomes a human being—a loving
and useful and finally a violent one, a woman who kills a man in revenge,
after Minna is stabbed. The ending of the novel leaves Sophia alone, absorbed
in reading *The Communist Manifesto*, dreaming of a time of liberation for
all. As at the end of *Villette*, the heroine's lover is probably—but not definitely—dead; as in Brontë's novel, the focus widens, in conclusion, from the
personal into the universal, by means of a borrowed rhetoric (here, literally
a borrowed quotation) that conveys the flavor and the promise of another,
better world. The ending of *Villette* is rewritten in atheist terms: the language
of Marx and Engels replaces Brontë's echoes of the Bible.

In *Summer Will Show*, the performer and her admirer act together on
the revolutionary, world-changing energies that Lucy Snowe experienced (and
denied) as she watched and heard the actress Vashti. Because of the other
woman who vividly figures the radical imagination in female form, who
began by boldly imagining herself in the roles of legendary heroic women
leaders, Sophia Willoughby can live as her world does not yet permit women
to live, expressing transformative power and passion.

IN A NOVEL published two years after Warner's, Rachel made what can
only be described as a cameo appearance, this time under her own name.
The author of the novel was an American, Rachel Field. *All This, and Heaven
Too* (1938) was a best-seller, a popular romantic fiction in the familiar mode
derived from Charlotte Brontë, about a plain, repressed, but fiercely passionate and ambitious governess and a warped, magnetic man. Based on a scandal
that had apparently touched a branch of Rachel Field's family, in France in
Rachel's time, it vindicates a woman whom history remembers as the mistress—and the motive—of a nobleman who murdered his wife. In Field's

story, Henriette Desportes-Déluzy is fiercely virginal and honestly passionate, in Brontëesque style. The daughter of Bonapartist aristocrats fallen on hard times, she is hired as a governess by the Duc de Praslin and his wife, a languid, excessively fertile, sexually aggressive Corsican who neglects her four children. The governess is prim and competent; the children soon come to prefer her to their torpid mother; and Henriette quickly fascinates the duke, who fastidiously disdains his blowsy wife and sees in the very different, independent-minded other woman "a little glimpse of what life might have been." Soon the two are going out together to the theater with one of the children, to see Rachel in *Judith*—hardly an appropriate choice for a child, Henriette remarks. (In the 1940 Hollywood film version of the novel, starring Bette Davis and Charles Boyer, the play is the more familiar *Phèdre*, "classic" and therefore respectable—quite as inappropriate. Rachel, by the way, appears in the movie only on a poster.) As gossips talk, and the newspapers publish hints, the charged, chaste friendship persists. The wife grows increasingly jealous, and forces the governess to leave. Poor Henriette's reputation is ruined, and she cannot find another position. She stays on in Paris, living frugally, seeing the duke very rarely, and always in the company of his children.

In the summer of 1847, some months after Henriette moves from the home of the Praslin family, the duchess is found murdered in her room. The duke is the chief suspect, and the woman reputed to be his mistress is suspected of complicity. Henriette is put in the Conciergerie, the prison where Marie Antoinette had been confined. Insulted and injured, she insists on her innocence, and maintains her dignity. (When Mlle Déluzy took her walks in the courtyard of the Conciergerie, Victor Hugo reported, she was conscious that all eyes, from all windows, were trained on her; she posed. Hugo judged her a clever but heartless woman, capable of a crime of egotism, not passion.)

Popular feeling against the duke is intense: as a peer of France, he cannot be prosecuted in the ordinary way, and when he is allowed to kill himself without confessing to his crime the people are enraged, against him and Mlle Déluzy. Hatred of Louis-Philippe and his ministry, and of aristocrats generally, is focused on the woman in the prison. (From Rachel Field's point of view, the Praslin affair helped bring down the government; and there is indeed some talk about it in Flaubert's *L'Education sentimentale*.) Henriette Déluzy is ultimately released for want of evidence, and she successfully escapes her questionable past by flight to democratic America, where, all passion spent, she will enjoy the calm devotion of a benign New England minister, Mr. Field.

But she is haunted by her sensational past. When the great actress Rachel comes to America, Henriette Déluzy Field goes to see her. Rachel Field picks up the trope of the woman who sees herself reflected in the great actress: having mediated between genres, shortening the distance between tragedy and bourgeois fiction, it blurs the distinction between "high" and popular fiction here. Henriette is thrilled by watching Phèdre, and sees in the passion Rachel makes manifest a mirror of her secret self. Like Phèdre, Henriette had experienced forbidden desire, and others had died violently as a consequence of it, as in the play. The exiled Frenchwoman goes backstage, and talks with her countrywoman about the parts they both have played in tragedy. Rachel, who knows Henriette's sensational story, says, "Drama has come to us both in different ways. Compared to what you have lived, my roles must seem like the charades of children." Henriette demurs. "Drama has marked both our lives," she acknowledges, but adds: "for me it took the form of a yoke; for you—wings." Rachel's exhausting performance has drained her; Henriette "could not help seeing how frail that body had grown." She takes leave of the restless, risk-taking actress, who lives her passions fully and is doomed not to be saved in a bourgeois heaven on earth, in a new world. She says, "I salute your genius." It is the tribute that Lucy Snowe could not pay her directly.

~

Notes

INTRODUCTION AND CHAPTER ONE

For stars, see Elizabeth Burns, *Theatricality* (London, 1972); Edgar Morin, *Les Stars* (Paris, 1972); Richard Dyer, *Stars* (London, 1979) and *Heavenly Bodies: Film Stars and Society* (London, 1986); Leo Braudy, *The Frenzy of Renown* (New York, 1986). Morin makes the point that stars are actors who save producers from financial ruin; I borrow his Hollywood examples.

The most useful biographies of Rachel in French and English are Sylvie Chevalley, *Rachel: J'ai porté mon nom aussi loin que j'ai pu* (Paris, 1989); Nicole Toussaint du Wast, *Rachel: amours et tragédie* (Paris, 1980); Joanna Richardson, *Rachel* (New York, 1957); Bernard Falk, *Rachel the Immortal* (New York, 1936); Louis Barthou, *Rachel* (Paris, 1926). M. Védel, *Notice sur Rachel* (Paris, 1859), is the most reliable and least tendentious work by one of her contemporaries. The book-length biographies and memoirs of Rachel also include Madame [A.] de B[arréra], *Memoirs of Rachel* (New York, 1858); Léon Beauvallet, *Rachel and the New World* (Paris, 1856; trans. Colin Clair, London, 1957); Jules Janin, *Rachel et la tragédie* (Paris, 1859); A.-P. Mantel, *Rachel: détails inédits* (Paris, 1858); Eugène de Mirecourt, *Rachel* (Paris, 1854); Samson, *Mémoires* (Paris, 1882); Mme Samson, *Rachel et Samson, souvenirs de théâtre* (Paris, 1898). See also Théodore de Banville, *Mes souvenirs* (Paris, 1882); Adolphe Crémieux, *Autographes* (Paris, 1885); Edmond Got, *Journal* (Paris, 1910); the pseudonymous Prince Georges de Hohenzollern, *Mademoiselle Rachel: souvenirs d'un contemporain* (Berlin, 1882); Arsène Houssaye, *Les Confessions: souvenirs d'un demi-siècle, 1830–1880* (Paris, 1885); Frances Anne Kemble, *Records of Later Life* (London, 1882); Ernest Legouvé, *Soixante ans de souvenirs* (Paris, 1886; trans. Albert D. Vandam, London, 1893); Adelaide Ristori, *Etudes et souvenirs* (Paris, 1887); Louis Véron, *Mémoires d'un bourgeois de Paris* (Paris, 1856).

For Rachel and Tragedy the *loci classici* are Jules Janin and Alfred de Musset,

"De la tragédie, à propos des débuts de Mlle Rachel," *Revue des deux mondes*, 1 November 1838; see also Musset's review of the "Reprise de *Bajazet*" in the same journal, 1 December 1838. Especially useful is the drama criticism of Théophile Gautier, collected as *Histoire de l'art dramatique en France depuis vingt-cinq ans* (Leipzig, 1858–59; repr. Geneva, 1968), 6 vols.; see also the theater reviews reprinted in the Pléiade edition of the works of Gérard de Nerval (Paris, 1984), and Matthew Arnold's essay "Rachel" in *On Actors and the Art of Acting* (Leipzig, 1875; repr. New York, Grove Press, n.d.). For a severely critical view of Rachel, see Charles Maurice, *La Vérité-Rachel: examen du talent* (Paris, 1850). See also C.-A. de Chambrun, *Quelques réflexions sur l'art dramatique de Mlle Rachel, ses succès, ses défauts* (Paris, 1853); Etienne Léon Lamothe-Langon, *Rachel* (Paris, 1838); E. Masseras, "Le dernier chapître de la vie de Mlle Rachel," in *Revue de France* (Paris, 1876); Auguste Vacquerie, "Mlle Rachel," *Profils et grimaces* (Paris, 1856). Rachel's influence on tragedy is considered retrospectively in André Bellessort, "Rachel et la tragédie française," *Heures de parole: sujets anciens, questions modernes* (Paris, 1929).

More and less "romanced" works about Rachel that have developed her myth since her death include James Agate, *Rachel* (New York, 1928); March Cost, *I, Rachel* (New York, 1957); A. de Faucigny-Lucinge (née Choiseul-Gouffier), *Rachel et son temps* (Paris, 1910); Hector Fleischmann, *Rachel intime* (Paris, 1910); Francis Gribble, *Rachel: Her Stage Life and Her Real Life* (London, 1911); Paul Hagenauer, *Rachel, princesse de théâtre et coeur passionné* (Paris, 1957); Arsène Houssaye, *La Comédienne* (Paris, 1884); Nina Kennard, *Rachel* (Boston, 1886); J. Lucas-Dubreton, *Rachel* (Paris, 1936); Martial-Piéchaud, *La Vie privée de Rachel* (Paris, 1954); and the frankly partisan but also scholarly Valentine Thomson, *La Vie sentimentale de Rachel d'après des lettres inédites* (Paris, 1910). There are at least two biographies of the actress in Yiddish, Abraham Cahan's *Rachel* (New York, 1938) and *Rachel* by Ch. Korenchandler (Paris, 1958).

The important (incomplete) collections of letters by Rachel, with interstitial commentary, are by Georges d'Heylli [Edmond Poinsot], *Rachel d'après sa correspondance* (Paris, 1882), and Gabriel Laplane, *Rachel: lettres inédites* (Paris, 1947). For other published letters, see Imbert de Saint Amand, *Mme de Girardin, avec les lettres inédites de Lamartine, Chateaubriand, Mlle Rachel* (Paris, 1875); Rachel, "Lettres inédites," *La Revue de Paris*, 1 May 1910, and "Lettres à l'aimé," *La Revue de France*, 15 December 1922; Léon Séché, "Les Amis d'Alfred de Musset: Rachel, lettres inédites," *La Revue*, 1 December 1906, and "Rachel et Mme de Girardin, documents inédits," *La Revue de Paris*, 1 June 1909; and Richmond Laurin Hawkins, *Rachel and Arsène Houssaye: Unpublished Letters*, Harvard Studies and Notes in Philology and Literature XV (Cambridge, Mass., 1933).

Rachel is one of several significant figures allotted essays in Théophile Gautier, *Portraits contemporains* (Paris, 1886); Sir Theodore Martin, *Monographs: Garrick, Macready, Rachel, and Baron Stockmar* (London, 1906); Mme [Béatrix] Dussane, *Reines de théâtre 1633–1941* (Paris, 1944); Marcel Pollitzer, *Trois reines de théâtre: Mlle*

Mars, Marie Dorval, Rachel (Paris, 1958); and especially Henry Knepler, *The Gilded Stage: The Years of the Great International Actresses* (New York, 1968). See also Robert Launay, *Figures juives* (Paris, 1921); Elizabeth Robins, *Twelve Great Actresses* (New York, 1900); and Marie-Louise Pailleron, *François Buloz et ses amis* (Paris, 1930).

The doyenne of modern scholarship on Rachel is Sylvie Chevalley: in addition to her recent biography, see her *Rachel en Amérique* (Paris, 1957); "La tournée de Rachel en Russie," *Revue de l'histoire du théâtre* IV, 1958; and "Rachel et les écrivains romantiques," *Romantisme* 38, 1982. See also Nikolai Solnzev, "Rachel vue par les artistes et les écrivains russes," *Revue de l'histoire du théâtre* IV, 1958; Lawrence Senelick, "Rachel in Russia: The Shchepkin-Annenkov Correspondence," *Theatre Research International*, vol. III, no. 2, February 1978; and John Stokes, "Rachel's 'Terrible Beauty': An Actress Among the Novelists," *ELH*, Winter, 1984.

I have quoted from the published collections of letters by Rachel and from letters in libraries in Paris (Bibliothèque de la Comédie-Française), Jerusalem (The Hebrew University), and Cambridge, Massachusetts (Harvard Theatre Collection). Most of the letters now in Israel are in Laplane's collection; most of those at Harvard are reprinted by Hawkins. I know of the existence of other letters which I have not been able to consult, and regret that the long-promised edition of Rachel's complete correspondence has not yet appeared.

I have cited accessible English editions whenever possible. Unless otherwise indicated, translations from the French are my own, made with the help of Elizabeth Houlding.

p. 4 "that supreme gift": "*ce don suprême qui fait les grandes tragédiennes, l'autorité.*" Théophile Gautier, *Histoire de l'art dramatique en France depuis vingt-cinq ans* V, p. 67.

8 "Rachel, who triumphed so magnificently": "*Rachel, qui avait obtenu de si beaux triomphes dans l'ancienne tragédie, était précisément douée de toutes les qualités modernes dans le talent comme dans la beauté.—Cette jeune fille élancée et mince, qui pourrait se faire une ceinture de son diadème, cet enfant au corps souple, aux mains fluettes, aux pied mignon, au front bombé, aux yeux pleins de sombres éclairs, à la lèvre arquée par le* sneer, *ne ressemble en rien aux femmes antiques, à hanches étroites, à flancs épais, à larges épaules, à front bas que nous font voir les statues grecques et romaines; toute la passion maladive du temps où nous vivons agite ces membres frêles, inquiets, nerveux et tirant de l'énergie morale la force que les anciens tiraient de l'énergie physique.—Cette fièvre moderne qui bouillonne sous toutes les froideurs de la vieille tragédie, et qui parvient toujours à trouver quelque échappement, est une des causes inconnues et inavouées du succès de la jeune tragédienne.*" Gautier IV, p. 71. In a paper, "Light and the Actor," presented at a conference, "Victorian Theater and Theatricality," at the Graduate Center of the City University of New York, 8 May 1992, Michael Booth suggests that the flashing eyes of actors described by Rachel's contemporaries

seemed remarkable because they reflected limelight, an innovation which made possible a follow spot that picked out the single actor on the stage, and was reflected by eyes as well as sequins, etc.

p. 9 "What can I tell you": *"Que vous raconterai-je de nos triomphes? Ils sont toujours à la hauteur de nos mérites."* Rachel to Louise de Saigneville, quoted by Sylvie Chevalley, *Rachel: J'ai porté mon nom aussi loin que j'ai pu*, p. 276.

10 "They wanted to orchestrate": *"On voulait un dernier triomphe pour la grande tragédienne; on n'eût qu'un immense concours de curieux."* "Rachel," in Michaud, *Biographie universelle* (Paris, 1880), p. 35.

"to inter the precious remains": Mme de B., *Memoirs of Rachel*, p. 370.

11 "Her acting is fascinating": *"Son jeu est fascinant; tant qu'elle est en scène, quoi qu'il se passe, vos yeux ne peuvent se détacher d'elle; cet être faible et fragile vous domine; je ne saurais estimer qui ne s'abandonnerait pas à son pouvoir pendant la représentation. Je crois voir encore cette moue orgueilleuse, ce regard rapide qui vous fouette."* Alexander Herzen is quoted by Nikolai Solnzev, "Rachel, vue par les artistes et les écrivains russes," *Revue de l'histoire du théâtre* IV (1958), p. 356.

"It was a marvellous sight": Charlotte Brontë, *Villette* (Harmondsworth, 1984), p. 339. All further quotations are from this edition.

12 "those lines": *"ces phrases qui résonnent sur l'idée comme une armure d'airain sur les épaules d'un guerrier, . . . ce style si arrêté, si net et si magistral, qui vient en avant comme un bas-relief fouillé par le ciseau."* Gautier VI, p. 181.

13 For the Second Funeral of Napoleon, see especially Victor Hugo, *Choses vues 1830–1846*, vol. 1 (Paris, 1913). Mary Shelley's letter about the funeral was written over a year after the event; see Betty T. Bennett, ed., *The Letters of Mary Wollstonecraft Shelley* III (Baltimore and London, 1988), p. 19.

15 "a tall, broad-chested, dark-eyed young prince": W. M. Thackeray, "The Second Funeral of Napoleon" (1841), in *The Complete Works of William Makepeace Thackeray XIX (Boston*, 1892), p. 335.

16 Susan Sontag, *Illness as Metaphor* (New York, 1978), esp. pp. 25, 62, 63.

17 For Rachel's will and Sarah Félix's willful or careless mismanagement, see Bernard Falk, *Rachel the Immortal*, p. 295 ff.

20 "She has had the funeral": Henry James, "Paris As It Is," 25 December 1875, *Parisian Sketches: Letters to the* New York Tribune *1875–1876*, edited by Leon Edel and Ilse Dusoir Lind (New York, 1957), p. 22. For Mlle Raucourt's funeral, see Roselyne Laplane, *Mademoiselle George* (Paris, 1987). For the funeral of Mlle Mars, see Hugo, *Choses vues* I, p. 236.

21 "Why was I chosen": Dumas is quoted by Hector Fleischmann, *Rachel intime*, p. 310.

23 "not a drop": See André Bellessort, *Heures de parole*, p. 220. Joseph-Isidore Samson, according to one historian of French Jewry, was himself a Jew. See David Cohen, *La Promotion des juifs en France à l'époque du second empire* (Paris, 1980).

p. 23 "the temperament of a bureaucrat": It is Gabriel Laplane who writes that Samson *"avait un tempérament de fonctionnaire . . . respectueux de l'autorité,"* while Rachel *"appartenait à la race sans racines."* Laplane, p. 64.

24 Félix's French is perhaps worth recording. *"Vous pouvez m'en croire, Monsieur, puisque je trouve en ce moment la force et le courage de vous écrire,"* he wrote, and protested that he was motivated by *"un sentiment de douloureuse et haute convenance."* Letter of 8 January 1858, Laplane, pp. 63–64.

"And so the history": James Agate, *Rachel*, p. 174.

25 "I had always believed that an artist's private life": *"J'avais toujours pensé que la vie privée d'un artiste n'était pas du domaine de la publicité; telle n'est pas votre manière de voir; je ne contesterais pas avec vous sur ce point, convaincue que mieux que moi vous devez connaître les limites imposées à la critique par les lois et les convenances."* Rachel's letter to M. Eugène Quinot of *Le Siècle* demanded a correction of an article announcing her conversion. Laplane, p. 126.

"We talked food all the way": *"Jusqu'à Marseille nous avons alors surtout parlé cuisine; c'était un prélat gourmand."* Rachel to her mother; repr. in Chevalley, *Rachel*, p. 376.

"All that we can say of Mlle Rachel": quoted by Falk, p. 307.

26 "in the half-light": *"Dans le demi-jour d'une alcôve qui ressemble à une chapelle, s'érige un lit d'albâtre . . . du plus étrange dessin. On dirait des tuyaux d'orgue, surmontés de masques antiques. Au pied du lit, regardant le chevet, une statue de Polymnie évoque dans les plis de sa tunique la beauté classique, égarée dans ce chef-d'oeuvre de mauvais goût. C'est sur ce lit, évoquant par avance la froideur de la pierre tombale, que Phèdre s'endormit et ne se réveilla plus."* H. Clouzot in *Bulletin de la société de l'histoire du théâtre* (1908), p. 147.

27 In England, according to a biographer of Mrs. Siddons, "the idea of an actress personifying the Tragic Muse had been in the air since Garrick's Jubilee, and, in that character, Romney, in 1771, painted Mrs. Yates. . . . It is small wonder that, on November 18th, 1785, a year and a half after Reynolds' masterpiece was exhibited, Mrs. Siddons herself condescended to be wheeled across the stage as Melpomene, in an attitude that reminded every one of the picture." Mrs. Clement Parsons, *The Incomparable Siddons* (New York, 1890; reissued 1962), p. 252. Around 1895, Gérôme—who embarked on a second career as a sculptor soon after painting *La Tragédie*—did a bust of Sarah Bernhardt with a full-length allegorical figure of Tragedy—red-haired like her—emerging from the drapery beneath her breast.

29 "It is the fate of actors": Virginia Woolf, "Ellen Terry," in Woolf, *Collected Essays* IV (New York, 1967), p. 67.

31 I have borrowed some insights into Delacroix's portrait of Talma from Claude Reichler, "Talma as Néron in *Britannicus*, or, Putting a Monster to Good Use," in *Yale French Studies* 76 (1989).

p. 31 his rival Ingres: Although he did not paint Rachel's portrait, Ingres did paint her into "The Birth of the Muses," a watercolor designed to be inserted into a model temple designed by the architect Hittorff as a gift from Prince Napoleon to Rachel. See John Whiteley, *Ingres* (London, 1977), pp. 86–87.

32 "the women of antiquity": Gustave Flaubert, *Sentimental Education* (Harmondsworth, 1964), pp. 67–68.

"thin, gaunt": Edmond and Jules de Goncourt, 11 April 1864, *Journal: mémoires de la vie littéraire* 2 (Paris, 1888–1917), p. 191, quoted in Anne, Margaret, and Patrice Higonnet, "Façades: Walter Benjamin's Paris," *Critical Inquiry*, vol. 10, no. 3 (March 1984), p. 408.

34 The French on the passport reads, *"Age de 35 ans; Taille 1,60 mètres; Cheveux bruns; Front haut; Sourcils bruns; Yeux bruns; Nez aquilin; Bouche moyenne; Menton rond; Visage ovale; Teint pâle."*

"Rachel was below average": *"La taille de Rachel était au-dessous de la moyenne; elle avait le front bombé, les yeux enfoncés et, sans être grands, très expressifs, le nez droit avec une légère courbe, cependant. Sa bouche, garnie de petites dents blanches et bien rangées, avait une expression railleuse et fière tout à la fois. Son cou était parfaitement attaché et sa tête, petite, au front bas, s'y reposait gracieusement. Elle était fort maigre mais s'habillait avec un art extrême qui faisait de cette maigreur presque une beauté. Sa démarche et son geste étaient aisés, tous ses mouvements souples, enfin toute sa personne remplie de distinction. Elle avait, pour me servir d'une expression en usage, des mains et des pieds de duchesse. Sa voix, qui était un contralto, avait peu d'étendue, mais grâce à l'extrême justesse de son oreille, elle s'en servait avec une extrême habileté et arrivait aux inflexions les plus fines et les plus délicates. Quand elle commençait à parler, son organe avait un peu d'enrouement qui se dissipait bientôt.*

Lorsqu'elle parût pour la première fois sur la scène française, sa taille n'avait pas encore reçu le développement qu'elle atteignit plus tard; il y avait dans ses traits petits, dans ses yeux rapprochés une sorte de confusion, s'il est permis de s'exprimer ainsi, et on la déclara laide. Plus tard, on l'a déclara belle. Elle n'était cependant ni l'un ni l'autre tout à fait, mais tous deux, selon l'heure, le jour, l'expression qui dominait son visage." Mémoires de Samson, pp. 311–12.

35 Roland Barthes, *Camera Lucida: Reflections on Photography*, translated by Richard Howard (New York, 1981), pp. 31–32.

Chapter Two

36 "Don't think": *"Ne croyez pas qu'on enterre si facilement les gens de ma race et de mon mérite."* This line from a letter of Rachel to her mother is the epigraph to Louis Barthou's *Rachel*.

"I would not advise an author": *"À la vérité, je ne conseillerais pas à un auteur de prendre pour sujet d'une tragédie une action aussi moderne que celle-ci. . . . Les personnages tragiques doivent être regardés d'un autre oeil que nous ne regardons d'ordinaire les personnages que nous avons vus de si près.*" Jean Racine, "Seconde préface de *Bajazet*"; English version is from *The Complete Plays of Jean Racine,* translated by Samuel Solomon, vol. II (New York, 1967).

p. 36 "Even if I had never seen Rachel": Henry James, "The Théâtre Français," in *French Poets and Novelists* (London, 1878), p. 414.

37 a *patrimoine* uniquely bound up in language: Rachel's bad spelling and lack of grammar, which legend exaggerates, were vastly more important than they would have been for an actress who was not identified with "high" literature, and more important in France than they might have been in, say, America. Theodore Zeldin writes: "An American professor who visited a French school in 1912 found, by tests, that French children of twelve could spell considerably better than American college freshmen. Good spelling, as the French Academy pointed out in 1694, was 'what distinguishes men of letters from the ignorant and from simple women'; the fondness for strict rules in this matter has increased very considerably with time, good spelling becoming a kind of social passport." Theodore Zeldin, *France: 1848–1945,* vol. II (New York, 1979–81), p. 175.

38 "She rose at nine": Brontë, *Villette,* pp. 339–40.

39 The freakish smallness of Rachel was much exaggerated: some contemporaries flatly asserted she was a dwarfish four feet six inches high; but Annenkov described her as "tall." Charlotte Brontë, according to the joiner who made her coffin, was herself four feet nine.

"I shall never forget it": Charlotte Brontë to Ellen Nussey, 24 June 1851, in T. J. Wise and J. A. Symington, eds., *The Brontës: Their Lives, Friendships, and Correspondences* III (Oxford, 1932), p. 251.

40 "I neither love, esteem, nor admire": Charlotte Brontë to Sydney Dobell, 28 June 1851, ibid., p. 253.

41 Delacroix reflects, "The unfortunate thing about an actor's talent is that after his death one cannot establish any comparison between him and his rivals, the men who competed with him for applause during his lifetime. All that posterity knows of an actor is the reputation which his contemporaries made for him, and our own descendants will probably place Malibran and Pasta on the same level; they may even believe that Malibran was the greater actress if they rely on the exaggerated praise of her contemporaries. When he was speaking of Mme Pasta, Garcia described her talents as cold and formal. . . . Unimaginative people, who are easy to please in matters of taste (and unfortunately they comprise the vast majority), will always prefer actresses of the type of Mme Malibran." The partisanship of Delacroix's friend Garcia is understandable: he was Malibran's brother. Delacroix, who preferred Pasta, was not disposed to compare Rachel to Malibran, as Musset did. See Hubert Wellington, ed., *The Journal of Eugène Delacroix* (Oxford, 1951; repr. 1980), p. 60.

p. 41 "RACHEL [ELISA FÉLIX] (1820–58), child of a poor Jewish family, and one of the greatest actresses France, or perhaps the world, has ever known." Phyllis Hartnell, ed., *The Oxford Companion to the Theatre* (London, 1957), p. 655. For Rachel as "the first international dramatic star," see Henry Knepler, *The Gilded Stage: The Years of the Great International Actresses*. For Rachel as probably the first to break the frame, see Jean Duvignaud, *L'Acteur: Esquisse d'une sociologie du comédien* (Paris, 1965), pp. 133–34: *"C'est Rachel, probablement, qui, la première, déborde le cadre de la notoriété pour vivre réellement sur le devant de la scène, transformant chacun des évènements de sa vie particulière en image du destin, d'un destin abstrait façonné du souvenir transposé des aventures représentées au théâtre."*

the humble musical instrument: Much joking has gone on about Rachel's profitable sale, in her lifetime, of the battered guitar she said she played as a child, #261 in the catalog of objects sold by her family after her death. An early Polish joke has it that the dupe she convinced to buy it was Walewski himself: Eugène Mirecourt seems to have originated this story, repeated by Mme Hamelin, "Une amie de Chateaubriand: lettres publiées par A. Gayot," *La Nouvelle Revue*, 15 August 1908. Others claim that the otherwise careful Jewish banker Achille Fould was the actress's dupe: cf. Falk, p. 144. A recent article about the actor Steve Martin, which describes his living room as "decorated with the genteel understatement of an upper-class British men's club," notes that "the only relic of Martin's show-business beginnings is a banjo on a chair in one corner." Peter de Jonge, "Cool Jerk," *The New York Times Magazine* (31 May 1992), p. 29.

42 For Corinne and the tradition of the "performing heroine," see Ellen Moers, *Literary Women: The Great Writers* (New York, 1985), p. 173 ff.

"on the stage she has always seemed to me": *Ellen Terry's Memoirs* (1932; repr. New York, 1970), p. 168. And see Nina Auerbach, *Ellen Terry: Player in Her Time* (New York, 1987).

"He judged her as a woman": Bretton's woman-artist distinction is a familiar one, made to defend against the truth that the artist is indeed a woman. Cf. George William Curtis, "Rachel," in *Literary and Social Essays* (New York, 1895), p. 120: "In our remarks upon this celebrated actress we have viewed her simply as an artist, and not as a woman. She appeals to the public only in that way. Perhaps the sinister stories that are told of her private career only serve to confirm and deepen the feeling of the intensity of her nature, she so skilfully presents the most fearful passions, not from the perception of genius alone, but from the knowledge of actual experience. Certainly no woman's character has been more freely discussed, and no public performer of any kind ever thought so little to propitiate her audience. She has seemed to scorn the world she fascinated; and like a superb snake, with glittering eyes and cold crest, to gloat over the terror which held her captives thrall."

p. 43 For "antitheatrical prejudice," the subject as well as the phrase, see the useful book by Jonas Barish, *The Antitheatrical Prejudice* (Berkeley, 1981).

"It is when we feel most": Virginia Woolf, review of Francis Gribble's *Rachel: Her Stage Life and Her Real Life*, in *Times Literary Supplement*, 20 April 1911; review reprinted as "Rachel" in Andrew McNeillie, ed., *The Essays of Virginia Woolf* I (New York, 1986), p. 352.

44 "it seemed to us we had lost": *"Nous connaissions à peine madame Dorval, et, cependant, il nous semble avoir perdu une amie intime: une part de notre âme et de notre jeunesse descend dans la tombe avec elle; lorsqu'on a de longue main, suivi une actrice à travers les transformations de sa vie de théâtre, qu'on a pleuré, aimé, souffert avec elle, sous les noms dont la fantaisie des poètes la baptise, il s'établit entre elle et vous, elle figure rayonnante, vous spectateur perdu dans l'ombre, un magnétisme qu'il est difficile de ne pas croire réciproque."* Théophile Gautier, *Histoire de l'art dramatique en France depuis vingt-cinq ans* IV, pp. 102–3.

"Like all true artists": *"Comme tous les vrais artistes, à mesure qu'elle avance dans sa carrière, Mlle Rachel augmente de fougue, d'ardeur, de violence. Au lieu de se refroidir, elle s'exalte: l'expérience lui sert à être plus libre, plus large, plus impétueuse. Ce qu'elle rendait autrefois par des nuances, elle l'indique aujourd'hui d'un ton magistral et fulgurant."* *Journal de Eugène Delacroix* III (Paris, 1932), entry of 3 January 1858, p. 170.

45 "There's a kinship": *The New York Times*, 10 June 1985.

47 "it is quite precisely amphibology": Roland Barthes, *Roland Barthes by Roland Barthes*, translated by Richard Howard (New York, 1977), p. 73.

"*Rachel* [Pronounced Ra-shell]" by Leila Taylor opened at the Belmont Theater in Los Angeles on 21 April 1928. A "comedy drama in three acts and three scenes," it starred Hedwiga Reicher, and was produced by Ruth Helen Davis. For Bernhardt on Rachel, see Sarah Bernhardt, *Memories of My Life* (New York, 1923), pp. 55–56.

49 "the great tragedienne": Mme de B., p. 17.

"Rachel did not accept": *"Rachel n'acceptait pas un pseudonyme; dès qu'elle fût libre, le nom qu'elle voulut immortaliser, ce fût son nom de fille d'Israël."* [Arthur Léon] Imbert de Saint-Amand, *Mme de Girardin* (Paris, 1875), p. 184.

50 On Ronald Reagan's name, see Michael Rogin, *Ronald Reagan the Movie, and Other Episodes in Political Demonology* (Berkeley, 1987), p. 11.

"last name was not known": Germaine de Staël, *Corinne, or Italy*, translated by Avriel H. Goldberger (New Brunswick, 1987), p. 20.

51 "what is proper to narrative": Roland Barthes, *S/Z*, translated by Richard Miller (New York, 1974), p. 191.

For "Rachel" in French literature, see Luce Arthur Klein, *Le Portrait de la juive dans la littérature française*, Paris, 1970.

"Rachel, there is something of Racine": *"Rachel, il y a du Racine dans le prénom que portera l'une des plus grandes tragédiennes du XIXe siècle.*" Toussaint du Wast, p. 17.

p. 52 "most cherished wish": "*mon voeu le plus cher est d'arriver à laisser au théâtre un grand nom, et à mes parents une belle et* honorable *fortune.*" Rachel to Sarah Félix, 13 June 1847, Laplane, p. 76.

"If Rachel's life remains": "*Si la vie de Rachel est, dans ses détails, ignorée du plus grand nombre en dépit de biographies qui lui ont été consacrées, son nom a conservé toute sa signification et toute sa grandeur. Il reste le symbole de l'art tragique. Il évoque un talent qui n'a plus jamais été égalé. Le nom de Rachel incarne aussi le souvenir d'une vie prodigieuse et émouvante, à l'image de la plus extraordinaire destinée.*" Pollitzer, p. 162.

53 "Many homosexuals": Arthur Gold and Robert Fizdale, *The Divine Sarah* (New York, 1991), pp. 235–36.

For "self-fashioning," see Stephen Greenblatt, *Renaissance Self-Fashioning: From More to Shakespeare* (Chicago, 1980). For a discussion of theatricality and its intersection with gay theory and with novels—among them those I discuss in Chapter 5—see Joseph Litvak, *Caught in the Act: Theatricality in the Nineteenth-Century English Novel* (Berkeley, 1992).

"I am jealous of the life": Gustave Flaubert, *Intimate Notebook 1840–1841*, translated by Francis Steegmuller (New York, 1966), p. 26.

54 The letters of Rachel and Bellevaut and the relevant lists of objects are in the archives of The Hebrew University. There are numerous extant copies of the catalog printed for the sale in April 1858.

"All the dead woman's old rags": "*toutes les hardes de la morte, hardes de femme, hardes de reine: les sorties de bal de satin piqué blanc, les robes d'Athalie, toutes les reliques de ce corps, tous les costumes de cette gloire accrochés en grappes comme aux murs d'une morgue, avec un aspect d'enveloppes fantômatiques, vêtements d'un rêve immobilisés et morts au premier rayon du jour.*

Quelques marchandes de ce regrat des nippes orgueilleuses et flétries s'en vont, le long, flairant dans la tunique de Camille l'accroc de l'épée de son frère.

"Passez, Messieurs et dames!" fait la voix glapissante du crieur, qui pousse par les épaules la foule hébétée qui bourdonne. . . . Voilà une petite chambre à coucher, un lit de bois noir, des rideaux de soie bleue et, jetés dans toute la chambre, des dentelles, des volants d'Angleterre, des garnitures de Malines, des mouchoirs de Valenciennes, tout le travail de patience d'une araignée au bagne. Une vieille est au chevet du lit, jaune et l'oeil allumé, cupide et juif, couvant toutes les dentelles. "Passez . . ." dit la voix.

E tutto, et voilà ce que laisse Rachel: des nippes, des diamants, des bijoux, des demi-reliures et des dentelles, un héritage de courtisane." Edmond and Jules de Goncourt, *Journal: mémoires de la vie littéraire 1856–1858*, vol. II (Monaco, 1956), p. 215.

p. 56 "I scarcely dare admit": "*À peine oserai-je dire que moi-même, dans une circonstance de ma vie ou j'éprouvai un chagrin profond, la passion du théâtre était telle en moi, qu'accablé d'une douleur bien réelle, au milieu des larmes que je versais, je fis malgré moi une observation rapide et fugitive sur l'altération de ma voix et sur une certaine vibration spasmodique qu'elle contractait dans les pleurs; et, je le dis non sans quelque honte, je pensai machinalement à m'en servir au besoin; et en effet cette expérience sur moi-même m'a souvent été très-utile.*" F.-J. Talma, *Réflexions sur Lekain et l'art théâtral* (Paris, 1856), p. 74.

57 "La Faustin had about her": "*Chez la Faustin . . . il y avait la saveur âpre, et sui generis qui se dégage d'une créature du peuple, dont elle était restée, et dont elle aimait la nourriture de crudités et de charcuterie.*" In her, "*la duchesse alternait avec la grisette*" (p. 236); she is "*la grande courtisane de Paris: la donneuse du plaisir amoureux le plus parfait qui existe sur la terre*" (p. 231). Edmond de Goncourt, *La Faustin* (Paris, 1882).

59 his *roman à clef:* Hector Fleischmann describes Houssaye's novel as "*un roman de clef aux serrures quelquefois dérangées*" (p. 74).

"Should the writers of scandalous tales": "*Si les faiseurs de chroniques scandaleuses s'avisaient un jour de parodier ma vie, contez-la dans toute sa simplicité; vous savez trop que je n'ai pas été élevée au Sacré-Coeur et que celles qui en sortent ne sont pas meilleures que moi, puisque je n'ai fait de tort qu'à moi-même, tandis que beaucoup de ces demoiselles ne passent par le mariage que pour le trahir.*" Houssaye, *La Comédienne* (Paris, 1884), p. vii. The other quotations from Houssaye are also from the introduction to *La Comédienne:* her "*incarnation la plus prodigieuse, ce ne fut ni Hermione, ni Phèdre, ni Tisbe, ce fut ce chef-d'oeuvre digne de Gavarni et de Balzac: 'Rachel Parisienne,'*" de Banville writes; Houssaye adds, "*Rachel pouvait à son gré se couvrir de joyaux ou de se parer d'un velours de quatre sous: elle était toujours dans sa plus haute distinction impérieusement dominatrice et dans sa grâce, ce qui est supérieur à tous les êtres créés: une dame parisienne!*"

60 "especially when": Heine is quoted by David Magarshack, *Turgenev: A Life* (London, 1954), p. 79. The rhetorical ploy of confounding genders and species, and real and imaginary creatures, so as to describe the transformative effect a performer has on her audience, was characteristic of the period. Janin contrasted the childlike young Rachel with "the proud male talent which she exhibits onstage." Of Fanny Elssler, he had asked, "Was it a woman, a youth, or a sprite? No one could tell, for she danced at the same time like a coquettish young woman, like a youth in love, and like a sprite on a fine May morning." *Journal des débats*, 30 January 1839; quoted in Ivor Guest, *The Romantic Ballet in Paris* (London, 1966), p. 175. Gautier described Elssler as a hermaphrodite (Guest, p. 151).

61 "If, when I take my seat": Joseph Barry, ed., *George Sand in Her Own Words* (New York, 1979), p. 432.

"It was no longer art": "*L'art n'existait plus, c'était la nature même, c'était la maternité résumée en une seule femme.*" Gautier IV, p. 148.

p. 61 a literary revolution: *"Aucun [artiste] ne peut se vanter comme elle d'avoir provoqué une révolution littéraire."* Laplane, p. 8.

62 "Do you know what you have to do": *"Savez-vous ce qu'il faut pour que mademoiselle Rachel vous sache gré de votre admiration? Allez au théâtre les poches pleines. Jetez des fleurs aux autres actrices, mais à elle, jetez-lui votre bourse, et si vous faites autour d'elle une litière d'écus où ses pieds embarrassent, si vous faites luire de l'or à ses yeux qui ne savent pas pleurer, vous lui donnerez l'émotion et la tendresse qui lui manquent."* La France musicale, January 1839; quoted by A. B[olé], *Mademoiselle Rachel et l'avenir du Théâtre-Français.*

"the hand of a child": Mme de B., pp. 79, 98.

63 "Renouncing": See Mme Samson, pp. 193–94.

"Rachel alone": F. Sarcey, "A Company of Actors (The Comédie Française)," *Papers on Acting*, with an introduction by Brander Matthews (New York, 1926), pp. 49–50.

65 "Cold impartiality": Quotations from the biographies by Valentine Thomson and A. de Faucigny-Lucinge are from pp. iii–iv and p. 255, respectively.

66 "first a great Jewess": James Agate, *Rachel*, pp. 20, 30; and see *Ego, The Autobiography of James Agate* (London, 1937), pp. 25–26.

68 "a story round that great name": William Archer's phrase occurs in an unpublished letter to Elizabeth Robins; Robins archives, Fales Collection, New York University Library. I owe this reference to Angela John.

69 "I thought her very pretty": quoted in Mary Lutyens, ed., *Young Mrs. Ruskin in Venice* (New York, 1965), p. 192.

70 "No doubt calumny has exaggerated": Sarah Josepha Hale, *Woman's Record; or Sketches of All Distinguished Women from the Creation to A.D. 1854* (New York, 1860), p. 774.

"Rachel possessed from childhood": *The Goncourt Journals, 1851–1870*, edited and translated from the journal of Edmond and Jules de Goncourt, with an introduction, notes, and biographical repertory by Lewis Galantière (New York, 1937), pp. 315–16.

Louis Jouvet's comments on Rachel and Talma occur in his *Tragédie classique et théâtre du XIXe siècle: extraits du cours de Louis Jouvet au Conservatoire (1939–1940)* (Paris, 1968). Of Rachel, he speculates, *"Quand Rachel entrait en scène, avec ce physique pauvre, ingrat, mais saisissant, un physique pas heureux, elle ne donnait pas cet appel sensuel que donnent certaines actrices; quand elle entrait en scène avec ce côté volontaire, israëlite, hostile, elle créait néanmoins dans le public une réaction; et cette réaction rendait le jeu intéressant, plus intéressant qu'avec quelqu'un qui vous rassure tout de suite."* (pp. 23–24).

CHAPTER THREE

p. 72 "My parents are poor people": *"Mes parents sont pauvres, mais il y a chez nous de la vieille race juive. Je suis une fille de la Bible, parce que je descends d'Israël et parce que mon père m'a appris à lire dans les prophètes et les patriarches; je ne comprends rien de ce qui est bourgeois et vulgaire; j'aime les sommets."*

75 For the legend of the Wandering Jew, see George K. Anderson, *The Legend of the Wandering Jew* (Providence, 1965); see also Marian H. Winter, *The Theatre of Marvels* (New York, 1964). For the *bibliothèque bleue,* see Theodore Zeldin, *France: 1848–1945,* vol. II, p. 378.

76 "Mlle Rachel was born": *"Mlle Rachel est née à Munf, canton d'Aarau (Suisse), le 24 mars 1820. Sa mère, Esther Haya, est juive; mais, Dieu merci! Rachel est française par son père, M. Félix, originaire de Metz. M. Félix, ainsi que la plupart des israélites, était un simple colporteur, parcourant les foires avec sa nombreuse famille."* Francis Girault, *Portraits contemporains* (Paris, 1843).

78 "Our age has no impress of its own": Alfred de Musset, *Confession of a Child of the Century,* translated by Robert Arnot (New York, 1910), p. 35 (translation modified).

79 "Bonaparte, c'est l'homme": Alfred de Vigny, quoted by Henri Lefebvre, *Musset: essai* (Paris, 1970), p. 34.

"the last flicker": *"Napoléon despote fut la dernière lueur de la lampe du despotisme; il détruisit et parodia les rois."* Alfred de Musset, *La confession d'un enfant du siècle,* in Musset, *Oeuvres complètes en prose* (Paris, 1960), p. 70.

For Napoleon plays, see Martin Meisel, *Realizations: Narrative, Pictorial, and Theatrical Arts in 19th Century England* (Princeton, 1983), pp. 202–3. Meisel quotes and translates from *Théâtre complèt de Alexandre Dumas* I (Paris 1863–1899), p. 302. He also quotes Janin: *"Déjà Bonaparte était partout, et l'on pouvait se demander qui donc regnait, Bonaparte ou Louis-Philippe,"* from his *Histoire de la littérature dramatique* I (Paris, 1855), pp. 61–62.

80 "to the place of execution": Michel Foucault, *Discipline & Punish: The Birth of the Prison,* translated by Alan Sheridan (New York, 1979), p. 13.

81 For the *saltimbanques* of Paris and Daumier, see T. J. Clark, *The Absolute Bourgeois: Artists and Politics in France 1848–1851* (Princeton, 1982), pp. 120–22.

"put Judaism": For Jews in France in the nineteenth century, see especially Phyllis Cohen Albert, *The Modernization of French Jewry: Consistory and Community in the Nineteenth Century* (Hanover, N.H., 1977), pp. 3, 61, 181. See also David Cohen, *La Promotion des juifs en France à l'époque du second empire (1852–1870)* (Paris, 1980); David Feuerwerker, *L'Emancipation des juifs en France de l'ancien régime à la fin du second empire* (Paris, 1976); Patrick Girard, *Les Juifs en France de 1789 à 1860* (Paris, 1976); Michael Marrus, *The Politics of Assimilation* (Oxford, 1971); Robert F. Byrnes, *Antisemitism in Modern France*

(New York, 1969). Daniel Stauben, *Scenes of Jewish Life in Alsace*, edited and translated by Rose Choron (Malibu, Calif., 1991) is a wonderfully evocative 1859 text that gives the flavor (sweetened by the influence of Sand and the pastoral tradition) of the life the Félixes abandoned. Marrus writes that the Russian, Galician, and Romanian Jews who came to France between 1876 and 1901 "usually moved to the Marais, behind the Hôtel de Ville and in the centre of the city" (p. 34). *The Jewish Encyclopedia* (1916) suggests they were there from the beginning: "Of the 1,733 Jews composing [the Jewish community in 1809] 1,324 were natives of Paris; the remainder were from Alsace, Lorraine, Germany, Austria, and Holland. Nearly all of these lived in the third and fourth arrondissements, where were situated the three Jewish markets (slaughterhouses), the temples, the societies (hebrot), the Central Consistory, and the Consistory of Paris." The present fourth *arrondissement* corresponds to the old sixth and seventh. See Albert, p. 211; and see Christine Piette, *Les Juifs de Paris (1808–1840): la marche vers l'assimilation* (Montréal, 1983): "*Globalement, [en 1809], les 6e et 7e arrondissements anciens contenaient environ 82 pour 100 de tous les Israélites de Paris—le 7e seul en comptant 65 pour 100—et une écrasante majorité de petites gens et d'indigents*" (p. 85). For Paris and Rachel's milieu and cultural trends involving Jews, see Jean-Yves Mollier, *Michel & Calmann Lévy ou la naissance de l'édition moderne 1836–1891* (Paris, 1984).

p. 82 For Adolphe Crémieux, see *Dictionnaire de biographie française* 9 (Paris, 1961), pp. 1187–92: "*par sa persévérance, il a réhabilité le Juif en Europe, et, en France, au dire de l'un de ses coréligionnaires, a préparé son avènement.*" See also S. S. Posener, *Adolphe Crémieux* (Paris, 1933).

83 "the remark": Byrnes, p. 97. For Jews and actors, see Jonas Barish, *The Antitheatrical Prejudice* (Berkeley, 1981), pp. 464–69; see also "On the Problem of the Actor," in Friedrich Nietzsche, *The Gay Science*, translated by Walter Kaufman (New York, 1974), pp. 316–17.

"*une mulâtresse*": At issue was a play about Toussaint l'Ouverture by Lamartine. Sylvie Chevalley relates the anecdote in "Rachel et les écrivains romantiques," *Romantisme* 38 (1982), p. 120.

For Mlle Judith on Jacques Félix, see *Mémoires de Mlle Judith et souvenirs sur ses contemporains, rédigés par Paul Gsell* (Paris, 1911). Judith writes severely, on p. 3: "*Le mari, d'ailleurs, ne faisait rien. Israélite d'Allemagne, il avait mené une existence nomade incompatible avec aucun travail régulier. Il aurait pu, sans doute, aider sa femme dans le petit métier qu'elle exerçait; marchande d'objets de toilette, de mouchoirs, de cravates, etc. Mais il préférait boire et fumer dans les auberges avec l'argent qu'elle lui apportait. Sa philosophie était sereine autant qu'immorale. Il vécut constamment aux crochets de quelqu'un. Quand sa femme se jugea bon de se reposer, ce fut de sa fille Rachel qu'il se fit le parasite.*"

p. 84 "The ear": Disraeli, *Coningsby, or The New Generation* (New York, 1907), pp. 234–35.

85 "Did you not think": George Eliot to John Sibree, Jr., 11 February 1848, quoted in Gordon S. Haight, ed., *The George Eliot Letters* I (New Haven, 1954), pp. 245–46.

86 "Père Rachel preens himself": Heinrich Heine, quoted in S. S. Prawer, *Heine's Jewish Comedy* (London, 1983), p. 755. In light of Prawer's diagnosis of Heine as afflicted by Jewish self-hatred, a slip or error here may be telling: Rachel customarily played Eriphile, not Iphigénie, in Racine's *Iphigénie*, and Hermione rather than the titular heroine of *Andromaque*. John Stokes writes of a similar lapse or deliberate change that "significantly Disraeli gives [Josephine] the name part [in *Andromaque*], that of the Trojan outcast, rather than the Greek heroine Hermione, which was the preferred role of the historical actress. Nevertheless, like Rachel, Josephine is a Jewish actress who will recreate the Greek heroines of a Christian dramatist. She will become, in Arnoldian terms, Hebrew and Hellene incarnate." Stokes, "Rachel's 'Terrible Beauty': An Actress Among the Novelists," *ELH* (Winter, 1984), p. 778. The Arnoldian terms were derived of course from Heine. On Félix's understanding of French poetry, see Védel, *Notice sur Rachel*, p. 7.

"gaslight fairy": I owe the quotation from Dickens to Doris Janet McReynolds, *Images of the Theatre in Victorian Literature* (University of Minnesota Ph.D. dissertation, 1970), p. 97.

87 "The first time I saw": *The New York Times Book Review* (19 June 1988), p. 34.

"a beautiful girl": Balzac, *Cousin Pons* (Harmondsworth, 1968), pp. 143, 146.

88 "Moi, je suis juive": *Juive* is rather prettier than *juif*, which is considered less polite than *israélite* or *hébreu*.

"Why should it have been": Jonas Barish, *The Antitheatrical Prejudice*, pp. 40–41.

89 "My dear Sarah, it is time to change": *"ma chère Sarah, il serait cependant temps de changer ta caractère. . . . Je suis humiliée de voir continuellement ma famille se traiter de telle sorte qu'on est à se demander si Dieu ne s'est pas trompé en nous retirant de la boue dans laquelle nous vivions avant mon entrée dans la carrière dramatique vous n'êtes ni les uns ni les autres dignes du bonheur que Dieu a versé chez nous depuis dix ans . . . il n'y a pas deux familles où le coeur existe moins que chez nous."* Rachel to her sister Sarah (n.d.; c. July 1848), Archives of The Hebrew University.

"She glows": *"Sarah se porte comme le jour, elle rayonne et ferait pâlir le soleil si elle le regard en face."* Rachel, 4 October 1856, Archives of the Comédie-Française.

95 "Everything in the theater": *"Tout au théâtre n'est qu'illusion; tout dépend du caractère, de la voix, de l'extérieur des individus, d'un penchant que l'on ne peut*

expliquer et qui les porte vers un genre plutôt que vers un autre. M. St-Aulaire cherchait à découvrir les instincts dramatiques, il ne les indiquait pas; il voulait que l'exercice du théâtre les lui demontrât, et il avait raison." Védel, p. 10.

p. 95 "that Jewish-looking girl": Edwin Forrest's letter, written in late 1834 to his friend William Leggett, is quoted in Richard Moody, *Edwin Forrest: First Star of the American Stage* (New York, 1960), p. 116.

"I was unable to reconcile": *"Je ne pouvais concilier cette nature frêle avec cette remarquable intelligence."* Védel, p. 14.

96 "Suddenly she moves": *La Vendéenne* was produced four years after an opera, *La Prison d'Edimbourg*, by Eugène Scribe and Eugène de Plenard, with music by Michel E. Carafa, enjoyed twenty-two performances at the Opéra Comique. For discussion of these and other productions, see Henry Adelbert White, *Sir Walter Scott's Novels on the Stage* (New Haven, 1927). Joanna Richardson quotes from Duport's play in *Rachel*, pp. 17–18; I have translated the passage.

97 "absolute bourgeois": I borrow the phrase, which he borrowed from an essay by Henry James, from T. J. Clark. See *The Absolute Bourgeois: Artists and Politics in France 1848–1851.*

100 For Bernhardt on the theater, see Gerda Taranow, *Sarah Bernhardt* (Princeton, 1972), p. 10.

102 "Voilà bien": Samson, *Lettre à M. Jules Janin* (Paris, 1858), p. 25.

103 "Mr. Barnum, America": Barnum boasts of this in Waldo P. Browne, ed., *Barnum's Own Story* (New York, 1927), p. 441, notes Leo Braudy, in a footnote in *The Frenzy of Renown*, p. 503.

"Racine and Corneille": *"Racine et Corneille revivaient parmi nous comme au grand siècle de Louis XIV."* Véron, *Mémoires d'un bourgeois de Paris* IV, p. 149.

"She makes Corneille": *"Elle fait de Corneille et Racine des génies contemporains et pleins d'actualité."* Gustave Flaubert is quoted in Toussaint du Wast, *Rachel: Amours et tragédie*, p. 77.

104 "the Mercury": See Charles Séchan, *Souvenirs d'un homme de théâtre* (Paris, 1883), p. 192.

"lives in amazing": For Véron's dinner party, see *The Journal of Eugène Delacroix*, p. 94.

"that strange physiognomy": *"Cette physionomie étrange, cet oeil plein de feu, ce corps grêle, cette voix si intelligente,"* Véron IV, p. 147. *"Pour compléter ces appréciations, je ferai remarquer combien il fallut à mademoiselle Rachel d'études, de puissance, de séduction, je dirai presque de profonde politique, pour soutenir dans tout son éclat sa réputation populaire pendant le long espace de seize années."* Véron IV, p. 174. Sixteen years of stardom does not seem extraordinarily long, today.

"they had the same": *"C'est la même netteté des vues, la même ardeur pour le but convoité, les mêmes ruses ingénieuses, les mêmes séductions calculées, la même fécondité d'expédients, la même tolérance philosophique qui ne comprend ni la vengeance, ni les haines, qui se contente de négocier. . . . J'estime qu'à l'élévation et à l'instruction près, mademoiselle Rachel montre dans les familières causeries autant d'esprit, autant de jugement, de bon sens et d'aperçus inattendus et piquants que le grand orateur et l'homme d'Etat de la monarchie de juillet. L'art oratoire (je ne dis pas l'éloquence) et l'art de la scène exigent presque les mêmes études, les mêmes pratiques, au rouge près."* Véron IV, pp. 174, 182. Compare Albert Vandam, writing as An Englishman in Paris, who saw much of Rachel between 1846 and 1853: "I have never met anyone, either man or woman, who exercised the personal charm that Rachel did. I have been told since that Bismarck had the same gift. . . . I have an idea that the charm of both lay in their utter indifference to the effect produced, or else in their absolute confidence of the result of their simplicity of diction." Vandam is quoted by Falk, *Rachel the Immortal*, p. 175.

p. 106 "I have often had": *"J'ai souvent eu l'honneur de faire asseoir à ma table Mlle Rachel, au milieu d'hommes distingués de ce temps-ci; j'ai vu autour d'elle M. le comte Molé, M. le général Changarnier, M. Ach. Fould, M. le duc de Soto-Mayor, alors ambassadeur d'Espagne à Paris, M. Sainte-Beuve, M. Eugène Delacroix, M. Meyerbeer, M. Auber, M. Halévy; etc., etc. La jeune artiste, de l'air le plus naturel, se montrait grande dame, et faisait preuve de toutes ces qualités d'esprit habiles à subjuguer même des hommes supérieurs, qualités rares que possédaient surtout certaines femmes du dernier siècle, dont les salons furent illustrés par l'assiduité des noms les plus célèbres."* Véron IV, p. 178.

"Rachel is exceedingly witty": *The Journal of Eugène Delacroix*, p. 94.

"A woman can arrive at": *"Une femme peut arriver à une position honorable, estimable et convenable, sans avoir peut-être ce vernis que le monde appelle à juste titre l'éducation: pourquoi cela? me demanderas-tu. C'est qu'une femme ne perd pas de son charme, au contraire, en gardant une grande réserve de maintien, de langage; une femme répond et n'interroge pas; elle n'ouvre jamais une discussion, elle l'écoute. Sa coquetterie naturelle lui fait désirer de s'instruire, elle retient, et sans avoir eu un commencement solide, elle a alors ce vernis qui quelquefois peut passer pour de l'instruction."* Georges d'Heylli, ed., *Rachel d'après sa correspondance*, p. 8.

CHAPTER FOUR

108 "Oh my sweet Racine": I adapt the translation from Joanna Richardson's *Rachel*, p. 211. The French reads: *"Oh! mon doux Racine, c'est dans tes chefs-d'oeuvre que je reconnais le coeur des femmes! Je forme le mien à ta noble poésie! Si la lyre de mon âme ne pleure pas toujours à tes accords divins, c'est que l'admiration laisse tout mon être dans l'extase."*

Mlle George supposedly remarked to Hugo apropos of Rachel, *"Voyez-vous, les tragédiennes sont des comédiennes, après tout!"* She is quoted in *Choses vues* I (Paris, 1913), p. 237.

p. 109 "High tragedy": *"La haute tragédie est l'école des grands hommes. C'est le devoir des souverains de !'encourager et de le répandre. Il n'est pas nécessaire d'être poète pour la juger; il suffit de connaître les hommes et les choses, d'avoir de l'élévation et d'être homme d'Etat. La tragédie échauffe l'âme, élève le coeur, peut et doit créer des héros. Sous ce rapport, peut-être, la France doit à Corneille une partie de ses belles actions. Aussi, messieurs, s'il vivait, je le ferais prince."* Napoleon in the *Mémorial de Ste. Hélène*, as quoted by C.-A. Sainte-Beuve, *Nouveaux lundis* (3d ed.) (Paris, 1880), pp. 206–7.

For intersections between history and performance, focused on a significant event in the mid-nineteenth century, the seminal work is Karl Marx, *The Eighteenth Brumaire of Louis Bonaparte* (Hamburg, 1885; New York, 1963). For fiction and history as melodrama, see Peter Brooks, *The Melodramatic Imagination: Balzac, Henry James, Melodrama, and the Mode of Excess* (New Haven, 1976); see also Linda Orr, *Headless History: Nineteenth-Century French Historiography of the Revolution* (Ithaca, 1990). For the social role of theaters in France, see Michèle Root-Bernstein, *Boulevard Theater and Revolution in Eighteenth-Century France* (Ann Arbor, 1984) and Frederick Brown, *Theater & Revolution: The Culture of the French Stage* (New York, 1980). For the history of the French theater since the Revolution, see especially Jacqueline de Jomaron, ed., *Le Théâtre en France, II, de la Révolution à nos jours* (Paris, 1989); also Marvin Carlson, *The Theatre of the French Revolution* (Ithaca, 1966), and *The French Stage in the Nineteenth Century* (Metuchen, N.J., 1972). See also Louis Allard, "La Comédie Française au temps de Mesdemoiselles Mars et Rachel," *La Revue théâtrale: revue internationale du théâtre*, no. 21 (1952), pp. 35–46. For theatricality in general, see Guy Debord, *La Société du spectacle* (Paris, 1967; trans. rev. ed. Detroit, 1977), and Jean Duvignaud, *L'Acteur* (Paris, 1965). For links between theatrical and other arts, especially in England, in the nineteenth century, see Martin Meisel, *Realizations: Narrative, Pictorial, and Theatrical Arts in Nineteenth-Century England* (Princeton, 1983). More generally, see Michael Goldman, *The Actor's Freedom* (New York, 1975), and Lesley Ferris, *Acting Women: Images of Women in Theatre* (New York, 1989).

110 The nineteenth-century cult of classicism: Of classicism in the nineteenth century, Theodore Zeldin writes, "That the revolution of 1789 should have strengthened the cult of antiquity was no temporary aberration, for that cult became even more widespread with the growth of schooling, and with the development of classical erudition, in archaeology, comparative philology and ancient religions. Théophile Gautier (1811–72) read the Iliad some thirty times in the original Greek. . . . The classics were admired not only as the source of French civilisation, as containing models of wisdom and simplicity, but also as an escape from the present." Zeldin, *France: 1848–1945*, vol. II, p. 407 ff.

111 "the infinite grace" Heinrich Heine, "The Romantic School," in Heine, *Selected Works*, translated and edited by Helen M. Mustard (New York, 1973), p. 189.

p. 112 For Talma's life, see Herbert F. Collins, *Talma* (New York, 1964). For Talma on the theater, see F.-J. Talma, *Réflexions sur Lekain et l'art théâtral* (Paris, 1856), p. 8.

113 *"Britannicus* and *Brutus"*: "Britannicus *ou* Brutus *cessent d'appartenir à un univers de référence dominé par la cour et l'Ancien Régime et deviennent des tragédies—des drames—historiques et profondément politiques. A travers cette réappropriation des auteurs classiques, Talma avait 'inventé' le théâtre national tant souhaité par les philosophes."* Jacqueline de Jomaron, ed., *Le Théâtre en France, II, de la révolution à nos jours,* p. 21.

"mode of excess": I mean to remind the reader of Peter Brooks, *The Melodramatic Imagination: Balzac, Henry James, Melodrama, and the Mode of Excess.*

114 "I would like to see you": *"Je voudrais aussi que vous fissiez moins de gestes; ces natures-là ne se répandent pas au-dehors; elles sont plus concentrées."* Napoleon is quoted in *Le Théâtre en France,* p. 153.

119 *"Rome, l'unique objet"*: Pierre Corneille, "Horace," IV, 5, and V, 3, in Corneille, *Théâtre complèt* I (Paris, 1950). Translations are Samuel Solomon's; see Pierre Corneille, *Seven Plays* (New York, 1969).

120 "practically unendurable": Annenkov is quoted in Lawrence Senelick, "Rachel in Russia: The Shchepkin-Annenkov Correspondence," *Theatre Research International,* vol. III, no. 2 (February 1978), pp. 106–7. On the deaths of heroines in Greek tragedy, see Nicole Loreaux, *Tragic Ways of Killing a Woman,* translated by Anthony Forster (Cambridge, 1987).

122 "Be it known": *"Soyez donc avertis . . . qu'au moment où je vous parle, il existe, au Théâtre-Français même, au* Théâtre-Français, *je le répète, une victoire inattendue, un de ces triomphes heureux dont une nation telle que la nôtre est fière à bon droit, quand, revenue à tous les sentiments honnêtes, au fier langage, à l'amour chaste et contenu, elle échappe aux violences sans nom, aux barbarismes sans fin. Quelle joie, en effet, pour une nation intelligente, de se voir tout d'un coup rendue à ces mêmes chefs-d'oeuvre indignement et si longtemps méconnus! O dieux et déesses! soyez loués, vous qui avez donné, avec tant d'immortalité, tant d'indulgence au chef-d'oeuvre!"* He describes Rachel as *"une petite fille ignorante, sans art, sans apprêt, qui tombe au milieu de la vieille tragédie!"* He goes on: *"Elle est née au milieu des domaines de la poésie; elle en sait déjà tous les détours; elle en dévoile tous les mystères. Les comédiens qui jouent avec elle s'étonnent de cette audace; la vieille tragédie espère; le parterre, ému et charmé, prête une oreille enchantée et ravie à ce divin langage des beaux vers dont nous sommes privés depuis la mort de Talma; fière et superbe, la foule s'abandonne à la toute-puissance de ces grands poètes, l'honneur de la France, l'orgueil de l'esprit humain."* Jules Janin, *Rachel et la tragédie,* pp. 53–54.

123 "We feel that his throat": Keats is quoted by Aileen Ward, *John Keats: The Making of a Poet* (New York, 1963), p. 150.

p. 123 "the panther of the stage": Lewes's most frequently reprinted essay on Rachel begins, "Rachel was the panther of the stage; with the panther's terrible beauty and undulating grace she moved and stood, glared and sprang." See George Henry Lewes, "Rachel," in *On Actors and the Art of Acting* (New York, n. d.), p. 31.

124 Rachel's offstage lapses in grammar: Rachel's posture and diction and aura of literary legitimacy provided her passport to social legitimacy; her notorious spelling was a sort of dirty little secret that belied her right to it.

125 a sword of gold: *"une lame d'or dans un fourreau d'argile,"* Janin, p. 55.

126 "The high rank": *"Le haut rang de l'actrice! . . . Non, mais le haut rang de la personne: car chacun de nous est pour ainsi dire doué en naissant d'un rang individuel dont il ne peut méconnaître les exigences, soit qu'elles l'entraînent à descendre, soit qu'elles l'obligent à monter. Si nous vivons chacun dans une condition qui nous est faite par la société, nous vivons dans un rang aussi qui nous a été imposé par la nature, et rien n'est plus curieux à observer, dans nos existences, que cette lutte, souvent dangereuse, entre la condition sociale et ce que nous appelons le rang natif ou naturel."* Delphine de Girardin, *Chroniques parisiennes 1836–1848* (Paris, 1986), p. 252.

"It's an accident, my dear man": *"C'est, mon cher, me dit-il, un hasard, une de ces natures qui savent en naissant ce que tant d'autres ne parviennent jamais à apprendre."* Védel, p. 16.

"those privileged by destiny": *"ces privilégiées du destin, de ces nobles de la nature qui portent sur le front majestueux, dans leur accent digne, dans leurs gestes gracieux, les titres indélébiles de cette féodalité instituée par la Providence et dont Dieu est le suzerain."* La Jeune Rachel et la vieille Comédie-Française (Paris, 1838), p. 168.

For the dandy see Ellen Moers, *The Dandy: Brummell to Beerbohm* (New York, 1960).

127 "had those qualities": Manette Salomon, the Goncourts write, *"possédait ce qui sauve les créatures d'en bas du commun et de la canaille: elle était née avec ce signe de race, le caractère de rareté et d'élégance, la marque d'élection qui met souvent, contre les hasards du rang et de la destinée des fortunes, la première des aristocraties de la femme, l'aristocratie de nature, dans la première venue du peuple:—la distinction."* Edmond and Jules de Goncourt, *Manette Salomon* (Paris, 1894), p. 220.

"playing to the public": *"plus au public qu'à son rôle, relève la couronne et me la présente. Indignée d'une interruption aussi vandale, digne vraiment d'un public d'opéra, je prends avec colère le malencontreuse couronne et je la jette brusquement de côté pour continuer Roxane. La fortune aime les audacieux; jamais preuve plus forte de cet axiome; trois salves d'applaudissements accueillirent ce premier mouvement irréfléchi."* Rachel to Delphine de Girardin, in d'Heylli, p. 139.

"The Comédie-Française is rejuvenated": *"La Comédie-Française retrouve une jeunesse nouvelle. Cela s'est accompli avec cette irrésistible facilité qui est le caractère des révolutions légitimes.*" Antoine de Latour, "Mlle Rachel," *La Revue de Paris,* December 1838. *"Une reine entre les comédiennes. . . . "* "*Adrienne Lecouvreur . . . cette illustre actrice qui essaya de révolutionner l'art dramatique au commencement du XVIIIe siècle. Mlle Rachel a réalisé cette révolution de nos jours.*" Francis Girault, "Mlle Rachel," *Des Actrices célèbres contemporaines* (Paris, 1843). Sandy Petrey argues that rhetorical confusion was characteristic of the discourse that insisted on the oxymoron "Citizen King," and obliterated the historical truth of the July Revolution with the meaningless term "July Monarchy." See his "Pears in History," *Representations* 35 (Summer 1991), for a discussion of the rhetorical making of the "King of the French," the rhetorical strategies used to discredit him, and, more generally, of "representation [as] a creative performance with the potential to change the world" (p. 69).

p. 128 "not only society women": *"non seulement les femmes du monde mais les jeunes filles de la plus haute condition aspirassent à l'amitié d'une femme de théâtre."* Sainte-Beuve is quoted by Toussaint du Wast, p. 50.

"passions so profound": *"Mais ce qui lui convient surtout, ce sont ces passions profondes dont on n'entrevoit l'abîme qu'à travers le sourire de l'ironie; ce sont ces douleurs contenues qui regardent au dedans d'elles-mêmes et analysent tristement leur propre désespoir."* Antoine de Latour, in *Revue de Paris* (1838), p. 277.

her Jewish audiences: *"C'est toujours ce rôle d'Hermione qui amena l'appel de tout ce que Paris, nous le croyons, pouvait contenir de fidèles enfants d'Israël."* L. pxxxx [sic], *Quelques observations sur l'art théâtral, la Comédie-Française, et Mlle Rachel* (Paris, 1842), p. 21.

"this young girl": *"cette jeune fille, cette poétique Rachel, qui porte au front une auréole de pureté, la plus belle parure d'une femme, comme, le soir, elle met le diadème, le plus riche ornement d'une reine."* A. B[olé], *Mademoiselle Rachel et l'avenir du Théâtre Français* (Paris, 1839), p. 19.

130 "People invite me": *"Ensuite on m'invite de tous les côtés chez des baronnes, des duchesses, des comtes, enfin si j'acceptais toutes ces invitations je n'aurais même pas le temps d'ouvrir un livre. La seule société qui convienne à un artiste, ce sont ses rôles, et non ces belles dames et ces beaux messieurs qui vous font des compliments bien flatteurs tant que l'on est chez eux, et ensuite vous abîment et vous déchirent."* Rachel to Sarah Félix, n.d., Archives of the Comédie-Française.

"precisely because she did not believe in it": *"Justement, je pense, parce qu'elle n'y croyait pas, parce qu'elle savait la part du snobisme et de l'esprit d'imitation dans cet empressement, parce que, sous la décente humilité qu'elle affichait pour la circonstance, elle demeurait une étrangère. Une étrangère attentive à plaire pour conquérir et dominer, une étrangère à qui rien de nos conventions ni de nos hiérarchies n'imposera jamais."* Mme [Béatrix] Dussane, *Reines de théâtre 1633–1941,* p. 160.

131 "Rachel, Rachel herself": George Sand is quoted by Gay Manifold, *George Sand's Theatre Career* (Ann Arbor, c. 1985), p. 144. Sand took an eccentric view

of Rachel: she was the only person to object—granted, it was in early 1848, when Rachel had perhaps gained weight after pregnancy and childbirth—to her "fat behind."

p. 133 "a Jewess's turban": Balzac, *Lost Illusions*, translated by Ellen Marriage (New York, 1901), p. 80.

In Musset's objections to Janin's review he cites *"la beauté du visage, la grâce des manières, la douceur du langage, qui peuvent appartenir à un homme aussi bien qu'à une femme."* He goes on: *"Dieu sait quelle rougeur eut monté au front du poète, si on avait cherché devant lui une interprétation obscène à son vers! Mais que voulez-vous? du temps de Racine, Robert Macaire n'existait pas."* Alfred de Musset, "Théâtre-Français: Reprise de *Bajazet*: Mademoiselle Rachel," *Revue des deux mondes*, 1 December 1838.

134 For a suggestive treatment of the theme of identity and Racine's *Esther*, see Eve Kosofsky Sedgwick, *Epistemology of the Closet* (Berkeley, 1990), pp. 75–82.

135 The poem and the footnote are quoted by Mollier, *Michel et Calmann Lévy*, p. 45: *"Quoique Juive, au milieu d'un peuple de chrétiens,/Rachel, nouvelle Esther, entre des Parisiens,/De mille Assuérus la sultane et l'idole/Chaque soir voit grandir sa superbe auréole."* The circumcision story seems to have been told first in *La Jeune Rachel et la vieille Comédie-Française* (1838), p. 164: *"L'enfant apportée à la synagogue, le huitième jour, y fut rachetée selon l'ancien usage, y subit la mystérieuse circoncision et fut marqué du nom charmant de Rachel."* The ritual *naming* of a Jewish female infant in the synagogue has been confused with the ritual for males.

136 "Genius, Goddess": *"Génie, Hymen, libérateur de Racine, déesse des Salons, Théâtre-Français personnifié, instituteur de ses comédiens, tragédienne cosmopolite, idole des Juifs, enfant gâté d'un faubour, huitième merveille de l'univers, magasin de bijouterie."* Le Courrier du théâtre, 21 January 1840.

"She could not get used to the silence": *"Elle ne peut s'habituer à ce silence; elle veut que son geste, elle veut que sa parole portent à l'instant même; sinon, elle hésite, elle se trouble, elle oublie, non pas son rôle, mais le drame dans lequel elle joue; pour reconquérir les applaudissements qui lui manquent, elle s'abandonne à toutes les exagérations de l'art dramatique; où elle était irritée, elle devient furieuse; où elle était grande, elle devient boursouflée."* Le Journal des débats, 17 February 1840, quoted in *Le Théâtre en France*, p. 132.

137 "her delivery": *"Sa façon de dire nette, serrée, saccadée, rageuse, si l'on peut s'exprimer ainsi, est en opposition avec les amples périodes, les circonlocutions élégantes, les phrases à longs plis de la poésie classique ... c'est de ce contraste même que résulte son succès."* Gautier II, p. 245.

"the whole issue": Molly Haskell, "Meryl Streep: Hiding in the Spotlight," *Ms.*, December 1988, p. 68. Quotations from Lewes are from his essay on Rachel in *On Actors and the Art of Acting*.

138 "she propped up": *The Era* of 16 May 1841 is quoted by Falk, p. 92.

p. 138 "it will be highly amusing": *"ce sera très amusant, car on m'assure qu'on ne comprend pas du tout la langue française là où nous devons aller jouer."* Rachel, quoted by Mme Samson, pp. 165–66.

139 "Everybody here is now raving": Frances Anne Kemble, *Records of Later Life* II (London, 1882), p. 99 ff. (Emma Woodhouse, Jane Austen's most power-loving heroine, is also criticized for lacking tenderness.)

"unworthy her acknowledged talent": Phrases from the English newspapers are taken from *The Era; The Illustrated London News; The Times;* and *The Morning Post,* 1841–55.

141 "greatly embarrassed by the conventions": Benjamin Lumley, *Reminiscences of the Opera* (London, 1864; repr. New York, 1976), pp. 51–52.

"a great *ébauche*": Thomas Carlyle, *On Heroes, Hero-Worship, and the Heroic in History* (London, 1879; repr. New York, 1980), p. 13.

142 "Mlle Rachel's wonderful impersonation": Queen Victoria is quoted in Richardson, p. 81 ff. One Englishman who refused to let Rachel persuade him to enthusiasm for Racine was Charles Dickens. "I have not seen Rachel yet, being unwilling to be forced to believe that anybody or anything could impart an interest to Racine," he wrote to Angela Burdett-Coutts in May 1841. "I mean to wait for *Mary Stuart*: I am told she is a wonder, and am prepared to think so." Edgar Johnson, ed., *Letters from Charles Dickens to Angela Burdett-Coutts, 1841–1865* (London, 1953), p. 31.

"It is delightful": Bernhardt is quoted by John Stokes, "Rachel's 'Terrible Beauty,' " p. 45. Macready is quoted by Richardson, p. 34.

143 "a kind of universal intelligence": Emerson saw Rachel in Paris in 1848 in *Phèdre* on May 9 or 13, in *Mithridate* on May 17 or 18, and in *Lucrèce* later in the month. In his journal he wrote, "The best part of her performance is the terror & energy she can throw into passages of defiance or denunciation. Her manners & carriage are throughout pleasing by their highly intellectual cast. And her expression of the character is not lost by your losing some word or look, but is continuous & is sure to be conveyed. She is extremely youthful & innocent in her appearance and when she appeared after the curtain fell to acknowledge the acclamations of the house & the heaps of flowers that were flung to her . . . her smile had a perfect good nature & a kind of universal intelligence." Elsewhere in his journal, Emerson explains why Carlyle disliked Rachel: "He saw Rachel in an impossible attitude, & learned that she could stand so, because her dress was loaded with lead. & he despises her ever since." This insight into the material basis of her "statuesque" poses is not corroborated elsewhere. Carlyle, Emerson notes, thought actors and actresses "all mad monkeys." Merton M. Sealts, Jr., ed., *The Journals and Miscellaneous Notebooks of Ralph Waldo Emerson* X (Cambridge, Mass., 1973), pp. 269, 543.

"Phèdre is separated": Lewes's review is reprinted in *Dramatic Essays: John Forster and George Henry Lewes*, with notes and introduction by William Archer and Robert W. Lowe (London, 1896), p. 92. The associations of Mme Tussaud were with French terror as well as popular culture; although her wax museum was in London, the proprietor was French, the niece of a Dr. Curtius, who had opened the first wax museum to the general public in Paris, in 1776, and begun to produce lifelike models of guillotined heads after the Terror. Mme Tussaud's wax museum had flourished in London since 1835.

p. 144 "We did not want": Mary Wallstonecraft, *Maria; or, the Wrongs of Woman* (New York, 1975), p. 149

"A classical education": Disraeli, *Coningsby*, p. 187.

147 Sandra M. Gilbert and Susan Gubar, in *The Madwoman in the Attic: The Woman Writer and the Nineteenth-Century Literary Imagination* (New Haven, 1979), trace connections between Laure in *Middlemarch* and Céline in *Jane Eyre*.

148 For the actress in England, see Christopher Kent, "Image and Reality: The Actress and Society," in Martha Vicinus, ed., *A Widening Sphere: Changing Roles of Victorian Women* (Bloomington, Ind., 1977). See also, more generally, Juliet Bair, "Private Parts in Public Places: The Case of Actresses," in *Women and Space: Ground Rules and Social Maps*, edited by Shirley Ardener (New York, 1981). For Nelly Ternan and actresses in England, see Claire Tomalin, *The Invisible Woman: The Story of Nelly Ternan and Charles Dickens* (New York, 1991), p. 14 ff.

149 "All the ladies-in-waiting": Heine is quoted in S. S. Prawer, *Heine's Jewish Comedy*, p. 327.

150 "Mlle Rachel is a great artist": *"Mlle Rachel est une grande artiste, elle veut bien mettre son talent à ma disposition, elle a un ton parfait. Je n'ai rien de plus à lui demander."* Mme Récamier is (allegedly) quoted by Martial-Piéchaud, *La Vie privée de Rachel*, p. 104.

she made and broke her liaisons: *"Elle noue, dénoue, et reprend ses liaisons avec la plus grande insouciance, elle vit de la plus complète liberté du corps et de l'esprit, comme si elle voulait se dédommager par une vie dissipée de ce vénérable et chaste sacerdoce qu'elle exerce sur la scène."* Laplane, p. 155.

For the type of *"grande amoureuse,"* see Simone de Beauvoir, *The Second Sex*, translated by H. M. Parshley (New York, 1953; 1974), pp. 712–43.

151 "I am *free*": *"Je suis libre . . ."* quoted by Chevalley, *Rachel*, p. 188.

152 "had two bracelets entirely": Agate, *Rachel*, p. 70.

"since you're willing to wag your tail": *"puisque tu veux bien remuer la queue en mon honneur, remue aussi les quatre pattes pour arriver à Paris."* Rachel, quoted by Toussaint du Wast, p. 96.

153 "My conduct": *"Ma conduite est irréprochable comme tu dis, mais cela n'empêche pas de faire des bêtises. Ne va pas être effrayé pour moi: ce ne sont que petites bêtises."* Rachel, quoted by Chevalley, p. 178.

"The Walewski": "P. S. *M. le Walewski me prie de vous dire mille choses (pensez-les aimables c'est ainsi qu'il entend.)"* Rachel to Adèle Samson, 15 March

1845, archives of the Comédie-Française. Walewski's biographer is Comte d'Ornano. See *La Vie passionante du Comte Walewski, fils de Napoléon* (Paris, 1953).

p. 154 *"boudoir de parade"*: Agate, pp. 78–79, repeats Hector Fleischmann's gossipy description. See also Nicole Toussaint du Wast for a description of the lavish decor.

"You ask whether my son is beautiful": *"Vous me demandez si mon fils est beau. Voulez-vous que je vous réponde franchement et que je vous dire sans détour ma façon de penser? Il est joli, très joli, et plus encore il promet de ressembler à son père."* Rachel, quoted by Chevalley, p. 169.

155 For Emile de Girardin, see Maurice Réclus, *Emile de Girardin* (Paris, 1934).

159 "The doubleness of Rachel's character": *"La dualité du caractère de Rachel se dénonce ici sans feinte. Femme, c'est-à-dire emportée, passionnée, toute en nerfs et en colères, elle méprisera Véron; juive, c'est-à-dire avisée, calculatrice, prévoyante et soucieuse, elle se servira de lui. D'un côté, son bonheur, sa dignité; de l'autre, son avenir, sa fortune. Et elle hésiterait? Et l'un passerait avant l'autre? Vous croyez donc que ce n'est pas une fille à père Félix?"* Fleischmann, p. 64.

160 "What a journey": *"Quelle route! Quelle fatigue!! Mais quelle dot!!!"* Also, *"je vous aime de tout mon coeur et me dis* le *plus dévoué de vos amis."* Rachel to Véron, in d'Heylli, p. 124.

"If by chance": The letter to Sarah, dated only "Berlin, 2 October," is worth quoting at length, with spelling and punctuation preserved: *"ab que c'est long trois mois de congé seule quand trouverai-je donc un homme indépendant qui pourra me venir voir dans ce long exil de congé. . . . je suis toujours sur une route de poussière et sale comme un petit cochon. Avoir un amant qui est à Paris ou bien à la campagne pendant que vous allez vous fatiguer à l'étranger . . . mieux vaut un vieux mari qui vous ne quitte pas ou bien rien de tout et alors se suffire à soi-même. Je me sens un peu refroidir pour le blond il est trop la bonne de son père. Si par un beau temps en te promenant tu recontrais un homme bien de taille et de mine, envoyé le moi poste restante à Munich où je serai d'un quinze jour."* Archives of The Hebrew University, Jerusalem.

"Un Souper chez Mlle Rachel": Jean Gooder, whose translation of Alfred de Musset I paraphrase here, writes, " 'Un Souper Chez Rachel' was written as a letter to Madame [Caroline] Jaubert on the night of 29–30 May, 1839. It was first published by Paul de Musset after his brother's death in *le Magasin de Librairie* on 25 March, 1859." Gooder's translation is of the version in the Pléiade edition of Musset's *Oeuvres complètes en prose* (Paris, 1960), which is based not on Paul de Musset's version but on a manuscript in the possession of Madame Jaubert's granddaughter. See *The Cambridge Quarterly*, vol. 15, no. 2 (1986).

161 "a revelation of two realities": Henry James, *The Tragic Muse* (Harmondsworth, 1984), p. 282.

p. 162 "Racinian tenebroso": Roland Barthes, *On Racine*, translated by Richard Howard (New York, 1983), p. 21.

"the will of Mlle Rachel": *"la volonté de Mlle Rachel et l'assentiment du public en ont fait une tragédienne."* Gérard de Nerval, *Oeuvres complètes* I (Paris, 1984), p. 1018.

George Sand wrote lovingly of Dorval's sensitive study of the role of Phèdre, insisting she was admired by connoisseurs but being no longer young lacked Rachel's erotic appeal; Rachel, she says, was too young, fearful, and restrained when she first played Phèdre, but later grew into it. Sand writes as if Dorval aimed deliberately to equal a standard Rachel had already set. See George Sand, "Histoire de ma vie," *Oeuvres autobiographiques* II, edited by Georges Lubin (Paris, 1971), pp. 239–40.

163 "the best-kept secret": Froma I. Zeitlin, "The Power of Aphrodite: Eros and the Boundaries of the Self in the *Hippolytus*," in Peter Burian, ed., *Directions in Euripidean Criticism: A Collection of Essays* (Durham, N.C., 1985), p. 71. Zeitlin makes the observation apropos of the Euripides heroine.

"Je le vis, je rougis": Jean Racine, "Phèdre" I, 3; *Oeuvres complètes* (Paris, 1950). The English is from "Phaedra," *The Complete Plays of Jean Racine*, translated by Samuel Solomon, vol. II (New York, 1967). For Racine and Sappho, see Joan de Jean, *Fictions of Sappho 1546–1937* (Chicago, 1989). The relevant lines, in a recent English translation of Sappho, are "my heart flutters in my breast/ whenever I look quickly, for a moment—/I say nothing, my tongue broken,/ a delicate fire runs under my skin,/my eyes see nothing, my ears roar,/cold sweat rushes down me,/trembling seizes me,/I am greener than grass,/to myself I seem/needing but little to die." Diane Rayor, *Ancient Greek Poetry: Archaic Lyric, Sappho and the Later Women Poets* (Berkeley, 1991), p. 57.

164 "Rachel begins": Annenkov, quoted in Senelick, "Rachel in Russia," *Theatre Research International*, vol. III, no. 2 (February 1978), p. 99.

165 "With her first step": *"Au premier pas qu'elle a fait hors de la coulisse, le succès n'était plus douteux; jamais physionomie d'un rôle ne fut mieux composée. Quand elle s'est avancée, pâle comme son propre fantôme, les yeux rougis dans son masque de marbre, les bras dénoués et morts, le corps inerte sous ses belles draperies à plis droits, il nous a semblé voir, non pas mademoiselle Rachel, mais bien Phèdre elle-même."* Gautier II, p. 328.

"Mlle Rachel understands Phèdre": *"Mademoiselle Rachel a compris Phèdre d'une manière particulière, et que nous croyons la bonne. Elle joue le rôle, non pas en femme passionnée, mais en victime. Son amour est comme une espèce de folie, de maladie vengeresse infligée par le courroux implacable de Vénus, qui n'hésite pas à perdre une innocente pour châtier un insensible qui dédaigne son culte."* Gautier III, p. 227.

166 "woman wasting away": Sir Theodore Martin, *Monographs: Garrick, Macready, Rachel, and Baron Stockmar* (London, 1906), p. 250. Martin asserts that Rachel had "a low moral nature," p. 267.

p. 166 "female criminality": *"La criminalité de la femme est plus dangereuse que celle de l'homme parce qu'elle est plus contagieuse."* C. Lucas, *De la réforme des prisons* (1838); quoted by Joan Scott, *Gender and the Politics of History* (New York, 1988), p. 133.

167 "Rachel they say is": Mary Lutyens, ed., *Young Mrs. Ruskin in Venice: Unpublished Letters of Mrs. John Ruskin Written from Venice between 1849–1852* (New York, 1965), p. 192.

"Her attraction": *"L'attrait qu'elle a pour moi, c'est l'attrait du danger."* "Judith" III, 5, in *Oeuvres complètes de Madame Emile de Girardin* VI (Paris, 1860).

For Madame Lafarge, see Mary S. Hartman, *Victorian Murderesses: A True History of Thirteen Respectable French and English Women Accused of Unspeakable Crimes* (New York, 1977), esp. p. 11; pp. 49–50. See also Flaubert's *L'Education sentimentale: "Quand il entra dans le salon, tous se lèverent à grand bruit, on l'embrassa; et avec les fauteuils et les chaises on fit un large demi-cercle autour de la cheminée. M. Gamblin lui demanda immédiatement son opinion sur Mme Lafarge. Ce procès, la fureur de l'époque, ne manqua pas d'amener une discussion violente."* (Gustave Flaubert, *Oeuvres* II [Paris, 1952], p. 42.) The editor's note to this passage in the Pléiade edition reads, *"Le procès de Mme Lafarge, 'fureur de l'époque' de Flaubert, passionne encore les hommes de la nôtre. Rappelons seulement ici que Marie Capelle, femme Lafarge, retirée dans la solitude provinciale du Glandier avec un mari qu'elle n'aimait pas, fut accusée de l'avoir empoisonné. Le procès occupa l'Europe entière."* The *Edinburgh Review* of July 1842 featured an article over thirty pages long by J. A. Roebuck, "Trial of Madame Lafarge: French Criminal Jurisprudence."

168 "predilection for prisons": In an 1843 letter from Brest to Delphine de Girardin, Rachel boasted of the courage that was required to enter into conversation with such "dregs of humanity." See d'Heylli, p. 143. For her letter to Sarah Félix describing the visit to Mme Lafarge, see pp. 150–53.

169 "those beautiful Grecian idols": *"de belles idoles Grecques qui firent un moment, sous le Directoire, rêver d'Athènes au peuple de Paris."* Lamartine, *Souvenirs et portraits* 1 (Paris, 1886), is quoted in the preface to Delphine de Girardin, *Chroniques parisiennes* (Paris, 1986).

"Distinguished and crowned": *"Distinguée et couronnée par l'Académie française en 1822 pour avoir chanté le dévouement des Soeurs de Sainte-Camille pendant la peste de Barcelone, Mlle Gay ne cessa de célébrer depuis en vers tous les évènements publics importants, les solemnités monarchiques et patriotiques,"* Sainte-Beuve wrote. *"On la vit un jour, au haut de la coupole du Panthéon, réciter son Hymne à sainte Geneviève, en l'honneur des peintures de Gros. Dans un voyage qu'elle fit à Rome en 1827, elle fut reçue au Capitole membre de l'Académie du Tibre.... Tout cela donna prétexte de dire autour d'elle et lui donna l'idée à elle-même qu'elle n'était pas seulement une Muse élégiaque, mais aussi la Muse de la Patrie."* Sainte-Beuve, *Causeries du lundi* III (Paris, 1852), is quoted on p. 11 of the preface to *Chroniques parisiennes*.

p. 170 "No woman has had": *"Jamais aucune femme n'avait eu ce triomphe tout viril depuis Vittoria Colonna; à qui vous ressemblez de traits, de génie, et, je crois, aussi d'héroisme."* Lamartine to Mme de Girardin, in Léon Séché, "Documents inédits de Rachel et Mme de Girardin," *La Revue de Paris,* 1 June 1909.

"When I was": Fanny Lewald's account of Heine's visit is quoted by S. S. Prawer, *Heine's Jewish Comedy,* p. 549. I quote Prawer's comment on the analogy. Alice Y. Kaplan reminds me, apropos of Heine's joke, that the carp is "the most Jewish of fishes," *carpe à la juive* being included in many French cookbooks—which of course have many more recipes for rabbit, the meat of the *terroir.*

171 "this is not a woman": *"cette femme n'est pas dans le caractère antique; c'est la chrétienne réprouvée, c'est la pécheresse tombée vivante entre les mains de Dieu: son mot est le mot du damné."* René de Chateaubriand, "Le Génie du christianisme," in Chateaubriand, *Oeuvres complètes* (Paris, 1978), p. 694.

"M. Nestor Roqueplan": *"M. Nestor Roqueplan me disait hier au soir: 'Les gens du monde en ce moment vont à la tragédie comme les lorettes vont à la messe.'"* Hugo, 27 April 1843; quoted by Louis Chévalier, *Montmartre du plaisir et du crime* (Paris, 1980), p. 61.

172 "Father Félix, who": *"le père Félix, qui s'est présenté jadis comme acteur au théâtre de Francfort, aurait pu se charger du rôle de Thésée, et la pièce se serait jouée tout à fait en famille; mais on a craint sa prononciation germanique, et il a bien fallu admettre un quatrième acteur d'un autre sang."* Gérard de Nerval, *Oeuvres complètes,* p. 820.

"a Rachelian progeny": *"tout une progéniture Rachélique . . . des acteurs non issus de Jacob en général, et le père Félix en particulier."* Nerval, p. 820.

173 "no particular knowledge": *"Mademoiselle Rachel, sans avoir de connaissances ni de goûts plastiques, possédait instinctivement un sentiment profond de la statuaire. Ses poses, ses attitudes, ses gestes s'arrangeaient naturellement d'une façon sculpturale et se décomposaient en une suite de bas reliefs. Les draperies se plissaient, comme fripées par la main de Phidias, sur son corps long, élégant et souple; aucun mouvement moderne ne troublait l'harmonie et le rhythme de sa démarche; elle était née antique, et sa chair pâle semblait faite avec du marbre grec."* Théophile Gautier, "Mademoiselle Rachel," *Portraits contemporains,* p. 423.

"If only you knew": *"Si vous saviez quels plis chastes et purs font dessiner à sa blanche tunique ses mouvements si nobles, ses gestes si contenus! Comme son oeil est d'un noir profond dans son masque de marbre pâle! comme la ligne de son cou, un peu amaigri, s'attache avec élégance à ses épaules!"* Gautier is quoted by Chevalley, *Rachel,* p. 172.

"Sculpture is as real": Théophile Gautier, *Mademoiselle de Maupin,* translated by Paul Selver (London, 1948), p. 244.

"her misunderstood beauty": *"Sa beauté méconnue, car elle était admirablement belle, n'avait rien de coquet, de joli, de français, en un mot;—longtemps même elle passa pour laide, tandis que les artistes étudiaient avec amour et reproduisaient comme un type de perfection ce masque aux yeux noirs, détaché de la face même de Melpomène!"* Gautier, *Portraits contemporains*, pp. 423–24.

p. 173 "Yes, the work of art": Anthony Hartley, trans., *The Penguin Book of French Verse* III *(The Nineteenth Century)* (Harmondsworth, 1957). Gautier's lyric, "L'Art," in his *Emaux et Camées* (1857), brings many of his characteristic themes together. It begins:

> *Oui, l'oeuvre sort plus belle*
> *D'une forme au travail*
> > *Rebelle,*
> *Vers, marbre, onyx, émail.*
> *Point de contraintes fausses!*
> *Mais que pour marcher droit*
> > *Tu chausses,*
> *Muse, un cothurne étroit.*

174 "The entrance of Mlle Rachel": *"L'entrée de Mlle Rachel au théâtre, lorsqu'au milieu des licenses poétiques du nouveau drame elle apparût subitement, drapée dans la tunique des statues, fut une révélation et un enchantement, quelque chose de semblable à l'effet que produisait cette grande Vénus trouvée à Milo, qui, à peine tirée de la poussière, réduisit au rang inférieur les prétendus chefs-d'oeuvre de l'art."* Paul de Saint-Victor is quoted in *La Grande Encyclopédie Larousse* (Paris, 1865), p. 605.
"in physiognomy and in attitude": *"de physionomie et d'attitude. L'armure d'acier, si invraisemblable qu'elle soit dans une prison, lui sied à merveille."* Nerval, p. 1046.
Under the aegis of a later republic, Brigitte Bardot and Catherine Deneuve would succeed her in that role.

175 For the contest between Mlles George and Duchesnois, see Roselyne Laplace, *Mademoiselle George, ou un demi-siècle de théâtre* (Paris, 1987), p. 42 ff.

176 "the most deserted theater in the universe": Charles Baudelaire, "The Salon of 1846," *Art in Paris 1845–1862, Salons and Other Exhibitions*, translated by Jonathan Mayne (Oxford, 1965), pp. 104–5.
"the female form": Marina Warner, *Monuments and Maidens: The Allegory of the Female Form* (New York, 1985), p. 225.
"Rachel is an antique statue": *"Rachel est une statue antique, c'est-à-dire, quelque chose comme le beau idéal."* Auguste Roussel, *Mlle Rachel et sa troupe en province, Satires* (Paris, 1849), p. 11. For a comparison of Mlles George and Rachel on the one hand, and Michelangelo and Raphaël on the other, see *La Tragédie et Mlle Rachel* (Amsterdam, 1846), p. 7.

177 "Her gaze": *"Son regard, ses yeux aggrandis par le douleur, exprimaient le plus violent désespoir, c'était la tête de Méduse."* *Mademoiselle Rachel: souvenirs d'un contemporain* (Berlin, 1882), p. 24.

p. 177 "beneath the sculptural folds": *"sous les plis de sa tunique sculpturale je vois s'agiter les serpents qui nous mordent le sein."* Théodore de Banville, quoted by André Bellessort, *Heures de parole: sujets anciens, questions modernes* (Paris, 1929), pp. 235–36.

"a severe classic figure": See George C. D. Odell, *Annals of the New York Stage (1850–1857)*, vol. VI (New York, 1931), pp. 448–49.

"cult of abstractions": quoted from *Revue et gazette des théâtres*, 29 September 1853, in Sylvie Chevalley, "La tournée de Rachel en Russie," *Revue de l'histoire du théâtre* IV (1958), p. 330.

In the nineteenth century: For another view of theatricality and the Victorians, see Nina Auerbach, *Private Theatricals: The Lives of the Victorians* (Cambridge, Mass., 1990). See also *Lady Audley's Secret*, in which the heroine, deciding to kill her nephew, "stopped in her rapid pacing to and fro—stopped as Lot's wife may have stopped, after that fatal backward glance at the perishing city—with every pulse slackening, with every drop of blood congealing in her veins, in the terrible process that was to transform her from a woman into a statue." Mary Elizabeth Braddon, *Lady Audley's Secret* (1862; repr. New York, 1974), pp. 203–4. Her story puts Lady Audley through a spectrum of actress-positions: she wears a mask to conceal her identity and cover up a crime, becomes statuelike when she gets the impulse to commit another, and responds to accusation, in the end, by assuming the grand statuesque manner of a tragic actress.

179 "a woman renowned": Germaine de Staël, *Corinne, or Italy*, pp. 21, 22.

"Pale as one": George Sand, *Lélia*, translated by Maria Espinosa (Bloomington, Ind., 1978), pp. 6, 89.

"reproduce the folds": *"ai-je pu reproduire ses admirables plis si bien fouillés par les ciseaux de Michel Ange, Canova, Lorenzetto, Morelli etc. etc., avant de les avoir vu. Mais aussi quel est mon orgeuil, je les avais devinés; la fille du peuple a su se draper à l'antique et les romains viennent de m'admirer et m'applaudir avec fureur, les couronnes et les bouquets ont à plusieurs fois dans les soirées caché les tapis de la scène."* Rachel, 16 September 1851; Laplane, pp. 78–79.

180 "he made the mistake": *"D'ailleurs, il a eu le tort de croire qu'on fait la Tragédie en faisant une tragédienne—fut-elle Mlle Rachel."* Edmond and Jules de Goncourt, *Etudes d'art: le Salon de 1852* (Paris, c. 1852), p. 143. Albert Blanquet admired Clésinger's busts of Rachel. *"Le marbre de Clésinger sera peut-être retrouvé un jour sous les ruines de la moderne Ninive comme la Melpomène d'un nouveau Parnasse,"* he raved; Blanquet, in *Galerie illustrée des célébrités des théâtres de Paris* (Paris, 1852), pp. 167–68.

"It was a rare and moving spectacle": *"Ce fut un émouvant et rare spectacle, ce premier acte, cette tragédienne qui entrait dans le drame, cette morte qui voulait vivre, ce marbre qui s'avançait vers les hommes et vers les femmes. Ce fut quelque chose de l'entrée du Commandeur au souper de Don Juan;—seulement, ici, c'était la statue qui avait peur."* Auguste Vacquerie, "Mlle Rachel," *Profils et grimaces* (Paris, 1856), p. 259.

p. 181 For demonic woman in the nineteenth-century imagination, see Nina Auerbach, *Woman and the Demon: The Life of a Victorian Myth* (Cambridge, Mass., 1982).

For Fru Heiberg, see Søren Kierkegaard, *Crisis in the Life of an Actress and Other Essays on Drama*, translated by Stephen Crites (London, 1967). The context suggests that the word translated as "luck" signifies a palpable happy and confident self-possession.

182 For Sarah Bernhardt as Joan of Arc at sixty-five, see Arthur Gold and Robert Fizdale, *The Divine Sarah* (New York, 1991), p. 243.

"the minister understood": Rachel's account of her impromptu political conference with Achille Fould in 1854 is in "Lettres à l'aimé," *La Revue de France* (15 December 1922), p. 675.

"Look, I'm all for Rachel": *"Voyez-vous, je suis pour Rachel; elle est fine celle-là. Comme elle vous mâte tous ces drôles de Comédiens français! Elle renouvelle ses engagements, se fait assurer des feux, des congés, des montagnes d'or; puis, quand c'est signé, elle dit:—Ah! à propos j'ai oublié de vous dire que j'étais grosse de quatre mois et demi, je vais être cinq mois sans pouvoir jouer!—Elle fait bien. Si j'avais eu ces façons, je ne serais pas à crever comme un chien sur la paille."* Mlle George is quoted by Victor Hugo, *Choses vues* I (Paris, 1913), pp. 237–38.

185 It was indeed the tocsin: *"C'était bien le tocsin révolutionnaire qui vibrait dans sa voix, et la fièvre de la vengeance qui faisait trembler son corps frêle."* Gautier VI, p. 75.

"she took her attitude": Lumley, p. 52.

187 "if her heart and soul": Letter of 15 April 1848 to *"Citoyen Verteuil, Secrétaire de l'administration du Théâtre de la République,"* which reads, *"J'y ai entendu la chante patriotique par notre grande tragédienne et l'ai trouvé entraînante par son énergie Républicaine, si son coeur et son âme le sont autant que son jeu, je la reconnais pour la première républicaine de la République de France."* Archives of the Comédie-Française.

"she came forward": Rowland E. Prothero, *The Life and Correspondence of Arthur Penrhyn Stanley*, vol. I (New York, 1894), p. 394. For R. W. Emerson on Rachel's *Marseillaise*, see his journal entries cited previously, and the letter to his wife of 25 May 1848 in Ralph L. Rusk, ed., *The Letters of R. W. Emerson* IV (New York, 1939), p. 77. See also the Marquis of Normanby, *A Year of Revolution from a Journal Kept in Paris in 1848*, vol. I (London, 1857), pp. 281–82: "The event of the evening was the 'Marseillaise' *(sung?)* by Rachel. It was the triumph of superabundant energy, really producing an irresistibly thrilling effect, though one shared the sentiments, forcibly articulated rather than melodised, as little as the gifted artist herself, and I believe one cannot state the case more strongly. There could exist no one less likely to celebrate a revolution, which must have been most opposed to all her social sympathies, and most damaging to her professional career. When one heard her, as it was called, sing the 'Marseillaise,' one was the more surprised to recollect that her brilliant career had commenced as a ballad-singer in the streets,—a fact which, to all who had the pleasure of her acquaintance in the days of her early triumph, she stated without either reserve or affectation; but which this musical exhibition would assuredly not have suggested." The marquis of course projects his politics. That he thought Rachel's frank acknowledgment of her past was no index to her "social sympathies" is a tribute to the legend, in which the insouciance of *La Grande* was taken to be an aspect of her natural rank.

p. 188 "very male hymn": *"Cet hymne si mâle pourtant et d'un si grand jet musical, mademoiselle Rachel a trouvé moyen de le rendre plus énergique, plus fort, plus farouche et plus formidable, par l'âpreté incisive, les grondements rancuniers et les éclats métalliques de sa diction."* Gautier V, p. 242. About Rachel's political views, the general opinion always has been that *"Elle frondait un peu, voilà tout, sans s'occuper de systèmes qu'elle ne comprenait pas."* See A.-P. Mantel, *Rachel: détails inédits* (Paris, 1858), p. 40. She herself was amused by her political position: refusing a dinner invitation, she wrote, *"On ne mange pas toujours quand on veut lorsqu'on a l'honneur d'être la première tragédienne de Sa Majesté le peuple français!"* Rachel, in d'Heylli, p. 69. In "Rachel et *la Marseillaise*," in *1848, révolutions et mutations au XIXe siècle*, no. 4 (Paris, 1988), Sylvia Chevalley concludes that the actress was not sincere in her revolutionary passion— and that her performances saved the Théâtre-Français.

"Rachel is the personified": Fanny Lewald, *Erinnerungen aus dem Jahre 1848* (Braunschweig, 1850), p. 195, quoted (and translated) in an unpublished paper by Irene Stocksieker Di Maio, "Landmarks and Language, Sites and Signs: Fanny Lewald's Observations on the 1848 Revolution in France." I am grateful to Professor Di Maio for making this available to me. Lewald's *Erinnerungen* is also the source of the anecdote, very different in tone, about Heine's visit to Rachel's house in the country.

190 For Rahel Levin Varnhagen, see Hannah Arendt, *Rahel Varnhagen: The Life of a Jewish Woman* (New York, 1974). Rahel is compared to Mme de Staël and described as *"l'anti-Corinne par excellence"* by Julien-Frédéric Tarn in *Le Marquis de Custine* (Paris, 1985), p. 472. Custine admired Rahel (before Rachel), and wrote an eloquent obituary after her death in 1833, praising her for disdaining eloquence, unlike de Staël, and speaking only to communicate, not to be admired.

191 "A nobleman can and must be": Johann Wolfgang von Goethe, *Wilhelm Meister's Apprenticeship*, edited and translated by Eric A. Blackall in cooperation with Victor Lange (New York, 1989), p. 175.

"ever attentive": *"'La Grande,' toujours attentive au vent capricieux du succès, fort peu tourné chez nous vers les choses républicaines, avait préalable-*

ment fait défection au premier rôle." Journal de Edmond Got 1822–1910, vol. I (Paris, 1910), p. 259.

p. 192 "that I sang *La Marseillaise"*: *"Rappeler mon zèle pour le théâtre chaque fois que le théâtre y a fait appel, et à cet endroit un mot à propos de la Marseillaise que je n'ai chantée que par dévouement dans un moment plus que critique, puisque sans elle après tout le Théâtre Français aurait péri comme tant d'autres dans ce naufrage des révolutions."* Rachel to Lockroy, in Laplane, p. 105.

"Tomorrow the republic": *"Demain la république quitte la France, notre climat ne lui est pas favorable. Demain sera l'Empire demain Paris sera illuminé, je regrette mon doux petit ange que tu ne puisses m'aider à accrocher mes lampions. Je suis un peu souffrante, je ne pourrai malheureusement voir aux Champs-Elysées l'entrée de l'Empereur à Paris."* Rachel to her son Alexandre Walewski, Paris, 1 October 1850; Archives of the Comédie-Française.

194 "ce que les Anglais appellent": "Revue des Théâtres," *Revue des deux mondes* III (1849), p. 1054.

For Houssaye's account of his appointment to the post of director of the Comédie-Française, see Arsène Houssaye, *Les Confessions: souvenirs d'un demi-siècle, 1830–1880*, vol. II (Paris, 1885).

197 "Travel makes one's youth": *"Les voyages, qui forment la jeunesse, déforment les cartons à chapeaux."* Rachel, quoted by d'Heylli, p. 153.

"I have traveled across": *"Je viens de traverser la Belgique, la Prusse, la Saxe et me voilà en Bohême après demain à Vienne, tout ce trajet en l'espace d'un mois!"* Rachel, letter of 26 August 1851, Archives of the Comédie-Française.

198 "Was it I who aroused": *"Vous auriez été satisfait de voir cette salle se soulever comme un seul homme. Etait-ce moi que montais le public ou le public que me montait? Je l'ignore; ce qu'il y a de certain, c'est que nous étions fort chauds tous les deux."* Rachel (sounding like Madonna), in "Lettres à l'aimé," *La Revue de France* (15 December 1922), p. 682.

199 "Life, finally, is sad": *"Toute jeune que je suis (car en verité quoiqu'en ait-dit le Constitutionnel) je me crois encore assez jeune, l'expérience m'est venue vite depuis quelques années; j'ai appris que la vraie gloire devait être indépendante. Qu'est-ce que nous donne mieux cette indépendance que la fortune! le désir très ardent que j'ai de devenir riche prend dailleurs sa source dans de très bons sentiments. La vie à finir est triste sans amis et rien ne me paraîtrait plus triste que de ne pouvoir en tout point satisfaire ceux que nous mènent gaiement au but eternel La mort."* Letter of 26 August 1851, Archives of the Comédie-Française.

Jean Chéry's recollections of Rachel on tour are recorded in an unpublished manuscript in the possession of the Comédie-Française. See also Sylvie Chevalley, "L'Amérique en 1855: notes de voyage de Jean Chéry," *The French-American Review*, April–June, July–September 1950.

200 "like a sovereign": *"comme une souveraine, non pas une souveraine pastiche de*

tragédie, avec une couronne en carton doré, mais une souveraine pour de vrai, contrôlée à la Monnaie.'' Rachel, in d'Heylli, p. 195.

p. 200 "Moscow will soon be taken": *"Bientôt Moscou sera pris; les Moscovites nous rendent avec usure ce qu'ils nous ont pris en 1812.''* Rachel to Rébecca Félix, 23 February 1854, *Catalogue de lettres autographes, etc.* (Paris, 1939), Bibliothèque de l'Arsénal. To Rébecca, Rachel also wrote victoriously on 18 March 1854, *"La Russie est à nous, j'ai laissé Moscou en feu.''* Laplane, p. 81.

201 "the fatal side": *"le côté fatal, l'ampleur majestueuse, les effets calculés, la pose et l'immobilité de statue coupées par des accès frénétique, la mélopée tumulaire déployée dans cinq tirades propres à son talent: la diction. Mme Ristori en manifeste l'autre côté, le plus sympathique à ses instincts; l'amour tendre et brûlant, la fièvre jalouse et les épouvantes secrètes, la pantomime expressive: la passion. Elle en fait une femme.''* Sébastien Rhéal (de Césena), *Les Deux Phèdre, Mme Ristori et Mlle Rachel. Lettre à M. Carini, directeur du Courrier franco-italien* (Paris, 1858), p. 20.

"the difference between talent and genius": For Lewes on Rachel and Ristori, see "Foreign Actors on Our Stage," in G. H. Lewes, *On Actors and the Art of Acting* (New York, n.d.), p. 144. For Fanny Kemble on the same subject, see Margaret Armstrong, *Fanny Kemble: A Passionate Victorian* (New York, 1938), pp. 369–70.

202 "My good old friend Michel": *"Mon bon vieil ami Michel, Je te fais juge de mon attachement de dévouement à ta très chère personne, n'oublies [sic] pas que je suis une tragédienne, que mes amours sont tout en Corneille dont j'ai les goûts mâles et virils.''* Quoted in Jean-Yves Mollier, *Michel et Calmann Lévy* (Paris, 1984), p. 300.

204 "Indeed, by virtue of the art": *"En effet, elle appartient, par l'art qu'elle exerce et par les chefs-d'oeuvre qu'elle représente, à tout ce que la république, à tout ce que la monarchie ont d'élégance, de courtoisie, de recherche, d'aristocratie et de raffinement. Athènes est une cour, la Rome d'Auguste est une cour; Louis XIV est un soleil qui donne sa clarté aux étoiles; les grands poètes Euripède et Sophocle, Corneille et Racine, s'adressent aux esprits choisis, aux âmes d'élite, aux passions élégantes, à la grandeur, à la toute-puissance, à la majesté; c'est dans un monde à part, et très difficile à contenter que s'agitent ces grands drames; ils parlent à l'âme des spectateurs choisis beaucoup plus qu'aux passions des foules assemblées.''* Jules Janin, "La Semaine dramatique: Mlle Rachel et la tragédie aux États-Unis," *Journal des débats,* 13 October 1855.

205 "May she stay there": *"qu'elle y reste! qu'elle y réussisse! qu'elle y soit écrasée de dollars! qu'elle s'y plaise, qu'elle y aime Racine, qu'elle l'épouse, et qu'ils aient beaucoup de tragédies!''* Auguste Vacquerie, "Mlle Rachel," *Profils et grimaces* (Paris, 1856).

206 "The Empire of France": *Mitchell's School Geography,* fourth rev. ed. (Philadelphia, 1854), pp. 244–45.

p. 206 For Harriet Beecher Stowe on Sojourner Truth (and Rachel), see her "Sojourner Truth, the Libyan Sybil," *Atlantic Monthly*, vol. XI, no. 66, April 1863; reprinted in Katharine M. Rogers, ed., *The Meridian Anthology of Early American Women Writers* (New York, 1991). Nell Irwin Painter, in a forthcoming biography, *Sojourner Truth: A Life, A Symbol*, argues that Sojourner Truth was a self-construction and an effect of various rhetorical tropes, much as I argue about Rachel. About Stowe she writes, "For all her fondness for Truth, or what she makes of her memory, Stowe reduces her to the status of a primitive whose observations might be witty, divinely inspired, but valuable only as entertainment." See Painter, "Sojourner Truth in Life and Memory: Writing the Biography of an American Exotic," *Gender and History*, vol. 2, no. 1 (Spring, 1990), p. 10.

207 the pistol-shot in *Lady Tartuffe*: Although stage directions for the play do not mandate a pistol-shot, a shot is crucial in an anecdote related in the play.

"O go not": the French is

> *On m'a dit:—"N'allez pas sur la rive lointaine*
> *Affronter au hasard la vie américaine.*
> *Ce monde est en travail; il demande des bras*
> *Et non pas du génie. Il ne comprendra pas*
> *La langue de Corneille, étrangère, inconnue. . . .*
> *N'allez pas!" m'a-t-on dit;—Et moi, je suis venue.*

See, e.g., Chevalley, p. 353.

208 "Some had put on their trousers": Beauvallet, *Rachel and the New World*, p. 123.

"Rachel made a great sensation here": W. W. Story to J. R. Lowell, in Henry James, *William Wetmore Story and His Friends* I (London, 1903), pp. 303, 301.

"because I imprudently failed": *"voilà ma position, j'ai eu froid en chemin de fer et depuis que je suis à Boston, je tousse comme une poitrinaire que je ne suis pas, je vous prie de le croire, malgré mon teint pâle et mon apparente maigreur, à part l'imprudence que j'ai eue de ne point me vêtir assez chaudement."* Rachel, letter in *La Revue de France* (1 May 1910), p. 46.

209 "I am making myself commercial": In the letter from Rachel to Louise de Saigneville, dated Boston, 8 October 1855, she laments that "notre belle langue française" is not much known in New York. She acknowledges the applause of Americans but writes, *"cela ne me fait plus rien plaisir pour que j'ai plaisir à être artiste j'ai besoin avant tout de savoir que je suis comprise et cela est impossible ici, je vous le répète je continue avec courage parce que je me fais commerciale je prends et j'entasse les dollars."* Archives of the Comédie-Française.

"My body and mind": *"Mon corps et mon esprit sont tombés à rien. Je ramène ma pauvre armée en déroute sur les bords de la Seine; et moi, peut-être, comme un autre Napoléon, j'irai mourir aux Invalides et demander une pierre pour reposer ma tête."* Rachel, letter in *La Revue de France* (1 May 1910), p. 44.

p. 211 "I have no more hopes": *"Je ne souhaite plus rien, je n'attends plus rien, et franchement, vivre de cette vie animale que je traîne depuis cette longue, doulou-reuse et triste maladie, plutôt cent fois se sentir renfermée entre quatre planches bien clouées et attendre qu'on fasse de nous et de notre boîte ce qu'on fait en ce moment des momies d'Egypte. Je ne mourrai peut-être plus de la poitrine, mais bien certainement je mourrai d'ennui. Quelle solitude morne s'est faite autour de moi! Songez que je suis seule avec un médecin polonais qui n'est que cela, une cuisinière et Rose, ma femme de chambre. Pourtant, j'ai constamment devant les yeux un ciel pur, un climat doux et ce fleuve hospitalier qui porte la barque du malade aussi doucement, aussi maternellement que la mère porte son nouveau-né; mais ces souvenirs majestueux de l'antique Egypte, ces ruines amoncelées de tem-ples merveilleux, ces colosses gigantesques taillés dans les flancs des montagnes de granit, tant d'oeuvres et de chefs-d'oeuvres dégradés par la mine des siècles, renversés de leurs piédestaux par des tremblements de terre, tout ce spectacle vu à l'oeil, sans compter ce que notre imagination lui prête encore d'effrayant, est trop lourd à supporter pour des êtres faibles, des esprits abattus."* Rachel, 10 March 1857; d'Heylli, pp. 232–33.

212 "At the foot of the Pyramids": *"Du bas des Pyramides, je contemple vingt siècles évanouis dans les sables. Ah! mon ami, comme je vois ici le néant des tragédiennes. Je me croyais pyramidale et je reconnais que je ne suis qu'une ombre qui passe . . . qui a passé. Je suis venue ici pour retrouver la vie qui m'échappe, et je ne vois que la mort autour de moi."* Rachel to Arsène Houssaye, Laplane, p. 233.

214 "Nothing survives": The heroine's last line, in Eugène Scribe and Ernest Le-gouvé's *Adrienne Lecouvreur*, is: *"Rien ne nous survit à nous autres . . . rien que le souvenir. Le vôtre, n'est-ce pas?"*

215 "Medea is to maternal love": *"Médée est à l'amour maternel ce qu'Othello est à l'amour, l'image de la passion qui tue."* Ernest Legouvé, preface to *Médée, Tragédie en 3 actes* (Paris, 1874).

"The objections to Madame Ristori's": Henry James, "Madame Ristori," in James, *The Scenic Art*, edited by Allan Wade (New Brunswick, 1948), p. 31.

216 Recent critics: On the *Medea* of Euripides, see Bernard Knox, "The Medea of Euripides," in his *Word and Action: Essays on the Ancient Theater* (Baltimore, 1979), and Helene P. Foley, "Medea's Divided Self," *Classical Antiquity*, vol. 8, no. 1, April 1989.

217 This did not stop him: Legouvé claimed that Rachel did receive him on her deathbed, and the story he told about her posing even there has been much recycled. A similar "event" colored reports of Josephine Baker's end: Phyllis Rose writes, "When she was sick, Maurice Chevalier came to Casablanca to perform and, hearing she was there, tried to pay a call on her. She refused to see him. In addition to her old dislike of him, she knew he had been perform-ing in Paris and regarded him as a collaborator. . . . [She] would not see him, and he gave out the story that she was dying, penniless, in a Casablanca

hospital. 'Don't leave me, Maurice,' he told reporters she had said. 'I am so unhappy.' Eventually the story spread and before long newspapers as far away as America were carrying the report that she had died in North Africa." Phyllis Rose, *Jazz Cleopatra: Josephine Baker in Her Time* (New York, 1989), p. 197. But Legouvé must be given his due: he lectured on women's history at the Collège de France in 1848, and his *Histoire morale des femmes* (Paris, 1849) was influential in the development of nineteenth-century French feminism. A feminist historian writes that "it appears that Legouvé's slogan of 'equality in difference' became the watchword for the organizers of the French women's rights movement during the late Second Empire and early Third Republic." See Karen Offen, "Ernest Legouvé and the Doctrine of 'Equality in Difference' for Women: A Case Study of Male Feminism in Nineteenth-Century French Thought," *Journal of Modern History* 58 (June 1986).

CHAPTER FIVE

p. 218 The quotation from Mario Praz is on page 191 of *The Romantic Agony*, translated by Angus Davidson (New York, 1956).

Leo Braudy's definition of fame is in *The Frenzy of Renown*, p. 15.

The quotation from George Rowell's *The Victorian Theatre: A Survey* (Oxford, 1956), is on p. 24.

Matthew Arnold wrote of Rachel to Arthur Hugh Clough, 24 May 1848; Howard Foster Lawry, ed., *The Letters of Matthew Arnold to Arthur Hugh Clough* (London, 1952), p. 81. Clough, evidently, did not think much of her. On 1 May 1848, he reported to his sister that he was "a little disappointed by Rachel as Phèdre," adding, very much in the Arnoldian vein, "but I am going again, to study *the thing*" (italics mine). Frederick L. Mulhauser, ed., *The Correspondence of Arthur Hugh Clough* I (Oxford, 1957), p. 203.

219 "merely mixed in": Roland Barthes, *S/Z*, translated by Richard Miller (New York, 1974), p. 102.

220 *Putnam's* VI, September 1855, and *Harper's* XI, October 1855, are quoted by Sylvie Chevalley, *Rachel en Amérique*, p. 35.

On the Victorian theater and the novel, see Gillian Beer, " 'Coming Wonders': Uses of Theatre in the Victorian Novel," in *English Drama: Form and Development, Essays in Honour of Muriel Clara Bradbrook*, edited by Marie Axton and Raymond Williams (Cambridge, 1977). Nina Auerbach has written on the subject in "Alluring Vacancies in the Victorian Character," *Kenyon Review* 8 (1986), as well as in her *Woman and the Demon; Ellen Terry: Player in Her Time;* and *Private Theatricals*. See also Alan S. Downer, "Players and Painted Stage: Nineteenth-Century Acting," *PMLA* 61 (1946). Joseph Litvak's *Caught in the Act: Theatricality in the Nineteenth-Century English Novel* (Berkeley, 1992) includes stimulating chapters on all three of the novels I discuss here. My thinking was influenced by portions of this book that were published earlier as articles. I am also indebted to Joseph Butwin, who lent me his 1971 Harvard Ph.D. thesis, *The Artist As Actor in English Fiction,* and to Doris Janet McReynolds, *Image of the Theatre in Victorian Literature,* University of Minnesota Ph.D. thesis, 1970.

p. 220 "her *distinction,* her simple": G. H. Lewes, "Rachel's Phèdre and Roxane" (6 July 1850) in William Archer and Robert W. Lowe, eds., *Dramatic Essays* III (London, 1896), p. 86.

221 "I am free to walk": Quotations from Charlotte Brontë's letters are from Thomas J. Wise, and J. A. Symington, eds. *The Brontës: Their Lives, Friendships, and Correspondence* III (Oxford, 1932), pp. 244–53. For a discussion of Brontë and the theater, see David Isenberg, "Charlotte Brontë and the Theatre," in *Brontë Society Transactions,* vol. 15, no. 3 (1968).

223 "When my children were very young": Elizabeth Gaskell, *The Life of Charlotte Brontë* (Harmondsworth, 1975), p. 94.

225 "each moment he came near me": Charlotte Brontë, in Wise and Symington III, p. 222.

"Rachel's acting": Cf. Rousseau, *Lettre à d'Alembert: "On frissonne à la seule idée des horreurs dont on paré la scène française, pour l'amusement du peuple le plus doux et le plus humain qui soit sur la terre! Non . . . , je le soutiens, et j'en atteste l'effroi des lecteurs, les massacres des gladiateurs n'étaient pas si barbares que ces affreux spectacles. On voyait couler du sang, il est vrai, mais on ne souillait pas son imagination de crimes qui font frémir la Nature."* Jean-Jacques Rousseau, *Discours sur les sciences et les arts, lettre à d'Alembert sur les spectacles* (Paris, 1987), p. 180.

All quotations from *Villette* are from the Penguin edition, pp. 334–47. For critical commentary on the Vashti episode, see Helene Moglen, *Charlotte Brontë: The Self Conceived* (New York, 1976); Sandra M. Gilbert and Susan Gubar, "The Buried Life of Lucy Snowe," *The Madwoman in the Attic* (New Haven, 1979); Steven Millhauser, "Villette," *Grand Street* (Winter, 1987); Mary Jacobus, "The Buried Letter: *Villette,*" *Reading Woman: Essays in Feminist Criticism* (New York, 1986); and Nancy K. Miller, "Changing the Subject: Authorship, Writing, and the Reader," *Subject to Change: Reading Feminist Writing* (New York, 1988). Christina Crosby, in "Charlotte Brontë's Haunted Text," *Studies in English Literature* 24 (1984), discusses "specularity" in the novel; Karen Lawrence, "The Cypher: Disclosure and Reticence in *Villette,*" *Nineteenth-Century Literature* 42 (March 1988), analyzes the two ways Lucy signifies, as a woman in society and as a writer.

226 "You get ice-cold shivers": H. C. Andersen is quoted in a *Times Literary Supplement* review, 15 February 1991, taken from Patricia Conroy and Sven H. Rossel, eds., *The Diaries of Hans Christian Andersen* (Seattle, 1991).

227 "Disguise makes a woman": J. Dusinberre, *Shakespeare and the Nature of Women*

(Basingstoke, 1975), p. 233, quoted by Juliet Bair, "Private Parts in Public Places: The Case of Actresses," *Women and Space: Ground Rules and Social Maps,* edited by Shirley Ardener (New York, 1981), p. 209.

p. 229 "After a first sight": Matthew Arnold, "The French Play in London" (1879), in R. H. Super, ed., *Works, IX: English Literature and Irish Politics* (Ann Arbor, 1973), p. 65.

230 "full of Parisianisms": Clough is quoted in Lionel Trilling, *Matthew Arnold* (New York, 1949), pp. 21–22. See also p. 270.

"mere head of steam": George Bernard Shaw, *Dramatic Opinions* II (London, 1917), p. 133, quoted in Alan S. Downer, "Players and Painted Stage: Nineteenth-Century Acting," *PMLA* 61 (1946), p. 561.

231 For Arnold's poems and useful notes on them, see Kenneth Allott, ed., *The Poems of Matthew Arnold* (London, 1965). Allott writes that Arnold first saw Rachel in London in July 1846, and that he arrived in Paris the following December and saw her ten times.

"She represented for him": Park Honan, *Matthew Arnold, A Life* (New York, 1981), pp. 483–85.

236 "a crude and casual": For Lewes as a critic of Rachel, and his influence on the novels of Brontë, Disraeli, and George Eliot, see John Stokes, "Rachel's 'Terrible Beauty': An Actress Among the Novelists," *ELH* (Winter, 1984), pp. 771–93. The phrase I quote is on p. 776, where Stokes observes in connection with it that Lewes had "acted Shylock as a sympathetic and wronged character in 1849." I am much indebted to this essay. For Lewes on Rachel, see his *On Actors and the Art of Acting,* and William Archer and Robert W. Lowe, eds., *Dramatic Essays: John Forster and George Henry Lewes* (London, 1896).

237 *Rose, Blanche, and Violet:* Patricia Thomson, in *George Sand and the Victorians,* notes that in Sand's *Rose et Blanche* (1831), which the title of Lewes's novel echoes, one of the heroines "goes to the theatre and sees Judith Pasta as Tancred, and is overwhelmed by the magnificence of the hall, the brilliance of the lights, the crowd of spectators. It is midnight when she returns through the dark streets to the convent, gliding along furtively, so much under the spell of the emotion which had been aroused that she does not know whether it is night or day." Thomson, p. 75, compares her to Lucy Snowe.

238 "enslaved by an impassioned sensibility": Margaret Fuller, *Woman in the Nineteenth Century* (New York, 1971), esp. pp. 103–4.

"a Sarah Siddons, a Rachel": Dinah Craik, *A Woman's Thoughts about Women* (Leipzig, 1860), pp. 45–50.

"Women, when they are young": Florence Nightingale, *Cassandra* (New York, 1979), p. 41. Helena Michie, in *The Flesh Made Word: Female Figures and Women's Bodies* (New York, 1987), comments on these passages in Craik and Nightingale on pp. 67–68.

p. 239 "the Rachels, the Duses": Simone de Beauvoir, *The Second Sex*, translated by H. M. Parshley (New York, 1953; 1974), pp. 782–83.

All quotations from George Eliot's *Daniel Deronda* are from the Penguin edition (Harmondsworth, 1967). For a discussion of theatricality in *Daniel Deronda*, see Litvak, *Caught in the Act*, as well as Nina Auerbach, "Secret Performances: George Eliot and the Art of Acting," in Auerbach, *Romantic Imprisonment* (New York, 1986); Catherine Gallagher, "George Eliot and *Daniel Deronda*: The Prostitute and the Woman Question," in Ruth Bernard Yeazell, ed., *Sex, Politics, and Science in the Nineteenth-Century Novel: Selected Papers from the English Institute, 1983–84* (Baltimore, 1986); Jacqueline Rose, "George Eliot and the Spectacle of the Woman," in Rose, *Sexuality in the Field of Vision* (London, 1986). See also Simon During, "The Strange Case of Monomania: Patriarchy in Literature, Murder in *Middlemarch*, Drowning in *Daniel Deronda*," *Representations* 23 (Summer, 1988).

240 how their names inform the way: Leonora Charisi or Alcharisi, The Princess Halm-Eberstein, remarks that for Jews one name is as real as another: "The Jews have always been changing their names," p. 701.

a stepfather: For conjectures that Gwendolen had an abusive stepfather see Judith Wilt, " 'He would come back': The Fathers of Daughters in *Daniel Deronda*," *Nineteenth-Century Literature*, vol. 42, no. 3 (1987).

241 "We went to see Rachel": George Eliot to Mrs. Charles Bray and Sara Sophia Hennell, 17 June 1853, in Gordon Haight, ed., *The George Eliot Letters* II, p. 104.

"Her acting is not acting": G. H. Lewes, *Three Sisters and Three Fortunes, or Rose, Blanche, and Violet* (New York, n.d.), p. 23.

242 "The belief": *Daniel Deronda*, pp. 298, 305. See Mary Wilson Carpenter, " 'A Bit of Her Flesh': Circumcision and 'The Signification of the Phallus' in *Daniel Deronda*," *Genders* 1 (March 1988).

243 "He wished I had been": *Daniel Deronda*, p. 694. The two interviews with the princess are in Chapter 51 and Chapter 53 of Book VII, "The Mother and the Son."

245 Helen Faucit: See George Eliot to Cara Bray, 16 April 1853: "I fell in love with Helen Faucit. She is the most poetic woman I have seen for a long while. Her conversation is not remarkable in any way but there is the ineffable charm of a fine character which makes itself felt in her face, voice and manner." *The George Eliot Letters* II, p. 98.

"Everything *specifically* Jewish": Joseph Litvak writes that there is a "power struggle between the good Jewishness of poetry and the bad Jewishness of theatricality" in *Daniel Deronda* (*Caught in the Act*, pp. 189–90). I would speculate that good and bad Jewishness seemed to George Eliot to be (agonizingly) collapsed in Rachel, and that to that extent the actress's figure inspired the novel.

p. 247 Woolf's Rachel: Louise A. DeSalvo, *Virginia Woolf's First Voyage: A Novel in the Making* (Totowa, N.J., 1980), pp. 69–70, comments on the connection between Woolf's review and her first novel, the heroine of which is named Rachel.

248 Quotations from *The Tragic Muse* are from the Penguin edition (Harmondsworth, 1978). Adeline R. Tintner has analyzed the narrative process through which Miriam Rooth is identified with Rachel in "Miriam as the English Rachel: Gérôme's Portrait of the Tragic Muse," *Critical Essays on Henry James: The Early Novels*, edited by James W. Gargano (Boston, 1987). See her *Henry James and the Lust of the Eyes: Thirteen Artists in His Fiction* (Baton Rouge, 1993).

249 parallel theatrical scenes: Mary Ann Caws connects these two scenes and comments on them illuminatingly as instances of "framing" in *Reading Frames in Modern Fiction* (Princeton, 1985), pp. 137–38.

For James and Fanny Kemble, see his essay, "Frances Anne Kemble," in *Essays in London and Elsewhere* (New York, 1893). See also Margaret Armstrong, *Fanny Kemble: A Passionate Victorian* (New York, 1938), esp. pp. 369–70.

250 "I may say that I know": F. O. Matthiessen and Kenneth B. Murdock, eds., *The Notebooks of Henry James* (New York, 1947), p. 26. In *The Melodramatic Imagination*, Peter Brooks observes that James would have preferred to write for the Comédie-Française. For James on that "ideal and exemplary world," see Henry James, Jr., "The Théâtre Français," in *French Poets and Novelists* (London, 1878), pp. 410–11. For James on Rachel, see *Notebooks*, p. 64.

"I don't see the princess": *"Daniel Deronda*: A Conversation," in James, *Partial Portraits* (London, 1919), p. 85.

251 About Ward's "tempting, challenging subject," James wrote to her more critically, "It seems to me, however, that, as I said, you have rather limited yourself—you have seen that concussion too simply, refused perhaps even to face it. I am afraid I have a certain reputation for being censorious and cynical: let me therefore profit by it with you and insist on one or two points in which I should have liked your story to be a little different; or at least upon *one*. I am capable of wishing that the actress might have been carried away from Kendal altogether, carried away by the current of her artistic life, the sudden growth of her power, and the excitement, the ferocity and egotism (those of the artist realizing success, I mean . . .) which the effort to create, to 'arrive' . . . would have brought with it." See Leon Edel, ed., *Henry James Letters* III (Cambridge, Mass., 1980), p. 59.

"the story of an actress": *Fortnightly Review* (April 1920), p. 857. Patricia Thomson is certain that *Miss Bretherton* "started James off on" *The Tragic Muse*. Conceding that the actress Mary Anderson inspired Ward's story, she argues that George Sand was "the vital source" for which Ward (and Geraldine Jewsbury) received "their literary stimulus to tackle the problems of the actress in society." Thomson, p. 238. It is perhaps also relevant here that Mary Augusta Ward wrote introductions to *Villette* and the other Brontë novels. A

president of the Brontë Society, she remarked—in her farewell address to that
group on 30 March 1917—on her own friendship with Charlotte Brontë's publisher and friend George Smith, "Dr. John in *Villette,*" and proudly claimed
another personal connection with Brontë through her uncle Matthew Arnold,
who had met the novelist when he was a young man.

p. 253 "a woman whose only being was to make believe": Joseph Litvak emphasizes
the sexual coloration of this passage, and reads allusions that link Medusa with
Miriam as signs of the heroine's gendered monstrousness; I think that the irony
and the emphasis on the aesthetic rather desexualizes Miriam, and makes her
a revisionary version of the *femme artiste.* My argument that Miriam Rooth,
commodified and spectacularized, denatures and unsettles the stock image of
the *femme artiste,* has been influenced by Catherine Gallagher's discussion of
the manipulation by women authors of the image of the prostitute. See her
articles: "George Eliot and *Daniel Deronda:* The Prostitute and the Woman
Question" in Yeazell, ed., *Sex, Politics, and Science in the Nineteenth-Century
Novel* (Baltimore, 1986), and "Who Was that Masked Woman? The Prostitute
and the Playwright in the Comedies of Aphra Behn" in Regina Barreca, ed.,
Last Laughs: Perspectives on Women and Comedy (New York, 1988). For the
aesthetic and theatrical underpinnings of James's novel and on its sources, see
the important long article by D. J. Gordon and John Stokes, "The Reference
of *The Tragic Muse,*" in John Goode, ed., *The Air of Reality: New Essays on
Henry James* (London, 1972).

254 Single-minded in her commitment: R. P. Blackmur observed of Miriam that
she "almost alone among James heroines never resigned, never gave up, never
renounced, whether in submission or to gain extra strength of being." See his
introduction to the Laurel Edition of *The Tragic Muse.*
"a large bright picture": *The Tragic Muse,* p. 375.

255 "the pure commodity": Walter Benjamin, "Paris: Capital of the Nineteenth
Century," in Benjamin, *Reflections,* translated by Edmund Jephcott (New York,
1979), p. 152.
"She made almost an income": *The Tragic Muse,* p. 494.
"She has in a supreme degree": Henry James, *The Scenic Art,* edited by Allan
Wade (New Brunswick, 1948), p. 129.

256 "the female grotesque": Mary Russo, "Female Grotesques: Carnival and Theory," in Teresa de Lauretis, ed., *Feminist Studies/Critical Studies* (Bloomington,
Ind., 1986).

257 "spell of intense astonishment": Carl Schurz, *The Reminiscences of Carl Schurz* I
(New York, 1907), p. 276 ff.

258 Recent criticism of Sylvia Townsend Warner's *Summer Will Show* (New York,
1936; repr. London, 1987) has not focused on the actress theme. Terry Castle
argues that *Summer Will Show* is an exemplary lesbian fiction that rewrites the
standard heterosexual plot. See her "Sylvia Townsend Warner and the Counterplot

of Lesbian Fiction," *Textual Practice* 4 (Summer, 1990). Claire Harman's introduction to the Virago edition emphasizes Warner's imagery, her Flaubertian objectivity, and her ultimately tragic view of revolution. In "Ideology, Ecriture, 1848: Sylvia Townsend Warner Unwrites Flaubert," *RSSI*, vol. II, nos. 2–3 (1991), Sandy Petrey presents a different political reading.

p. 260 a Jewish Corinne: Minna is also suggestive of performers like Ruth Draper, who recited their own sketches in London in the 1920s and were popular in lesbian clubs and cafés.

261 Mlle Déluzy, as she walked in the court of the Conciergerie, seemed to many to be carrying on like an actress: *"Elle sait que beaucoup de regards sont fixés sur elle de toutes les fenêtres. Les gens qui l'ont vue disent qu'elle prend des poses."* Hugo, *Choses vues* II (Paris, 1913), p. 278.

History remembers the Duc de Praslin (his family name was Choiseul, part of the name of one of Rachel's aristocratic biographers) as a cad as well as a wife-killer; the *Dictionnaire de biographie française* (Paris, 1959) further observes that the letters the duchess sent him after their 1837 separation *"témoignent d'une grande élévation de pensées."* ("Choiseul [Praslin]", vol. 8, p. 1214.) Mlle Déluzy is recalled as having been the duke's mistress as well as "la maîtresse de la maison" during the years he lived separately from his wife, in the same household. Rachel Field's novel uses the conventions of governess fiction to file a belated brief for her heroine: the reader is meant to be persuaded that, like Jane Eyre, Mlle Déluzy maintained her innocence in spite of her passion.

Index

~

italicized page numbers refer to illustrations

Illustrations

Rachel M. Brownstein is Professor of English at Brooklyn

College and the Graduate Center, City University of New York.

She is also the author of *Becoming a Heroine*.